STUDIES IN MODERNITY AND NATIONAL IDENTITY

Sibel Bozdoğan and Reşat Kasaba, Series Editors

Studies in Modernity and National Identity examine the relationships among modernity, the nation-state, and nationalism as these have evolved in the nineteenth and twentieth centuries. Titles in this interdisciplinary and transregional series also illuminate how the nation-state is being undermined by the forces of globalization, international migration, electronic information flows, as well as resurgent ethnic and religious affiliations. These books highlight historical parallels and continuities while documenting the social, cultural, and spatial expressions through which modern national identities have been constructed, contested, and reinvented.

Modernism and Nation Building: Turkish Architectural Culture
in the Early Republic
Sibel Bozdoğan

SIBEL BOZDOĞAN

MODERNISM AND NATION BUILDING

TURKISH ARCHITECTURAL CULTURE IN THE EARLY REPUBLIC

University of Washington Press

Seattle and London

Publication of *Modernism and Nation Building* is supported by a grant
from the Graham Foundation for Advanced Studies in the Fine Arts.

Publication is also supported by a grant from
the Institute of Turkish Studies, Washington, D.C.

Library of Congress Cataloging-in-Publication Data

Bozdogan, Sibel.
    Modernism and nation building : Turkish architectural culture in the early republic /
  Sibel Bozdogan.
        p.   cm. — (Studies in modernity and national identity)
    Includes index.
    ISBN 0–295–98110–5 (alk. paper) ISBN 0–295–98152–0 (alk. paper) (pbk.)
      1. Architecture—Turkey. 2. Architecture, Modern—20th century—Turkey. 3.
Nationalism and architecture—Turkey. 4. Turkey—History—1918–1960. I. Title. II.
Series.

NA1368.B69 2001
720'.9561'09041—dc21

                                                                    00–069048

To my parents, Necla and Mehmet Bozdoğan, children of the early republic iN.

Contents

Preface

I BEGAN CONTEMPLATING this book more than ten years ago in Turkey when I was doing research on the late Sedad Hakkı Eldem. If I had stayed in Turkey as I had always thought I would (one never knows!), I probably would have been intimidated by the immensity of the task and put it aside for other, more focused projects. It was only after I found myself "settled" in the United States (still a tentative concept for me) that the idea became more urgent. First, it became professionally important for me to locate myself in what I saw as an emerging scholarly field encompassing the study of transnational and cross-cultural histories of modern architecture and their relationship to culture and politics. Second, and equally important, was a personal dimension: working on this book became my connection to the country I had left behind and never stopped thinking about since then. Every new development in Turkish culture and politics, every new book on Turkey, and every trip there each summer reflected back on my research material, giving me new interpretive insights and delaying the completion of the book.

In the end, the making of the book was spread over many years, many fragmented periods of research, many seminars, conferences, and informal discussions in which the ideas were elaborated, and many moments of doubt over the feasibility of such an all-encompassing cultural and architectural history. Many people have become part of it in different capacities—as resources, as interlocutors, or simply as supporters who did not hesitate to place their trust in someone with architectural training who was turning cultural historian. It is impossible for me to list or remember everyone along the way. But with my sincerest apologies for any unintended omissions, I would like to thank the following institutions and individuals.

Most of my research in Turkey was done with a grant from the Social Science Research Council in New York, and I thank everyone involved for supporting my proposal. Additional funding for research expenses came from a Humanities and Social Sciences Research Grant and from the Ford International Career Development stipend, both at the Massachusetts Institute of Technology. In Ankara, at different times between 1994 and 1999, I used the resources of the Middle East Technical University, the Chamber of Turkish Architects (with special thanks to Bayar Çimen), the National Library, the Prime Ministry Archives of the Turkish Republic, and the Library of the Turkish Parliament. In Istanbul, I relied on the resources of Istanbul Technical University, Mimar Sinan University, and the Atatürk Library of Istanbul Municipality. In the United States, in addition to the Rotch Libraries and Visual Collections at MIT, I consulted the Weidener and Fine Arts Libraries of Harvard University, and I thank the Aga Khan Program for facilitating my access to them. The Department of Architecture at MIT reduced my teaching load for a semester during the writing of the first draft, and I thank Stanford Anderson for that. I also thank the Institute of Turkish Studies in Washington, D.C., which provided a subvention grant for the final publication of the book.

My deepest gratitude goes to Diane Ghirardo, Gülsum Baydar Nalbantoğlu, Gwendolyn Wright, and Yıldırım Yavuz for reading the manuscript carefully and critically, making helpful suggestions, and above all encouraging me at the most needed moments. An anonymous reviewer also read the manuscript and gave much-appreciated comments. In addition to them, I want to acknowledge my indebtedness to İnci Aslanoğlu not only for reading an initial draft of the first part and sharing her knowledge with me but also for installing in me an interest in the topic many years ago through her own work. Sarah Shields and Aydan Keskin Balamir also read parts of the first draft and made insightful comments, and I thank them warmly. Among my colleagues in architecture, I am grateful to Roy Landau, Kenneth Frampton, Francesco Passanti, and Akos Moravanszky not only for their general interest in and support of my work but also for the inspiration their work has given me toward a critical historiography of modern architecture. I also thank Stanford Anderson and Mark Jarzombek for reading the manuscript and for giving "transnational and cross-cultural histories of modernism" an important place in the History, Theory, and Criticism section of the Department of Architecture at MIT during the years I taught there. Some of the ideas in the first chapter of this book were developed during those years at MIT, in a seminar I co-taught with Nasser Rabbat, and I cherish those exchanges. I would also like to express my appreciation to Maristella Casciato, Bernd Nicolai, Vittorio M. Lampugnani, Guiseppe Semerani, Jorge Francisco Liernur, and Augustus Richard Norton for the recognition they gave my work by inviting me to give talks on modern Turkish architecture. Among my friends and colleagues in Turkish studies, Feroz Ahmad, Ayfer Bartu, Alev İnan Çınar, Haldun Gülalp, Çağlar Keyder, Şevket Pamuk, and Jenny White were particularly supportive over the years. I owe it to them that I was able to present earlier versions of this work to interdisciplinary audiences as lectures, conference papers, and published articles.

Above all, it is the graduate students with whom I have worked or exchanged ideas in seminars and conferences who have given me the greatest enthusiasm and motivation in writing this book. The larger field within which I have situated my work on Turkish modernism—a field that spans the history of modern architecture outside

Europe and North America—has been our shared theoretical terrain. It is through the work of these younger scholars that the field is growing rapidly and challenging the traditional conceptions of the discipline of architectural history, theory, and criticism. Among them, I want to express my appreciation for the work of Esra Akcan, Ritu Bhatt, Asia Chowdhury, Ahmet Ersoy, Nathaniel Fuster-Felix, Yehchin Hsu, Brian McLaren, Alona Nitzan-Shiftan, Anoma Pieris, Panaiyota Pyla, Maha Yahya, and Zeynep Kezer. I also wish to thank Aslıhan Demirtaş, Ömer Kanıpak, Yael Navaro-Yasin, Neşe Yeşilkaya-Gürallar, and Zeynep Yürekli for sharing their work on different aspects of early republican culture and architecture with me.

Among the people who helped me with the production of this book, I thank Necati Yurtseven in Turkey and John Cook in Cambridge for responding to my endless requests for photographic reproduction over the years. Many others generously allowed me to use individual photographs from their collections; I have acknowledged them separately in the figure sources. My sister, Hande Bozdoğan, not only kept me sane and smiling with long overseas phone calls but also was a reliable resource for any material I needed from Turkey. My very special thanks go to Michael Duckworth, the editor of the University of Washington Press without whose commitment and support neither this book nor the larger series in which it appears could have been possible. The same goes to Jane Kepp, the talented copy-editor who did marvels with my manuscript, making it possible for me to finally visualize it as a book rather than the draft of a potential book.

As much as this book is indebted to the many people who intersected its path at different points in fruitful ways, the writing of it was ultimately a lonely enterprise. Most of the time I wrote it "on the side," during the time left over from full-time teaching and parenting. It took much longer than it should have, its progress fluctuating with the ups and downs in my life and career, and it was finally finished under circumstances dramatically different from those in which I began writing it. Throughout all this, a few people have been so indispensable to my well-being that I want to single them out, with full knowledge that whatever I write will be insufficient to express how much I appreciated and needed them. First, I thank Feridun Özgören for opening up the world of Turkish classical music for me—a world in which I found refuge and relaxation when nothing else worked. Second, I thank Leila Kinney for being the intelligent colleague, great girlfriend, and walking companion that she is. She, too, was trying to write a book between full-time teaching and parenting, and with her there, it was less lonely. Third, I thank Reşat Kasaba, my colleague and co-editor, my best friend of nearly thirty years, and the single most important contributor to the conception, elaboration, and realization of this book. In his immense generosity and kindness, he listened to every idea I ran by him, read and commented on every paper I wrote, invited me to his conferences, and read the manuscript a few times over. Above all he believed in the importance of writing a book of this sort when I myself had doubts. "Rethinking modernity and national identity in Turkey" became our shared obsession in our separate but parallel lives in the United States. Fourth, I thank Peter Parsons, who listened patiently to my ideas and challenged them in constructive ways, read my drafts, helped me out on a daily basis, and endured my moments of depression with grace. As colleagues and intellectual companions, we learned, discussed, and taught "the culture and architecture of modernity" together. In addition, I always turned to his capacities for handling practical matters that would have left me helpless and to his overall wisdom in life whenever I seemed to lose my sense of purpose. Finally, I thank our son, Sinan Bozdoğan Parsons, who, for the first ten years of his life, grew up with the making of this book and still does not blame it for all the time I would otherwise have given to him.

Sibel Bozdoğan
Brookline, Massachusetts
January 2001

MODERNISM AND NATION BUILDING

Introduction

MODERNISM ON THE MARGINS OF EUROPE

> Some time ago, by the "Sweet Waters of Europe" at the far end of the Golden Horn, I heard the whine of countless gramophones on the *caiques* plashing the water. And I reckoned that Abdulhamid was dead, the Young Turks had arrived, that the Bazaar was changing its signs and that the West was triumphing. And already today we have Ankara, and the monument to Mustafa Kemal! Events move fast. The die is cast: one more centuries-old civilization goes to ruin.
>
> —Le Corbusier, L'art decoratif d'aujourd'hui, 1925

FOR LE CORBUSIER, the making of modern Turkey over the ruins of the Ottoman Empire was just one example of what he saw as the disappearance of balanced, harmonious cultures everywhere with "the arrival of the twentieth century."[1] He dated "the advent of modern times" in Turkey to the appearance of the Young Turks on the scene, just before his own first visit to Istanbul in 1911.[2] He observed that what the Young Turks had started then had been carried to its logical conclusion by Mustafa Kemal, the nationalist hero who proclaimed the Turkish republic in Ankara in 1923, dismantling a six-centuries-old Islamic civilization. Indeed, the new republic had recently passed its most radical and, to this day, most contentious decrees, abolishing the Ottoman sultanate and the Islamic caliphate. A series of Westernizing institutional reforms was under way to shape the entire social, cultural, and architectural fabric of Turkey along European models. It was only a matter of years before Le Corbusier himself would be hailed as a great visionary and his works and ideas would mobilize a new generation of young Turkish architects.

Why, then, do Le Corbusier's words have such a melancholy ring? Many Western commentators writing in the 1920s expressed ambivalence toward the new nationalist government in Turkey, if not outright nostalgia for Ottoman culture and society.[3] Although Le Corbusier shared the general orientalist nostalgia, his agenda was a different and personal one, little related to the historical events under way in Turkey. While evoking the necessity and historical inevitability of the disappearance of old civilizations, his nostalgic remarks were intended mainly to draw attention to the loss of "harmonious cultures" everywhere and to justify his own mission to re-create that lost harmony in the modern world.

During his first visit to Istanbul in 1911, like other European orientalists before him who went to the East in search of the "exotic" and the "authentic," Le Corbusier had despised the modernizing agenda of the Young Turks, including the new architecture they sponsored. Instead, he had admired "the simplicity of their fathers" who had built the classic mosques and the wooden houses of old Istanbul—those "architectural masterpieces," as he called them, the spatial and constructional qualities of which he registered in his mind and in his sketchbooks. As recent scholarship on Le Corbusier confirms, in those formative years he was looking at the cultural artifacts and vernacular architectures of eastern Europe and Turkey as conceptual models for a possible modern vernacular.[4] They were his sources of inspiration to begin contemplating the possibility of a similar harmony, this time between twentieth-century culture and its designed objects. Yet in the official modernist polemic of the 1920s and 1930s (to which Le Corbusier himself significantly contributed), these "non-European" cultural influences became merely anecdotal. Instead, the ocean liners, grain elevators, and airplanes of the industrial West took center stage as the exclusive sources of twentieth-century modernism.

The official history of modern architecture was written in the West with Le Corbusier as its main author and protagonist at once. According to this account, which has become a part of the mainstream cultural history of the twentieth century, "modernism," or the "Modern Movement" as it was then called, encompassed a revolutionary aesthetic canon and a scientific doctrine in architecture originating in Europe during the interwar period. Use of reinforced concrete, steel, and glass, the primacy of cubic forms, geometric shapes, and Cartesian grids, and above all the absence of decoration, stylistic motifs, traditional roofs, and ornamental details have been its defining features in twentieth-century aesthetic consciousness. For most people, the works of masters such as Le Corbusier, Walter Gropius, and Mies van der Rohe epitomize this modernist aesthetic. Its European origins notwithstanding, it is a doctrine that has claimed universal validity and rationality. The new needs, tools, and technologies of complex industrial societies that informed this modernist vision were presented as the needs, tools, and technologies of a rationally progressing universal history—an epochal force that no nation, culture, or geography could escape.

The most effective organization working for the dissemination of these ideas was the International Congress of Modern Architecture (CIAM), which inaugurated its annual meetings in 1928 in Europe. A year before that, a major housing exhibition in Stuttgart, Germany (the Weissenhof Siedlung, 1927), had given a unified image and great publicity to the leading modernist architects of Europe. In 1932 the movement crossed the Atlantic Ocean, and the term "international style" was coined for this architecture after the famous exhibition by that title at New York's Museum of Modern Art. In a very short time during the 1930s, the architectural and urbanistic precepts of the Modern Movement were embraced by an entire generation of architects, planners, and bureaucrats everywhere as the most progressive and thoroughly rational expression of the modern zeitgeist in the making. As we will see later in this book, its arrival in Ankara, the new capital of modern, postimperial, republican Turkey, was celebrated as a historical moment marking the country's entry into the twentieth century.

The greatest ideological appeal of the Modern Movement was its claim to transcend ideology. During the interwar period, many new regimes and diverse political systems, from socialism in Weimar Germany and postrevolutionary Russia to fascism in Italy, Zionism in mandate Palestine, and Kemalism in Turkey, embraced the progressive discourse of the Modern Movement. Republican Ankara in the 1930s was one of the earliest manifestations of the historical alliance of modernism with nation building and state power—an alliance from which the term "high modernism" would be born. By the time high modernism reached its epitome in the post–World War II period, it designated not so much the particular aesthetic canon of the Modern Movement (which gave way to new, more monumental, and more sculptural forms after World War II) as its larger political project. Le Corbusier was, without doubt, the mastermind of high modernist vision in architecture and urbanism—"the revolutionary architect par excellence," as most of his contemporaries and many Turkish architects of the 1930s saw him. The proliferation of the high modernist vision beyond the margins of Europe to other continents and cultures, from postcolonial India to Latin America, shaped much of the history, culture, and built fabric of the twentieth century. The new capitol complexes of Chandigarh and Brasilia are only the most ambitious and famous of its numerous expressions in architecture and urbanism.[5]

As James C. Scott notes in his compelling account of high modernism, the term is not confined to architecture and urbanism. "High Modernism is the most visionary and ultimately devastating ideology of the twentieth century," Scott explains, "a particularly sweeping vision of how the benefits of technical and scientific progress might be applied, usually through the state, in every field of human activity."[6] That high modernism tends to simplify reality, making it legible and ultimately controllable, and that it sees the past as an impediment to the realization of an idealized future are two of Scott's observations that are particularly pertinent to an analysis of Kemalist Turkey in the 1930s. There are certain conditions, Scott argues, that have particularly favored the blossoming of the high modernist faith. These include "crises of state power, such as wars and economic depressions, and circumstances in which a state's capacity for relatively unimpeded planning is greatly enhanced, such as the revolutionary conquest of power and colonial rule."[7] The presence of both of these conditions in Turkey at the time modernism "arrived" in Ankara cannot be missed. The country had barely emerged from decades of warfare extending from the Balkan Wars and the First World War to the nationalist War of Independence. The construction of a new nation had to be accomplished in the midst of dire economic conditions, not to mention the impact of the depression of 1929. Finally and most importantly, after the consolidation of single-party rule under Mustafa Kemal's Republican People's Party (RPP), there was a new revolutionary regime in power with an all-encompassing project of modernization and civilization at the top of its agenda.

With its predilection for social engineering and top-to-bottom modernization and its self-declared revolutionary premises, the Kemalist regime embraced the high modernist faith as one of its founding ideologies. The architectural culture of the early Turkish republic amply illustrates how high modernism as an ideology appealed particularly to "planners, engineers, architects, scientists and technicians" who "wanted to use state power to bring about huge, utopian changes in people's work habits, living patterns, moral conduct and worldview."[8] Modern architecture was imported as both a visible symbol and an effective instrument of this radical program to create a thoroughly Westernized, modern, and secular new nation dissociated from the country's own Ottoman and Islamic past. In this respect, architecture in early republican Turkey can be looked at as a literally "concrete" manifestation of the high modernist vision.

In this book I offer evidence for the essentially ideological appropriation of modernism in Turkish architectural culture of the 1930s. At the same time, I address how this imported ideology was interpreted, justified, modified, and contested in ways unique to the Turkish experience. The architectural culture and production of the early republican period bear ample testimony to the ambiguities, complexities, and contradictions resulting from encounters between imported ideas and local realities, not just in Turkey but everywhere. This book is also about these complexities and contradictions, which make it problematic to explain the Turkish case (or any other case, for that matter) exclusively from the general high modernist blueprint.

The "New Architecture" (*Yeni Mimari,* as the Modern Movement was called in Turkey) came to Turkey in the 1930s largely through the example of German and Central European architects who worked and taught in Turkey throughout the early republican period. Their more conservative brand of modernism, which can be observed in the architecture of Ankara (mostly a stripped-down classicism), bore little resemblance to the canonic aesthetic of "international style" in the 1930s (with its slick, white boxes, transparent walls, and advanced industrial materials). The discourse celebrating Turkey's entry into the heroic world of the Modern Movement notwithstanding, modern architecture in early republican Turkey was conspicuously heavier than the celebrated examples of the Modern Movement in Europe. Buildings were constructed more traditionally, with smaller openings and, in many cases, pitched tile roofs, largely as a result of the poverty and constraints of the building industry. Modernist Turkish architects were themselves profoundly contradictory in their comments about modernism. Sometimes they privileged its aesthetic component (as is implied by the term "international *style*") by celebrating the "harmonious composition of geometric volumes." More often they rejected the stylistic implications of an aesthetic understanding of modernism in favor of the principles of "rationalism and functionalism," which, they believed, were the objective and scientific criteria determining modern form. Mostly they tried to reconcile the two.

As much as young Turkish architects wanted to embrace the Modern Movement, in the passionately nationalist climate of the early republic the word "international" was even more objectionable to them than the word "style." In the same way that republican leaders wanted to import the positivism, science, and progress of modernity without its liberal philosophy or its socialist overtones, republican architects wanted a modernism without its international connotations. As will be evident throughout this book, the entire architectural culture of the early republic was one big effort to reconcile the "modern" with the "national." Some argued that because the Modern Movement was the most rational response to site, context, and program, it was, by definition, "national." As a corollary to this, others argued that traditional Turkish architecture (classical Ottoman monuments and vernacular houses) embraced such rational designs in terms of function and construction that it was already "modern" in concept. Analogous to (and inspired by) the way Italian rationalist architects elaborated the concepts of "Italianità" and "Mediterraneità" to appropriate modernism for the Fascist state,[9] Turkish architects tried to "nationalize the modern" for a better ideological fit with Kemalism. Any study of early republican architecture in Turkey needs to take into account this ambiguous and very particular sense of what "modern" was all about and resist the tendency to read modern Turkish architecture in terms of exclusive binary oppositions between national and international or between tradition and modernity. At a time when any emphasis on either supranational or subnational affiliation was anathema to republican ideology, modernism could not be international in its affiliations, nor could national architecture be truly local, traditional, or regionalist.

Both the European modernism of the 1930s and the idea of a "national style" that had been a recurrent obsession in Turkish architectural culture since the late Ottoman period are important backdrops for this book. It was the specific ways in which the two interacted and negotiated in the 1930s, however, that gave early republican architecture its unique character. One central idea informing this book is that a distinction should be made between modern architecture and high modernism, counter to the tendency to collapse the two together. Modern architecture, as it first emerged in Europe around the turn of the century, was before everything else a critical discourse that defied received notions and established canons of architecture. It commenced from the idea of exploring a critical, antistylistic, and continuously self-transforming approach to art and architecture, irreducible to an official style or program in the same way that modernity is irreducible to the grand political project of high modernism. As Scott puts it in the context of social theory, "one of the great paradoxes of social engineering is that it seems at odds with the experience of modernity generally. Trying to jell a social world, the most striking characteristic of which appears to be flux, seems rather like trying to manage a whirlwind."[10] The same could be said for modern architecture. To turn it into an official style and ideology—simple, legible, and recognizable as such (geometric, undecorated, abstract building forms)— seems very much at odds with its theoretical premises, which emphasize formal indeterminacy, response to context, and response to changing needs, materials, and techniques. Therefore, the initial identification of modernism with nation building under the auspices of an authoritarian state in Turkey is itself problematical—a premise waiting to be questioned rather than taken for granted.

⊙ ⊙ ⊙

THE HISTORY OF modern architecture and urbanism outside Europe and North America is a relatively recent and rapidly growing field of research. Until the last two decades or so of the twentieth century, nineteenth- and twentieth-century architectures in Asia, the Middle East, Africa, and Latin America were topics doubly marginalized, not only by historians of modern architecture but also by area specialists. As is widely known and discussed today, the reasons for this had much to do with the initial constitution of the discipline of art and architectural history on primarily Eurocentric and orientalist grounds.[11] For many art historians in the so-called area studies, non-Western cultures were interesting mostly insofar as they remained "others" with respect to the West. Thus their attention and scholarly specialization were focused heavily on the classic periods or "golden ages" of Islamic, Indian, Chinese, and other cultures. Modern architecture was regarded as an imported and "alien" discourse not indigenous to these societies—a much-lamented symbol of the "contamination" of their authentic cultural expressions. Little attention, if any, was devoted to the efforts of non-Western cultures to make modern architectural concepts, forms, and techniques originating in Europe their own. "Modern" was assumed to be an exclusively European category that non-Western others could import, adopt, or perhaps resist but not reproduce from within. In the case of Turkey, not only twentieth-century modernism but also the histories of Ottoman baroque, neoclassic, and other European architectural imports of the nineteenth century were, until recently, little known to an English-speaking readership.[12]

Much of area studies has been predicated on a belief in the essential differences between cultures. Twentieth-century modernism embraced the opposite—a belief in the essential "sameness" of human beings as the scientific, objective, biological underpinning of what were to be inevitably uniform modern lives. Consequently, neither perspective has helped much to open up a space for the study of modernism outside the industrialized West. Area specialists and orientalists have looked at non-Western cultures as strictly "bounded domains," the essences of which were in the past. Historians of modern architecture, on the other hand, have focused exclusively on the social, technological, and intellectual determinants of modernism, the sources of which were in the West. Hence they have regarded modern architecture and urbanism in non-Western contexts simply as extensions of Western developments and therefore as of little interest and originality in themselves—unless, of course, a famous European architect or planner happened to be working in some overseas territory. Until the fairly recent appearance of publications on India's colonial heritage and the work of modern Indian architects, for example, what was known about modern architecture in India was confined to Le Corbusier in Chandigarh.

In the aftermath of the critique of orientalist and Eurocentric perspectives in nearly every discipline, the foregoing picture has been changing dramatically. Orientalist constructions of "other cultures" as timeless and essentialist categories have been radically challenged at least since the publication of Edward Said's groundbreaking work in the late 1970s.[13] An entire new field of cultural studies has emerged, drawing attention to the hybridity and complexity of non-Western societies, "modern" in their own ways and not necessarily following the patterns delineated by the history of the industrial West. At the same time, critical histories of modern architecture have also been dismantling the idea of modernism as a thoroughly rational and universal doctrine that the architecture of every nation would sooner or later emulate. The scholarly trend now is to expose multiple and heterogeneous trajectories, even within European modernism itself, not to mention hitherto unexplored contexts and countries from Latin America to East Asia. As a result, the last twenty years have seen a boom in scholarship and published literature on the plurality of modern experiences, histories, and cultural transformations of non-Western societies. There is a wealth of new research on colonial architecture and urbanism, modern architecture and national identity, and postcolonial architecture.[14] This book is informed by these studies in many ways and was motivated by, among other things, the conviction that such studies of "other modernisms" challenge not only essentialist categories of non-Western cultures as static but also assumptions of a linear, homogeneous, and universal history of modern architecture. Looking at different experiences in different places and circumstances is the most effective way by which we can ensure that modern architecture, traditionally reified by both its supporters and its opponents, becomes historically situated, contextualized, and, most importantly, politicized.

It is not surprising that the categories "power" and "politics" have been at the center of much of the work in this field, because it is through these categories that asymmetries in cultural and architectural history emerge most clearly. The primary reason for the privileging of politics is a simple one. In most countries outside western Europe and North America, modernization was not a profound societal experience resulting from the nineteenth-century "great transformation" into an industrial, urban, and market-oriented order.[15] It was an official program conceived and implemented either by colonial governments or by the modernizing elites of authoritarian nation-states that most of the time placed a high priority on architecture and urbanism as a form of "visible politics." In Turkey, too, from the reformist bureaucrats of the Ottoman

Empire in the nineteenth century to the republican leaders in the 1920s and 1930s, successive generations of modernizers sought to "catch up" with Western civilization and progress by importing Western institutions, forms, and techniques. Architecture, by its very nature, has always been a powerful symbol as well as an effective instrument of reform and change in the modern world. As a result, modern architecture in non-Western contexts has often been a *representation* of modernity without its real material and social basis—namely, industrial cities, capitalist production, and an autonomous bourgeoisie.

Although one can rightly argue that modern architecture has been a representation of modernity and a foil for modernization *everywhere*, including the industrialized West, this process has nevertheless been far more evident and transparent outside the West. As a result, the study of modern architecture in non-Western contexts compels us to go beyond traditional categories of art history, formal analysis, or discussion of "origins," "influences," and so forth, and to delve into the historical and political contexts in which forms acquire meaning—which may be different from their original meanings in the West. Traditional assumptions about the "autonomy" of architectural form (which have been under critical scrutiny everywhere for some time now) are even more conspicuously contested by the example of "other modernisms." With the proliferation of studies of the latter, the emphasis has been shifting from architecture as an autonomous, self-referential discipline to what we might call the *politics* of architecture.

While the top-to-bottom character of modernization in non-Western contexts inevitably brings the issues of power and politics to the forefront of architectural history, it is also important not to read the history of modern architecture *exclusively* through the lenses of current critical perspectives focused on power and politics. In this book I hope to make a more nuanced assessment of the modernist vision, discriminating between its critical premises and its ultimately authoritarian implementations, between what it meant to its contemporaries and what it means to us today. Modern architecture in non-Western contexts, or anywhere for that matter, may be seen as a form of cultural and environmental oppression imposed upon people by bureaucrats, architects, and planners—as indeed numerous cultural critics have seen at least since Jane Jacobs.[16] Power, however, is not only about oppression but also and literally about empowerment, and it is the factor of historical agency associated with the modernist vision that has made it so appealing to non-Western nations—nations that for centuries were cast as "ahistorical." New nation-states such as Turkey and many postcolonial governments in the twentieth century initially adopted modern architecture and urbanism as what they perceived to be statements of national independence, pride, and progress. Whatever our retrospective critical assessments may be, to its contemporaries modernism was an expression of the desire of "other cultures" to contest their "otherness" and to claim subjectivity in making their own history.

In this book, my approach to the architectural culture of early republican Turkey is informed by an awareness of the profound ambiguity of the modernist project of the 1930s, including its modern architecture. Perhaps there is a personal and generational explanation for this. Unlike the generation born into the early republic—my parents, my teachers, and the first generation of historians who studied modern Turkish architecture and to whom this book is greatly indebted[17]—I can maintain a critical distance from that period in order to see through modernism into the authoritarian politics. I can question the republican modernist vision with the hindsight of all the developments, critical ideas, and scholarship of the last two decades. I can take issue with its larger claims to scientific truth and with its mandate to transform society for the better and to construct a thoroughly transformed future largely dissociated from culture, context, and history.[18]

At the same time, I am equally distanced from the emerging younger generation of architectural historians who have been focusing, with much critical force and insight, on the ideological programs and authoritarian politics of early republican architecture.[19] Unlike most of these younger scholars, I have caught the tail end of the republican vision through personal memories—family outings in Youth Park, the Atatürk model farm and forest, and the Çubuk Dam in Ankara—the legacies of republican public space that I discuss later in the book. I lived my childhood and youth within the lingering legacy of the Kemalist project, just before the dismantling of the ethos of the early republic and the demolition or transformation of its most representative physical spaces after 1980. Perhaps as a result of this relative historical proximity, I still take the optimism, energy, and excitement of the early republican architects to heart. I am fascinated by their heroic feelings of nation building and history making, which come across in contemporaneous documents, testimonies, photographs, and publications. Such evidence suggests to me that, emerging out of a highly popular nationalist war of independence and conceived by the hero of the war, Mustafa Kemal Atatürk, Turkey's modernist vision was more popular than is typically suggested by other cases of high modernist social engineering "forced upon" traditional societies. Interestingly, James C. Scott did not include Mustafa Kemal in his "Hall of Fame of High Modernism," which features other famous figures from Saint-Simon and Lenin to Robert Moses and the Shah of Iran. I believe that, without negating the high modernist legacy of Kemalism, there are good historical reasons to justify this exclusion. Deified as a secularist and Westernizer by many Turks, detested for the same reasons by others, but ultimately revered as a soldier and national hero by all, Atatürk left a legacy that continues to be one of the more complex and enduring legacies among twentieth-century modernizers and nation builders.

The Modern Movement may have been conspicuously out of place in a war-torn, traditional Muslim society without the industrial infrastructure to justify its aesthetic and constructional precepts. Yet its introduction into Turkey was elevated to epic proportions in the architectural culture of the 1930s. It was hailed as the visible proof that Turkey was a modern European nation with no resemblance to the exotic and orientalist aesthetic tropes by which the Ottoman Empire had typically been represented in the past. Like Salman Rushdie's Indian immigrant in a Western metropolis who is "a disguise inventing his own false descriptions to counter the falsehoods invented about him," the modernist vision of the early republic embodied "as much heroism as pathos."[20] I hope my account conveys these ambiguous and simultaneous feelings of both pathos and heroism, of both state power and popular empowerment, of both alienation and liberation—feelings without which modernism loses its richness and historical complexity.[21] That the current cultural climate in Turkey is increasingly more polarized between a staunch, uncritical defense of the republican modernist vision and an indiscriminate condemnation of its Westernizing, secularizing agenda testifies to the importance and urgency of accounts that complicate the picture.

⊙   ⊙   ⊙

FINALLY, SOME METHODOLOGICAL notes are necessary to explain the sources and structure of this book. As is evident from its subtitle, the concept of "architectural culture" has been central to it.[22] Very simply, the concept of architectural culture starts from the premise that one should look at architecture not as an autonomous, self-referential discipline interested in forms and form-making alone, but rather as a larger institutional, cultural, and social field with important political implications. The concept of architectural culture implies a cultural historian's approach to the buildings, projects, and architectural texts that collectively constitute a "discourse" about architecture, in the original sense of this helpful but now clichéd term. The architectural culture of a particular place and time includes all the institutional practices—architectural schools, publications, exhibitions, competitions, and professional associations—that produce, reproduce, discredit, or lend credibility to discourses about architecture.

A cultural approach does not mean that architecture can be reduced to discourses about architecture or that buildings are unequivocal and transparent expressions of the ideas that are claimed to have informed them. Most of the time the most prolific producers of the discourse (such as Aptullah Ziya, Behçet Sabri, and Bedrettin Hamdi in the Turkish scene in the 1930s) are not the most prolific or the most interesting designers of the period (such as Seyfettin Arkan or Şevki Balmumcu). In other cases the two functions overlap in the personalities of individual architects (such as Zeki Sayar and Sedad Hakkı Eldem). Yet even then their published writings, theories, and programs fall short of fully explaining their built work or revealing the tacit agendas, unacknowledged influences, and simply personal aesthetic choices involved in their designs. More specifically, the doctrines of rationalism and functionalism that are at the center of the official discourse of modernism often prove to be no more than clichés that leave out the complex cultural, aesthetic, and personal considerations that go into the making of the best modernist work. The idea behind the study of architectural culture is not to explain the work through what was said and written about it but to see the ways in which what was said, written, and built *collectively* confirm, interpret, contest, or negotiate the political and ideological agendas of the time.

As the foregoing tenets of the cultural approach suggest, the primary sources for this study were contemporary publications and visual sources of the early republican period, as well as the surviving buildings and surviving people. I surveyed the most representative official, professional, and popular publications of the "long 1930s." I took this quintessentially Kemalist "long decade" to span the period from the graduation and professional organization of the first modernist Turkish architects in 1928 to the architectural competition for Mustafa Kemal's mausoleum in 1942, the symbolic closure of the early republican period. With the utopian modernist vision of the Kemalist revolution at its height at home and the establishment of the Modern Movement as the dominant aesthetic and ideological canon abroad, the 1930s constitute a particularly fascinating decade with a strong visual component, to which contemporary photographs testify. The historical overlap between modernism and techniques of reproduction, photography, and advertisement in Europe has been the topic of many recent studies.[23] The Turkish scene in the 1930s affirms the importance of these new means in disseminating a visual culture of modernity mostly by the agencies and publications of the state. Thus contemporary photographs, postcards, and posters were also consulted, and in many cases they have been as important and informative as published textual material.

Although the *architectural* research for this book was focused on "the long 1930s," the larger cultural and political framework within which the research is meaningful spans the period from the Young Turk revolution of 1908 to the end of the RPP's single-party regime in 1950. There are many good reasons why there is a clear definition and coherence to this larger period, not just in architectural history but in the history of modern Turkey in general.[24] The overarching reason that concerns the structuring of this book is the strong ideological grip of Turkish nationalism on all aspects of politics, life, and culture throughout this period. For this reason, four chapters focusing on modernism as an aesthetic canon of the Kemalist period proper are bracketed by an introductory chapter looking at what came before modernism and a final chapter looking at what followed the rejection of the modernist canon. Taking issue with the common tendency to divide the architectural history of the early republic into stylistically defined periods—that is, a succession of "national" and "international" styles[25]—I regard *the continuity of the nationalist framework* as the defining feature of early republican architectural culture, regardless of stylistic shifts.

The thematic ordering of the book follows a loosely chronological structure, but each chapter stands on its own in exploring one component or theme in the architectural culture of the early republic. The first chapter reviews the legacy of the Ottoman revivalist "national style" that preceded modernism in Turkish architecture. The casting of this style as modernism's academic, stylistic, and anachronistic "other" constituted the first high-modernist gesture that depicted the past as "an impediment, a history that must be transcended" and the present as "the platform for launching plans for a better future."[26] The rest of the book offers historical context and evidence for three important and recurrent terms that collectively summarize the aspirations of early republican architectural culture: "architecture of revolution" (*inkilap mimarisi*), "new architecture" (*yeni mimari*), and "national architecture" (*milli mimari*). The primary question that preoccupied early republican architects was how to find an architecture that embodied all three attributes at once.

Chapters 2 and 3 address the meaning and implications of the term *inkilap mimarisi* (architecture of revolution)—a key term designating an idealized but largely formless quest of the early 1930s. Chapter 2 looks specifically at the official discourse through which modern architecture came to be the primary visual expression of the republican "revolution," as it was called, and shows how modern forms were mobilized to serve the ideological agenda of the regime. Chapter 3 focuses on the significance of the industrial and technological icons of modernism in the revolutionary consciousness of the republic and in the specific discourses of progress and civilization espoused by Kemalism. It highlights parallels with and divergences from the ways in which the modernist avant-garde in Europe exalted the same technological icons.

How the professional discourse of Turkish architects—their struggle for legitimacy and state commissions and their particular readings of modernism to strengthen their professional claims—took shape around the term *Yeni Mimari* ("the New Architecture") is discussed in chapter 4. Chapter 5 then looks at images and ideas of the modern house, the most paradigmatic domain claimed by modernist architects everywhere in the 1930s, as well as the symbol of the republican desire to extend the "civilizing mission" of the Kemalist reforms into the private realm. Nowhere is the ambiguity of modernism more evident than in the architecture of the house (*mesken mimarisi*, as Turkish architects called it). On one hand, it was a theme that symbolized the democratic potential of the New Architecture, whereby architects could claim service to "the people" rather than to wealthy patrons, states, and institutions. On the other hand, the perception of the house as a means for reforming lifestyles epitomized the penetration of the state, through experts, architects, and planners, to the traditionally resistant domain of privacy, family life, and domestic order.

By the late 1930s, nationalist attacks on modernism had already intensified in Turkey, portraying its abstract, geometric forms as the mark of an alienated, individualistic, and cosmopolitan society. Chapter 6 focuses on the intensification of the *milli mimari* (national architecture) debates in the late 1930s, discussing how vernacular building traditions—especially the timber "Turkish houses"—were appropriated by modernist architects in an effort to "nationalize the modern." It also looks at how, after the death of Mustafa Kemal Atatürk in 1938, the more "futuristic" revolutionary spirit declined, giving way to the influences of contemporary German and Italian nationalist trends in architecture and to the inspiration of Central Asian and pre-Islamic Turkish monuments. The resulting departure from the modernist aesthetic of the early 1930s toward a more classicized and monumental modern architecture representative of state power and nationalist historiography is covered in this last chapter, bringing this heroic era of modern Turkish history to a close.

One of the major difficulties of writing a book of this nature and scope has been the question of the multiple readerships that I wished to engage with it. First and most obviously, I expect this book to be of interest to my own disciplinary constituency—namely, historians of modern architecture. Second, I expect it also to appeal to area specialists—to those in Turkish and Middle East studies in this case. Third, I hope that an even larger interdisciplinary and nonspecialist audience concerned with questions of modernity and national identity in general will find it interesting and informative. It was frustrating at times to write with all of these constituencies in mind. (Does one explain who Le Corbusier was for nonspecialist readers outside the field of architecture? Does one give basic historical information such as the date of the proclamation of the Turkish republic for readers unfamiliar with the history of Turkey and the Middle East?). But what ultimately transcended the fear of compromise on each side was the conviction that something rich and original can come out of a cultural history of this sort—insights that can be gained only by crossing the boundaries between architectural history and area studies everywhere.

1

First Moderns

THE LEGACY OF OTTOMAN REVIVALISM

> Since young poets started to compose in the modern meter and since some
> novelty fans started to conduct Turkish *saz* music with a baton, a notorious
> *medrese* architecture, which we do not know what to call, has proliferated
> among our architects. Domes reminiscent of the turban taken off the head
> of the religious fanatic have started to mushroom under the Turkish sky.
> Hotel, bank, school, ferry landing, all are now a caricature of a mosque,
> missing a minaret on the outside and a *minber* inside. . . . This kind of
> return to the past is a degeneration, a reactionary architecture [*mürteci*
> *mimari*].
>
> —Ahmet Haşim, *Gurabahane-i Laklakan,* 1928[1]

COMPLETED IN 1909, the Central Post Office in Sirkeci on the tip of
Istanbul's historical peninsula is an impressive monumental building designed by the
Turkish architect Vedat Bey (fig. 1.1). It incorporates a number of stylistic references
to classical Ottoman architecture (pointed arches, ornate tile work on the spandrels
above the arches, domes over the corner towers) in an otherwise conspicuously
European building. The use of the tall Corinthian order on the upper floors of the
main façade and the symmetry and axiality of the plan follow a distinctly École des
Beaux-Arts *parti* testifying to the European training and cultural references of its
architect, like those of many other educated Ottoman elites of the time. The building's most spectacular feature is a reinforced concrete and iron truss structural system
that allows a large span over a spacious central hall lit by a glass roof. This central
space evokes a feeling not unlike that of comparable European buildings of the time,
such as Otto Wagner's Postal Savings Bank in Vienna (1906), one of the canonic buildings of early modern architecture, completed only three years before the Sirkeci post

Fig. 1.1. The first major National Architecture Renaissance building in Istanbul—the Central Post Office, Sirkeci (1909), by Vedat Bey.
Top: Front elevation showing the symmetrical, axial arrangement and the use of pointed arches, corner domes, and the tall Corinthian order on the upper floors. **Bottom:** Interior view of the main hall showing the reinforced concrete structure and the glass roof of the skylit hall.

office. Like Wagner's bank, Vedat Bey's post office was a modern urban structure in a busy, imperial, cosmopolitan, and rapidly changing city.

The design and construction of the Central Post Office coincided with a major event in the history of modern Turkey: the Constitutional Revolution of 1908, which brought the European-educated "Young Turks" to power during the final years of the Ottoman Empire. On 23 July 1908, the constitution and the parliament, suspended some thirty years earlier by Sultan Abdulhamid II (1876–1909), were restored. After the brief euphoria of 1908, however, the revolution's dreams of liberal reform turned into authoritarian politics, and power was consolidated in the hands of the Committee of Union and Progress (CUP), the military and political organization of the Young Turk movement. Leaders of the CUP deposed Sultan Abdulhamid II in 1909, suppressed their conservative and liberal opponents in the next few years, and ruled the country until the First World War, while Sultan Mehmet Reşat V (1909–1918) remained on the throne as a figurehead. At the same time, they initiated important urban modernization, sanitation, and transportation projects in the hope of reviving the empire and breathing life into the "sick man of Europe." As Bernard Lewis, the prominent historian of modern Turkey, remarked, "Young Turks may have failed to give Turkey constitutional government; however, they gave Istanbul its drains."[2] They also gave a new face to public buildings, as exemplified in the architecture of the Sirkeci post office. Between 1908 and 1918 a new architectural style emerged in Turkey, symbolizing many of the ideological aspirations and cultural complexities of the late empire.

Retrospectively labeled by historians of architecture the "First National Style,"[3] but known to its contemporaries as the "National Architecture Renaissance," this rather eclectic Ottoman revivalism dominated architectural discourse and practice in Turkey from about the turn of the century well into the 1930s. The basic idea was to combine decorative elements derived from classical Ottoman architecture (especially semispherical Ottoman domes, wide roof overhangs with supporting brackets, pointed arches, and ornate tile decoration) with beaux-arts design principles (symmetry and axiality, in particular) and new construction techniques (reinforced concrete, iron, and steel). Like classical and Gothic revivals in nineteenth-century Europe and the United States, it was used extensively for banks, offices, cinemas, and other public buildings in the imperial capital. In a manner also reminiscent of the use of stylistic revivals in industrial and utilitarian buildings in the West, it was adopted for smaller utilitarian structures of modern life such as the ferry stations built in Istanbul between 1913 and 1917 (fig. 1.2).[4] After the nationalist War of Independence and the proclamation of Ankara as the new capital of the republic in 1923, major public buildings continued to be built in this style in Ankara and other Anatolian cities.

In spite of the visible mark that the National Architecture Renaissance left in many Turkish cities, it has been largely neglected in architectural historiography and design education until quite recently.[5] Historians of Ottoman and Islamic architecture have typically focused on the sixteenth-century classical period epitomized by Sinan's

Fig. 1.2. The National Architecture Renaissance as the "corporate style" of Şirket-i Hayriye, the Ottoman passenger ferry company in Istanbul. Three examples of the many ferry stations built between 1913 and 1917: **Top:** Beşiktaş, by Ali Talat Bey, 1913; **middle:** Haydarpaşa, by Vedat Bey, 1915; **bottom:** Büyükada, by Mihran Azaryan, 1915.

work. For many of them, the turn-of-the-century Ottoman revivalism was too stylized, too Westernized, and too modernized to be discussed within the Ottoman tradition—it was too much a departure from the tradition's "purity" and "authenticity."
On the other hand, historians of modern Turkish architecture, especially those with
professional training as architects, have tended to approach Ottoman revivalism with
the biases of a doctrinaire modernism that took shape in the 1930s. From this perspective, modern architecture was identified with the formal canons of the Modern
Movement, and Ottoman revivalism was seen as modern architecture's academic, stylistic, and anachronistic "other" that had to be left behind in order to capture the zeitgeist of the modern age. The idea of "dressing up" modern building types, modern
materials, and modern construction techniques in ornate historical "envelopes"—the
basic idea behind nineteenth-century revivalism everywhere—was criticized as
"untruthful" and "deceptive" from the vantage point of a modernist ethic. The stylistic unity of all Ottoman revivalist buildings, "from hotels and banks to schools and
ferry landings," as the prominent author Ahmet Haşim observed in 1928, was seen as
a violation of the functionalist and rationalist principles of modernism, which man-
dated a programmatic differentiation of exterior form.

From a less stylistic and more historical perspective, one can talk about the
National Architecture Renaissance as the first "modern" discourse in Turkish architectural culture.[6] It was the first systematic engagement of Turkish architects with new
building types, construction techniques, and design principles. Above all, it was the
first large-scale mobilization of architecture for identity construction and nation
building. Or one can talk about the National Architecture Renaissance as the last
breath of Ottoman-islamic architecture before its final eclipse in the republican period—a last reference to the architectural heritage of the empire even in that dramatically transformed, Westernized, and stylized form. Both are accurate descriptions of
Ottoman revivalist architecture at the turn of the twentieth century. By the same
token, the architects who designed and built in that style were at once the last
Ottoman and the first republican architects, their careers coinciding with important
institutional transformations toward the making of a modern architectural profession
in Turkey. Most important of all, it was this ambiguity of cultural signification—the
ambiguity of a style that could accommodate modern functions yet refer back to a
glorious Ottoman-islamic past—that lent itself to different readings and interpretations that have shifted over time.

To begin with, turn-of-the-century Ottoman intellectuals, artists, and architects
were concerned primarily with preserving the Ottoman state, which they identified
with the sultan and the empire. For most of them, an Ottoman revivalist architectural style symbolized, before everything else, the patrimony of the Ottoman state: it was
a "patriotic" architecture for an ethnically and religiously heterogeneous *Ottoman*
"nation." This interpretation was short-lived, however. As many historians have
pointed out, the last vestiges of this Ottomanism were shattered during the cata-
strophic losses of the Balkan Wars and especially the First World War, when Turkish

nationalism emerged from the trenches of Gallipoli as the victorious ideology to carry Turkey into the republican period. For the Turkish nationalists of the CUP and their followers in the early republic, the National Architecture Renaissance was primarily a *Turkish* national style. Its Ottoman forms and motifs were recharged with "Turkish" rather than Islamic or imperial cultural meanings. It was this "Turkification" of Ottoman architecture in the final years of the Ottoman Empire that sanctioned its continued use during the first decade of the Kemalist republic, a time when everything else Ottoman was radically rejected. Furthermore, the republican leaders, in search of legitimacy at a time of competing ideologies, tacitly (and strategically) accepted that this style's implicit references to Islam and to the sultan would appeal to a traditional population still loyal to those symbols.

By 1931, however, once the single-party regime of the Republican People's Party (RPP) was consolidated and the secular, Western-oriented cultural politics of the republic firmly established, Ottoman revivalism was rapidly abandoned in favor of an imported "New Architecture" (*Yeni Mimari*), as the Modern Movement came to be called in Turkey. This was the beginning of an ideologically charged binary way of thinking, based on contrasts between the old and the new, the traditional and the contemporary, the reactionary and the progressive—in terms of which the entire architectural discourse of the 1930s was construed and legitimated. Ahmet Haşim's views on the National Architecture Renaissance are representative of official republican sentiments toward this style in the heyday of Turkey's radical transformation along Western lines under the auspices of Kemalism. "This reactionary architecture [*mürteci mimari*]," Haşim wrote in 1928, "dressed in a robe and a turban, this imitation of a tomb or a *medrese* [madrasah, or school for Islamic religious instruction], does not deserve to be called an 'architectural renaissance.' What they call a 'newborn' is in fact a very old man."[7] What is especially significant in this characterization is the association of Ottoman revivalism with reactionary forces (*irtica*), signifying a resistance to progress.[8] It captures how, in that dramatic period of transition, architecture was viewed through the perspective of an ideology that presented itself as a unique, progressive, and radical break with the nation's own imperial, "anachronistic," and "backward" past.

In the light of these shifting interpretations, one concludes that Ottoman revivalism, the prevailing architectural idiom between 1908 and 1931, was far from being a clearly delineated style with a fixed ideological meaning. Rather, it was the architectural expression of a process through which the cultural significance of Ottoman forms was negotiated and transformed over a few decades. The rest of this chapter traces the legacy of the Ottoman revivalist National Architecture Renaissance through the three phases just outlined: its origins in Ottoman patriotism, its appropriation by Turkish nationalism, and finally its rejection by the Kemalist revolution. It also highlights the corresponding institutional, educational, and professional transformations in art and architecture before the radical switch to European modernism in the 1930s. The premise is that for a critical understanding of the architectural culture of the early republic, it is necessary to begin with Ottoman revivalism—which was in fact a constitutive aspect of the modernist architectural culture of the 1930s, albeit in the form of its stylistic and ideological "other."

Patriotism and Ottoman Revival

ONE CAN TALK about Ottoman revivalism as a "modern" discourse in a historical sense if one makes a basic distinction between "modernism" as a particular artistic and architectural trend of the early twentieth century and the broader term "modernity." The latter involves, among other things, a clear self-consciousness, on the part of nations as well as individuals, of history and change and of one's own position with respect to change—a claiming of one's subjectivity and a recognition of one's need for self-representation and self-transformation. In this latter sense, the term "modern" does not have a narrowly fixed historical reference, nor is it the exclusive monopoly of European history: there can be different "moderns" in different places and times. Although Western Europe has been the historical source and geographical locus of this modern self-consciousness, the rest of the world was intimately connected to it, either as colonial extensions of Europe or as old empires caught in Europe's expanding sphere of economic and cultural influence. For these societies, modernity was, by definition, a process of catching up with a historical phenomenon the parameters of which were delineated elsewhere.

The National Architecture Renaissance and the idea of Ottoman revival on which it was predicated represent the first self-conscious and systematic attempt to codify Ottoman architecture as a rational aesthetic discipline. It was a contrived response to the new and unprecedented programmatic requirements of modern life, as distinct from a predominantly craft-based building practice limited to traditional building types such as the mosque, the tomb, the *medrese,* and the *hamam* (public bath). Although its stylistic vocabulary was derived from the traditional types, it was precisely the progressive disappearance or transformation of the "life-worlds" represented by these types under the impact of modernization that made the idea of an architectural "renaissance" based on Ottoman precedents conceivable in the first place. "Where old ways are alive, traditions need be neither revived nor invented," observed the historian Eric Hobsbawm.[9] As such, the National Architecture Renaissance can indeed be seen as an "invented tradition" in the way Hobsbawm formulated it, arising from the desire to construct an identity that is "unchanging and invariant" in a rapidly changing modern world. It is the historical self-consciousness implied in the very idea of "revival" that makes the National Architecture Renaissance a "modern" discourse.

Above all else, the idea of Ottoman revival entails an aspiration to claim a place for Ottoman architecture among the "modern styles" or revivalisms of the nineteenth century. This was, in effect, a repudiation of the classification of Ottoman architecture as a "non-historical style," which was the norm in classic architectural texts of the nineteenth century, informed as they were by orientalist and Eurocentric visions.[10] As we know today, after at least twenty years of critical theorizing on orientalism and the politics of representation, the very constitution of the discipline of architecture in the West was based on this nineteenth-century distinction between the "Western tradition" in architecture and its non-Western "others." The Western tradition was thought to represent a dynamic historical evolution from classical antiquity to modern revivalism, whereas non-Western traditions were regarded as frozen in their golden or classic ages, incapable of modern transformations. In that context, the National Architecture Renaissance was not only the first self-consciously "modern" discourse in Turkey but also, by the same token, the first "anti-orientalist" one, claiming its historicity and refusing to be a "nonhistorical style," as Sir Bannister Fletcher classified Ottoman architecture in 1896.[11]

The historical roots of this anti-orientalist and modern self-consciousness go back to the Young Ottoman movement in the second half of the nineteenth century. Young Ottomans, mostly intellectuals, bureaucrats, and journalists educated in Europe, were the first to begin thinking about the empire as a political community or an "Ottoman nation." It should be immediately added that many scholars characterize the Young Ottoman movement as a "proto-nationalist" movement in which Islam and the patrimony of the Ottoman sultan, rather than ethnicity and language, still constituted the primary elements of social cohesion and solidarity.[12] Nevertheless, many of the elements that Benedict Anderson, in his classic work on nationalism, has identified as playing a major role in "imagining a nation"—maps, the census, the first novels, and especially the first newspapers—had in fact emerged in the Ottoman Empire in the 1860s.[13] It is no coincidence that the stylistic vocabulary of the National Architecture Renaissance goes back to the seminal text *Usul-i Mimari-yi Osmani* (Principles of Ottoman Architecture), produced in 1873, in the heyday of the Young Ottoman movement. This volume compellingly reflects the desire of educated Ottoman elites to redress the balance of excess Westernization in the preceding Tanzimat period and to install a new sense of patriotism that included pride in the artistic and architectural heritage of the empire.[14]

Commissioned to Ibrahim Edhem Pasha, the minister of public works during the reign of Sultan Abdulaziz (1861–1876), *Usul-i Mimari* was prepared for the empire's participation in the Vienna International Exposition of 1873 and was published in three languages (Ottoman, French, and German).[15] Founded upon "the realization that the progress [of Ottomans] in the exalted realm of Fine Arts is possible only by recourse to the resplendent works of their past," this massive volume was the result of a systematic study and documentation of classical Ottoman buildings, monuments, and decorative details. The idea was to abstract from them the underlying system of architectural orders, compositional principles, and geometric rules that the authors of the text claimed to possess universal validity and practical applicability for different programs and sites. The universalistic aspirations of the text are of particular importance: the principles of Ottoman architecture were offered to the rest of the world as alternatives to and of no less importance than the principles behind neoclassic or neo-Gothic styles.

The theoretical models, analytical methods, and representational techniques informing the 1873 text were unmistakably European, particularly French, reflecting the educational background of the Ottoman artists and intellectuals involved in its production. In the manner of Viollet-le-Duc (1814–1879), who looked for rational principles underlying historical precedents,[16] the authors of *Usul-i Mimari* studied Ottoman precedents as the possible sources of a contemporary Ottoman architecture, "modern" and infused with "national character" at the same time. In the manner of Claude Perrault (1613–1688), who codified the "correct" orders of classical architecture to demonstrate the superiority of the "moderns" over the "ancients,"[17] they codified the three Ottoman orders: the conic, the diamond, and the crystalline, roughly corresponding to the Doric, the Ionic, and the Corinthian, respectively. The extensive use of these Ottoman orders in National Architecture Renaissance buildings of the 1920s demonstrates that they constituted a solid vocabulary upon which a "national style" could rely half a century later (fig. 1.3). Finally, in the manner of Owen Jones (1806–1889),[18] they classified Ottoman decorative patterns, abstracting them out of tiles, woodwork, mother-of-pearl inlay details, and so forth, and making them available for use in the ornamental programs of Ottoman revivalist buildings.

This re-presentation of Ottoman forms and details in the format of European architectural discourse is symptomatic of what is, in essence, the profound ambiguity of nationalist consciousness in non-Western contexts. At the same time the authors of *Usul-i Mimari* sought to restore the dignity of Ottoman architectural heritage and claimed its theoretical equality to European styles, they simultaneously confirmed the superiority of the European constructs of knowledge from which they borrowed their analytical frameworks, methods, and techniques. They were "anti-orientalist" to the extent that as Ottoman intellectuals and architects they claimed a historical subjectivity—that is, an active role in the making of a modern Ottoman architecture which, they implied, was not outside the progressive historical evolution of architecture. At the same time, as rationalist, self-knowing, post-Enlightenment subjects in the European sense, they adopted the same objectifying constructs of knowledge—the same systematic study, classification, and ordering of knowledge—that European orientalists had applied to non-Western "others."

As many scholars have pointed out in discussing this phenomenon, nationalist thinking outside the industrialized West was an inherently contradictory project. "It reasoned within a framework of knowledge whose representational structure corresponded to the very structure of power that nationalist thought sought to repudiate."[19] As we will see in chapter 3, this profound dilemma would reach its crest under the Westernizing impetus of the 1930s, to be captured by the Kemalist slogan "being Western in spite of the West." As profound as the contradictions of nationalist modernization might be in the non-Western world, however, the adoption of Western constructs of knowledge need not always and necessarily mean a total submission to

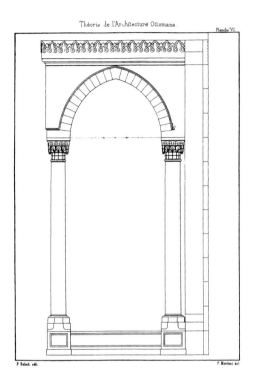

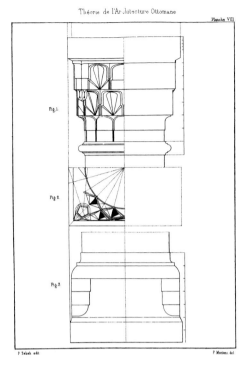

Fig. 1.3. Top: The "crystalline order" (*tarz-i mimari-yi mücevheri*) from the book *Usul-i Mimari-yi Osmani,* 1873. **Bottom left:** Use of the crystalline order in the entrance portico of the Ethnography Museum, Ankara (1925–1928), by Arif Hikmet Koyunoğlu. **Bottom right:** Detail of the column capital.

Western powers. Nor does the wholesale repudiation of these constructs need be the only conceivable form of resistance. After all, power is not only about oppression, even if this was the dominant feature of the colonialism and imperialism through which non-Western others encountered Western power. Power is also about "empowerment"—the possibility of people's becoming active participating subjects rather than passive objects of history.[20] A text like *Usul-i Mimari* suggests how the appropriation of European architectural theories by non-European "others" and the reprocessing of those theories toward self-representation could actually mark a critical moment.

Nothing illustrates this critical moment more explicitly than the paintings of Osman Hamdi Bey (1841–1910), a prominent Ottoman artist, intellectual, and public figure, founder of the Istanbul Archaeology Museum (1881) and the Academy of Fine Arts (1882), where the first architectural school was located. Closely connected to the authors of *Usul-i Mimari* and himself a French-educated member of the Young Ottoman generation, Osman Hamdi Bey was shaped in both life and career by the same modern and anti-orientalist self-consciousness that informed the 1873 text.[21] In many of his paintings, Osman Hamdi Bey employed the European orientalist genre of painting that he learned in the atelier of Jean Leon Gerome in Paris, reversing, however, the stereotypical image of the orient represented by the exotic (and erotic) scenes of the harem, the bazaar, and the *hamam*. These paintings of the 1890s and 1900s depict a different, rational and dynamic orient where people, including women, stand upright, read, debate, stroll in the streets, and engage in productive activities—that is, they depict a progressive Muslim society engaged in the pursuit of knowledge, science, and progress (fig. 1.4).

Not surprisingly, in the context of recent critical debates concerning the Western canon in art, Osman Hamdi Bey's paintings have drawn the attention of many scholars in the West. Some commentators use them to salvage the term "orientalism" from the negative connotations that have been attached to it since Edward Said's work first appeared.[22] The more critical and sophisticated analyses, however, observe the potential in these paintings for exposing the biases of the Western orientalist canon and hence for complicating and expanding it, more in the way Said himself intended.[23] In spite of their conspicuously oriental surroundings, the characters in Osman Hamdi Bey's paintings resist being categorized as essential, unchanging, stereotypical "others." They are characters with personalities and temporality, depicted in scenes of learning, daily life, and domestic bliss. They maintain their "difference" from European identities, but no longer as "inferior others": difference is rendered neutral rather than hierarchical.[24]

There are interesting chronological and ideological parallels between Osman Hamdi Bey's "corrective enterprise" and the emergence of the National Architecture Renaissance around the turn of the century. Like Osman Hamdi Bey, the proponents and leading designers of the National Architecture Renaissance were educated in Europe but were at the same time deeply committed to the welfare of the Ottoman

state and its artistic and architectural heritage. For them, Ottoman architecture was not something frozen in the mosques and *medreses* of the classical age, incapable of adapting to the modern world. Nor was it something "exotic" and trivial like the orientalist and pseudo-islamic styles popular in Europe throughout the nineteenth century. Ottoman architecture was a rich tradition (already documented in *Usul-i Mimari-yi Osmani*

Fig. 1.4. "Girl Reading" (*Rahle Önünde Kız*), by Osman Hamdi Bey (1880)—an "orientalist" painting defying orientalist stereotypes.

in 1873) that contained the necessary stylistic vocabulary for the creation of a "modern" and "national" architecture for the late empire. This, they argued, would be an architecture capable of reflecting not only the contemporary needs and technological developments of the turn of the century but also the pride and patriotism of the Ottoman nation. It would be a rebirth—a National Architecture *Renaissance*.

There was much in the nineteenth-century architectural scene at large to justify these sentiments of patriotism and the desire for an Ottoman renaissance. First, some of the orientalized and pseudo-islamic styles that had been feeding the European imagination in the public spectacle of the great expositions had also made their way to Istanbul throughout the century.[25] For example, the onion domes of the Taksim Army Barracks gatehouse by Kirkor Balyan (c. 1850) and the large horseshoe arch of the Ministry of Defense gatehouse by the French architect Marie-Auguste Antoine Bourgeois (1867) were orientalized designs that defied historical appropriateness in favor of an exotic effect. The Young Ottomans must have especially resented that in these examples, stylistic references to the more exotic Alhambra and Taj Mahal had been selected over references to local Ottoman precedents. More pervasive, however, was the profusion of European styles and influences (neoclassic, baroque, and French Empire styles in particular) that had dominated Ottoman architecture, especially after the beginning of the Tanzimat period (1839). When Young Ottoman thought was fermenting during the reigns of Sultan Abdulaziz (1861–1876) and Sultan Abdulhamid II (1876–1909), the architectural scene in Istanbul was indeed a cosmopolitan mix of eclectic and revivalist styles, from neoclassic to art nouveau, mostly the work of European, Levantine, and non-Muslim Ottoman architects.[26] In principle, the National Architecture Renaissance was the patriotic reaction of Ottoman architects to this cosmopolitan mix of styles. At the same time, it was itself informed by the same eclectic and cosmopolitan architectural culture of the late nineteenth century that was institutionally reproduced through the training of the architects. The other dimension of the "modernity" of Ottoman revival (the first one being the rise of a patriotic, protonationalist consciousness) had to do with the institutional and educational setting within which this style emerged.

The radical modernization of Ottoman architectural and engineering education along European lines dates to the first half of the nineteenth century, when the Office of Royal Architects (Hassa Mimarları), the traditional training ground of Ottoman architects in the classical period, was dissolved.[27] In 1883, through the initiative of Osman Hamdi Bey, the Academy of Fine Arts (Sanayi-i Nefise Mekteb-i Âlisi) was established as a royal school with four main sections: architecture, painting, sculpture, and calligraphy. A year later, the Civil Service School of Engineering (Hendese-i Mülkiye Mektebi) was established and offered courses in architecture. Until after the turn of the century, architectural education in these schools was conducted by European or Levantine architects, among whom Alexandre Vallaury and August Jasmund were the two prominent names. Both had designed major buildings in Istanbul, including Vallaury's Public Debt Administration Building (1897) and Jasmund's Sirkeci Railroad Station (1880–1890)—both of them stylistically orientalized designs with an eclectic mix of Ottoman and Islamic references. The National Architecture Renaissance entailed an implicit critique of the work and instruction of these teachers by younger designers, among whom two Turkish-Muslim architects assumed leadership as both practitioners and educators: Vedat Bey and Kemalettin Bey.

Vedat Bey (1873–1942) was a well-connected, École des Beaux Arts–trained architect who, upon his return from Paris in 1898, worked for the Municipality (Şehremaneti) as well as the Ministries of Postal Services and War. He occupied the post of royal chief architect during the reign of Sultan Mehmet Reşat (1909–1918) and designed major public buildings of the Young Turk era in Istanbul before moving on to work in Ankara during the first years of the republic. In addition to his seminal role as a teacher in the architectural section of the academy, he offered job training to his students and apprentices in the construction of his own buildings. For example, Mimar Muzaffer (1881–1920), chief architect of the city of Konya and designer of important buildings in the Ottoman revivalist style during the 1920s, was initially an apprentice to Vedat Bey during the construction of the Sirkeci Central Post Office.[28]

Kemalettin Bey (1870–1927) was a graduate of the Civil Service School of Engineering, where he later held a teaching position. He studied at the Charlottenburg Technische Hochschule in Berlin at a time when Germany and the Ottoman Empire were drawing increasingly closer on economic and political issues. Kemalettin Bey's extensive knowledge of Ottoman precedents was derived from his restoration work as chief architect for the Ministry of Endowment's Scientific Commission for Repairs and Construction (Evkaf Nezareti İnşaat ve Tamirat Heyet-i Fenniyesi).[29] Under his leadership, this office became an important educational institution, training architects, engineers, and craftsmen who then disseminated the National Architecture Renaissance to remote corners of the country. His small mosques in Istanbul, such as the Bebek Mosque (1913), bear testimony to his mastery of and passion for Ottoman architecture, the revival of which, he believed, would restore the lost glory of the empire. A passionately religious and conservative man, as Yıldırım Yavuz characterizes him, Kemalettin Bey was deeply disturbed by the decline and immanent disintegration of the Ottoman Empire.[30]

That Vallaury and Jasmund initially taught and mentored Vedat Bey and Kemalettin Bey, respectively, underscores the continuity of an academic method and eclectic pedagogy that emphasized the blending of local traditions with contemporary techniques. The prevailing architectural curriculum that constituted the pedagogical premises of the National Architecture Renaissance was modeled after that of the

Fig.1.5. Student work showing the classical training of Turkish architects at the Academy of Fine Arts. **Left:** An elevation drawing by Arif Hikmet Koyunoğlu. **Overleaf:** Watercolor renderings of the classical orders by Sedad Hakkı Eldem, done when he was a second-year student in Giulio Mongeri's studio.

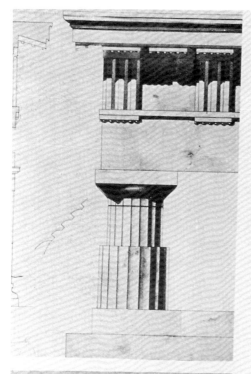

MIKYAS ⅟₄
TAFSILAT · ⅟₄
LATIF 889

French École des Beaux Arts system. Classical composition, drawing, and rendering constituted the core of the curriculum; façade composition took precedence over the plan, and axiality and symmetry dominated the designs. After an emphasis on art education in the first year, the second year was devoted to the study of classical Greek and Roman styles, with a specific focus on monochrome studies of light and shadow. In the third year, neoclassic and neo-Renaissance projects, almost exclusively for large institutional buildings, were as-

Fig. 1.6. Classical training of students in the Civil Service School of Engineering. A light-and-shade-rendered student drawing in the École des Beaux-Arts tradition, late 1920s.

signed to be rendered in watercolor (fig. 1.5). The final year requirements were measured survey drawings of classical Ottoman buildings and a final project to be designed according to the precepts of the National Architecture Renaissance. Architectural courses in the Civil Service School of Engineering followed a similarly academic program based on the study of classical orders and their artistic rendering (fig. 1.6).

The launching of the National Architecture Renaissance as the official style of the Young Turk era became possible in the aftermath of the Constitutional Revolution of 1908, when important new initiatives and staff changes were undertaken at the Academy of Fine Arts. A conspicuous change was the emergence of Turkish-Muslim artists and architects on a cultural scene traditionally dominated by Europeans, Levantines, Armenians, and Greeks. In the architectural studios, Vedat Bey succeeded Alexandre Vallaury as head of the section. A Milan-trained Italian architect, Giulio Mongeri (1873–1953), who was the third major name of the National Architecture Renaissance in Turkey, worked with him as the other influential teacher in the architectural studios.[31] In the Civil Service School of Engineering, where Jasmund had taught, Kemalettin Bey took over the architectural courses offered to engineering students. In the painting studios of the academy as well, European and Levantine teachers were replaced by younger Turkish-Muslim artists educated in Europe. The academic art instruction of Salvatore Valeri and Warnia Zarzecki was taken over by members of the so-called 1914 generation—a group of Turkish painters who studied in Paris and upon their return in 1914 introduced impressionism into Turkey.[32]

Also in 1914, in order to accommodate female art students, a sister school to the Academy of Fine Arts was established (Inas Sanayi-i Nefise Mektebi) under the directorship of Mihri Müşfik Hanım (1886–1954). She was a talented artist and a colorful personality, "herself a living testimony to the mixture of the 'alafranga' (Western) and 'alaturka' (Turkish) ways, sometimes veiled, sometimes elegantly dressed in high heels and straw hats adorned with flowers."[33] Although architecture remained an exclusively male profession until the 1930s, women started making their appearance in other arts, literature, and some professions, and a Turkish women's movement was initiated in the atmosphere of freedom that came with 1908. Further illustrating the "modernity" of this period at the academy, the practice of working with nude models in the painting and sculpture studios was established in 1917—an unprecedented step in a traditional and predominantly Muslim society.

The first attempts toward modern professionalism in art and architecture were also made in the aftermath of the Constitutional Revolution, which encouraged the establishment of independent associations and professional societies.[34] The Society of Ottoman Painters (Osmanlı Ressamlar Cemiyeti) was established in 1909, and more systematic annual art exhibitions were organized in the Galatasaray Lycée after that date.[35] Again in 1909, the Society of Ottoman Engineers and Architects (Osmanlı Mühendis ve Mimar Cemiyeti) was established, to remain active until 1922. It published a journal and propagated the ideals of scientific and technological progress. In general, however, professional boundaries between painters, architects, and engineers were blurred in those years, and the establishment of a separate professional organization exclusively for architects had to wait until the arrival of European modernism in the late 1920s.[36] In her comprehensive analysis of the professionalization of Turkish architects, Gülsüm Baydar Nalbantoğlu points out the difference between the Society of Ottoman Engineers and Architects and Western professional associations, which were interested primarily in setting professional standards and monopolizing the construction market. Unlike their Western counterparts, she argues, members of the Ottoman society saw their alliance predominantly in idealistic terms. "Their technologism was consistent with the political ideology of the modernist constitutional government, and the product of a political consciousness more than a professional one."[37]

There is no doubt that the numbers and prominence of Turkish-Muslim artists and architects increased dramatically in the Young Turk era and even more dramatically after the War of Independence. Celal Esat Arseven (1875–1971), a leading art his-

torian and public figure of the early republic, related that, defying his family's desire to see him a military officer, he attended painting classes at the academy in 1890
as one of only three Turks among many Greeks and Armenians.[38] Arif Hikmet
Koyunoğlu (1888–1982), a younger architect of the Ottoman revivalist "national
style," wrote that when he entered the academy in 1908, architecture was not a
respectable profession among Turkish-Muslim families, who did not want their sons
to be "master masons," a vocation associated with Armenians, Greeks, Jews, and
Levantines.[39] Some two decades and many wars later, among the 39 architects registered in the recently established Fine Arts Association (Guzel Sanatlar Birliği) in 1931,
there were 22 Turkish names, 10 Armenian, 6 Greek, and 1 Italian.[40] Still later, in the
1940 roster of the Turkish Architects Union (Türk Yüksek Mimarlar Birliği), 171
Turkish names were listed, three of them belonging to women, along with the names
of 18 Armenians, 11 Greeks, and 4 others (Jews and Italians).[41] It is important to add
that of these non-Muslims, all but 2 Armenians and 6 Greeks had graduated before
1923. The displacement of Armenians during the First World War and the exchange
of populations with Greece after 1922 were without doubt the primary factors in the
changing demographics of the architectural profession. The 1940 roster suggests,
however, that there were still considerable numbers of non-Muslim architects in
Istanbul who, compared with provincial non-Muslims, were relatively unaffected by
these dramatic historical events.

In spite of the increase in the numbers of Muslim-Turkish architects, the term
"nationalism" needs to be used cautiously in relation to the architectural culture of
1908–1918. Unlike the Kemalist nationalists after them, turn-of-the-century Ottoman
intellectuals, artists, and architects were concerned primarily with preservation of the
Ottoman state through identification with the sultan and the empire. For most of
them, the primary bond for holding the Ottoman "nation" together was still the patrimony of the Ottoman state rather than ethnicity and language. Ottoman-islamic art
and architecture were the shared culture of the Ottoman state and belonged to all the
peoples of that state. The idea of "nation" was still an inclusive concept designating
a political community or "commonwealth" that represented the ethnically and religiously heterogeneous, cosmopolitan character of the empire. Hasan Kayalı compellingly argues that "Young Turk" is an unfortunate misnomer for the turn-of-
the-century Ottoman modernizers and liberal constitutionalists, since not all of them
were Turks.[42] Architecture presents an analogous picture at the level of individual
designers. Many non-Muslims contributed to the making of the National Architecture Renaissance, and architects such as Giulio Mongeri (see fig. 1.10), Alessandro
Valeri, and Mihran Azaryan produced some of the most remarkable designs in this
style (see fig. 1.2).[43]

This patriotic Ottomanism, however, within which the National Architecture
Renaissance was born, gave way to the nascent ideology of Turkish nationalism some-
where around the First World War, with corresponding shifts in architectural culture.
Especially the younger generation of Turkish architects, who received their training

from Vedat Bey, Kemalettin Bey, and Giulio Mongeri between 1908 and 1918, embraced Ottoman revival as primarily a *Turkish* national style, above and beyond its function in representing the Ottoman state and its Islamic culture. Although they largely shared the Ottomanist commitment to the empire as the protector of all Muslims, most of them perceived the "Turkish nation" to be the essential core of Ottoman society.[44] Some of the most important and prolific architects of this generation were Tahsin Sermet, who graduated from the academy in 1909, Arif Hikmet Koyunoğlu (graduated 1914), Necmettin Emre (1913), and Sedad Çetintaş (1918). It was through their work that the National Architecture Renaissance was refined, "Turkified," and carried over into the republican era (literally to Ankara and other Anatolian towns) with a new ideological bent.

"Turkification" of Ottoman Forms

THE EFFORTS OF the Young Turks to modernize the Ottoman state, its institutions, and its buildings went hand in hand with the emergence of Turkish nationalism in the first decades of the twentieth century. Whether we follow scholars who portray nationalism as a product of modernity or those who see modernity as defined by nationalism,[45] the final years of the Ottoman Empire were marked by a strong relationship between the two phenomena. Whereas during the last decades of the nineteenth century, the relationship between the idea of Ottoman revivalism and Islam was analogous to that between Gothic revivalism and Christianity, increasingly after the turn of the century Ottoman forms were symbolically recharged with "Turkishness." This was not unlike, for example, the manner in which the later Victorians looked at Gothic revivalism as a symbol of "Englishness" as much as or more than a symbol of the good Christian society that Pugin and Ruskin had advocated earlier.[46] By 1918, Ottoman revivalism in architecture unequivocally meant Turkish national style.

It should also be added that in the case of the late Ottoman Empire, a complementary development in Egypt around the same time—the emergence of an Arab-Egyptian nationalist consciousness—was another important factor in the increasingly nationalist perception and portrayal of Ottoman revivalism. The "Turkification" of Ottoman architecture, especially the rejection of Arab-islamic motifs in favor of classical Ottoman ones, was paralleled in Egypt by a corresponding appeal to Memluk rather than Ottoman precedents as the basis of an "Egyptian national style." Two buildings compellingly illustrate the Egyptian case. In the early nineteenth century, the Mosque of Muhammed Ali in Cairo (1830–1848) had been designed with a conspicuously Ottoman monumentality, a central-domed plan, and slender "pencil minarets," reflecting the imperial ambitions of its patron, who modeled himself after the Ottoman sultans. As Nasser Rabbat explains, some forty years later, at the time when an Ottoman revivalist "national style" was in the making in Istanbul, the Rifa'i Mosque in Cairo (1869–1911) was built in the neo-Memluk style—the new symbol of Egyptian national identity, which distanced itself from any Ottoman references.[47] This parallel suggests a great deal about the reciprocities that operate in identity construction, which is by definition a differentiation of the "self" from similarly delineated "others."

Şerif Mardin, the leading scholar of Ottoman-Turkish modernization, has written extensively about a progressive undermining of religion by the imposition of Western notions of nationhood that overlooked the significance of Islam as the primary basis of social cohesion and as people's existential foothold in a fast-changing world.[48] As he argues, the roots of this gradual undermining of religion extend back to the Tanzimat reforms of 1839. It was after the consolidation of power of the nationalist wing of the CUP in 1913, however, that the primacy of Islam in the official definition of Ottoman identity was replaced by an emphasis on Turkishness. The emerging definition of nationhood on the basis of shared cultural, historical, and linguistic heritage, rather than shared religion under the patrimony of the Ottoman sultan, differentiated the new nationalist ideology from the earlier patriotism of the Young Ottomans. The classical texts of Turkish nationalism were written in this period, especially after the founding of the nationalist organization Turkish Hearth Society (Türk Ocaği) in 1912 and the publication of its journal, *Turkish Homeland* (*Türk Yurdu*).

The well-known distinction between culture and civilization (a distinction central to the classic theories of modernity as a transition from *Gemeinschaft* to *Gesellschaft*) was a significant theme in preparing the context within which the idea of a national style in architecture was elaborated. The leading ideologue of Turkish nationalism was Ziya Gökalp, whose theories provided ample ideological justification for the making of a "national style" out of Ottoman revivalism. Before everything else, Gökalp differentiated "nationality" (the Ural-Altaic group of Turkic peoples) from "religion" (the Islamic community, which was supranational), although both were constitutive of Turkish identity. As much as Ottoman culture (and architecture) represented the Islamic community to which Turks belonged by religion, it was nonetheless a specifically *Turkish* culture, distinct from the cultures of other nationalities within the Islamic community. Second, on the basis of the sociological theories of Emile Durkheim and Gabriel Tarde, who identified the locus of social life in "culture groups" and "civilization groups," respectively, Gökalp formulated his well-known distinction between "culture" (*hars*) and "civilization" (*medeniyet*). This was a distinction between "beliefs, moral duties, aesthetic feelings, and ideals of a subjective nature," on one hand, and on the other, "scientific truths, hygienic or economic rules, practical arts pertaining to public works, techniques of commerce and of agriculture—all of an objective nature."[49] From this he observed that whereas civilization could be borrowed from the West, culture had to reside in the nation's own people and history. He wrote in 1918:

> As there is no contradiction between the ideals of Turkism and Islamism, there is none between these and the ideal of modernism. The idea of modernity necessitates only

the acceptance of the theoretical and practical sciences and techniques from Europe. There are certain moral needs, which will be sought in religion and nationality, as there were in Europe, but these cannot be imported from the West as if they were machines and techniques. . . . Culture is national, civilization is international.[50]

The Turkish nationalism of Ziya Gökalp (ironically himself of Kurdish origins) was anticosmopolitan in cultural terms. From his perspective, it was not the high culture of Ottoman sultans but the folk culture of Turks that could be the real source of "national culture"—as it would indeed be in the late 1930s. Nonetheless, aside from being an already established building practice since 1908, the National Architecture Renaissance seemed to offer a literal translation of his eloquent arguments into architectural terms. Elements derived from classical Ottoman architecture (i.e., Turkish culture) were combined with European academic design principles and construction techniques (i.e., Western civilization).

This recharging of Ottoman forms and details with "Turkishness" coincided with major wars and historical transformations in Turkey. The First World War concluded with the Ottoman capitulation to the Entente powers and the organization of the independence struggle in Anatolia under the nationalist leader Mustafa Kemal. Such events, especially heroic battles such as the Gallipoli defense and defeats such as the Arab revolt during the First World War, reinforced the unleashing of a process of national self-identification, primarily self-identification as a nation of Turks, distinct from other Muslims whom the patrimony of the Ottoman Empire had traditionally embraced. Nationality thus replaced religion as the primary signifier of identity. The National Architecture Renaissance made its way to Ankara in the midst of these dramatic historical events. Many Turkish artists and architects, distressed by the occupation of Istanbul, identified with the nationalist cause of Mustafa Kemal, some of them actively joining the War of Independence.[51]

The small CUP headquarters in Ankara, with a prominent overhanging roof, pointed arches, and other Ottoman details, was one of the first examples of the National Architecture Renaissance in an otherwise insignificant Anatolian town (fig. 1.7). It was designed in 1917 by İsmail Hasif Bey (1878–1920), who was then killed in the War of Independence, and it was transformed into the first National Assembly building in 1920. Today it is the Museum of the War of Independence. In the collective consciousness of the republic, it is the symbol of the historical awakening of the nation to self-consciousness. Literally it has been the backdrop to many paintings and photographs showing the opening day of the National Assembly, with Mustafa Kemal giving his speech in front of the building (fig. 1.7). After the proclamation of Ankara as the new capital of the republic, the construction of major public buildings in the Ottoman revivalist "national style" was undertaken in a very short time and under the most unfavorable conditions, with serious shortages of funds, materials, and labor. Concentrated in what is today known as "old Ankara," near Ulus Square (literally,

Fig. 1.7. The first major "national style" building in Ankara, associated in Turkish collective consciousness with the birth of the nation. Initially built as the CUP headquarters in 1917 by İsmail Hasif Bey, it was used for the first National Assembly in the early 1920s and is today the Museum of the War of Independence. **Top:** 1990s photograph of the building. **Bottom:** "That Day" (*O Gün*), 1937 painting by Refik Epikman depicting the opening of the National Assembly in 1920.

Fig. 1.8. One of the earliest "national style" buildings in the new capital, Ankara: the Ministry of Finance (1925) by Yahya Ahmet and Mühendis İrfan. Postcard, circa 1930.

Nation Square), these buildings bear strong associations with the nationalist sentiments of the first decade of the republic.

One of the earliest examples (with a symmetrical façade, wide overhangs, and blue tiles) is the Ministry of Finance (1925), designed by Yahya Ahmet and Mühendis İrfan (fig. 1.8). Adjacent to the first National Assembly building, Vedat Bey's RPP headquarters (1926) was built with a rusticated stone façade, blue glazed tiles at the top, and a three-arched loggia on the second floor overlooking the entrance plaza. It was used as the second National Assembly building for a large part of the early republican period and is today the Museum of the Republic. Across from it, the Ankara Palas (1924–1927) was constructed as a luxurious hotel to host foreign dignitaries and the higher bureaucrats of the new regime (fig. 1.9). The joint work of the two leading architects of the National Architecture Renaissance, Vedat Bey and Kemalettin Bey, it is arguably the most paradigmatic structure of the Ottoman revivalist national style in Ankara. Its symmetrical design, pointed arches, and ornate entrance portal topped with a nonstructural dome illustrate the classical and academic design precepts of the National Architecture Renaissance. It was "a monument to modernity and civilization," as two architectural historians put it, "with its grand ballroom, pressurized water and central heating systems, its Western type toilets and bathtubs and its powerful electric generator—a unique feature in this rural Anatolian town accustomed to dim kerosene lamps."[52]

Not far from these buildings, the more ornate bank buildings by Giulio Mongeri are located along the Bankalar Caddesi (Avenue of the Banks), representing the National Architecture Renaissance at its most mature (fig. 1.10). These buildings still

evoke the more cosmopolitan and imperial feeling of the architecture of the late empire in Istanbul. The most prolific architect of this period in Ankara, however, was Arif Hikmet Koyunoğlu (1888–1982), from the younger generation, who was a student of Vedat Bey's and Giulio Mongeri's. He rose to prominence with the construction of the Ministry of Foreign Affairs (1927), the Ethnography Museum (1925–1928), and the Türkocağı (Turkish Hearth) building (1926–1930), which were among the last paradigmatic works of the National Architecture Renaissance before the switch to European modernism (fig 1.11). As recorded in the architect's memoirs, an enthusiastic Mustafa Kemal periodically visited these buildings during their construction, illustrating the

Fig. 1.9. The Ankara Palas (1924–1927), the most paradigmatic "national style" building in Ankara, as seen from the garden of the second National Assembly building. It was designed by the two leading practitioners of this Ottoman revivalist style, Vedat Bey and Kemalettin Bey. Postcard, circa 1930.

endorsement of the National Architecture Renaissance by the national hero himself.[53] The design and construction of the Türkocağı building was a major nationalist event, earning admiration and praise from Ziya Gökalp himself, the ideologue behind the Turkish Hearth organization. The closing of this nationalist organization and the replacement of its function by the new cultural and ideological program of the RPP later in 1932 (see chapter 2) were events that Arif Hikmet remembered in his memoirs with "deep sorrow."[54]

Throughout the 1920s, lesser-known buildings of the National Architecture Renaissance were constructed in Konya, Izmir, Kütahya, Afyon, and other cities of the republic, especially for government buildings, municipal palaces, schools, and post offices

Fig. 1.10. A view of the Avenue of the Banks in Ankara, circa 1930. The Ottoman Bank (Osmanlı Bankası, 1926) is in the front, with the Agricultural Bank (Ziraat Bankası, 1926–1929) visible behind it on the right. Both buildings by Giulio Mongeri. **Fig. 1.11.** Contemporary postcard showing "national style" buildings by Arif Hikmet Koyunoğlu in Ankara: the Turkish Hearth building (1927–1930) in the foreground and the Ethnography Museum (1925–1928) in the background. The Turkish Hearth building was used as a "People's House" after 1932 and today houses the National Gallery of Art (Devlet Resim ve Heykel Müzesi).

Fig.1.12. Proliferation of the Ottoman revivalist "national style" in provincial towns throughout Anatolia. **Top:** Municipal offices in Havran, with characteristic pointed arches and wide eaves, circa 1933. **Bottom:** A domed corner building in Bandırma, today used as a hotel.

(fig. 1.12). Schools were particularly important building types representing the ideals of the new regime, and in the 1920s they were built according to an Ottoman revivalist prototype design produced by the Ministry of Public Works (Nafia Vekaleti). All were based on the same plan: a symmetrical layout with entrances on the central axis and three-window bays projecting on the elevation at each end, two stories; pointed arches for windows; and a wide, overhanging roof. Some examples are the Gazi and Latife schools in Ankara, designed by Mukbil Kemal (1924), the Gazi Mustafa Kemal elementary schools in Konya (1926–1928) and Denizli (late 1920s), the Republic School (Cumhuriyet Mektebi) in Yozgat, and the elementary and high schools in Afyon (fig. 1.13).[55]

Konya and Izmir were particularly proud of their public buildings in the national style. In Konya the city architect, Mimar Muzaffer, a protégé of Vedat Bey's, and Mimar Falih Ülkü, who continued the practice after Muzaffer's death, built the impressive Konya Central Post Office building. In Izmir, the ideological appeal of the National Architecture Renaissance was particularly strong after the liberation of the city from Greek occupation in 1922. The term *milli* (national) was used extensively in conjunction with new public buildings, as in the case of the Milli Sinema (National Cinema, 1926) and the Milli Kütüphane (National Library, completed in 1933), both by the architect Tahsin Sermet. Another graduate of the Istanbul Academy of Fine Arts, Necmeddin Emre, was the other prominent architect of the Ottoman revivalist style practicing in Izmir; he was particularly known for his Izmir Türkocağı (Izmir Turkish Hearth) building of 1925.[56] Although the works of Vedat Bey and Kemalettin Bey and other major national-style buildings in Ankara, Istanbul, and Izmir are covered in monographic studies, there is no comprehensive survey covering the extent of construction in this style in the provinces and by lesser-known architects.

In order to understand the significance of the National Architecture Renaissance during the first decade of the republic, it is necessary to consider the specific historical, political, and ideological context of the transition from an Ottoman-islamic identity to a nationalist Turkish one. This issue frequently eludes architectural historians who, viewing the stylistic Ottoman references of the National Architecture Renaissance through the post-1931 biases of the Modern Movement, consider it an anachronistic style for a modern, secular, Western-oriented nation. Thus, the fact that construction in this style continued throughout the 1920s, in the midst of the most radical Westernizing institutional reforms of the Kemalist republic, is often assessed as a temporary aberration to be explained by circumstantial factors and later rectified in the 1930s.[57] What is missing in this assessment is that it was the profound ambiguity of this style—that is, the simultaneity and interchangeability of the Turkish and Islamic connotations of Ottoman forms—that made it especially appropriate. An Ottoman revivalist national style was capable of symbolizing the glory of the Ottoman-islamic past of the Turkish nation and thus of legitimating the new nationalist regime in the eyes of a traditional population loyal to the religious patrimony of the Ottoman dynasty. Apart from the obvious practicality of continuing an already established building practice, it was the symbolic ambiguity of the National Architec-

Fig. 1.13. Prototype elementary schools designed in the Ottoman revivalist "national style" of the 1920s: Gazi and Latife elementary school (**top**) in Ankara (1924), photograph 1990s; Cumhuriyet (Republic) elementary schools in Yozgat (**middle**) and Afyon (**bottom**), photographs circa 1933.

ture Renaissance—its capacity to signify both the old empire and the new nation at once—that made it a politically and ideologically convenient choice in a volatile period of transition.

This ambiguity of the National Architecture Renaissance can be likened to the ambiguity of the word *millet*, which, as many scholars have pointed out, was used increasingly to mean "nation" as defined on the basis of a shared historical, cultural, and linguistic heritage.[58] Nonetheless, for a long time the word still carried the religious connotations of its older meaning in the Ottoman period, when it designated the different *religious* communities of the empire. In the 1920s, when the population's primary allegiance was still more to Islam and the empire than to the new nation, Mustafa Kemal must have seen the power of this religious symbolism to make the secularizing reforms more palatable. Especially in the aftermath of his radical decision to abolish the Ottoman dynasty (1922) and the office of the caliphate (1924), which was the supreme religious authority for all Muslims, it was a particularly effective symbolism. After all, the nationalist War of Independence had been won with the overwhelming support of religious leaders from various parts of Anatolia who had mobilized the population around Mustafa Kemal. Many of these religious figures were members of the first National Assembly in 1920, as portrayed, for example, in the famous photograph "Prayer for Victory" (1921) showing Mustafa Kemal praying with open hands in front of the National Assembly, next to deputies in turbans and religious garb. The sentiments of these people and their constituencies (as well as any possibility of opposition from them) had to be handled carefully through, among other things, reverence to the symbols of Islam and the sultan. It is for this reason that the Ottoman references of the National Architecture Renaissance were not an aberration in the 1920s. They were an appropriate architectural expression of the specific circumstances of these crucial years when many religious codes were semantically recharged in what Şerif Mardin calls "the vibrating of an important traditional chord with the people."[59]

As Mardin has pointed out on many occasions, this representation of the nation as a secular religion is best illustrated by the title *gazi*—literally, "a fighter for the Islamic faith"—adopted by Mustafa Kemal in this period. A 1923 painting by Tahirzade Hüseyin titled "Gazi Büyük Mustafa Kemal Paşa Hazretleri" (The Great Gazi, His Highness Mustafa Kemal Pasha) is particularly illustrative (fig. 1.14). Mustafa Kemal's portrait is framed by angels in the same representational genre as that of miniature paintings depicting the life of the Prophet. That many of the National Architecture Renaissance school buildings of the early republic were named after the "Gazi" further strengthened these symbolic associations. The last building designed by Kemalettin Bey before his death was the Gazi Teachers College in Ankara (1926–1930), after which the National Architecture Renaissance gave way to modernism. It may be interesting to add that, like the Ottoman-islamic motifs of this national style, the poems of Mehmet Akif Ersoy (who also wrote the lyrics of the Turkish national anthem) are full of such religious codes adapted to the new nationalist consciousness.

Fig. 1.14. "Gazi Büyük Mustafa Kemal Paşa Hazretleri" (1923). Painting by Tahirzade Hüseyin portraying Atatürk in the representational genre of Islamic miniature paintings that depict the Prophet's life.

For example, in these poems the soldiers who fought in Gallipoli or in the War of Independence are "as glorious as the lions of Bedr," a reference to the holy wars of the Prophet, and the Kaaba, the holiest structure of Islam, becomes their gravestone.

The overtly religious terms in which the new nationalist spirit was cast in the first decade of the republic were also evident in the nationalist press coverage of the opening of the Türkocağı building in Ankara in 1930. *Türk Yurdu,* the official publication of the nationwide Türkocağı organization, published a special issue on the building with twelve plates showing exterior views, the marble entrance hall, the ornately carved ceiling, interior views, and other details. With allusions to the holiest places of Islam, the commentary said: "This building in Ankara, the Kaaba of the Turk, rising on a small hill—a national *arafat*—is a magical work combining matter with spirit."[60] In this "Kaaba," however, cultural and social events were to take place—art exhibitions, lectures, concerts, operas sung in Turkish with all-Turkish casts—not unlike other republican spatial practices of replacing the mosque complex with secular public spaces of cultural, educational, and recreational functions. Other nationalist newspapers hailed the building as "the work of pure Turkish sons: architect Hikmet Bey, masons Kayserili Hakkı and Hüseyin Usta," emphasizing the "Turkishness" of this stylistically "Ottoman" architecture.[61] That these sentiments were voiced at precisely the same time the new architectural establishment was growing increasingly critical of the National Architecture Renaissance bears testimony to the complex and conflicting undercurrents in Kemalist culture in this first decade of the republic.

In the institutional setting as well, the increasing grip of Turkish nationalism on young artists and architects was evident during and after the First World War. Gulsum Baydar Nalbantoğlu writes that as early as 1913, Academy of Fine Arts students rebelled against Giulio Mongeri and demanded "to learn Turkish architecture from Turkish instructors inspired by the Süleymaniye and the Selimiye [mosques] rather than St. Peters in Rome."[62] Yet in the turmoil of the transition from empire to nation, the importance and self-esteem that Turkish-Muslim architects enjoyed as practitioners of the National Architecture Renaissance were to be glorious but brief. As the old generation of eclectic and revivalist foreign architects—the Jasmunds and Vallaurys of the empire—gave way to Turkish architects at the academy and in practice, more radical changes were in the making. By the late 1920s, the academicism of Ottoman revival was already under attack, and the new republican regime was initiating an era of construction by a new group of foreign architects, this time bringing German and central European modernism to Turkey. While Kemalettin Bey was working on the Gazi Teachers College in Ankara in 1927, the National Architecture Renaissance was already a subject of intense debate and criticism, causing Kemalettin Bey much despair just before his death.[63] The same year, the academy curriculum was radically reformed along modernist lines, preparing the way for the demise and ultimate rejection of the National Architecture Renaissance. As for its three leading practitioners, Kemalettin Bey died in 1927 and Giulio Mongeri resigned from the academy in 1928, to be followed by Vedat Bey in 1930.

Rejection of Ottoman Forms

FROM AN ARCHITECTURAL point of view, the proliferation of the National Architecture Renaissance in the first two decades of the twentieth century can be seen as a belated revivalism at a time when early modernist experiments were already under way in Europe. Particularly interesting in terms of Turkey's encounter with these experiments was an ill-fated architectural competition for the German-Turkish House of Friendship in Istanbul in 1916. The project was intended as a celebration of the strategic alliance between the two nations, especially after a much-celebrated visit by Kaiser Wilhelm II in 1889—an alliance that eventually drew the empire into World War I. Many of the prominent early modernist architects in Germany participated in this competition, including Peter Behrens, Theodor Fischer, Paul Bonatz, Martin Elsaesser, and Germen Bestelmeyer (who won).[64] Notably, there were two unconventional schemes, by Hans Poelzig and Bruno Taut, respectively, who were both associated with the expressionist movement in Germany. Poelzig's cascading terraces towering above Istanbul's historical peninsula and Taut's domed structure with allusions to Byzantine architecture are remarkable projects in the history of early modern architecture. What is worth pondering is the complete absence of any exchange or influence between the designers of these visionary projects and Ottoman architects of the time. This absence is curious, especially in the light of Suha Özkan's verification that both Vedat Bey and Kemalettin Bey, the two leading architects of the National Architecture Renaissance, participated in the jury deliberations in Berlin as representatives of the Ottoman Empire.[65] It is likely that, immersed in the emerging Ottoman revivalist "national style," the two Ottoman architects took little interest in the new modern trends, which departed radically from classic and revivalist traditions. The interruption of this competition by the war was another reason for the absence of a sustained dialogue around these projects—an interruption that would be rectified after 1927, when the modernization of Turkish architectural culture would be entrusted to the Germans once again. A few of the same German architects who participated in the House of Friendship Competition in 1916 (notably Paul Bonatz, Martin Elsaesser, and Bruno Taut) would later come back to build important public buildings in republican Turkey in the 1930s and 1940s.

The demise of the National Architecture Renaissance started around 1927 and was completed by 1931. With the RPP's assertion of an unambiguously Western-oriented and secular cultural politics and the suppression of all opposition and debate in matters of national identity, references to Ottoman architecture rapidly became anathema for republican architects. Construction in Ottoman revivalist style came to a near end, and the "New Architecture" (*Yeni Mimari*)—the unadorned cubic compositions of European modernism—was enthusiastically received. In some cases, existing classical, eclectic, and Ottoman revivalist buildings were refaced in a new modern façade, as, for example, in Aptullah Ziya's conversion of the Teachers' School in Adana, which was published in the journal *Mimar* in 1933 with "before" and "after" photographs.[66]

Today the physical fabric of Ankara bears the traces of this shift in the architectural style of its major public buildings. Whereas the National Architecture Renaissance buildings of the 1920s are located in the older section of the city to the north, the austere German and central European modernism of the 1930s characterizes the newer southern extension of the city, appropriately called "Yenişehir," the "New City." Atatürk Boulevard, the prestige axis running north-south, joins the two sections of the city. In a small stretch at the center one can simultaneously observe the domes, Ottoman orders, pointed arches, and ornate tile and marble decorations of the National Architecture Renaissance buildings adjacent to the distinctly modernist aesthetic of the work of foreign architects, all of it built around the same time. For example, two ministry buildings, both dating from 1927 but displaying different stylistic choices, mark the two ends of this stretch: to the north, Arif Hikmet Koyunoğlu's Ministry of Foreign Affairs, and to the south, Theodor Post's Ministry of Health (fig. 1.15). On closer inspection, however, one can see that apart from the former's ornate façade of Ottoman motifs and the latter's unadorned façade, both buildings are symmetrical with formal, monumental entrances, testifying to the classical training of their architects. I will return to this issue later.

Even in the older section of the city, contemporaneous photographs of İstasyon Caddesi (Station Avenue) show the conspicuously modern forms of the Court of Financial Appeals (1928–1930), by the Swiss architect Ernst Egli, across from the ornate and domed Ankara Palas (fig. 1.16). Construction on Egli's building began only a year after completion of the Ankara Palas. The temporal simultaneity and physical proximity of the two styles suggest much about the actual complexity of the cultural and ideological scene during the first decade of the republic. A contemporaneous postcard testifies to the fact that, until the intensification of the polemical confrontation between the National Architecture Renaissance and the New Architecture, early republican Ankara was equally proud of its Ottoman revivalist and European modernist buildings (fig. 1.17). For a brief period, stylistic discrimination on ideological grounds seems not to have been an issue, compared with the larger pride of constructing a capital city from scratch. Even for the 1930s there is evidence in popular publications that outside architects' professional circles, no one particular style, but "architecture" in general, symbolized the constructive energy of the republic, the act of "nation building" in the literal sense (see fig. C.1). The official architectural culture of the republic, however (as represented by schools, publications, professional associations, and practice), propagated and reproduced the critique of Ottoman revivalism forcefully and effectively. After 1931, architecture became a major aspect of the larger republican revolutionary discourse and its claim of "a radical break with the Ottoman past."

In reality, the transition from the final decades of the Ottoman Empire into the new republic was far more complex and overlapping than what is often polemically posited as a radical break. The National Architecture Renaissance of the 1910s and

Fig. 1.15. Coexistence of the "national style" and the "New Architecture" in Ankara at the end of the 1920s: two government buildings completed at the same time along prestigious Atatürk Boulevard. **Top:** Ministry of Foreign Affairs (1927), by Arif Hikmet Koyunoğlu. **Bottom:** Ministry of Health (1927), by Theodor Post. Postcards, circa 1930.

1920s and the republican modernism that replaced it in the 1930s shared some common political and ideological grounds that underlie the *stylistic* opposition in terms of which the two periods are often discussed in architectural history. Both were self-conscious attempts at identity construction through architecture, and both flourished under state-sponsored modernization programs. Both were closely identified with authoritarian state power under single-party rule: respectively, the Committee of Union and Progress (CUP), which eliminated all opposition in 1913, and Mustafa Kemal's Republican People's Party (RPP), which consolidated its power in 1931.

Perhaps most significantly, both Ottoman revivalism and republican modernism were shaped, to a large extent, by a distaste for the stylistic eclecticism and cosmopolitan character of late-nineteenth-century Ottoman architecture, the work of Armenian, Greek, Levantine, and European architects living and working within the empire. Whereas the architects of the Young Turk era sought to combat the nineteenth-century "contamination" and "degeneration" of Turkish architecture by returning to the true principles, or "golden age," of Ottoman architecture in its classical period, their republican successors chose to abandon Ottoman architecture altogether in the 1930s. The difference was one of form and style. In 1934, in an important piece titled "Nationalism and Art," young republican architect Aptullah Ziya (Kozanoğlu) outlined what he called "the historical process of contamination since the Tulip Era."[67] This process, he argued, robbed the arts of the empire of their purity and their "Turkish character" and enslaved them to elements of Arab and Persian culture, as well as of the neoclassic, baroque, and empire styles of the West. He directed his anticosmopolitan criticism and contempt at foreign architects ranging from Ignace Melling, who, he claimed, "introduced foreign taste to the country at the end of the eighteenth century," to Alexandre Vallaury at the end of the nineteenth. Of Vallaury's Public Debts Administration building (Düyun-u Umumiye Idaresi), Aptullah Ziya had only this to say: "[It is] a building itself unsure of what it wants to represent, other than perhaps what its name stood for—namely the capitulation of the empire to foreign powers."[68] What underlay Aptullah Ziya's nationalist and anticosmopolitan discourse was something more than simply a critique of the orientalist distortions of Ottoman architecture: it assumed the essential "Turkishness" of Ottoman architecture, categorically rejecting any non-Turkish influence from either Europe or from other Muslim cultures. As already discussed, the Ottoman architects of the National Architecture Renaissance were, by comparison, less "nationalist" than patriotic (or "protonationalist") and far more cosmopolitan in their culture and upbringing, with a number of prominent non-Muslims in their own ranks. When it came to architectural style, however, they, too, shared the view that eclectic and orientalized styles contaminated the original purity of classical Ottoman architecture, and they sought to restore it to its classical grandeur and dignity.

In other words, beyond the obvious formal and stylistic contrast, the National Architecture Renaissance and the New Architecture of the 1930s were two different expressions of the same project of modern identity construction at a dramatic historical

Fig. 1.16. View of Station Avenue in Ankara, 1930s. On the right is the recently completed Court of Financial Appeals (1928–1930), by Ernst Egli. Across from this modern building can be seen the dome of the Ottoman revivalist Ankara Palas (1924–1927).

Fig. 1.17. Postcard of Ankara, circa 1930, showing the national capital's pride in the construction of public buildings regardless of stylistic difference.

moment. Whether in the form of fixing a classical period in the past as the most appropriate architectural paradigm for the present (i.e., Ottoman revivalism) or in the form that Alan Colquhoun has called a "flight into the future" (i.e., republican modernism), the two were equally "historicist" in their philosophical premises.[69] Both embraced a progressive model of history in which they sought to locate a place and identity for Turkish architecture. The common assumption that Ottoman revivalism is "historicist" and therefore "not modern" is more symptomatic of the formal-stylistic biases of architectural culture than of any rigorous investigation of what these terms may mean. Such an assumption overlooks the fact that historicism has nothing to do with historical *forms*; it simply designates a linking of architecture with a larger historical project and, as such, is itself a mark of modern consciousness.

After the resignation of Vedat Bey and Giulio Mongeri, the directorship of the architectural section of the Academy of Fine Arts was given to the Swiss architect Ernst Egli (1893–1974), who introduced European modernism to the country, as we will see in chapter 4. The legacies of Vedat Bey, Kemalettin Bey, and Giulio Mongeri, among the first generation of republican architects, is a contentious topic even to this day, often revealing less about their pedagogical programs than about the modernist biases of architectural culture in the 1930s. Many of the younger architects criticized them through the anti-academic, rationalist criteria of modernism. Behçet Ünsal, who graduated in 1933, wrote that "in the Mongeri studio, architecture was understood as the art of façade design," and "site plan was altogether unnecessary for Vedat Bey, who believed that 'if you make a good design it will fit any site.'"[70] Sedad Hakkı Eldem, a graduate of 1928 and arguably the most prominent Turkish architect of modern Turkey, attributed his accomplished career to his early determination to break away from what he was taught at the academy by Vedat Bey and Mongeri.[71]

By contrast, the older architects who graduated in the 1910s, the most prolific designers of the National Architecture Renaissance, expressed deep gratitude and praise for their teachers for instilling in them a love and appreciation of Ottoman architectural heritage, even after they switched to modernist designs in the 1930s. And many of them did switch. Of these, Arif Hikmet Koyunoğlu moved back to Istanbul in the 1930s and designed and built a number of modern, undecorated apartment buildings with no traces of Ottoman stylistic motifs. Sedad Çetintaş (1889–1965), who had a deep reverence for classical precedents and even published a book titled *Turkish Architectural Monuments: The Ottoman Period*,[72] designed a modern building for the RPP in 1934 (see fig. 2.25). Similarly, Necmeddin Emre, the prominent practitioner of the National Architecture Renaissance in Izmir, designed the Gazi Elementary School in a conspicuously modern form in 1934 (see fig. 4.7). There are still no comprehensive studies of or monographs on these architects, whose careers spanned the most dramatic transformations in modern Turkish history. Many interesting and still unexplored questions can be posed by such studies: Which architects, among those who made their reputations in the National Architecture Renaissance, disappeared from the scene in the 1930s, and which ones tried to adapt? When they tried to adapt, was their modernism different from that of the younger architects educated in the anti-academic and empirical methods of the European Modern Movement? Was their modernism perhaps more comparable to art deco or the *moderne* style of the 1930s elsewhere—a form of stripped-down classicism continuing the beaux-arts precepts in modernist disguise?

Although these important questions are beyond the scope of this book, there is ample evidence to suggest that the "radical break" proclaimed by the architectural discourse of the 1930s was not, after all, that radical, even in architectural terms. In a 1937 interview, long after his teachings had been abandoned at the academy, Vedat Bey said that during the transition period he had seen few irreconcilable conflicts between his generation's notions of architecture and the new modernist emphasis on undecorated simplicity. Refusing to dismiss modernism as a whole, he argued that "modernism coming out of the hands of architects well versed in classicism is well suited especially for buildings such as schools, barracks, etc., which by their very nature should be simple and plain."[73] There is the suggestion here of a more pluralist understanding of architecture in which architects can have more than one stylistic choice, depending on circumstances and program, and by implication a less ideological approach to architecture. Indeed, a number of student projects from the architectural course at the School of Engineering dating from the early 1930s illustrate this coexistence of academic and modernist approaches to design, rather than a total replacement of the former by the latter. Next to renderings of classical orders there are plain modern designs for schools, hospitals, and villas (see fig. 4.5), as well as a cinema project for which the student work can best be characterized as art deco or *moderne* rather than either eclectic-revivalist or functionalist-modernist.

Whether or not they acknowledged any formative value in the teachings of Vedat Bey, Kemalettin Bey, and Mongeri, it can be argued that the work of the transition generation carried some of the old sensibilities, if not the old stylistic Ottoman motifs. Many public buildings of the 1930s display a concern with symmetry, proportions, axiality, and façade detailing characteristic of academic teaching. Colonnades (but not arcades), loggias, tall columns (but not Ottoman orders), stone basements, axial entrances, borders around windows and doors, and the detailing of reinforced concrete as if it were masonry are some of the features that evoke a *feeling* of classicism. One also finds this feeling of classicism in the work of modern architects from Auguste Perret, whom Sedad Hakkı Eldem and other 1928 graduates greatly admired, to Theodor Post, whose Ministry of Health was one of the first buildings of German modernism in Ankara. It is possible to say that in a stripped-down and "modernized" way, classicism never totally disappeared from the architectural culture of the early republic, and if anything, it became even stronger at the end of the 1930s and into the 1940s.

One example of the National Architecture Renaissance in Ankara illustrates what else might have been possible in the evolution of Turkish architecture if the abrupt and ideologically charged break of the 1930s had not separated a generation of architects from the classical sensibilities of Ottoman revival. The Vakif Apartments (Vakıf Apartmanları), designed by Kemalettin Bey for the Ministry of Endowments in the final years of his life and completed in 1928, after his death, were a remarkable project covering an entire urban block (fig.1.18). Residential units occupied the perimeter of the block on the upper floors, with the ground floor reserved for shops and access to a theater-auditorium located at the center of the block. The affinities between Kemalettin Bey's design and a well-known icon of early modern architecture—the Auditorium Building by Adler and Sullivan in Chicago (1887–1889)—are difficult to miss, especially in the plan's concept of locating the theater within the block. Like the landmark Chicago auditorium, the Vakif Apartments were a distinctly modern urban type equipped with the latest technological amenities of their time (central heating, electricity, elevators, and modern sanitary fixtures that were successfully incorporated into the design) yet not entirely cut off from history and culture. Kemalettin Bey's evocation of an "Ottoman feeling" without any direct use of Ottoman motifs and precedents resembles Adler and Sullivan's evocation of the Romanesque in an otherwise modern building.

This comparison suggests that an evolutionary, rather than a revolutionary, path to modern architecture could have been a real historical option in Turkey. This option, or any other possibility of smoother transition and exchange between revivalism and modernism, was aborted with the "arrival" of the Modern Movement as the official architectural expression of the Kemalist revolution.

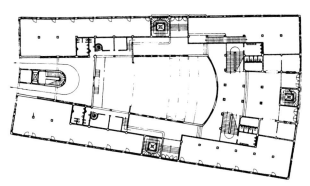

Rölöve 9. Ankara, Ikinci Vakıf Hanı, yer katı planı

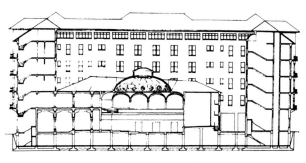

Rölöve 10. Ankara, Ikinci Vakıf Hanı, boyuna kesit

Fig. 1.18. A modern urban type in Ankara: apartments for the Ministry of Endowments (Vakıf Apartmanları, 1928) by Kemalettin Bey. A theater is placed in the middle of the block with street-level access, and residential units are located along the perimeter on the upper floors. **Top:** Photograph circa 1930. **Bottom:** Ground floor plan and longitudinal section.

2

İnkilap Mimarisi

ARCHITECTURE OF REVOLUTION

Gentlemen, it was necessary to abolish the fez, which sat on the heads of our nation as an emblem of ignorance, negligence, fanaticism and hatred of progress and civilization. [It was necessary] to accept in its place the hat, the headgear used by the whole civilized world; and in this way, to demonstrate that the Turkish nation, in its mentality as in other respects, in no way diverges from civilized social life.

—Mustafa Kemal Atatürk, *Nutuk,* 1927[1]

When making a revolution in the way we dress ourselves, the great Turkish nation did not contemplate modernizing the fez but accepted the hat. When revolutionizing the script, it did not propose to change and revise the old script but adopted the Latin alphabet. Similarly, Turkish architects of today abandoned domes, floral ornaments and tile decoration. They are marching on a new and logical path.

—Behçet and Bedrettin, "Türk İnkilap Mimarisi," 1933[2]

AFTER THE DEPARTURE of the last Ottoman sultan, Vahdeddin Mehmed VI (1918–1922), in 1922 and the proclamation of the Turkish republic in 1923, a series of Westernizing institutional reforms was launched under the personal directive of Mustafa Kemal, the national hero and founder of the republic. These Kemalist reforms can be looked at as one episode in a much longer history of institutional reform in Turkey that has tried, at least since the Tanzimat reforms of Sultan Mahmut II (1808–1839), to modernize the state without a corresponding "great transformation" in society, economics, and productive forces. At the same time, the scope and radicalism of the Kemalist reforms distinguish the republican period from everything that preceded it, lending it its revolutionary aura. The most radical of these

56

reforms were the abolition of the caliphate, the ultimate religious authority for all Muslims, and of the *şeriat* (*sharia*), the Islamic law (1924), the adoption of the Swiss civil code (1926), and the replacement of the old Ottoman-Arabic script with the Latin alphabet (1927). Collectively, they amounted to nothing less than a total civilizational switch from a traditional order grounded in Islam to a Western and secular one. To this day, the word *inkilap* designates this founding idea of switching civilizations that marked the making of modern Turkey out of the disintegrating Ottoman Empire. Translated into modern Turkish as *devrim* (revolution), it was written into the 1931 program of Mustafa Kemal's Republican People's Party (RPP) as one of the six pillars of Kemalism: republicanism, secularism, nationalism, populism, statism, and revolutionism.

The revolutionary self-consciousness of the Kemalist *inkilap* is most evident in the way it represented itself in the image of the French Revolution. The secular and scientific outlook of the Enlightenment had been the single most important source of inspiration for Turkish modernizers in general, even before the republican reformers appeared on stage. Many scholars and intellectual historians have dealt extensively with the influence of Enlightenment ideas and Jacobin politics on the reformist thinkers of the Ottoman Empire in the nineteenth century and the continuation of this mental structure into the Kemalist republic.[3] Nonetheless, with the establishment of the secular republic in 1923, the inspirational force of the French Revolution became far more pronounced. One remarkable artistic expression of this is the 1933 painting "İnkilap Yolunda" (On the Path of the Revolution), by Zeki Faik İzer, one of the leading modernist artists of the period, who was also influenced by cubism and other avant-garde currents in Paris. Adapted from the famous Delacroix painting of 1830, "Liberty Leading the Nation," this painting is an allegorical expression of the republican revolutionary ethos (fig. 2.1). It portrays the *inkilap* as a popular insurgence of the Turkish people, guided by Mustafa Kemal himself, against the darkness and anachronism of Turkey's ancien régime: a violent upheaval (soldiers, bayonets, flags) equipped with scientific knowledge and youthful energy (books, torch light, young people in Western clothes).

Like modernization in most other non-Western contexts, the modernization of Turkey was an official program to be implemented from above by the reformist elites of a paternalistic state. In the conspicuous absence of all the historical conditions within which the industrialized West had attained the heights of "contemporary civilization," Kemalism was overcome by a desire to "skip stages" in a heroic leap. Like all other "ideologies of delayed development," as one scholar calls them, "Kemalism was essentially revolutionary and, in Manheim's usage, 'utopian,' its ideological position based on a zealous futurism to catch up with western civilization."[4] Considering this sense of historical restlessness, it is not surprising that the recognizable symbols and exterior forms of modernity, rather than its substance, rapidly became the primary preoccupation of republican modernizers. The publications of the 1930s display

a pervasive obsession with the image of the new republic abroad. They wanted to show the world how the country was succeeding in shaking off its "oriental malaise" (*şarklılıktan kurtulmak*) and beginning to participate in contemporary civilization (*asrileşmek*). The words "modern" (*modern*) and "contemporary" (*asri*) were used synonymously throughout the decade as adjectives designating the new and desirable qualities of anything that became an object of Kemalist reforms— from lifestyles to women's appearance, from cities to homes and kitchens. These qualities were presented, almost invariably, as contrasts to the undesirable characteristics of their old or traditional counterparts under the late Ottoman Empire.

Fig. 2.1. "On the Path of the Revolution" (1933), by Zeki Faik İzer. Allegorical representation of the Kemalist revolution after the model of "Liberty Leading the Nation" (1830), by Eugene Delacroix.

This tendency to reduce the idea of "civilization" to the norms and forms of Western civility was epitomized in the so-called hat law (*şapka kanunu*) of 1925, by which the fez, the turban, and other forms of traditional garb with religious connotations were outlawed. In his historical Kastamonu and İnebolu speeches of August 1925, Mustafa Kemal personally explained what "a civilized and international" men's clothing "worthy of and appropriate for our nation" consisted of. "Boots or shoes on our feet," he specified, "slim trousers on our legs, shirt and tie, jacket and waistcoat, and, of course, to complete these, a cover with a brim on our heads. This head covering is called a hat."[5] Two years later, in his famous speech to the National Assembly, he would justify the hat law in unequivocally civilizational terms and declare the old fez to be "an emblem of ignorance, negligence, fanaticism, and hatred of progress and civilization."

This assumption that form could transform content, along with a belief in the power of representation, was by no means unique to the modernizing elites of the new republic. It was a characteristic of reform as a top-to-bottom process, as espoused by modernizers from the Jacobins of the French Revolution in the eighteenth century to the reformist bureaucrats of the Ottoman state in the nineteenth, with their respective choices of appropriate clothing and headgear.[6] What was unique to the Kemalist program in the 1930s was the inordinate time and energy invested in changing the form of things and the official production, supervision, and dissemination of a distinctly republican *visual* culture of modernity.

Architecture, by its very nature, constituted a central element of this visual culture of modernity, and in the spirit of the hat revolution, republican architects sought to dissociate this culture from any connection with the forms and stylistic features of Ottoman precedents. The Ottoman revivalist "national style" that had dominated Turkish architectural education and practice from about the turn of the century to the 1930s was rapidly abandoned in favor of the European Modern Movement. That the Modern Movement came to be known in popular parlance as "cubic architecture" (*kübik mimari*) is itself indicative of the formal biases of the republican culture of modernity. Although many architects rejected such stylistic and formalist definitions of modernism (see chapter 4), they nonetheless promoted the formal and aesthetic canons of the Modern Movement as the most appropriate expression of the rationalist and positivist ideals of Kemalism. Especially the new generation of architects who graduated from the Academy of Fine Arts after its radical switch from the classical beaux-arts system to modernism became the flag bearers of the Modern Movement, or the "New Architecture" (*Yeni Mimari*), as they preferred to call it.

In a series of paradigmatic essays published in *Mimar*, the new professional journal of Turkish architects launched in 1931, Behçet Sabri and Bedrettin Hamdi established just such a rhetorical connection between the Kemalist reforms and the Modern Movement in architecture. In the first essay, they juxtaposed the title "Mimarlıkta İnkilap" (Revolution in Architecture) with a photograph of Le Corbusier's Villa Savoie of 1929 (fig. 2.2), thus linking the canonic forms of the Modern Movement with the word *inkilap*, which in Turkish collective consciousness is synonymous with Kemalism.[7] This identification was further strengthened in the follow-up essay by an explicit analogy between the rejection of "domes, floral ornaments, and tile decoration" and the rejection of the fez and the Ottoman script in favor of the Western-style hat and the Latin alphabet. "There can be no doubt," concluded Behçet Sabri and Bedrettin Hamdi, "that the architecture of the Turkish revolution [*Türk inkilap mimarisi*] will be an entirely different thing from Ottoman architecture. The domes, moldings, and forms of that architecture have become history. There is no return from

Mimarlıkta inkılâp

Mimar Behçet ve Bedrettin

Modern bir köşk. Mimar Lecorbusier 1929

Yeni, mimarlık bir süs bir ayrılış için değil; ukalâlık için değil; ihmal edileni elde etmek için, ihtiyaç için, zaruret için doğdu. Onun yaşayamıyacağı mevzuubahs bile olamaz. Belki; bu hayat başka bir mecraya girinceye kadar bu gözler ve insan kafası başka bir güzellik mefhumunu hissedinceye kadar... O zaman ise, yeni bir teknik bir vasıta keşfedilmiş olacaktır ki bu da, bugünkü mimarlık san'atı âbidesini bir basamak daha yükseltmek içindir.

Fig. 2.2. Title page of the 1933 article "Revolution in Architecture" by Behçet Sabri and Bedrettin Hamdi, published in *Mimar,* the professional journal of Turkish architects. The caption for the photograph of Le Corbusier's Villa Savoie (1929–1931) reads: "The New Architecture was not born as an ornament; it was born out of necessity. It will live on until the day life enters another epoch and the human mind comes up with another concept of beauty arising out of new technical means which will have been invented then. At that point, the architectural art of today will have been elevated to the next step."

the path of progress. Even to pause along this path means regression."[8] They urged the state to provide opportunities, through commissions and competitions, for young Turkish architects to demonstrate their commitment to the republic by designing its buildings in the progressive spirit of the Kemalist revolution. Thus the conveniently ambiguous term *inkilap mimarisi* collapsed two meanings into one: it signified both the Modern Movement (i.e., revolution in architecture) and the particular building program of the new Kemalist regime in Turkey (i.e., architecture of revolution).

The identification of the Modern Movement with a new political order or ideology was by no means unique to Turkey. Modern forms were used by revolutionary regimes or political systems ranging from fascism in Italy and Stalinism in the Soviet Union to Zionism in mandate Palestine during the building of Tel Aviv. It was a characteristic feature of interwar modernism in many countries, where the scientific and progressive discourse of the Modern Movement legitimated new regimes and in turn, identifying with these new regimes, legitimated and benefited the architectural profession in that great era of state patronage. Retrospectively explaining modernism's alliance with fascism in the 1930s, for example, the Italian architect Ernesto Rogers said, "We based ourselves on a syllogism which went roughly thus: Fascism is a revolution, modern architecture is revolutionary, therefore it must be the architecture of Fascism."[9] Replacing the word "fascism" with "Kemalism," the same statement could have been made by most young Turkish architects of the 1930s, as it was in fact made by many in publications of the time. Aptullah Ziya, who visited the Mostra della Rivoluzione Fascista of 1932 in Rome, wrote: "Today a new art is born in Italy. With the support of the state, it is prospering in the hands of young Italian artists and progressing in giant steps. Italians have created a Fascist architecture. The Turkish nation has accomplished a revolution much greater and higher than what Fascist Rome calls a revolution. But one thing is still missing. This revolution has not been adorned with works of art and architecture."[10]

As many other architectural historians have pointed out, there were also pragmatic reasons reinforcing the switch from the National Architecture Renaissance to modernism.[11] After decades of war, skilled labor for traditional crafts in stone, marble, and tile decoration was scarce, putting serious constraints on the republican building program. Especially in the aftermath of the economic crisis of 1929, the unadorned simplicity and austerity of modern forms became an appealing option, with their connotations of rationality and economy of means (without necessarily being rational or economical, given the state of the building industry in Turkey). Yet the primary explanation for the enthusiastic reception of modernism in the Turkish architectural establishment of the republic remains an ideological one. The ambiguity of Ottoman forms in signifying the empire and the nation simultaneously, the very reason for their ideological appeal in the 1920s, was no longer appropriate for a state intent on dissociating itself radically from its dynastic imperial legacy and its traditional Islamic culture. Modernism offered precisely the kind of abstraction and formal novelty devoid of historical associations that matched this ideological agenda.

The acceptance of the ideological as "natural" permeates many accounts of this period in the historiography of modern Turkish architecture. Üstün Alsaç, for example, observes a major contradiction between "the idea of a national style based on tradition" and "the revolutionary principles of the Kemalist revolution, which sought to destroy the old order." He writes: "Traditional architectural elements embodied qualities that would have kept the symbols and memory of the Ottoman Empire alive. *Naturally* [my emphasis] this could not have been permitted in the initial years of the *inkilap*."[12] The irony is that it was precisely during the "initial years of the *inkilap*"— the 1920s—that Ottoman motifs and precedents flourished in Turkish architecture, for reasons discussed in the previous chapter. It was only in 1931, when the power and authority of the RPP were consolidated and all forms of opposition suppressed, that references to Ottoman culture acquired their negative connotations and the new was pitted against the old in every aspect of life.

The New against the Old

THAT ENLIGHTENMENT NEEDS its civilizational "other" finds ample evidence in the official discourse of the republic in the 1930s. Binary oppositions such as anachronism versus progress, tradition versus modernity, and obscurantism versus enlightenment were all embodied in the contrast between the old and the new—a prominent theme in the Kemalist culture of the 1930s. The new was valorized and celebrated not only in itself, as a symbol of progress, but more often in juxtaposition with the contrasting image of the old, now discredited as the mark of backwardness. In the propaganda posters of the RPP, designed to promote Kemalist reforms, the pedagogical function of the binary opposition between the old and the new was most evident (fig. 2.3). These posters tried to convey, for example, the civilized nature of the

Fig. 2.3. The "old versus new" construct in propaganda posters of the Republican People's Party, 1930s. **Left:** The "difficulty" of the old Arabic script is contrasted with the benefits of the new script, which "made it easier for everyone, young or old, to read and write and triggered the literacy campaign of the republic." **Right:** "Revolution in attire and marriage": traditional clothes and Islamic polygamy are contrasted with the new Western-style clothes and the new civic code banning polygamy.

nuclear family in modern, Western-style clothes, juxtaposed with the anachronism of the traditional, polygamous Muslim man in religious garb, trailed by his veiled wives. Or as part of the national campaign for literacy, they promoted the practicality and simplicity of the new alphabet, contrasting it with the old Ottoman script, the "difficulty" of which, it was argued, made it an emblem of illiteracy and obscurantism.

The official propaganda publication of the republic, *La Turquie Kemaliste* (published by the Ministry of Interior in French, English, and German, primarily for a foreign audience), featured many such juxtapositions as a rhetorical strategem to prove the success of the new nation in shaking off the "oriental malaise." Photographs of clean, modern school buildings filled with healthy children in their school uniforms were juxtaposed against descriptions of outlawed *medreses* in dilapidated buildings. The new textile mills, power plants, dams, and agricultural machinery of the republic were proudly featured in contrast with descriptions of the toiling peasants and craftsmen of the old empire. In a Ministry of Interior publication of 1938, enthusiastic excerpts from the foreign press on the accomplishments of the new regime in Turkey were translated and illustrated with a series of "before and after" photographs.[13] The new model villages built near Ankara were placed next to images of mud-brick huts with thatched roofs captioned, "The old villages of the empire." The new tree-lined boulevards in Ankara were contrasted with dirt roads and ox-drawn carts, captioned "Roads and transportation in the old empire" (fig. 2.4).

There is something about these images that is remarkably similar to the use of the same "old versus new" construct for the modernist polemic in the architectural culture at large in the 1930s. The purity, simplicity, and rationality of modern form were often contrasted with the exuberant, ornamental, and, by implication, aristocratic forms of the past—as, for example, in F. R. S. Yorke's 1934 book *The Modern House* (fig. 2.5). In the professional journal of Turkish architects, the New Architecture was characterized as "open and joyful" (*açık ve sevinçli*), in contrast with the "obscurity and solemnity or grimness" (*anlaşılmaz ve korkulu*) of the old architecture.[14] The choice of modernism over historical styles was not simply an aesthetic choice but was imbued with a progressive political message as well. In 1936, Norbert Von Bischoff, a diplomat of the Austrian embassy in Ankara, commented on this progressive political content of modern form when he wrote about the new presidential residence of Mustafa Kemal Atatürk, designed by the Austrian architect Clemenz Holzmeister (see fig. 5.21). Flattering both the building's Austrian architect and its Turkish patron, he connected the choice of a modern design with the democratic spirit of the modern age. "Among the leaders of today" he wrote, "there is only Atatürk who lives in the real spaces, furnishings, and technical spirit of the twentieth century, far away from the pompousness of a classical or baroque palace."[15]

Numerous books by foreign travelers and observers in the 1930s recorded the dramatic changes in Turkey under the new regime.[16] They expressed opinions ranging from the celebratory to the critical or simply nostalgic for the exoticism of the empire. Many of them contained the same "old versus new" commentaries, sometimes illus-

Fig. 2.4. "Old versus new" photographs from a government publication, Republican Turkey through Foreign Eyes, 1938. **Left:** Comparison between "villages of the empire" and "the model village of Etimesgut outside Ankara." **Right:** Comparison of "roads and transportation during the empire" with "Atatürk Boulevard, Ankara." The modernity, orderliness, and rationality of the second image is highlighted in each pair.

DESIGN

FOR

MODERN

LIVING

Fig. 2.5. "Old versus new" as part of the modernist polemic in architectural culture at large. A page from F. R. S. Yorke's *The Modern House* (1934).

trated by the same photographs published in *La Turquie Kemaliste*. Turkish publications mentioned and quoted the favorable views of these foreign authors on every occasion. The republican need for self-affirmation through Western eyes appears to have been central to the cultural and political consciousness of the period. Conversely, any hint of nostalgia on the part of foreigners for the traditional culture and architecture of the Ottoman Empire was vehemently resented by representatives of the republic and by most educated Turks, underscoring the anti-orientalist premises of Kemalism.[17] Modern architecture and urbanism were, by definition, the most potent visible symbols of this desire to create a new and thoroughly modern nation. That Le Corbusier lost a major urban commission in Turkey when he suggested that the Turkish government spare the old wooden houses of Istanbul from any modern intervention illustrates the strength of these republican sentiments. In a much later interview, Le Corbusier recollected: "If I had not committed the most strategic mistake of my life in the letter I wrote to Atatürk, I would be planning the beautiful city of Istanbul, instead of my competitor Henri Prost. In this notorious letter, I foolishly recommended to the greatest revolutionary hero of a new nation to leave Istanbul as it was, in the dirt and dust of centuries."[18]

Ironically, it was the "dirt and dust" of old Istanbul against which the newness and cleanliness of Ankara were celebrated as a republican icon. The "old versus new" construct was employed extensively in visual and literary representations of Ankara. Istanbul, the city that had been the seat of imperial power and religious authority for five centuries, was delegated to serve as Ankara's "other" in every respect. Not only in architectural and urban terms but also in terms of less visible qualities, "the purity, moral superiority, and idealism" of the new capital were contrasted with "the imperial and dynastic traditions, the cosmopolitan contamination and decadence" of Istanbul.[19] During the heightened nationalism and anticosmopolitanism of the 1940s, these sentiments grew even stronger, as illustrated by a 1943 issue of *La Turquie Kemaliste* that proclaimed, "Ankara is a city of the future, Istanbul is a city of the past." In one passage, addressed to a foreign audience, the negative tone of the references to the ethnic mix of Istanbul is particularly symptomatic of Ankara's nationalist position at the time:

The average visitor who has spent a few days rushing from Hagia Sophia to the Great Walls and quickly around the old Hippodrome goes home to tell the folks about Turkey. He is no better equipped than the stay-at-homes who get their ideas out of novels about the sultans. For in Istanbul he has probably eaten Russian food, got his views on the government from a Greek porter, been guided by an Armenian courier, and concentrated exclusively on the relics of a past now intentionally forgotten by the average Turk, who looks ahead to better days. He who really wants to know the Turkey of today and tomorrow should take the first train for Ankara.[20]

Ankara was declared the capital of the new Turkish republic on 13 October 1923, in a dramatic historical decision to distance the new regime from its Ottoman past.

From the start of the nationalist struggle in 1919 until the abolition of the caliphate in 1924, Turkey had been, in essence, "a country with two capitals: the center of Islam in Istanbul and the center of the state in Ankara."[21] Until about 1927 there was substantial opposition to the idea of Ankara as the capital. The urban historian Gönül Tankut appreciates the soundness of Mustafa Kemal's intuitions in calculating the importance of a "center of gravity" for the distribution of the services of justice, education, and health. She challenges the theory that Ankara was not actually "selected" but that the war government simply stayed in Ankara, making it a de facto capital.[22] With or without deliberation, the selection and construction of Ankara as a modern capital became a national saga feeding the republican imagination.

References to Ankara in official and popular publications of the time as "the heart of the nation" (ulusun kalbi) point to more than the geographical centrality of its location within the boundaries of modern Turkey. It was a powerful metaphor for the organic unity of the nation, as in the other nationalist slogan of becoming "one body, one heart." Another metaphor for Ankara, derived from the city's strategic importance during the nationalist war, was that of a benevolent mother who gave birth to the Turkish republic. The latter, in turn, became "a grateful offspring dutifully caring for her: adorning her arid land and poor neighborhoods with beautiful buildings and glorious institutions, with modern construction, wide boulevards, and public squares with monuments and statues."[23] Designating it "a European city in Asia," a 1936 article proudly stated: "The construction of Ankara has effectively transformed the map of Europe. We can now claim that Europe starts in Ankara. Was not this the purpose of our revolution"?[24]

Many scholars writing about the politics of urban design discuss how planned capitals such as Ankara, Brasilia, and Islamabad are conceived, before everything else, as expressions of the pride and hard work of nation building and thus cannot possibly derive their image and character from an existing city.[25] The less there is on site, the greater the pride and glory in making the capital "out of nothing," as a popular school song about Ankara goes in Turkey. Perhaps the most heroic visual expression of this is an image from La Turquie Kemaliste that depicts a utopian city of abstract, geometric buildings reminiscent of avant-garde constructivist tectonics (fig. 2.6). At the corner of the image, a rugged and empty mountain site is shown as if to emphasize the emergence of this utopian city out of the bare land. Ankara's own insignificant past conveniently allowed republican modernizers to perceive and portray it as a tabula rasa upon which their grand vision could be implemented.

Ankara was not a tabula rasa, to be sure. The city around the citadel area had lived through flourishing times, once in the Roman period and again in the seventeenth century during the Ottoman Empire. In her poignant critique of the modernizers' disregard for the traditional local population of the city, Zeynep Kezer emphasizes the "duality" in early republican Ankara that was obscured by the more canonic representations of the modern capital. "Lurking behind its picturesque imagery and legendary conception," she writes, "behind the strip development of

Fig. 2.6. "Ankara Construit." Modernist aesthetic of cubic blocks representing the new capital. Illustration from *La Turquie Kemaliste,* April 1935.

institutional buildings and ostentatious villas neatly lined up along its main boulevard, there was another Ankara. This was an Ankara missing from its representations;
an Ankara that seldom, if ever, appeared as a context from which the discourse and
images about the new capital were drawn."[26] Indeed, in contemporaneous publications, references to the "malaria-ridden town," to dusty or muddy streets, and to the
"dim light of kerosene lamps at night" often functioned as backdrops to highlight the
achievements of the republic in building a modern city in contrast to what existed
before.

The ethos of new Ankara was intimately connected with the work of foreign
architects and planners who were invited to the country, starting with the German
planner Hermann Jansen (1869–1947), who won the international competition for the
Ankara master plan in 1927. Nine years later, an article in a popular magazine
observed: "For the first time in four thousand years of Turkish history, houses are not
huddled around the citadel seeking refuge from it. Ankara is spreading down below,
along the wide plain and according to a comprehensive urban plan, supervised for the
last seven years by Professor Jansen."[27] Appropriately titled "How Old Ankara Is
Becoming Younger," the article was illustrated with the sketch of a traditional wood-
en house and, facing it on the opposite page, a photograph of one of the new "cubic"
apartment buildings along Atatürk Boulevard, with obvious pride in the latter.
Paradoxically, it was not the modernist urbanism of Le Corbusier but aesthetic and
preservationist principles of urban design going back to Camillo Sitte in the 1880s
that informed Jansen's master plan of Ankara. This was most evident in his concern
for and attention to the historical fabric of the "old city" around the citadel. The overall absence of a land-use and planning policy in the government program, however,
soon plagued Jansen's plan, and when his propositions against land speculation
proved unpopular among influential people close to the government, his contract was
terminated in 1939.[28]

After approval of the Jansen plan in 1932, other prominent European architects
were invited to work in making the "new" face of Ankara. Not only does their work
constitute the topic of numerous studies beyond the scope of this book,[29] but it also
provided the official icons of modernism endlessly reproduced in publications, photographs, and postcards of the 1930s. First, as the foremost showcase of the new
regime's modernity, the entire Government Complex was commissioned to the
Austrian architect Clemenz Holzmeister (1886–1983). Culminating at the Grand
National Assembly, the Government Complex was conceived as a triangular
superblock on the southernmost end of the "new Ankara" (Yenişehir), the place farthest removed from the old Ankara of the citadel area (fig. 2.7). Second, in the same
years during which Holzmeister was designing the Government Complex, the Swiss
architect Ernst Egli (1893–1974) was brought in to transform architectural education
at the Academy of Fine Arts along modernist principles, as I will take up in chapter 4.

In addition to Egli and Holzmeister, some of the most prominent veterans of
Weimar Germany were also invited to work in Turkey, including Martin Wagner,

Fig. 2.7. Cover page of *La Turquie Moderne,* 1 November 1935, featuring the new project for the Government Complex in Ankara by Clemenz Holzmeister. The triangular superblock of ministries culminates with the Grand National Assembly at the far end of the central axis.

Bruno Taut, Martin Elsaesser, Franz Hillinger, Wilhelm Lihotzky, and Margarete Schütte-Lihotzky. Not just in architecture and planning but in all fields of higher education and professional expertise, foreigners became the true "architects" of Kemalist Turkey as the world drew closer to another major war. After 1933, more than two hundred German, Austrian, and Swiss professors, including some forty architects and planners, worked in Turkey as teachers, administrators, and consultants, playing key roles in the establishment or improvement of major university departments in Ankara and Istanbul.[30] Although the majority of these were refugees (mostly, though not exclusively, Jewish) who opposed the National Socialist regime in Germany, the Turkish government also contacted the Reich officially, inviting German professors to work in Turkish institutions.

At a time when the entire infrastructure of university education was being assembled by foreign professors invited by the republican regime, buildings of higher education became the first and highly celebrated examples of European modernism in Ankara, most of them lined up along prestigious Atatürk Boulevard. The most significant modern buildings of higher education were designed within the architectural office of the Ministry of Education (Maarif Vekaleti), perhaps the most important state department through which modernism was introduced into Turkey. Regine Erichsen notes that a key figure in the architectural progressivism of the ministry was the director of higher education, Cevat Dursunoğlu, who served as a cultural attaché in Berlin between 1933 and 1935 and played a key role in the invitations to Martin Wagner and Hans Poelzig.[31] Hans Poelzig (1869–1936) died before he made it to Turkey, but Martin Wagner spent many years there as a teacher, planner, and consultant to the Turkish government. Both Ernst Egli and later Bruno Taut (1880–1938) directed the Ministry of Education's architectural office, which became a supplemental training ground for the students they taught at the academy.

Ernst Egli's most significant school buildings in Ankara were the State Conservatory of Music (1927–1928), the Higher Agricultural Institute (1928), the Commercial Lycée (1930), the İsmet Paşa Girls' Institute (1930), and the Faculty of Political Sciences (1935–1936). These were widely published in Turkish and German architectural magazines and were praised as the first examples of the "New Architecture" (*Yeni Mimari*) in Turkey.[32] In these projects, Egli established the basic and most recognizable features of German modernism that became the trademark of republican Ankara—namely, flat roofs used partly as terraces, plain surfaces, borders around windows or continuous window sills, and the use of tall colonnades for entrances (fig. 2.8). In the State Conservatory of Music, Egli arranged the school around a central courtyard with a colonnade on three sides in a gesture that can be connected to his appreciation of regional vernacular architecture (see chapter 6). In the Higher Agricultural Institute he used an L-shaped layout, again with a tall colonnade marking the entrance to the administration wing on the central axis of the campus. His two buildings along Atatürk Boulevard, the Commercial Lycée and the İsmet Paşa Girls' Institute, were less classicized in their formal expression, with a more "modern" composition of horizontals and verticals, rounded corners, and asymmetrical arrangements.

Bruno Taut's reputation as a school builder is even more remarkable, considering the short two years he spent in Turkey before his untimely death in December 1938. In addition to his most prominent work, the Faculty of Humanities in Ankara (1937), he also designed and built, together with Franz Hillinger, Cebeci and Atatürk high schools in Ankara, Cumhuriyet Girls' High School in Izmir, and Boys' High School in Trabzon, all during 1937–1938 (fig. 2.9). The Faculty of Humanities is an impressive, austere building with square windows punched over the entire facade, which is finished in stone and topped with an inscription of Atatürk's famous words: "Hayatta en hakiki mürşit ilimdir" (The true guide in life is science). The asymmetrical entrance canopy with its rounded wall and single corner column offers a more modern accent in an otherwise heavy and classical-looking building. The use of alternating stone and brick courses on the elevations of the auxiliary block is an important if subtle testimony to Taut's reverence for the traditional building practices of Ottoman architecture—in this case the Ottoman walling technique.[33]

What is important to note is that what these architects of German and central European origin brought to Turkey was an austere, heavy, and official-looking modernism. It is difficult to categorize this architecture as belonging to "international style" or the Modern Movement as disseminated by Le Corbusier and the International Congress of Modern Architecture (CIAM) in Europe. The latter entailed a much lighter aesthetic, with large glazed areas in conjunction with steel or reinforced concrete frames—an aesthetic different from that of the heavy colonnades, stone fac-

Fig. 2.8. Buildings of higher education in Ankara by Ernst Egli, the first major European architect to introduce the "New Architecture" to Turkey. **Top:** Higher Agricultural Institute (1928). **Middle:** State Conservatory of Music (1927–1928). **Bottom:** İsmet Paşa Girls' Institute (1930).

Fig. 2.9. Buildings of higher education by Bruno Taut. **Top:** Faculty of Humanities, Ankara (1937–1938). **Bottom:** Boys' High School, Trabzon (1937–1938).

ing, and small window openings of the buildings in Ankara. The "newness" of Ankara's modernism rested not in any visible connection to the aesthetic canons of the Modern Movement but simply in its being what the old was not. Ankara's new buildings were technically more advanced and "scientifically designed," which often meant an emphasis on functional and programmatic considerations and, most conspicuously, an absence of ornament and stylistic motif. Most historians of modern Turkish architecture draw attention to the specific features of this German or "Viennese" school, pointing out the difficulty of considering its buildings "true representatives of the Modern Movement."[34] Others, however, use the terms "international style" and "rationalist-functionalist architecture" interchangeably to designate the modern buildings of new Ankara in the broadest sense. Such broad usage of these terms overlooks the fact that despite international polemics by CIAM to the contrary, modern architecture was far from being monolithic in the 1930s.

In addition to educational institutions, a number of parks, sports facilities, and places of public recreation were built in Ankara in the 1930s that also became urban and architectural icons of republican modernity. As in other nationalist contexts of the time, Italy and Germany in particular, early republican culture was permeated by a strong cult of youth and health. The idealized qualities of being "young" and "healthy" signified a state that had successfully broken ties with "the *old* empire" or "the sick man of Europe," as the Ottoman Empire was known in the nineteenth century. Ankara was the ultimate embodiment of youth and health, and these attributes found their more literal spatial expression in places of public recreation and collective sports where the regeneration of the body and, in turn, of the nation was to take place. Of these, the "19 May Sports Stadium,"[35] the appropriately named Youth Park (Gençlik Parkı), the Atatürk model farm and forest (Atatürk Orman Çiftliği), and the picnic grounds of the Çubuk Dam outside the city are particularly representative public spaces of the 1930s. They carried an important ritualistic function above and beyond providing sports facilities or simply offering access to nature. For example, the stadium (1934–1936), designed by the Italian architect Paolo Vietti Violi, was the stage for many celebrations of national holidays, most symbolically the "Youth and Sports Holiday" of 19 May, when male and female students paraded in their shorts and conducted exercises in athletics and gymnastics (fig. 2.10). In a published description of the project, Vietti Violi touched upon the militaristic connotations of sports activities in the 1930s: the stadium complex was "a grandiose and exceptional program that necessitated the creation of a wide road for military parades."[36]

Youth Park (1936–1937), located across from the stadium along Station Avenue (Istasyon Caddesi), was conceived as a large urban park with an artificial lake to provide much-needed greenery and water in arid Ankara (fig. 2.11). Initially conceived under Jansen's 1934 plan, it was then modified by the landscape architect and planner Theo Leveau, who worked for the Ministry of Public Works. The enthusiasm for this visionary project and its conception as a modern public space for popular recreation

were described in the 1935 issue of *Journal of Public Works* (*Nafia Isleri Mecmuasi*) as follows:

The lake, with its central spout shooting water up to a height of 30 meters, the pools, and the artificial waterfalls will provide an attractive view. The rose garden to the north of the lake will be an intimate and enchanting place to stroll and relax. To the east of the lake, a spacious area is reserved for popular gatherings and entertainment. A luxurious restaurant-casino with a spectacular view will be constructed on the small island in the lake, accessible by two footbridges. A playground, a swimming pool for children, a popular café–tea garden, and an open amphitheater will adorn the periphery of the lake. An aviary, an English garden, and a large greenhouse will complete the project.[37]

Most of these items were built in the late 1930s; an amusement park was added to the initial scheme, and the entire park was inaugurated on the 19 May holiday of 1943. Serving as what Zeynep Uludağ calls "a school for socializing the people into modern citizens," the park was a stage set for weekend outings of Ankara families who could sit in the tea gardens, stroll in the park, or enjoy the artificial lake in small rowboats. Youth Park remains, to this day, one of the most popular legacies of republican spatial practices. The "luxurious restaurant-casino" on the artificial island was not built in Youth Park as intended, but the same idea was implemented at Çubuk Dam outside Ankara,

Fig. 2.10. Nationalist cult of youth and health: gymnastics and sports performances in the "19 May Sports Stadium" in Ankara (1936), designed by the Italian architect Paolo Vietti Violi. The citadel of old Ankara is visible in the distance. The photograph was taken from the covered seating area, which was protected by a cantilevered, reinforced-concrete canopy. Contemporary postcard published by the Ministry of Interior Press Office.

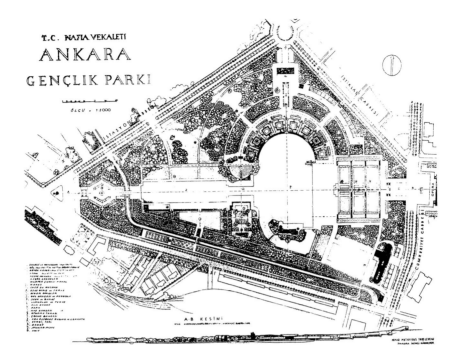

which became another popular public space for recreation, picnicking, and entertainment. Its restaurant-casino building, particularly spectacular at the time, became the gathering place of mixed-gender crowds for elegant dining and entertainment (fig. 2.12). The larger significance of Çubuk Dam as a symbol of the technological conquest of nature and thus of the republic's success in building its modernist utopia is taken up in more detail in chapter 3.

The Atatürk model farm and forest, established as a model state enterprise for agriculture (vineyards, orchards, vegetable gardens, poultry, and dairy), industry (brewery, soda, ice cream), and commerce, was also conceived as a popular place for recreation, picnicking, and family entertainment. Ernst Egli designed the brewery (1933–1934), the brewery workers' housing, and a public bath (1936–1938), as well as the farm residence of Atatürk (Marmara Köşkü, 1930). "Dreaming of the welfare of the people he loved," as *La Turquie Kemaliste* stated it,[39] Atatürk personally supervised the maintenance of the tree-shaded promenades and the management of the parks, restaurants, cafés, swimming pool, and zoological garden, all contained within the farm's grounds. Scientific methods of farming, the planting of an evergreen forest in the middle of the arid Anatolian plateau, and mod-

Fig. 2.11. Site plan of Youth Park in Ankara (1935), the paradigmatic national space for public recreation, with its large artificial lake in the middle. The park was initially conceived by Hermann Jansen in his 1934 master plan for Ankara and then was modified by the landscape architect and planner Theo Leveau for the Ministry of Public Works.

ern irrigation techniques were patriotic themes in the 1930s. They represented the idealized acts of taming the wilderness, mastering nature, and ultimately reclaiming the land as national property. It should be noted that these were the same themes that mobilized other nationalist regimes and movements at the time, motivating projects ranging from the draining of the Agro Pontina marshes in Fascist Italy to the Zionist utopia of redeeming and settling the land of Palestine.

In the more typical tendency of architectural history to focus on the modern *buildings* of the 1930s, it is frequently overlooked that popular public spaces—particularly recreational parks and municipal gardens (*belediye bahçesi*)—played an equally significant role in nation building. If not to the scale and scope of Ankara's Youth Park, many other republican cities acquired similar public spaces and urban infrastructures during the 1930s. Izmir's Kültürpark (1936), which became the site of the Izmir International Fair (see chapter 3), had many features similar to those of Youth Park in Ankara, including an artificial lake with an island for "a casino and dancing platform." Individual architectural tropes like these "island casinos" warrant separate and more extensive study, because they were powerful expressions of the republican vision of a thoroughly Westernized, mixed-gender public, dining in style, listening to jazz bands, and dancing without inhibition. These spaces, many of which still bear their original aesthetic and environmental qualities, had important democratic implications even when actual access to the more refined establishments remained the province of a small elite. Postcards of many Turkish cities in the 1930s testify to the extent to which such public spaces, with their pools, meticulous land-

Fig. 2.12. The restaurant-casino of Çubuk Dam outside Ankara (1936). The curving modernist form cantilevered over the water alludes to the "ocean-liner aesthetic" of the 1930s common to comparable buildings of the Modern Movement in Europe.

scaping, casinos, tea gardens, zoos, and amusement parks, became truly "popular" spaces where people of all ages, classes, and genders came to stroll, to see, and to be seen (fig. 2.13). The presence of women in these public places was in itself a celebrated theme, "a gendering of the modern" underscoring the Kemalists' pride in having liberated Turkish women from the oppressive seclusion of tradition.

Fig. 2.13. Contemporary postcards of municipal parks (*belediye parkı*) in Samsun (**top**) and Mersin (**bottom**)—a repeatable and recognizable national image throughout Anatolia. Geometrically shaped pools with water jets, carefully delineated flower beds, regularly planted trees, lamp posts, and benches were characteristic features of these public parks, which often lay close by the more formal "republic squares" (*cumhuriyet meydanı*) with their government buildings and Atatürk statues.

Gendering the Modern

By characterizing the Ottoman past as static, corrupt, backward, and fatalist, republican culture employed, in effect, the same orientalist tropes that Europeans had used over the centuries, only this time in order to transcend them with the spirit of its own revolution. It is therefore not surprising that the two primary symbols of republican modernity were both visualized as direct responses to two corresponding themes in typical orientalist representations. The first, as already discussed, was the construction of Ankara as a modern capital, which sought to counteract orientalist images of Istanbul, city of the sultans, with their associated connotations of imperial decline and decay. The second was the idealized image of the new Kemalist woman, which would undo exotic fantasies of the Ottoman harem. A number of cover illustrations for the republican weekly *Yedigün* are particularly interesting. Images of modern, Western-looking women (collaged from European publications) were superimposed upon background images of old Istanbul (fig. 2.14). The new woman facing the beholder was healthy and young; the city behind her was ancient and aging. The spatial or architectural link between the two images—an open window or an iron grill like those found in traditional Ottoman architecture—introduces a further layer of signification that can be read as either a connection or a separation, or both.

A 1930 editorial in the nationalist publication *Türk Yurdu*, with the self-explanatory title "The Difference between the Old System of Government and the Republic," illustrates the workings of the "old versus new" construct in a chain of associations that runs through politics, women, and architecture.[40] Whereas the article is about the shift in the political system from dynastic empire to republic, the two pairs of photographs printed on facing pages show the two major symbols of this shift without any reference to them in the text. In one pair, the dilapidated wooden buildings of the old Ankara citadel area are shown next to the new Atatürk Boulevard, then under construction. In the other pair, a veiled woman of the Ottoman Empire is juxtaposed with a "liberated" woman of the republic, dressed in a straw hat, pleated skirt, and high-heeled shoes. Throughout the 1930s, modern architecture, modern Ankara, and modern women were connected in republican consciousness, and all three were associated with the qualities of beauty, youth, health, and progress—the qualities specifically idealized by the Kemalist *inkilap* and repeatedly juxtaposed with their old counterparts.

With this we can turn our attention from Ankara to the other major symbol of republican modernity, the Kemalist woman. The centrality of women for the Kemalist project of modernity, the importance attached to their education and participation in public life, is the topic of numerous studies and publications.[41] The ideologically charged contrast between the old and the new was nowhere as strong as in the image and position of the new Kemalist woman in society, in the aftermath of the new civil code of 1926. In spite of the code's inadequacies and double standards from today's perspectives, it was as progressive as its Western models were at the time. It abolished

Fig. 2.14. Cover illustration from *Yedigün,* a popular weekly family magazine of the mid-1930s. In a number of successive issues, in a literal representation of the "old versus new" construct, images of Western-looking modern women were collaged against a background of views of Istanbul.

polygamy, prevented child marriage, and, even when it remained on paper, granted women the right to chose their spouses, initiate divorce, inherit, and maintain property.[42] With this major legal reform, the ground was prepared for the increased presence of women in various professions and, perhaps more significantly, in public space, a challenge to the orientalist stereotype of secluded Muslim women in private interiors.

The current feminist critique of the Kemalist reforms is a compelling one: it holds that these reforms were essentially a paternalistic program casting women as objects of nationalist modernization rather than as subjects in their own lives—as individuals with unique capacities and desires. Nonetheless, this does not alter the progressiveness of the reforms as viewed in their own time, especially by women themselves, who felt empowered by their new rights and new visibility in public life. In 1931, in her book *The Turkish Woman*, dedicated to "the great leader Atatürk," the feminist writer and founding member of the Women's Association (Kadınlar Birliği), Nezihe Muhittin, described the contrast between "old and new women" as follows:

What was the woman of fifteen years ago but a "monster" both in appearance and in personality? Today's woman is civilized: civilized in the way she looks, civilized in the way she thinks. . . . The woman who, only yesterday, was nothing other than a cook and a nursing mother, today finds all the professions awaiting her with open doors. She who yesterday would consider going to the doctor an embarrassment and a sin is today a doctor herself. She who could not put two words together without sweating and blushing under her veil is proudly seated at the judge's bench today. . . . Yesterday and today . . . we can multiply these examples indefinitely.[43]

Representations of women in photographs, paintings, and posters of the 1930s constitute a rich source of documentary evidence for the study of republican modernity in general. What is important for the discussion here is the prominent *spatial* and *architectural* component of the republican discourse on women. Images of modern women, like images of modern buildings (and often the two were juxtaposed), were visible proofs of the success of the new nation in dissociating itself from the Ottoman past. Among the most canonic photographs of the Kemalist *inkilap* are those of unveiled women in educational and professional settings—as students, artists, lawyers, doctors, even aviators (fig. 2.15; also see fig. 3.12). There were also photographs of women in the public spaces of parks, sports events, fairs, and national holidays. Images of modern women as inhabitants of modern spaces were preferred propaganda statements.

The idealized qualities of the new woman—simplicity, health, youth, unadorned beauty, practicality, and, most importantly, a "scientific" worldview—were precisely the same attributes for which modern architecture was celebrated. The topic of health and hygiene, for example, was an obsession of national proportions in representations of republican modernity. Scientific explanations about environmental and personal hygiene were proposed to justify the looks of both buildings and people in conformi-

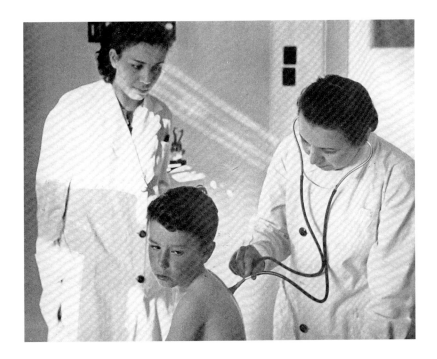

Fig. 2.15. Photographs of the "new Kemalist woman" in different professions—medicine (**top**) and the arts (**bottom**)—from *La Turquie Kemaliste,* February 1939. Such images were circulated extensively in official publicity material as testimonies to the success of the new republic in liberating Turkish women.

ty with Western models. For example, republican arguments against the veiling of the women often resorted to factors of rationality and healthiness, the same reasoning upon which the modernist polemic was conducted in architecture, including many Turkish versions of the Corbusean quest for sun, air, ventilation, and greenery. Along with the common anti-orientalist, image-conscious, and "civilizational" objections to veiling, there were strictly technical objections on grounds of hygiene and aesthetics. An essay titled "When Will Istanbul Be Free of the Veil?" by a medical doctor, Ali Rıdvan, illustrates the point, which was further strengthened by the authority of its author's profession:

The veil: this black robe of death. If only people knew how hazardous it is for women. This black cloth which blocks all the healthy rays of the sun and transmits only its heat is the enemy of health. Its color and its unaesthetic shape are additional offenses to the sight. When you add to all of these the face veil, which reminds one of the tortures of the Inquisition, the creature suffering inside this elected prison has to be the object less of our pity than our anger.[44]

In popular publications of the time there were many direct associations between images of modern women and images of modern architecture, both contrasted with their traditional counterparts. For example, in 1934 the popular weekly *Yedigün* featured "a cubic building," just completed to house the offices of the Istanbul daily *Son Posta,* with the following commentary: "It is adjacent to the old Zaptiye building, a huge block, its width, mass, and color reminding one of old-time *hans* [office buildings] designed by unschooled architects. The new and elegant 'cubic' building of *Son Posta* rising in its shadow is like a delicate and charming young girl standing next to a motherly, awkward, and stupid old woman."[45] In this case "the delicate and charming young girl" was a small, two-story building with an asymmetrical entry, a flat roof, and a modernist volumetric composition, designed by the prominent early republican architect Aptullah Ziya.[46]

In another issue of the same magazine, proudly contrasted with "the poor veiled women of the empire, secluded behind window screens," the physician Bayan Saadet, a young woman radiologist, was featured with the subtitle, "The Woman Doctor Who Commissioned an Apartment Building."[47] The photo montage showed Bayan Saadet (head uncovered, blouse with an open neckline) posing in front of a distinctly modern apartment building (flat roof, curving corners, cantilevered balconies) appropriately named after her profession: the Rontgen Apartmanı (fig. 2.16). Published earlier in a 1933 issue of the architectural magazine *Mimar,*[48] the Rontgen apartment building was the work of Zeki Sayar, the editor of *Mimar* and designer of numerous modern villas and apartments in Istanbul. Whereas the architectural magazine emphasized the "scientific, rational, and modern" qualities of the building in technical language, the *Yedigün* article was focused on its female patron.

The identification of modern architecture with the new Kemalist woman was not just a matter of symbolic association. In a more literal and directly architectural "gendering of the modern," new buildings for the education of women were often

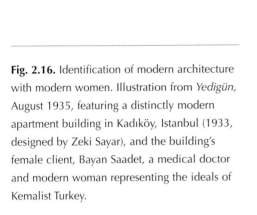

Fig. 2.16. Identification of modern architecture with modern women. Illustration from *Yedigün*, August 1935, featuring a distinctly modern apartment building in Kadıköy, Istanbul (1933, designed by Zeki Sayar), and the building's female client, Bayan Saadet, a medical doctor and modern woman representing the ideals of Kemalist Turkey.

Bayan Saadet ve Kadıköyündeki meşhur Rontgen apartımanı

designed and built in a conspicuously modernist aesthetic. As women's appearance and visibility became the primary symbol of the Kemalist *inkilap*, educational buildings for women became the most representative structures of the New Architecture in the early republic. For example, Margarete Schütte-Lihotzky's unbuilt scheme for an extension of the Girls' Lycée in Ankara exemplified the boldness and optimism of the republic's modernist vision in architecture (fig. 2.17).[49] It consisted of a circular structure containing an assembly hall on the lower level and reading and music rooms above. The circular form was supported by a ring of reinforced concrete columns and was connected to the existing building by a glass corridor. A single-story wing of six classrooms was attached to this pavilion at the lower level, along a tree-lined promenade. The project suggested that not only were the young women of the republic different from their mothers, but so were the buildings within which they were educated and socialized into Kemalist ideals.

Among the defining institutions of the republic were the girls' institutes (*kız enstitüleri*), or vocational schools. In 1927, Western education experts were invited to Turkey, and in 1928–1929, upon the recommendation of the Dewey report, girls' institutes were founded under the Ministry of Education. Although desegregated basic education for every child became the centerpiece of republican nationalism, girls' institutes became the paradigm of "good education" for the daughters of middle-class families. By 1940 there were about thirty-five girls' institutes in different cities and sixty-five evening girls' vocational schools (*akşam kız sanat okulları*) open to older women past the normal school age.[50] The purpose of these schools was to make

enlightened wives, mothers, and homemakers out of Turkish girls at a time when cultural and societal sanctions against women's working outside the home were still strong, despite the Kemalist reforms' official endorsement and encouragement of it.

In chapter 5, I will have more to say about the role of these institutes in making modern wives and mothers, trained in the latest, most efficient and "scientific" methods of housekeeping. Although no comprehensive study of the architecture of girls' institutes exists, published examples such as the İsmet İnönü Girls' Institute in Manisa in western Turkey show the association of girls' education with distinctly modern buildings (fig. 2.18).[51] Another example, the Ali Çetinkaya Girls' Institute in Afyon (1937–1938), included in İnci Aslanoğlu's survey of early republican architecture, confirms the pervasiveness of modernist formal gestures (horizontal window

Fig. 2.17. Perspective drawing of an unbuilt project for an annex to the Girls' Lycée in Ankara by Margarete Schütte-Lihotzky (1938). The project, consisting of the circular building (assembly hall, music and reading rooms) and the single-story classroom wing attached to it, was connected to the existing Lycée by a glazed corridor.

bands, circular windows, cantilevered balconies) in these buildings.[52] One paradigmatic example that occupies special status as a republican icon of modernity is the İsmet Paşa Girls' Institute in Ankara, designed by Ernst Egli and inaugurated in 1930 with much publicity and media coverage. It is a four-story building with a balanced composition consisting of a horizontally accentuated facade flanked on the two ends by vertical stair shafts, along with a flat roof, rounded balconies, and continuous window sills—a characteristic expression of the modernist aesthetic as it was adapted in

Turkey (see fig. 2.8). Photographs of the front and rear elevations of the building were published in Celal Esat Arseven's *Yeni Mimari* in 1931, an important document that celebrated the switch from Ottoman revivalism to European modernism. Feature essays were devoted to the İsmet Paşa Girls' Institute in popular magazines, celebrating both its architectural modernism and its new program to educate women well adapted to Western lifestyles, manners, and cuisine. *La Turquie Kemaliste* published photographs of young girls standing in front of the building in their school uniforms (fig. 2.19), and *Yedigün* published interviews with the teachers and students of the institute.[53] The two most powerful symbols of the Kemalist *inkilap*, architecture and women, were thus combined in the aesthetic and programmatic specificity of one building.

While an undecorated and geometric modern aesthetic constituted the formal discourse of the Kemalist revolution, there was also a strong typological component to it that to this day identifies particular building types or programs as quintessentially republican. Buildings and projects representative of the state and the ideological agenda of the RPP constituted an "architecture of revolution" (*inkilap mimarisi*) in the more literal sense of the term. Of these, government buildings, often inscribed with Atatürk's words and facing a formal government square (*hükümet meydanı*) with an Atatürk statue in the middle (bust, equestrian, standing figure), represented the presence of the state in every city and town. So did post offices and railway stations, which symbolized the extension of Ankara into every corner of the nation. The buildings most representative of the RPP's ideological agenda, however, were those for the education and indoctrination of the people along Kemalist ideals—the spaces in which the regime sought to make a nation out of a heterogeneous and traditional population. What follows is an overview of how architecture was instrumentalized for this ideological mission.

Educating the Nation

THE INSTITUTIONAL AND architectural infrastructure for "educating the nation" had a clear priority on the republic's ideological agenda. A nationwide literacy campaign in the new Latin alphabet, the closing of religious schools, and the establishment of universal national education (*tevhid-i tedrisat kanunu*) were among the first acts of the republican regime. Contemporaneous photographs and paintings testify to the cultural significance of the theme of education: they portray healthy schoolchildren in their uniforms, women being taught how to read and write, and coeducational village schools where boys and girls were introduced to scientific learning and republican ideals (fig. 2.20). Schools as well as centers for popular education (*Halkevleri,* or "People's Houses") and projects for new villages and agricultural resettlement programs (*köy mimarisi*) were the centerpieces of republican building activity, planned and supervised directly by the RPP. Whereas banks, offices, and

Fig. 2.18. Plain and "cubic" modernism as the dominant architectural-aesthetic expression of the progressive function of educational buildings for girls. İsmet İnönü Girls' Institute in Manisa, 1930s.
Fig 2.19. Young girls in their uniforms in front of the İsmet Paşa Girls' Institute, Ankara (1930), one of the first major modern buildings designed by Ernst Egli.

Fig. 2.20. Educating the nation: "Registration for School" (*Okula Kayıt*, 1935), painting by Şeref Akdik depicting an idealized scene of the republic's literacy campaign in Anatolian villages.

department stores were associated with the discredited cosmopolitanism of the late empire, and mosques with the reactionary forces of religion, educational buildings of all kinds became emblems of the scientific and progressive ideals of the Kemalist revolution. Their construction was synonymous with nation building itself.

While the celebrated modern buildings of higher education in Ankara testify to the exceptional role played by the architectural office of the Ministry of Education, it was the design of more anonymous, repeatable, and recognizable prototype schools that represented the unifying agenda of the nation-state. Until the switch to modernism around 1931, the National Architecture Renaissance was still the recognizable style of prototype elementary and secondary schools in almost every city or provincial town. Often they were named after Atatürk as war hero—that is, Gazi schools (see fig. 1.13). After 1931, while the style of the prototype schools changed, the practice of working with prototypes continued within the Ministries of Education and Public Works, and it also became a topic of important and interesting debates within the emerging architectural profession. Zeki Sayar, the founding editor of *Mimar* and an important architect of the 1930s, wrote extensively about the problems of prototype design, touching on the theoretical incompatibility of the prototype idea with a contextualist modernism, about which more will be said in chapter 6. In the first issues of *Mimar*, criticizing the prototype schools built in Istanbul in 1928 (Nişantaşı, Kadıköy, and Azapkapı were the examples he cited), Sayar emphasized the different characteristics of each urban site in terms of terrain, slope, orientation, and other factors. Calling for "a scientific approach to site selection" and designs for "a particular rather than a hypothetical site," he voiced an insightful but unelaborated objection to the idea of stamping school buildings with an official style to represent the state: "It is not right to build schools like uniforms. An official and serious style fit for a government building will make the school 'boring' in appearance. Today it is impossible to distinguish schools from other state institutions such as government offices, police stations, and law courts. . . . It is enough and desirable that schools are built in a local expression [*mahalli mimari*], but not in an official style [*resmi üslup*]!"[54]

Most young architects involved with the journal *Arkitekt* (the new name of *Mimar* after 1934) shared Sayar's rationalist approach to school design, as well as his criticism of prototype schools designed within the Ministry of Public Works. Projects published in the journal illustrate certain aesthetic and organizational principles that prescribed what came to stand for a modern school building "designed from the inside out," a critical response to the Gazi schools of the 1920s. Blocks of two or more stories were arranged in L- or U-shaped plans to define a courtyard and assembly plaza; the gym was attached to one end as a distinct block, and the classrooms, on single-loaded corridors, were oriented to the east or the south. As exemplified by a secondary school project by Abidin Mortaş (fig. 2.21), elevations reflected what was behind them (bigger windows for classrooms, horizontal bands of windows for corridors, and vertical slits for circulation shafts and auditoriums). Plain volumetric compositions, flat roofs, and occasional circular windows projected a modernist aesthetic.[55] It was often explained in the project descriptions that corridor and stair widths, classroom sizes, and the number of stalls in the bathrooms were calculated "according to scientific formulas based on number of students" and that the desks, display windows, and other interior furniture were designed "according to children's scale."[56] Health and hygiene—an abundance of sunlight, ventilation, and germ-free plain surfaces—were the main themes in architects' discourses about school buildings.

Unlike the Ministry of Public Works, the Ministry of Education favored site-specific designs for schools, endorsing prototype designs only for the special case of "village schools," considered "not [to be] of great artistic significance, limited by meager budgets, and unconstrained by the specificities of urban sites."[57] The different types of village schools were classified according to the number of students and the primary material of construction (fig. 2.22).[58] Sizes varied from one to three classrooms, based on a maximum of sixty students per classroom, and each type was designed in three variants for different local materials—stone, adobe, and wood. Model designs were also prepared for teachers' lodgings in two types, one for bachelors and another for families, either as separate units next to the school or incorporated into the main school building, possibly as a second phase of construction. The prototype village

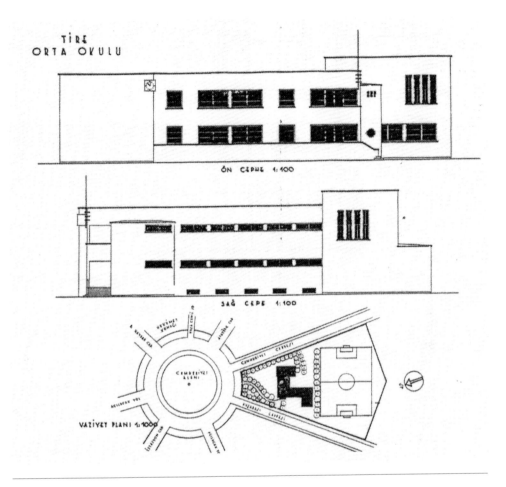

Fig. 2.21. A representative example of modernist school design in the 1930s: project for a middle school in Tire by Abidin Mortaş, as published in *Arkitekt,* 1937. Different functions are grouped in different blocks in an L-shaped layout defining an outdoor assembly area. Flat roofs and undecorated cubic volumes reflect a distinctly modernist aesthetic. Different window sizes and forms of windows reflect what is behind them: large windows for the classrooms, narrow horizontal bands for corridors, circular windows and/or vertical slits for stair shafts and double-height spaces such as the gym.

schools for Anatolia (1938–1939) designed by Margarete Schütte-Lihotzky for the Ministry of Education were of the two-phase kind, in which at its largest the school contained two or three classrooms with separate living quarters and a small kitchen for two teachers. The materials were specified as wood, mud brick–clay, brick, or rough stone. Schütte-Lihotzky's perspective drawing of this three-classroom type of village school for 150–180 students depicts an idyllic Anatolian landscape with the school building located atop a hill overlooking the village, in aesthetic harmony with the whitewashed walls and red tile roofs of the village houses below (fig. 2.23).

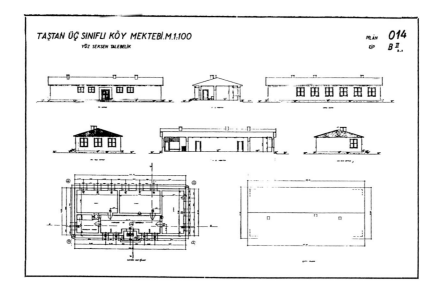

Fig. 2.22. Prototype school design for Anatolian villages: a three-classroom type with 180-student capacity to be built in stone. From the Ministry of Education publication *Plans of Village Schools and Teachers' Lodgings,* 1935. **Figure 2.23.** Perspective rendering of a prototype village school for Anatolia (1939) by Margarete Schütte-Lihotzky. The school sits prominently on a hill, dominating the other buildings of the village.

Whereas school building was carried out by the Ministries of Education and Public Works, the centers of popular education and indoctrination, the so-called People's Houses (*Halkevleri*), were directly commissioned by and connected to the RPP, making them overtly ideological symbols of the republic. The People's Houses organization was established in 1932, at the height of the RPP's systematic program to disseminate a nationalist consciousness following the foundation of two other major republican organizations, the Turkish Historical Society (Türk Tarih Kurumu) in 1931 and the Turkish Language Society (Türk Dil Kurumu) in 1932. Through the People's Houses and the RPP's official journal, *Ülkü* (Ideal), which began publication in 1933, the RPP sought to propagate the principles of the Kemalist revolution and to instill a strong idealism, especially among the young, for serving the nation and bringing "civilization" to every corner of the country. The inaugural issue of *Ülkü* described its mission this way: "*Ülkü* is being issued to nurture the spirit of the young generation that has left the dark ages behind and is marching toward a bright future. It is issued to mobilize the revolutionary elements in society . . . and to establish the union of minds, hearts, and action among those committed to this great mission. . . . In the writings, analyses, and commentaries of *Ülkü*, the ideas of republic, nation, and revolution will be primary."[60]

In his comprehensive work on the organization of People's Houses, Anıl Çeçen traces their ideological sources to similar organizations in other revolutionary regimes, from the Jacobin clubs of the French Revolution to the *narodnik* movement in czarist Russia.[61] Most conspicuously, however, as covered in numerous essays in *Ülkü*, People's Houses were modeled after the Italian Dopo Lavoro cultural organizations and the Fascist youth clubs, Balilla for boys and Piccole for girls.[62] The establishment, organization, and operation of the People's Houses constitute a vast topic beyond the scope of this cultural history of architecture.[63] But as a paradigmatic republican building type directly in the service of the regime and designed mostly along the aesthetic canons of modernism, they constitute a major theme in the architectural culture of the 1930s, as a recent book by Nese Gürallar Yeşilkaya testifies.[64] They were the Turkish counterparts of the well-known *case del fascio* in Italy, which epitomized the brief overlap in the 1930s between the ideals of rationalist architects and authoritarian regimes. Symbolically, they were the most important *secular* centers of assembly and socialization, replacing the traditional social function of the mosque as well as its architectural prominence in the urban order.[65] That two of the first women architects in Turkey, Leman Tomsu and Münevver Belen, made their reputations with designs for People's Houses further accentuates the progressive connotations of this building type.

People's Houses were established with the stated objective of teaching the people the meaning, necessity, and ideals of the Kemalist *inkilap*, explaining to them "why certain things were abandoned, why others were imported from the West, and why many things were reconstructed under the auspices of the republic."[66] Throughout the

1930s, among many other contributors to *Ülkü*, Nusret Kemal and Mehmet Saffet wrote extensively on people's education, Aptullah Ziya wrote about the architecture of the village, Ali Sami Boyar, about art, Abdülhak Şinasi, about monuments and museums, and Zeki Nasır, about health and hygiene. "Popular training" (*halk terbiyesi*) constituted one of the most important and recurrent themes in the journal, also illustrating the republican belief in the power of representation (through publications, posters, radio, and film). In 1933 Hamit Zubeyr described the "instruments of popular training" as follows: "Training the people means molding a unified social body and a unified nation out of ethnically, linguistically, and civilizationally diverse groups living in our country. It means the cultivation of the spirit in such a way that the thinking, feelings, and desires of individuals will fully coincide with national ideals. . . . Words, publications, art, music, film, and radio are among the most effective vehicles of popular training."[67]

Each People's House was organized in at least three of nine designated activity areas: language-history-literature, the arts, performances, sports, social work, vocational training, library-publications, museums-exhibitions, and village work. Their political and ideological functions notwithstanding, the progressive role played by the People's Houses is evident in these activities. It was in People's Houses that many provincial Turks living in small towns first encountered theater, classical music, books, and art exhibitions. It was in these buildings that many people engaged in sports or learned typing, accounting, mechanics, vine growing, sewing, embroidery, and hat making. Art was perceived by the RPP as a powerful pedagogical vehicle to educate the people (*mürebbi sanat*) and to win their hearts for the revolution: "It is obvious that to conquer the minds of the people, one has to start by conquering their hearts. That hearts can best be captured by the fine arts has been amply demonstrated by experience. . . . The eye and the ear are the most receptive organs for persuasion, and the international languages of painting, sculpture, music, and architecture, which are capable of directly addressing these organs, are the branches most worthy of our full attention."[68]

People's Houses were not just built to house the cultural, educational, and social activities of the RPP but were also formally identified with the party. The extensive use of republican iconography—flags with the RPP emblem of six arrows, Atatürk statues, and inscriptions of Atatürk's words and party slogans—complemented the architecture of these buildings. For example, in the project for Gebze People's House by Selim Sayar (1939), a large blank wall facing the street was allocated for inscriptions and party propaganda, an idea that was epitomized in Italy by Guiseppe Terragni's canonic Casa del Fascio in Como (1932–1936). In her study of the architecture of People's Houses, Neşe Gürallar Yeşilkaya identifies two other ideologically charged architectural elements: a balcony or platform on which party notables could address the public and the vertical accent of a tower to serve as a landmark. The latter, she explains, symbolized not only republican ideals of production and progress, by alluding to the verticality of factory chimneys and silos, but also the triumph of secularism over religion, by rising to a height taller than the minaret of the mosque.[69]

Towers with abstract geometric designs, signs in modern lettering, and night illumination were indeed characteristic elements of the RPP propaganda machinery and were used extensively as temporary commemorative structures erected for national holidays (fig. 2.24). Yet any explanation of these architectural elements exclusively in terms of ideological motives confined to Turkish politics would be inadequate; it must also be recognized that similar towers constituted an aesthetic norm of modern public buildings everywhere in the 1930s. A number of contemporaneous buildings in Europe incorporated towers in designs for comparable programs and became sources of influence and inspiration for Turkish architects. Among these, the Hilversum Town Hall by Dudok in Holland (1928–1930) and the Revolution Square Town Hall by Cancellotti, Montuori, Piccinato, and Scalpelli in Sabaudia, Italy (1934), were published in *Arkitekt* and were well known to Turkish architects.[70] More will be said in chapter 4 about these formal and aesthetic tropes of modernism that were internal to the discipline of architecture.

People's Houses initiated activities in fourteen cities in 1932, some taking over the old Turkish Hearth (Türkocağı) buildings erected in the 1920s, in the heyday of the National Architecture Renaissance. New People's Houses were funded and commissioned by the local branch of the RPP, sometimes through architectural competitions and sometimes through direct selection of a local architect.[71] Throughout the 1930s, popular magazines like *Yedigün* published model designs for People's Houses "for small towns that do not yet have one."[72] By the end of the decade, in 1939, there were 163 People's Houses in different cities and towns, and by 1946, at the movement's peak (before its closure in 1950, when the RPP lost power), the number of People's Houses had reached 455.[73]

The representational importance of People's Houses was expressed first in the prominent urban locations of these buildings, which were often sited as landmarks directly facing the major street or government square. Second, their importance was reflected in the quality of materials and meticulous detailing employed in their construction. It was the strong modernist statement of their architecture, however, that endowed them with progressive and revolutionary connotations. Examples commissioned through competitions and published in *Arkitekt* were especially paradigmatic in terms of formal features and facade aesthetic. Most projects had flat roofs, although as a result of technical problems some were later covered over by a pitched tile roof, as in the case of Zonguldak People's House by Abidin Mortaş and Zeki Sayar (1933) or the Bursa People's House by Münevver Belen (1938). Different components of the program were expressed on the facade in different window sizes and shapes; curved facades, projecting and cantilevered elements, towers, and circular windows were arranged in modern compositions of interlocking blocks. The project for Kadıköy People's House by Rüknettin Güney (1938) is a particularly representative

Fig. 2.24. Festive commemorative structures for the Republican People's Party: "Light Tower" (**top**) and the RPP tower (**bottom**), both designed by Seyfi Arkan for the tenth anniversary of the republic in 1933. The use of electric illumination, abstract planes, and propaganda writing is reminiscent of the constructivist structures of the 1920s in the Soviet Union.

example of this modernist aesthetic, with the assembly hall–gym block culminating in a rounded end and lit through a row of circular windows (fig. 2.25). L-shaped plans with rounded corners for the entrance were also common, as in the case of Yalova RPP Headquarters–People's House by Sedad Çetintaş (1934) and the unbuilt winning design for the Sivas People's House by Nazif Asal and Emin Necip Uzman (1938) (fig. 2.25).

In terms of plan arrangement, the larger spaces of the hall-auditorium and gym were typically located in a separate block easily readable in exterior form while the rest of the program—offices, spaces for activity groups, library, and classrooms—constituted the main block. The blocks were arranged so as to define an open space or courtyard for meetings, concerts, public festivals, and weddings. The program also included offices for RPP officials, sometimes designed as a separate building connected to the People's House by a colonnade, as in Manisa People's House by Asım Kömürcüoğlu (1938). In other cases, party offices were located on the upper floor(s), as in the Karamürsel and Gerede People's Houses by Leman Tomsu and Munevver Belen (1936).[74] In unusual cases such as the Eskişehir People's House by İzzet Baysal (1936, demolished), the entire program was designed on the upper floor of a long, two-story block, and ground level was reserved for shops to bring revenue to the RPP. Construction of People's Houses was typically of reinforced concrete for floor slabs and the structural walls and columns, with brick infill. After 1940, however, the use of stone and pitched tile roofs gradually replaced the earlier materials that had produced such pristine geometric forms, launching a new trend in national expression.

Colonizing the Countryside

Parallel to the elaborate organization of popular education through People's Houses, the RPP's program for "colonizing the countryside" through village architecture (köy mimarisi) represented another major spatial component of republican ideology. Turkey was an overwhelmingly agrarian country, with more than 80 percent of its population living in rural areas in the 1930s. The contribution of villages to the national economy was a strong incentive for modernizing them. The training of peasants (köycülük) constituted one of the most important branches of activity in the RPP program. Not only the modernization of existing villages and agricultural lands but also the resettlement of refugees from the Balkans and other lost territories of the empire were major challenges encountered by the republican regime in its first decade. By 1933, sixty-nine model villages had been built by the state,[75] and the "modern and scientific standards" employed in their construction were contrasted with the "poor and primitive condition of peasants in the old empire," in the characteristic manner of "old versus new" (see fig. 2.4).

It was after the consolidation of the RPP's power (1931), however, and under the auspices of the People's Houses (1932) that villages and peasants became primary

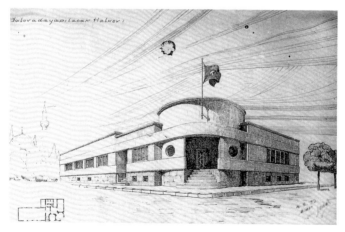

Fig. 2.25. The pervasiveness of modern forms (flat roofs, geometric blocks, rounded corners, and circular windows) in the design of "People's Houses" in the 1930s. Model photographs of winning competition projects for the Kadıköy Halkevi, Istanbul, by Rüknettin Güney (**top**), and the Sivas Halkevi by Nazif Asal and Emin Necip Uzman (**middle**). **Bottom:** Perspective drawing of the Yalova Halkevi by Sedad Çetintaş.

objects of the "civilizing mission" of Kemalism. It was an ideological, cultural, and educational mission to be taken to the remotest, harshest, and most inaccessible corners of the country with revolutionary zeal, idealism, and sacrifice (fig. 2.26). In the pages of *Ülkü*, this call was described with explicit analogy to and admiration for "American missionaries" and the "civilization-bearing" colonizers in Africa.[76] What the young Turkish "village missionaries" (*köy misyonerleri*) were expected to undertake was regarded as a much higher form of battle (against ignorance and backwardness) than all the conventional battles of the past, including the glorious siege of Vienna by Ottoman armies more than two centuries earlier:

The era of combating the cannibals in African jungles in order to spread Christianity is over. Nor would one any longer consider it bravery to force the gates of Vienna with swords. The missionary work of today is listening to the problems of the people whose blood, feelings, and sweat we share in our bodies and spirit, and to search for solutions to these problems. The bravery of today is to force the walls of illiteracy, conservatism, laziness, and despair, which are more formidable than the most formidable fortifications.[77]

In this ideological climate, the "scientific planning" of villages and the design of their buildings—the "architecture of the village" (*köy mimarisi*), as it was called—was

Fig. 2.26. Cover of *La Turquie Kemaliste,* April 1938, celebrating the Anatolian peasant and the working of the land under the guidance of Kemalist idealism.

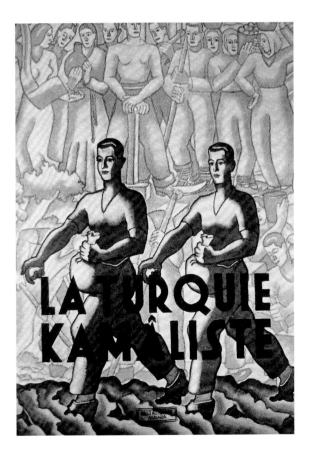

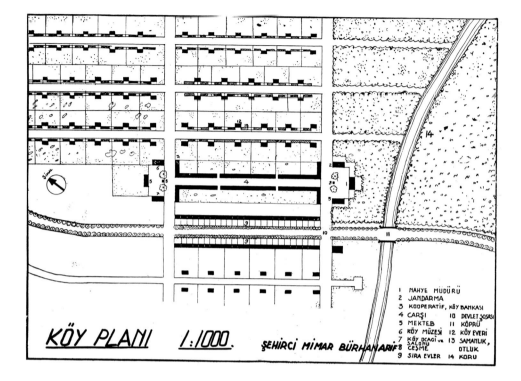

KÖY PLANI 1:1000.   ŞEHİRCİ MİMAR BÜRHAN ARİF

1 NAHYE MÜDÜRÜ
2 JANDARMA
3 KOOPERATİF, KÖY BANKASI
4 CARŞI   10 DEVLET ŞOSASI
5 MEKTEB   11 KÖPRÜ
6 KÖY MÜZESİ   12 KÖY EVERİ
7 KÖY OCAĞİ ve   13 SAMANLIK,
   SALONU   OTLUK
8 CEŞME
9 SIRA EVLER   14 KORU

Fig. 2.27. Model village project based on a uniform grid by the "urbanist architect" Burhan Arif (1935).

presented as a distinct area of specialization for architects, legitimating their claims to serve the regime as "agents of civilization." "Villages are of paramount significance in nation building," wrote Abidin Mortaş in 1935, "and they must be designed and supervised by the professional architect, responding to the local traditions, building techniques, and materials of the village."[78] This plea was illustrated by a plan for a model village by the "urbanist architect" Burhan Arif. A linear shopping street terminating in a small square at each end occupied the village center in a symmetrical arrangement (fig. 2.27). One of the squares was given to state functions and held government buildings; the other was the cultural square containing the school, the museum, the village hall, and the fountain. As the ultimate expression of scientific rationality and efficiency, identical village houses in detached and row-house variants were laid out in a rectangular grid suggestive of a thoroughly flat site. The diagrammatic simplicity and exaggerated rationality of the proposal, like the rubber-stamp designs of most model villages built by the state, disregarded most traditional rural settlement types in which village houses of different sizes and qualities typically huddled together in clusters.

Most conspicuously, the absence of the mosque, the primary landmark of most Turkish villages, was a strong architectural statement affirming the secularizing agenda of the RPP. Architects shared this secular enlightenment ideal, and Aptullah Ziya expressed their suspicion of mosques as follows:

Edifying and electrifying the villages never occurred to the rulers of the Ottoman Empire, with the exception of some mosques they built in Anatolian villages. These mosques had no other effect than strengthening the religious loyalty of the peasants to the sultan and thus turning the oppression of the individual to a collective oppression. The worst thing about a village mosque, which has been the only cultural and social center for the village, is that in its four walls it offers a bastion for the reactionaries who are the organizers of oppression and ignorance.[79]

An even more remarkable example of the idealized diagrammatic approach to planning new villages is a 1933 project attributed to Kazım Dirlik, inspector general of Thrace (fig. 2.28).[80] This "ideal republican village" (*ideal cumhuriyet köyü*) was laid out in perfect concentric zones for residential units, for health, educational, and sports facilities, and for commerce and light industry, all radiating from the center of the circular plan. According to Gülsüm Baydar Nalbantoğlu, it was "unmistakably inspired by Ebenezer Howard's Garden City diagrams."[81] Nalbantoğlu argues that "republican model villages consisted of neatly arranged rows of identical houses reminiscent of the disciplinary environments of nineteenth-century factory towns." Her evocation of a "disciplinary environment" is appropriate for this plan in light of the fact that the perfectly geometric centralized plan was indeed a symbol of reformist utopia, from Renaissance ideal cities to Jeremy Bentham's "Panopticon" in the nineteenth century. It was the most symptomatic formal expression of Enlightenment ideals that informed the RPP's village architecture program.

In 1936, Zeki Sayar further elaborated on the civilizing role of the architect and the necessity of imposing the plans and ideas of experts even when they conflicted with traditional settlement patterns and lifestyles:

Although we must consider the habits and lifestyles of the peasants when we are constructing the new villages, we should not hesitate to go against these traditions wherever they clash with contemporary social and hygienic standards. The new village plans should also provide the users with the means for civilized living. A revolution in lifestyles is also necessary to teach them to sleep on individual beds rather than together on the earth, to teach them to use chairs and tables rather than sitting and eating on the floor. Kitchens, stoves, and bathrooms should be standardized into a number of different types so as to obtain the most economic and functional results.[82]

These writings by Zeki Sayar, titled, without any hint of irony, "Interior Colonization" (*İç Kolonizasyon*), illustrate architects' more "professional" approach to the building of new villages and resettlement of the land. He criticized the earlier model villages built during the first decade of the republic, the inadequacies of which, he argued, were evident by looking at all the additions and alterations the peasants had made to render them habitable. In order to improve on these early examples, he emphasized the necessity of resorting to the technical expertise of architects. He declared it a "civilizational imperative" to eliminate the use of mud bricks (*kerpiç*), "a primitive material utterly unfit for construction by the state," and advocated the extensive use of concrete and cement (*çimento*) in "village buildings, sanitary infra-

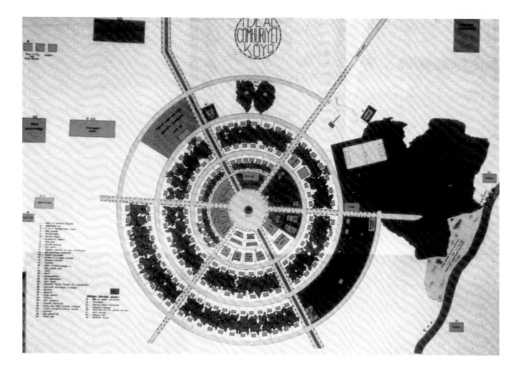

Fig. 2.28. Circular plan of an "ideal republican village" (1933) by Kazım Dirlik, inspector general of the Thrace region.

structure, irrigation canals, stables, and garden walls."[83] He called for the "rational and scientific" design of multiple house plans for each village, depending on family size and site characteristics, rather than building the entire model village with one type of house. At the same time, he argued that the economies of standardization and serial production should be exploited in the selection of construction materials and the design of building components (windows, doors, and fixtures).

Theoretically, the most interesting aspects of Sayar's writings are the parallels he drew between the building of new model villages in Turkey and the construction of agricultural colonies elsewhere in Europe to return idle industrial workers to the land after the Great Depression. Germany was presented as the nation most successful in building agricultural colonies and new villages, "not by individuals and private efforts but by state initiative according to National Socialist economic policies."[84] Site plans and photographs of model villages in Germany were published in *Arkitekt* along with detailed drawings of model farms and rural houses. That "the German government considers the German peasant to be the primary source of the national blood" was observed with admiration. "In order not to repeat the mistakes of earlier model villages built in Anatolia," Sayar concluded, "we, too, like the Germans, must give great importance to science, specialization, and organization."

Turkey, however, had not experienced the massive industrialization or social and environmental ills of urbanization that had sparked the antiurban sentiments of

German nationalism, and so Sayar's embracing of German models was devoid of historical basis. More convincing were parallels drawn between Turkey and the new Zionist Jewish settlements in Palestine or the Italian agrarian colonies in the reclaimed marshes of Agro Pontino and the conquered lands of North Africa.[85] The revolutionary zeal of Kemalism and the idealism of the RPP program most closely resembled those of Zionism and fascism, respectively. This congruence between the three ideologies largely accounts for the common architectural vocabulary of rationalist modernism proposed for these colonies: flat roofs, grid plans, plane surfaces, village squares with clock towers, and faith in reinforced concrete.

The writings by architect Aptullah Ziya in *Ülkü* represent a more "populist" approach to village architecture, one that was less interested in examples from other countries than in the principles of a native program "born out of the village—out of its needs, earth, materials, and trees."[86] His point of departure was an analysis of the vernacular architecture of existing villages under three groups based on location (plains, mountains, and forests), with further differentiation based on the primary material of construction (stone or wood). He then outlined and illustrated with a drawing his own hypothetical proposal for a model village on the Anatolian plain—a village with a perfectly geometric layout and diagrammatic buildings reminiscent of Owenite ideal communities in the nineteenth century (fig. 2.29).[87] The site plan was a perfect square with the village square–coffeehouse at the center, encircled by rows of small houses, with a linear arrangement of farms on the periphery. The material for the whole scheme was specified to be mud brick, with flat earth roofs, contrasting

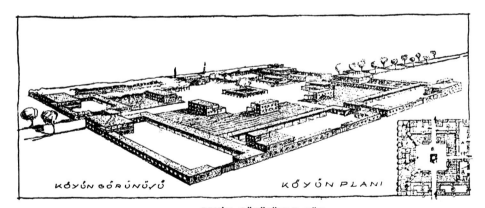

KÖYÜN GÖRÜNÜŞÜ — KÖYÜN PLANI

BENİM GÖRÜŞÜMLE KÖY:
A — Köyü saran çiftlikler B — Köy meydanını saran ufak evler C — Meydan ortasında köy kahvesi D — Köy meydanı E — Köy bahçesi ve a-ğaçlığı F — Köy mektebi.
1 — Çiftlik evi —2 — Çiftlik ahırları — 3 Ziraat makine ve âlâtı hangarları.

Fig. 2.29. Design for an ideal village by Aptullah Ziya (1933), laid out on a square plan with a communal center for cultural and educational activities.

GÜN GEÇİMİNDE KERPİÇ KÖY YAPISI

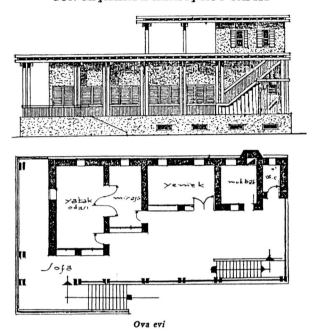

Ova evi

GÜN GEÇİMİNDE KERPİÇ KÖY YAPISI

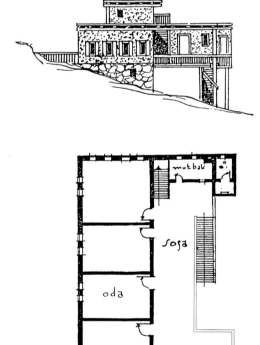

Dağ evi

Fig. 2.30. Aptullah Ziya's model designs for prototype village houses to be built in mud brick, based on the traditional "exterior *sofa* [hall]" plan type. Plans and elevations of two variants: one for a steep mountain site and the other for a flat plain.

starkly with Zeki Sayar's aversion to these materials. The village school was the only other public building identified on the diagram, and any sign of a mosque was again conspicuously absent. Aptullah Ziya explained the idea behind the central placement of the village coffeehouse: "The peasant should receive ample air and light; he should not be cold in his house. He should have a coffeehouse and a radio at the village square, and if not a cinema or a theater, he should at least have a place for itinerant films and plays that might be visiting the village. The village coffeehouse is the library, the meeting place, the club, and the cinema of the peasant: it is a 'modern temple.'"[88]

In another issue Aptullah Ziya gave the drawings (plans and elevations) for three types of mud-brick houses for a mountain site, for a plains site, and for a larger farm-house (fig. 2.30).[89] All had mud-brick walls, wooden floors, and flat roofs with clay earth over a straw mat supported by wooden beams. The traditional wisdom of vernacular building was acknowledged: the designs were oriented to the sun, the flat earth roofs offered a cool place to sleep at night, and the toilets were placed as far away from the houses as possible, "in the same way that villagers have always built." Although this reverence for vernacular traditions differentiated the tone of Aptullah Ziya's writings in *Ülkü* from Zeki Sayar's in *Arkitekt,* both architects shared the RPP ideals of civilizing the village and infusing the peasants with nationalist consciousness. "There are many citizens of our country who would consider it an insult if you called them a 'Turk,'" complained Aptullah Ziya. "It is our responsibility to construct their villages and to make them talk, dress, and live like the rest of us."[90]

What is fascinating about the 1930s is that the term "colonization" was devoid of all of its negative connotations: it signified a progressive and enlightened state bringing civilization to the countryside. The majority of writings in both *Arkitekt* and *Ülkü* portrayed village planning as the necessary intervention of enlightened reformers, the active agents, upon backward and silent peasant populations, the passive receptors of enlightenment. With few exceptions, the fundamental differences and the absence of communication between these two sides and the implied relations of power in this civilizing project were unattended in the writings of the 1930s. As Nalbantoğlu observes, the "silence" of the peasants would come to an end only after 1950, when their large-scale migration to cities would begin transforming the physical and social fabric of Turkish cities in unprecedented ways.[91]

3

Aesthetics of Progress

IMAGINING AN INDUSTRIAL NATION

If civilization [*medeniyet*] is the name of a stage in the domination of nature by the human will to power, what else is culture [*kültür*] but the accumulation, over time, of the rational means of this victory? . . . Many are waiting for a cultural renaissance in our country. But few would accept that this is possible only after a "precultural" stage: the name of this stage is "a society of advanced technique."

—Yakup Kadri Karaosmanoğlu, "Kültür ve Medeniyet," 1933[1]

It is impossible to create art in this century by borrowing motifs from the temple that the Egyptians constructed for their deities or the acropolis that the Greeks built for their gods. Nor from the temple of Vesta through which the Romans showed off their grandeur, or the fountains and mosques of the Turks. These cannot be the source of art in the twentieth century, when airplanes are hovering in the skies and ocean liners are crossing the sea at phenomenal speeds.

—Aptullah Ziya, "Yeni Sanat," 1932[2]

ALTHOUGH THE REPUBLICAN definition of "contemporary civilization" (*muasır medeniyet*) was frequently reduced to norms and exterior forms of "civility," as we saw in the previous chapter, many republican intellectuals, artists, and architects defined civilization as a broader concept, irreducible to the way women, cities, buildings, or kitchens looked. It designated what they perceived to be the universal trajectory of progress that every nation had to follow—a teleological destiny that could not and should not be resisted. This was the common philosophical premise that the Modern Movement and Kemalism shared. The former claimed to be the destiny of architectural evolution everywhere, the latter presented itself as the last stage in the historical evolution of the Turkish nation, and both claimed to reflect the spirit of "contemporary civilization" in the twentieth century. The favorable reception of European modernism in Turkish architectural culture of the 1930s must be understood, before everything else, in the context of this teleologically defined project of civilization that gave Kemalism its revolutionary creed.

Long before the Kemalist *inkilap,* doctrines of positivism and rationalism originating in post-Enlightenment France had been the most influential currents of thought shaping the consciousness of Ottoman-Turkish intellectuals. At least since the end of the eighteenth century, Ottoman reformers had diagnosed the "sickness" and decline of the empire to be a consequence of lagging behind the scientific spirit of the Enlightenment and the technological and industrial progress of Europe. Around the turn of the century, the leading nationalist ideologue, Ziya Gökalp, had put it in the following terms: "For us today, being contemporary with modern civilization [*asrileşmek*] means to make and use battleships, cars, and airplanes that the Europeans are making and using. When we see ourselves no longer in need of importing manufactured goods and buying knowledge from Europe, then we can speak of being contemporary with it."[3] Gökalp's distinction between this science-and-technology-based notion of universal civilization (*medeniyet*) and a more spiritual notion of national culture (*hars*) had been an important source of inspiration behind the Ottoman revivalist architecture of the 1910s and 1920s.

With the Kemalist republic, the term "civilization" was reconceived more broadly, not just as the superior tools, technologies, artifacts, and knowledge of the West but as a historically inevitable process of social evolution in which scientific and technological development assumed historical agency. In an important 1933 essay titled "Culture and Civilization," Yakup Kadri Karaosmanoğlu, a leading novelist, intellectual, and political figure of the period, rejected Ziya Gökalp's earlier distinction between the two terms.[4] Instead, he outlined a new, unified concept of "contemporary civilization" grounded in scientific and technological progress that, he argued, was the prerequisite for the desired artistic and cultural regeneration of the nation. This progressive model of history, which subsumed the category "culture" under the broader term "civilization," marked a conspicuous departure from Gökalp's formulation and a move toward the idea of a single contemporary civilization to be shared by all modern nations. Civilization and the culture that went with it constituted an indivisible conceptual totality. Importing one without the other was impossible.

Mustafa Kemal Atatürk's own words frequently alluded to this idea of civilization in eloquent terms. "Civilization is a sublime force that pierces mountains, crosses the skies, enlightens and explores everything from the smallest particle of dust to the stars," he said.[5] In these words, Atatürk allegorically endowed "civilization" with a supernatural power to overcome every hardship and to redeem Turkish society as a whole. More significantly, it was a matter not of choice but of *necessity* to follow this "sublime force," represented in the real world by the social and material progress of the West. As Atatürk emphasized on every occasion, to resist Western civilization would be a futile resistance to history in the making: "We lived through pain because we did not understand the conditions of the world. Our thinking and our mentality will have to become civilized. Take a look at the entire Turkish and Islamic world. Because they failed to adapt to the conditions and rise, they found themselves in such catastrophe and suffering. We cannot afford to stop anymore. We have to move forward. . . . Civilization is such a fire that it burns and destroys those who ignore it."[6]

It is on these premises that scholars of nationalism talk about Atatürk's remarkable success at overcoming the "anti-Western sentiments and xenophobia" that typically characterize nationalism outside the Western world. Like Nehru after him, Atatürk was the paradigmatic modernizing nationalist hero whose primary ideological and rhetorical strategy was constructed around the compelling idea that civilization is *one*, whereas nations are *many*, and participation in this singular universal civilization is a necessity for national progress.[7] In spite of its vagueness in real terms (or perhaps because of it), this would prove to be a powerful formulation that allowed republican leaders, intellectuals, and artists to be Westernizing modernists and fervent nationalists at the same time. By the same token, it was a formulation that alienated the more uncompromisingly religious, anti-Western, and anticolonial nationalists, such as the poet Mehmet Akif Ersoy and some proponents of the National Architecture Renaissance, who were still committed to the "Islamic civilization" of the Ottoman Empire. It is telling that, whereas in Mehmet Akif's poetry "[Western] civilization" was a "single-toothed monster" representing the Christian aggressor on the battlefields of Gallipoli, Atatürk embraced *all* the dead of Gallipoli—Australian and British soldiers as well as Turkish—when he dedicated the Gallipoli monument in 1934. The Australians and British may have been the adversaries in war, but they were members of the larger "civilization" to which the new Turks of the republic aspired to belong in peace.

In Kemalism's idealized formulation, contemporary civilization was not the exclusive monopoly of Europe or of any Western nation because it happened to originate there. Rather, it was the stock of accumulated scientific knowledge, methods and tools, worldviews and lifestyles that constituted the very substance of historical evolution of humanity and should be seen as the property of all nations. How else could one sustain the passionately anticolonialist, anti-imperialist, and hence anti-Western sentiments of nationalist insurgence and, at the same time, justify the most radically Westernizing reforms hitherto implemented in a traditional and predominantly Muslim society? The Kemalist slogan of "being Western in spite of the West" neatly summed up this profound contradiction common to postcolonial nation building in many countries. In the case of Turkey, the slogan was made further viable by the fact that unlike many other new nations of the postcolonial era, Turkey was never officially colonized by Western powers and could even claim to be itself a "European" power at some point in its history.[8] Thus, in spite of the nationalist anticolonial rhetoric of Kemalism, which had fueled the War of Independence, Turks could approach the West with less resentment than could many other non-European nations. Instead, resentment could be directed toward the rulers of the late Ottoman Empire for failing to understand the conditions of the modern world and to push the nation forward into civilization.

That the Kemalist emphasis on "universal civilization" was not a negation of "national culture" needs to be underscored. In fact, no other period of modern Turkish history has seen such obsession with national culture as the 1930s, precisely the time when the idea of universal civilization assumed such a mythical and all-encompassing status. Republican intellectuals were fascinated by German philosophers' arguments for *Kultur* as much as they were by the rationalist and positivist ideas of French thinkers, Auguste Comte in particular, seeking possible ways of synthesizing them into a singular concept. Much intellectual effort was devoted to demonstrating the compatibility of Turkish culture with universal civilization and disproving any irreconcilable antagonism between them. It was argued that modernism, far from being an alien import, was in fact the uncovering of what was already rational and modern in Turkish culture, forgotten behind layers of obscurantism and backwardness. The Modern Movement in architecture was seen "not as a meaningless rupture with the old" but as "a revealing of what was hidden in the old and enhancing it with new truths."[9] This unresolved tension between the idea of "revolution" and the need to justify it as a necessary redemption of history can be clearly observed in republican discourse, especially in the portrayal of the Kemalist *inkilap* as a rational unfolding of Turkish history into the more advanced stage of contemporary civilization. This chapter focuses on certain textual themes such as technology, industry, and progress that were central to the Kemalist notion of "contemporary civilization" and to its powerful iconography in the 1930s. The visual and spatial embodiment of these themes in the architecture of infrastructure, factories, and industrial exhibitions was an especially powerful marker of republican modernity.

Civilization, Progress, and the Arts

The official discourse of the republic was strongly and self-consciously revolutionary, as is attested by the inclusion of "revolutionism" (*inkilapçılık*) among the six pillars of the Republican People's Party (RPP), the ideological foundations of the new republic. In the first issue of *Ülkü*, the RPP's journal, a long article by Mehmet Emin discussed the difference between a "revolutionary" (*inkilapçı*) and a "progressive" (*terakkisever*) in terms reminiscent of Sir Isaiah Berlin's *The Hedgehog and the Fox*.[10] "Although both believe in the necessity of progress," Mehmet Emin wrote, "the revolutionary negates any obstacle and proceeds with a passionate heart while the progressive calculates the possible problems systematically and moves in a piecemeal manner."[11] Seeing themselves in the former category, the Kemalists portrayed revolution as a necessarily radical upheaval uninhibited by obstacles and uncompromised by piecemeal strategies. At the same time, like all other revolutions, the Kemalist *inkilap* had to seek historical legitimacy. While enforcing its vision upon society, it had to seek consent and "win the hearts and minds of the people," as RPP literature often stated, in the same way that modernism had to be explained and justified in order not to be "just another style."

This need for historical legitimacy explains the attraction of many republican intellectuals, architects, and artists to the basic progressive model of history that has been shared by different forms of modern thought from Marxism to the Modern Movement. From this perspective, modern architecture was viewed as a thoroughly rational and scientific "fact" of the modern era and as a natural and logical consequence of the historical evolution of architecture, reflecting its latest stage of development and holding a claim to truth that hitherto-existing styles no longer held. Hence, in an inherently ambiguous formulation, what was celebrated as an "architecture of revolution" (*inkilap mimarisi*) was also rationalized and legitimated as natural evolution to a higher and better state. Nowhere is this more evident than in a 1929 essay titled "Cubism in Architecture and the Turkish Tradition" by Müderris İsmail Hakkı (Baltacıoğlu), one of the earliest proponents of modernism when sentiments in favor of an Ottoman revivalist "national style" were still strong. "Artistic periods arise out of a social idea," wrote İsmail Hakkı. "To say that an artistic movement is alive means that it is the product of a living [social] idea. Greek art is the art of classical cities; Gothic art is the art of medieval Christian society. In the same way, cubism must be the art of our times, that is, the art of contemporary democracies." [12] After expressing his reverence for the Ottoman revivalist National Architecture Renaissance, İsmail Hakkı characterized it as simply the style of a bygone epoch, rendered obsolete in the face of contemporary technological and sociological developments:

With the new post office building, Vedat Bey initiated a new era of romantic thought that combined the classical age with the new needs of the time. This era witnessed the emergence of a great architect like Kemalettin Bey and many other young artists. . . . Each epoch produces its own art. [Today] when it is possible to build flat roofs, it makes no sense to modernize the dome. *The dome is not a national motif; it was merely a constructional necessity of the past* [my emphasis]. [13]

What is most significant in this quotation is that İsmail Hakkı portrayed the dome, the major stylistic motif of the National Architecture Renaissance, not as a "national element" but simply as a "technical" one that was surpassed by modernism. This is one of the earliest expressions of what was to become the dominant theme of architectural discourse of the 1930s—namely, legitimating modernism on rational and scientific rather than ideological grounds and resorting to progressive historicism to justify the abandoning of Ottoman precedents. On every occasion, modernist architects emphasized that Ottoman revivalism had to be replaced by the Modern Movement, not out of caprice or revolutionary zeal but as a historically necessary step if Turkey was to be in tune with the times. Furthermore, as Burhan Arif wrote in the first volume of the architects' professional journal, *Mimar*, modern architecture and urbanism simply sought to recapture the most desirable aesthetic qualities of historical precedents in a contemporary form:

In the hands of architects who have understood the needs and philosophy of contemporary life and who struggle to adapt the accumulated wisdom of city building to the social organization of modern times, New Architecture is producing works that match the classical beauty of historical periods. When we look at the large housing projects of Martin Wagner and Professor Gropius in Berlin, we can almost see the streets of the Roman forum, of antique Pergamon, or the shady streets of old Istanbul with green courtyards behind walls.[14]

When Behçet Sabri and Bedrettin Hamdi illustrated their 1933 essay "Revolution in Architecture" with a photograph of Le Corbusier's Villa Savoie (see fig. 2.2), the caption under the photograph read: "The New Architecture was not born as an ornament; it was born out of necessity. It will live on until the day life enters another epoch and the human mind comes up with another concept of beauty arising out of new technical means which will have been invented then. At that point, the architectural art of today will have been elevated to the next step."[15] A year later, in an essay titled "The New and the Old Architecture," they elaborated on the idea of progress in art and architecture in a way reminiscent of İsmail Hakkı's arguments before them:

As in all fine arts, what changes in architecture is the means and solutions: the principles remain the same. Look at the monuments of past epochs that did not have the means of our contemporary civilization. A Greek temple, an Egyptian pyramid, and the Ottoman baths in Ayasofya are among the masterpieces of architecture. However, yesterday's masterpieces were created by religious beliefs; today's works are shaped by positive thinking. . . . There is no old and new architecture: there are only civilized and primitive solutions [to architectural problems].[16]

Likewise, in the cultural scene at large, many authors sought to portray the Kemalist *inkilap* not as destruction of the past (since the past was, after all, the locus of national identity) but as its redemption to a higher level of social evolution, represented by contemporary Western civilization. For example, a 1930 editorial in the popular illustrated magazine *Resimli Ay* rejected the common assumption that the terms "revolution" and "culture" were mutually exclusive because of their association with "destruction" and "creation," respectively. It argued that "the progress of culture is its movement toward higher stages of historical evolution, and the [Kemalist] *inkilap* is nothing but an acceleration of this process of social evolution. Therefore it represents the highest creative moment of culture."[17] What is significant in this argument is that "culture" is defined not as an autonomous domain but as an agent of history: it is charged with a mandate not just to reflect but to trigger and accelerate the flow of history.

Undoubtedly such arguments served to reinforce the self-affirming posture of the Kemalist reforms against their critics, who questioned the wisdom of abandoning centuries-old Ottoman culture in a matter of few years. On these grounds it could be argued that to break away from Ottoman culture was not an arbitrary ideological decision but simply the need to follow the flow of history and capture the zeitgeist of the modern age. It was also on these rationalist grounds that modernism in art and architecture could be justified as a historical imperative. From the moment of its arrival in Turkey, the progressive discourse of the Modern Movement found a perfect match in the rationalist and positivist biases of Kemalism. There is ample evidence in the publications of the 1930s that scientific justifications precluded doubt or dispute, equating both Kemalism and modernism with the unfolding of truth.

In the published speeches of Mustafa Kemal, this notion of scientific necessity or historical inevitability is a recurrent theme, not only as the basis for the legitimacy of the reforms but also as the basis for his own authority and leadership in making them happen. For example, in his historic speech delivered to the National Assembly in 1927 as his personal account of the nationalist war and the subsequent reforms, Mustafa Kemal alluded to his awareness of events to come *before* their actual unfolding. "I had observed the potential for progress latent in the conscience and in the future of the nation," he said. "I had to carry this knowledge in my conscience as a national secret and gradually to see its implementation in all aspects of our social organization."[18] Mehmet Emin's discussion of "revolutionism" in *Ülkü* confirmed this with the following words: "It is always a chosen individual who feels the excitement of revolution in his soul before everyone else: this can be a leader, a hero, or a genius."[19]

There is a conspicuous affinity between the spirit of these words and the basic Hegelian schema of teleological destiny with its concomitant notion of "heroes" (who are the agents of rationally unfolding history) and "victims" (who are yet unaware of this irresistible grand plan in history). As is well known, modernist architects, too, envisioned themselves as heroes who knew that "the sun is mirrored even in a coffee spoon,"[20]—that is, that design (of objects or buildings) was capable of reflecting the larger course of history. This notion of zeitgeist, or "spirit of the age," was the very basis upon which the modernist avant-garde sought credibility and gradually transformed itself into the artistic-architectural establishment of the first half of the twentieth century. The spirit of the age became a concept that explained everything, rather than being itself a concept to be explained. Modern works were and had to be that way because they could not possibly or rationally be otherwise, given the laws of history and nature. In Turkey, too, the official culture of the 1930s continuously evoked the zeitgeist of the modern age, which, it was argued, all nations should seek to capture in their political, social, cultural, and artistic endeavors. From this, it was a short step to the argument that the zeitgeist of the twentieth century was embodied primarily in the technology, machinery, and industry of the West, producing unprecedented wealth and well-being. To be "Western in spite of the West" meant, above all, appropriating this technology, machinery, and industry for the nationalist goals of the Kemalist *inkilap.*

A more explicit longing for "the society of advanced technique" that Yakup Kadri Karaosmanoğlu posited as the prerequisite for the cultural and artistic regeneration of the nation can be found in Burhan Asaf's discussion "Why Do We Not Have Art?" published in the same journal, *Kadro*.[21] Identifying the transition from craft to machine production as the primary principle shaping human history since the industrial revolution, Asaf characterized the nineteenth century as "the pagan phase of machine civilization." In this phase, he explained, machinery enslaved man for the production of utilitarian objects while the idea of art remained tied to old conceptions based on craft. With explicit reference to the art historian Heinrich Wölfflin, he argued that this "duality of the nineteenth-century weltanschauung" could be overcome only when painters, sculptors, musicians, architects, and literary figures came in direct contact with the machine. They had to understand the machine thoroughly, he wrote, and eventually conquer it as the basic matter of art. He concluded with a vision of the future reminiscent of the artistic ideals of Soviet productivism: "Machines, which have hitherto produced utilitarian objects only, will create objects of art. To achieve this stage, however, artists will have to get into their overalls, take control of the machine, and, giving it a soul, make it a sensitive tool just like the hand of the craftsman."[22]

Another prominent republican author, Nurullah Ata, made a similar point in 1934 in *Yedigün*. Criticizing the stubborn craft enthusiasts' biases against the machine in matters of art, Ata narrated his own recent realization that photography was an art form, albeit with different tools from those of painting.[23] Along similar lines, the first issue of *İnsan*, a cultural journal to which leading intellectuals and artists contributed in the late 1930s, defined the goal of the "Turkish renaissance" in terms of three aspirations. First, the transition from craft to industry and "from semicolony to nation" had to be accomplished. Second, Turkey had to progress from a closed and mystical system of social relations to an international and humanist one. Third, the fatalist mentality uninterested in this world had to give way to a mentality of "paradise on earth" by which the creative power of the people could be unleashed.[24] It should be pointed out that although *İnsan* was not an architectural publication, it included translations of Le Corbusier's most influential writings on modern architecture and urbanism and on "the age of the automobile, mass production, steel, concrete, and glass," with commentaries by leading Turkish intellectuals such as Hilmi Ziya Ülken.[25]

It cannot be missed that Burhan Asaf's "duality of the nineteenth century" between utility and art foreshadowed Sigfried Giedion's classic account of modern art and architecture as the final overcoming of the same duality in the twentieth century. According to Giedion, modernism was the realization of the zeitgeist of the modern age in art and architecture, after those disciplines' blindness to it for most of the nineteenth century.[26] As Giedion, a student of Heinrich Wölfflin's, explained it, his account was derived largely from Wölfflin's notions of zeitgeist and weltanschauung—

the very concepts that informed Burhan Asaf's essay. Moreover, Asaf's longing for a future society in which the difference between craft and machine production would be eliminated was remarkably similar to that expressed in the paradigmatic 1922 essay "Art, Handicraft, Technology" by the German architectural critic Adolf Behne. Nurullah Ata's observations on photography and painting almost paraphrased Behne's characterization of the transition "from the factura of the brush to the factura of light" or "from the craftsmanly to the technical," when painting gave way to photography.[27] Collectively, such published writings about the relationship between the Kemalist *inkilap* and the art and architecture expected to arise from it suggest that a number of Turkish authors were familiar with the intellectual sources of European modernism. German philosophical and art historical sources, especially, were cited in support of arguments concerning how art and architecture had to express the essence of their own epoch and how the Modern Movement expressed the zeitgeist of the machine age.

At the same time, Le Corbusier enjoyed a special status as the great popularizer of these arguments and the charismatic polemicist for modern architecture and urbanism. In 1931, in an inaugural issue of *Mimar*, Le Corbusier was idolized as an architect who was "not just a reformer but a true revolutionary [*inkilapçı*]," the mastermind of "contemporary urbanism [*muasır şehircilik*]."[28] Aptullah Ziya, one of the most prolific architects and architectural critics of the 1930s, evoked the well-known Corbusean connection between modern architecture and the technological icons of the new epoch. As quoted at the beginning of this chapter, he wrote that the inspiration for the "new art" (*yeni sanat*) of the twentieth century (and of the Kemalist *inkilap*) could no longer be the monuments of the past but should be sought in airplanes "hovering in the skies and ocean liners . . . crossing the sea at phenomenal speeds." The official republican daily, *Hakimiyet-i Milliye,* published excerpts from Ludwig Hilbersheimer's writings on the need for the architect "to employ the same rational thinking, the same precision and economy, that an engineer applies to building a machine, a ship, a car, an airplane, or a bridge."[29] The enthusiastic reception the New Architecture won in Turkey has to be understood in the context of this republican fascination with the industrial sources and technological icons of modernism.

Technological Icons of Modernism

As the cultural historian Leo Marx explains it, the "industrial iconography" of the nineteenth century signified the replacement of the idea of technology as discrete artifacts and machines, or the so-called mechanical arts, with an entirely new conception of technology as the primary agent of social change.[30] In Turkey, too, the industrial and engineering achievements of the West (especially of the United States, its mythical status enhanced by geographical distance) were the material bases of "civilization" that generations of Turkish reformers longed for. As early as 1918, the journal *Sanayi* (Industry) undertook publication with the claim to be "the guiding light for all the minds infused with the national ideal";[31] it continued to be published in the republican period under the new title *Endüstri*. Collaged images of turbines, pistons, machinery, factory chimneys, and propellers were used as cover designs for the magazine throughout the 1930s, reminiscent of Russian avant-garde collages or the cover designs for *Das Neue Frankfurt* in Weimar Germany. From the turn of the century onward, images of skyscrapers, grain silos, bridges, railroads, airplanes, and assembly lines, along with anecdotes of Henry Ford's life and career, were published extensively in illustrated popular magazines. Even in a poor, agricultural, and war-weary country like Turkey, where such images lacked any real material basis, the proliferation of such industrial iconography created a favorable context in which a polemic for modern architecture could be situated.

To give some examples of these popular images of industry and technology, I begin with *Muhit*, the "illustrated family magazine," which began publication in 1928, in the midst of the transition from the old script to the Latin alphabet. A 1929 editorial featured a long, self-explanatory title: "It is necessary to change: If societies do not change, they will be forever condemned to barbarism and nomadism."[32] The illustrations at the tops of the pages depicted, respectively, a sailboat being passed by an airplane overhead, a horse-drawn carriage being outraced by an automobile, and an earlier version of the locomotive being overtaken by a bigger steam engine. There was an illustration of the Brooklyn Bridge (itself a modernist icon glorified by the famous Mayakovski poem around the same time) towering above small tugboats, and another illustration showing a silhouette of skyscrapers dwarfing a little wooden hut below. In 1932, *Muhit* ran an article titled "The Daring Enterprise of Metropolitan New York," featuring the specifications of the Radio City complex and Rockefeller Center, with perspective and axonometric views of the skyscrapers.[33] In the same issue, a translated piece titled "What Is Mechanization and What Kind of Society Results from It?" was illustrated with photographs of a factory in Pittsburgh and a portrait of Henry Ford, arguably the figure most influential in the eyes of the modernist architectural avant-garde in Europe between the wars.

What is remarkable in these early popular images of industry and advanced technology is a sense of science fiction—a fascination with unfamiliar forms of machinery, vehicles, and buildings but little information (and sometimes misinformation) about their actual context, location, or designers. It is as if the idea was to claim them for a universal future for humankind independent of the particularities of place and nation and to evoke a linear path of progress along which Turkey aspired to march. For example, in 1924, just a year after the proclamation of the republic, an article in *Resimli Ay* contrasted the metropolitan condition of "civilized countries" with "our small and humble capital city under construction in Ankara." The accompanying illustration was that of a futuristic skyscraper city with airplanes flying above and multilevel subway systems below ground (fig. 3.1)—an unattributed variant of New

منتقل مدنى شهرلرينه رمنظر و. ايكى قانى ارلاه سرقاتلر كرق كوكربلر اننزه مدده. مقاره ال.ون خانه ودره.شهيرى
بودرون بزل محمد. ارنوابلره. رامواريلره قفيض امنشده. لوالدرد. ارنورين. رامواى نضالىنلرماقان ربقتهامنشىره.

Fig. 3.1. "Cities of the Future": illustration of a modern metropolis published in the popular magazine *Resimli Ay,* March 1924. The image of skyscrapers and underground networks inspired by New York City was a common visual trope in the architectural culture of the 1920s at large.

York fantasies endlessly reproduced, from Harvey Wiley Corbett's "The City of the Future" (1913) to Hugh Ferris's *The Metropolis of Tomorrow* (1929).[34] Similarly, in 1929 a single-page illustration in *Muhit* titled "Modern Cities" showed the model of a scheme for the Alexander Platz in Berlin encircled by the streamlined forms of Mendelsohnian buildings (fig. 3.2). With no identification of the project, however, the commentary simply read: "A major characteristic of civilization is its tendency to be bored by the mainstream and to look for new means to respond to new needs."[35]

Although American technological and industrial achievements continued to fascinate modern Turkey throughout the 1920s and 1930s, Kemalist Turkey had no real contact with American experts, engineers, and firms. For historical and political reasons, the country relied almost exclusively on Germany for expertise; in any case, Kemalism found a better match in the statist, anticapitalist appropriation of technology that was articulated by German thinkers, leaders, and engineers.[36] While popular magazines continued to feature futuristic images of American technological wonders, official Turkish publications of the 1930s focused more specifically on the actual industrial and technological accomplishments of the new republican regime. Most representatively, *La Turquie Kemaliste* extensively published photographs of factories, power plants, bridges, dams, and agricultural machinery, sometimes collaged into posters, underscoring the propaganda function of this industrial iconography (fig. 3.3). With the implementation of the first five-year industrial plan (1934) and the

Fig. 3.2. "Modern Cities": futuristic image of a modern metropolis published in the illustrated popular magazine *Muhit,* 1929. The lower image is taken from the Alexander Platz competition in Berlin, 1928, but is not identified as such.

Fig. 3.3. Industrial imagery representing the aspirations and accomplishments of the new republic. **Left:** Contemporary postcard of the Kayseri textile mills of Sümerbank, published by the Ministry of Interior Press Office. **Right:** The collage "Ankara Construit" from *La Turquie Kemaliste,* February 1937.

establishment of major state industries, especially Sümerbank for textiles (1933) and Etibank for mining (1935), industry and technology were celebrated as centerpieces of nationalism. As Benedict Anderson noted in his classic book on nationalism,[37] the naming of these state industries after the ancient civilizations of the region, those of the Sumerians and the Hittites, respectively, is particularly representative of how nationalist narratives operate. While their names grounded the nation in a remote and mythical past rooted in the land—the archaic component of nationalism—the programs of Sümerbank and Etibank symbolized the futuristic industrial aspirations of Kemalism—the utopic component of nationalism.

The establishment of the Turkish Iron and Steel Works, especially the construction of its blast furnaces, in Karabük in 1937 by an English firm, H. A. Brassert and Company, was elevated to epic proportions.[38] Such new enterprises toward industrialization were regarded as continuations of the nationalist War of Independence on a different front, this time against the forces of nature—a theme frequently evoked in the writings of republican intellectuals. In 1933 Şevket Süreyya wrote: "The national liberation movement means the transformation of a backward society into an advanced and organized nation. Hence the most important thing is that the real struggle is not between men, but between men and nature. The struggle with nature is the main principle, the highest goal, and the most vital symbol of all national liberation movements, including and especially that of Turkish nationalism."[39]

A powerful allegorical representation of this theme can be found in the competition for two large murals to decorate the main passenger hall of the new railroad terminal in Ankara, designed by Şekip Akalın and completed in 1937 (see fig. 6.17). The winning pair of murals, by Nurettin Ergüven, each measuring four by twenty-one meters, depicted the Turkish national saga in two stages, "Before the Treaty of Lausanne" and "After the Treaty of Lausanne."[40] The first one showed heroic scenes of the nationalist war; the second was devoted to the postwar accomplishments of the republic in the form of technology, industry, and transportation. It showed a train entering a village, concrete bridges, harbors and docks, irrigation canals, agricultural scenes, factories with smoking chimneys, the construction of Ankara, highways, and airplanes, evoking similar examples of Soviet social realism around the same time.

By the mid-1930s, slogans such as "electrification of Turkey" and "covering the motherland with an iron web of railroads" expressed the goals of national economic policy.[41] Networks of communication and transportation—railways, roads, bridges, and tunnels—were particularly significant in representing a new territorial consciousness of nationhood. Like newspapers, which were instrumental in the spread of nationalism by making every corner of the country accessible and linked to every other, these networks and structures of transportation contributed to the mental mapping of the "imagined community." Their importance for republican self-consciousness and self-representation is amply documented in official publications. In 1934, for example, the first issue of the *Journal of Public Works* (*Nafia İşleri Mecmuası*) published a lengthy report on the history and present status of bridge construction in Turkey. After paying homage to the masonry tradition of Sinan and other Ottoman builders, the report began with the first bridge built during the republic, which continued the same masonry tradition: the Garzan Bridge on the Siirt-Diyarbakır road in southeastern Turkey, built in 1923. This thirty-six-meter single-span bridge, constructed "in a distant and difficult terrain and in the absence of advanced scientific means," wrote the author, himself a civil engineer, "demonstrated the republic's love of construction and the determination and courage of our engineers."[42] The rest of the report described the new reinforced concrete bridges of the republic, with their increasingly greater spans and slenderer aesthetic.

Railroads, one of the major state enterprises identified with the early republican period, had a particularly symbolic status as transmitters of the Kemalist *inkilap* to every corner of the nation. The journal *Ülkü* hailed "the railway policies" of the new regime as an instrument for realizing the goals of the *inkilap* and a representation of how the regime approached large-scale national issues.[43] Photographs of trains and new station buildings, statistics, and maps proudly announcing kilometers of new rail lines constructed since the proclamation of the republic were published in *Demiryolu*

(Railroads), the official publication of the State Railroads, an administrative unit connected to the Ministry of Transportation (fig. 3.4). The new railroad stations built during the early 1930s followed a standardized design with a conspicuously modernist aesthetic that was intended to be the most appropriate architectural expression of the progressive function of the railroads. Photographs of the Sivas, Malatya, and Manisa railroad stations, among others, show identical façades displaying this new aesthetic: symmetrical, undecorated arrangements of plain vertical and horizontal volumes with flat roofs and geometric façade articulations (fig. 3.5).[44] In many provincial cities, the most modern-looking residential neighborhoods (plain single-family or row houses with gardens) were built around the new station buildings (istasyon mahalleleri) for the employees of the State Railroads.

The celebration of bridges, industrial plants, and railroads as aesthetic objects followed similar recent developments in European architectural culture. Grain elevators and silos, for example, the well-known Corbusean archetypes of modern architecture, were such objects of architectural and aesthetic interest for Turkish architects, who admired their basic composition of unadorned masses and volumes and their utilitarian design precepts. The professional journal Arkitekt published photographs and detailed descriptions of the new reinforced concrete grain silos built in Turkey since 1933.[45] Constructed with European technology and know-how (Ankara and Konya silos were built by MIAG, a German construction firm; Eskişehir and Sivas silos were built by Froment Clavier, a French firm), they were presented as archetypes of modern functional building that Turkish architects could learn from. New technologies such as prefabricated reinforced concrete slabs and panels assembled on site, or new methods such as mechanized loading, unloading, and processing systems, were particularly highlighted in these descriptions.

Dams and power plants, too, were aesthetic objects worthy of designers' attention. Most prominently, Çubuk Dam near Ankara, completed in 1936, was endlessly reproduced in official publications and postcards (fig. 3.6). Not only was it clear testimony to the new republic's mastery over nature, but also it exemplified an impressive aesthetic refinement of a utilitarian program, not unlike the case of the Dnieprostroy Dam in the Soviet Union, designed by the constructivist architects Vesnin Brothers in 1927–1932. Çubuk Dam was published in Arkitekt, which gave only the technical and constructional details—the amount of concrete, the conditions of the soil, the structural calculations of the wall—in the typical "scientific" discourse of expertise that architects adopted in their journal.[46] Beyond this discourse, however, the dam's photographic appeal clearly resulted from its elegant modernist composition. The giant curve of the dam was counterbalanced by the undulating concave-convex form of the restaurant-casino at water's edge at the bottom of the valley (see fig. 2.12). Attached to the powerful sweep of the dam's concrete curve, a curious small, templelike commemorative portico marked the end of the approach from the landscaped park. Classical Ottoman columns of the crystalline order supported this portico, which was inscribed with the words of Atatürk—a small relic of the National Architecture

Fig. 3.4. Cover of the special issue of *Railroads* celebrating the tenth anniversary of the republic, 29 October 1933, and representing progress in transportation.

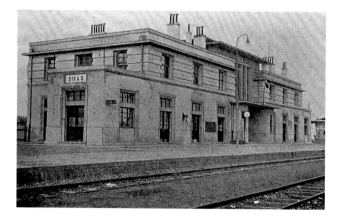

Fig. 3.5. Prototype design for railroad stations across the country in the 1930s: a repeatable and recognizable modern image symbolizing the extension of the central state into the provinces. Three examples with identical designs: Malatya Station (**top**), Manisa Station (**middle**), and Sivas Station (**bottom**).

Fig. 3.6. A major technological and cultural icon of republican modernity: Çubuk Dam outside Ankara (1936), with a public park and a restaurant-casino (also see fig. 2.12). Contemporary postcard published by the Ministry of Interior Press Office. **Fig. 3.7.** Commemorative portico with classical details attached to the giant curve of Çubuk Dam, Ankara, 1936.

Renaissance in what was otherwise a showcase of republican modernism (fig. 3.7). Besides the main structure of the dam, its filter station (1935–1936), a balanced geometric composition of horizontal volumes, rounded corners, and a vertical tower, also testified to the aesthetic potential of industrial and utilitarian buildings (see fig. 4.6).[47] A discussion of this particular aesthetic trope in early republican architecture follows in chapter 4.

Factories were particularly significant, both as quintessential modern buildings and as built manifestations of republican success in catching up with "contemporary civilization" (fig. 3.8). Since the nineteenth century, foreign architects and engineers had on occasion been commissioned to design factories in Ottoman Turkey. This practice was extended and systematized under the republican regime, and although there has been little research on this topic, some of the most prominent European names in modern architecture designed industrial buildings for Turkey during the first decade of the republic. One of them was the British architect-engineer Sir Owen Williams, a pioneer in the use of reinforced concrete mushroom columns, who reportedly designed a cotton-crushing mill in Adana in 1926. Another was Rob Mallet-Stevens, the prominent French modernist architect, who designed a distillery in Istanbul in 1930.[48] The German architect Fritz August Breuhaus designed the sugar factories, administration buildings, housing, and social services in Eskişehir and Turhal, two of the most important early republican industrial complexes.[49]

It was the factories of Sümerbank, however, an institution that singularly symbolized the ideals of nationalist industrialization in the 1930s, that were elevated to the status of major republican icons and extensively covered in official publications (see fig. 3.3).[50] From the inception of the five-year industrial plan of 1934, Sümerbank's publications reported the construction of fifteen factories.[51] These included the textile factories in Bakırköy (1934), Kayseri (1935), Bursa (1935), Ereğli (1937), Nazilli (1937), and Malatya (1937), as well as the paper mills of İzmit (1936), the iron and steel mills of Karabük (1937), and artificial silk factory in Gemlik (1935). The cotton mill in Kayseri (1934–1935), attributed to a Russian architect, is an interesting example evocative of postrevolution Soviet experiments. It was conceived as a small factory town, including workers' housing, social club, cinema, swimming pool, day-care center, infirmary, and sports facilities in addition to the main factory building (fig. 3.8). At least one foreign traveler described it as "the largest cotton mill in the Near East."[52] Its perspective drawings and models were featured in *La Turquie Kemaliste* in 1934 to illustrate "New Turkey's Five-Year Industrial Plan."[53] The textile factories in Nazilli and Bursa were also conspicuously modern designs.[54] They displayed clear formal distinctions between different components of the program and were informed by functional considerations such as receiving northern light in the main sheds. Most of the buildings were conceived as simple, undecorated geometric volumes with details such as metal railings and circular windows, which in the context of modernist architectural culture of the 1930s signified the "machine aesthetic" of ocean liners.

There was, however, one particular building of the 1930s that epitomized the

Fig. 3.8. Modern architectural design of industrial buildings in the early Republic. **Top:** "Yüniş" textile factory in Ankara, circa 1930. **Bottom:** General view of the textile mills of Sümerbank in Kayseri (1934–1936), the pride of republican industrialization in the 1930s.

ocean-liner aesthetic of the Modern Movement as popularized by Le Corbusier in Europe in the 1920s. Literally above the water like a ship, the summer residence of Atatürk in Florya, Istanbul (1934–1936), was the work of Seyfi Arkan (1904–1966), "the first true Turkish modernist," according to many commentators.[55] After graduating from the Academy of Fine Arts in 1928, Arkan had spent four years in the Berlin Technische Hochschule, and with a solid reputation as an uncompromising modernist, he was selected for the Florya project by Atatürk himself. Bringing to mind other famous contemporaneous modernist buildings, such as the De La Warr Pavilion at Bexhill, England, by Eric Mendelsohn and Serge Chermayeff (1933), Arkan's "ship building" is a remarkable example of this new modern type that explored the aesthetic potentials of reinforced concrete. It is a horizontally elongated composition projecting over the sea and connected to the land by a walkway, the intersection of the two marked by a vertical element (fig. 3.9). The fully glazed circular projection of the main space and the thin cantilevered projections of the flat roof were characteristic elements of the modernist aesthetic of the time. The long open corridor, like the deck of a boat, the row of circular windows, or "portholes," and the white metal railing of the decks unequivocally connect this building to the image of ocean liners.

Perhaps even more prominent an image than the ocean liner was the airplane, with its concomitant metaphor of flight, which, as cultural historians point out, was "an imaginative turning point deeply implicated in the modernist avant-garde movement."[56] Le Corbusier's passion for flight and airplanes was favorably received in Turkey, where the founder of the republic himself took a personal interest in civil aviation. A mural of Atatürk pointing to the skies decorates one wall of the Turkish Aviation Society (Türk Hava Kurumu); it is inscribed with his famous aphorism, "The future is in the skies" (*istikbal göklerdedir*). The school for civil aviation, the "Turkish Bird" (Türk Kuşu), was housed in a modern building in Ankara designed by Ernst Egli in 1937, and photographs of it appeared on numerous postcards, in *La Turquie Kemaliste,* and in other official publications (fig 3.10). The reinforced concrete building with its flat roof and roof terrace, its semicircular projection on the front façade, and its circular windows at roof level effectively associated the theme of aviation with a modernist aesthetic, evoking the progressive claims of both.

Aviation was an important theme of republican modernity in more than one way. It was the subject matter of art, as, for example, in the famous painting "Aviators" by Nurullah Berk (with all its futurist elements: propeller, aviator hats, goggles), which was exhibited in the "Revolution and Arts" exhibition of 1933 in Ankara (fig. 3.11). It was the subject matter of propaganda postcards published by the Ministry of Interior, as in one portraying a young Turkish aviator (fig. 3.11). Most recognizable, however, were photographs of Sabiha Gökçen, the first woman aviator and military pilot of Turkey, which were circulated in official and popular publications and featured on magazine covers (fig. 3.12). In these particular images, the two most powerful symbols of republican modernity, the Kemalist woman and technological progress, were combined as ultimate testimony to the success of the new nation.

Fig. 3.9. A paradigmatic modernist building of the 1930s: Atatürk's summer residence in Florya, Istanbul (1934–1936), designed by Seyfi Arkan. Floating over the water like a ship, the building makes references to the Corbusean "ocean-liner aesthetic," especially with its "deck" spaces, portholes, and metal railing. View of the approach from land (**top**) and the curved "deck" on the sea (**bottom**).

Electricity was yet another important theme of modernity, portrayed as an agent of civilization in both the literal and metaphorical senses of the term "illumination." While state publications celebrated the "electrification of Turkey," popular magazines described fully electrified "houses of tomorrow" in which electricity would be applied to everyday lives and domestic spaces. Architects, too, wrote about the electrification of the home as the defining feature of contemporariness (*asrilik*), even proposing novelties such as electrically heated and illuminated beds.[57] There were no significant prototype designs comparable to, for example, the "Casa Elettrica" of Italian rationalist architects Luigi Figini and Gino Pollini for the Societa Edison in Italy. Nonetheless, the Turkish counterpart of that organization, the Société Anonyme Turquie d'Installation Électrique (SATIE), promoted the symbolic association between electricity and modernism. Its advertisements depicted modern buildings, modern interiors, and modern lifestyles with household appliances. In 1934, SATIE commissioned Sedad Hakkı Eldem, then a young architect at the start of his career, to design its offices in Fındıklı, Istanbul (fig. 3.13). Eldem's modern building, reflecting the influence of Corbusean principles (especially with its flat roof, *pilotis*, and free plan), is one of the few exceptions to the architect's otherwise "Turkish-style" *ouvre* (which I discuss in chapter 6). It testifies to the strong modernist image that the electric company wished to project. Similarly, Rebii Gorbon designed a store for the display of electrical and gas appliances as a distinctive two-story modern building on a triangular lot with the sign "House of Electricity" (*elektrik evi*) prominently displayed above the entrance (fig. 3.14). With its flat roof, horizontal window band turning the corners, reinforced concrete construction, and mushroom columns on the

Fig. 3.10. Another modernist icon of the new Ankara: the "Turkish Bird" Civil Aviation School (1937–1938), designed by Ernst Egli. Photograph from *La Turquie Kemaliste*, April 1938, showing the building just completed.

Fig. 3.11. Images of aviation and aviators, a central theme in the representation of Kemalist Turkey's aspiration to catch up with the zeitgeist of the modern age. **Top:** The painting "Aviators" by Nurullah Berk, a member of the avant-garde "Group D," was exhibited in the "Revolution and Arts" exhibition in Ankara in 1933, celebrating the tenth anniversary of the republic.
Bottom: Contemporary postcard of a "young Turkish aviator" published by the Ministry of Interior Press Office.

Fig. 3.12. Aviation and modern women, two symbols of the republican revolution juxtaposed. Cover of the popular republican weekly *Yedigün* (28 July 1937) featuring Sabiha Gökçen, Turkey's first female pilot and Atatürk's adopted daughter.

main floor, the House of Electricity was a small showcase of modernity, both in form and content.[58]

It was the public use of electricity, however, that made it an icon of republican modernity. Lighted structures and illuminated signs were among the most important devices of Kemalist propaganda, again similar to the political function of light in contemporaneous fascist and socialist contexts. Among the temporary commemorative structures celebrating the tenth anniversary of the republic,[59] the illuminated towers designed for the RPP by architect Seyfettin Arkan were particularly remarkable in their constructivist statement: abstract prismatic towers of thin, cantilevered slabs lit from below (see fig. 2.24). Illuminated night views of such structures and of major government buildings and public parks were among the most familiar postcard images of the 1930s, especially during national holidays and unique events of national significance such as the Izmir International Fair. In the case of the latter, architectural descriptions of the Kültürpark fairgrounds included heavy emphasis on the electrical system (tenvirat işleri)—the use of neon lights, projectors, and "sodium and mercury

Fig. 3.13. Offices of the Société Anonyme Turquie d'Installation Électrique (SATIE) in Fındıklı, Istanbul (1934), by Sedad Hakkı Eldem, displaying the Corbusean principles of flat roof, horizontal band windows, *pilotis,* and free plan. **Figure 3.14.** "House of Electricity," a store for electrical appliances in Kadıköy, Istanbul (1937), by Rebii Gorbon. The plain "cubic" volume of the building, the transparency of the ground floor, and the use of reinforced concrete mushroom columns on the lower level are some of the most conspicuously "modern" features of the building.

Fig. 3.15. Electricity and night illumination as an expression of progress and a source of republican pride. Night view of the 1938 Izmir International Fair. Contemporary postcard issued by the Fair Organization Committee.

lamps," as well as the lighting of paths, pavilions, landscaping, and artificial lakes, all captured in night views (fig. 3.15).[60] Such images suggest that electricity was a key ingredient in the spirit of celebration, youth, optimism, and progress embodied by the spaces of public gathering and recreation, a spirit that reached its zenith in the exhibition spaces of the republic.

Public Display of Industry and Progress

As James C. Scott has pointed out, a fascination with productivity is a defining feature of the high modernist vision, and it was particularly appealing to nationalist regimes that saw it as a "technological fix to class struggle."[61] In Turkey's case, although there was little talk about "class struggle" or "classes" in the socialist sense, there was another gap that industrial progress and material well-being were expected to bridge. That was the gap between the peasant and the city dweller, the country and the city. In the preface to his comprehensive history of Sümerbank, Zafer Toprak emphasizes the priority that was placed on consumer goods in the 1930s. "The initiatives taken by Sümerbank," he writes, "opened the closed village economy, created unity between urban and rural communities, and played an important role in uni-fying the villager with the market."[62] Nowhere is this emphasis on consumer goods produced by state enterprises for the well-being of a thoroughly unified nation seen better than in posters by Ihap Hulusi (Görey) (1898–1986), the most prolific graphic designer of the early republican period and the maker of Sümerbank's "corporate image." Numerous posters for Sümerbank textiles and for state monopolies such as tobacco and alcohol, as well as advertisements for banks and for household appliances such as radios and refrigerators, bear his signature. What is particularly interesting in many of these posters is the harmonious coexistence of the peasant and the city dweller, with the products of industry offering fulfillment of their respective aspirations in life—parallel but never in conflict (fig. 3.16).

Sümerbank's imposing central offices in Ulus Square, Ankara, also underscored the significance and stature of that institution as the ultimate symbol of state productivity in republican Turkey. An international competition for the building's design was held in 1934, with participation by prominent Turkish, German, and European

Fig. 3.16. Advertisement posters designed by the prominent graphic artist İhap Hulusi for RCA radios (**left**) and Sümerbank textiles (**right**). The harmonious juxtaposition of the peasant and the urban citizen was a central theme of the nationalist vision in the 1930s.

Fig. 3.17. Projects entered in the international architectural competition for the Sümerbank central offices in Ulus Square, Ankara (1934). Projects by Martin Elsaesser, the commission-winning architect (**top left**), Fritz August Breuhaus (**top right**), Albert Laprade (**bottom left**), and the Turkish architects Behçet Sabri and Bedrettin Hamdi (**bottom right**). The last displays a conspicuously more modernist aesthetic (asymmetrical, undecorated, lighter, and more transparent) than the heavier and more "classical" designs of the European architects.

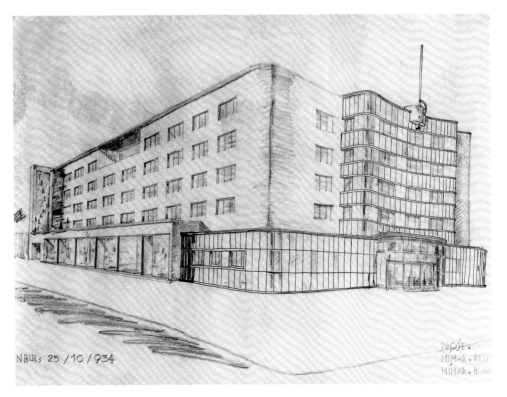

NBUL: 25 /10 /934

Fig. 3.18. Construction photographs of the Sümerbank building by Martin Elsaesser. **Top:** May 1937, midway through construction, showing the enormous scale of the building with respect to the urban fabric of old Ankara around the citadel. **Bottom:** September 1937 view of the top floor under construction, showing the reinforced concrete mushroom columns and circular skylights.

architects (fig. 3.17).[63] Although first prize was awarded to Seyfi Arkan's project, the commission eventually went to the German architect Martin Elsaesser. The scale of the building, the use of the latest reinforced concrete structural systems (such as the mushroom columns of the top floor carrying a slab punctured for skylights), and the central location of the building in the heart of the old city all contributed to the overall effect. As can be seen in the construction photographs (fig. 3.18), the scale of the urban fabric was completely transformed, the old buildings of the citadel area in the background were dwarfed, and the entire public space of Ulus Square was redefined.

In 1929, the National Economy and Savings Society (Milli Iktisat ve Tasarruf Cemiyeti) was established to educate and encourage the people "to live economically, to combat waste, and to use national products." It convened a Congress of Industry in 1930, followed by a Congress of Agriculture in 1931, toward the Society's aim of "increasing national production and improving its quality." Although improving "the quality, strength, and elegance" of national products was a stated objective, no systematic effort to focus on matters of design, craft, or production followed from it. One can speculate that if efforts had been directed toward these issues in the manner of the arts and crafts schools in England at the turn of the century or the Deutsche Werkbund in Germany, the history of modernism in Turkey might have been very different. Nonetheless, the primary contribution of the National Economy and Savings Society to Turkish modernism was its emphasis on exhibitions, which, in the 1930s, became showcases for modern architecture and republican public space. The society had 210 branches in different cities in 1933. Its pedagogical mission included propaganda posters, the journal *Economy and Savings,* preparation of brochures, school plays, poems, and educational material, the institutionalization and celebration of "Savings and National Products Week," and, above all, the organizing of exhibitions. The society also led Turkey's participation in exhibitions elsewhere, such as the Budapest International Exposition of 1931, for which Sedad Hakkı Eldem designed the Turkish pavilion.

In 1933, on the occasion of the tenth anniversary of the republic, the society prepared a major "Exhibition of National Economy" featuring agricultural and industrial products, textiles, olive oil, sugar, carpets, maps of railroad construction, and charts of electrification. In the brochure published for the occasion, futuristic aspirations for industry and technology were mixed with references to archaic Turkish culture, connecting the two in a sweeping gesture of nationalist narrative. In descriptions of the exhibits on railroads, for example, the Turkish engineers and workmen who "spanned the large bridges and dug the deep tunnels" were presented as descendents of "the Gray Wolf that dug through the iron mountain."[64] This was an overt reference to the nationalist legend about the Turks' origin in and migration from Central Asia. The "old versus new" construct, too, was an important rhetorical device in distinguishing republican accomplishments from "the neglect and poverty" of the late Ottoman Empire: "In the dynastic empire, the meaning of the word "exhibition" was limited to the *tespih* [prayer beads] and spice stands that opened in the courtyard of Beyazıt Mosque in the month of Ramadan. In the new Turkish republic, which is building up its national industry, the modern concept of exhibition has been accepted as a progressive necessity."[65]

The connection between the modernist design of exhibition spaces and the progressive claims of political regimes in the 1930s is a well-known theme in the history of architecture. Among many important exhibitions of the 1930s, the Mostra della Rivoluzione Fascista of 1932 in Rome was of particular significance and inspiration for Turkish architectural culture. It was visited by the Turkish architect Aptullah Ziya and was featured in popular publications as well as in the professional journal *Arkitekt*. That it was organized to celebrate the tenth anniversary of Mussolini's march on Rome suggests a parallel to the idea of comparable exhibitions to celebrate the tenth anniversary of the Turkish republic, including the previously mentioned Exhibition of National Economy in 1933.

That same year, an international competition for the new Exhibition Hall (Sergi Evi) in Ankara, commissioned by the National Economy and Savings Society, was concluded and construction started. The journal *Mimar* praised the society's decision to open a competition rather than commissioning the job to a foreign architect as was the norm. It expressed architects' gratitude for the society's "profound understanding of the concept of native artists and architects, just like the concept of native/national products in the economy," and it concluded with a plea for other state institutions to do the same.[66] "Only in this way," it argued, "can real Turkish artists create a worthy Turkish architecture by feeling it, and only then can works foreign to Turkish culture be avoided." The irony was that the selected project, by the Turkish architect Şevki Balmumcu (1905–1982), was the work perhaps most representative of a European modernist aesthetic, with affinities to Italian rationalist and Russian constructivist projects of the 1920s.

The competition brief explicitly stated that the design of the Exhibition Hall should be in "the style of modern architecture" (*modern mimari tarzında*). From the twenty-six entries in the competition, two projects were selected as finalists. The first was that of the Italian architect Paolo Vietti Violi (who also designed the stadium in Ankara). When the estimated cost of Vietti Violi's design (400,000 Turkish lira) was found to be too high, Şevki Balmumcu's project was selected for construction. It was a long, horizontal volume with rounded ends, balanced by an asymmetrically placed entrance block and the inevitable vertical clock tower to complete the composition (fig. 3.19). The long body of the building, with its horizontal band windows and rounded ends, coupled with the reinforced concrete tower like a chimney, was evocative of a huge ship, making the building a conspicuously modernist icon along prestigious Atatürk Boulevard. The symbolism of technology and industry, embodied by both the form and the program of the building, was further accentuated by placing utilitarian and technical components of the building (water tanks, heating and venti-

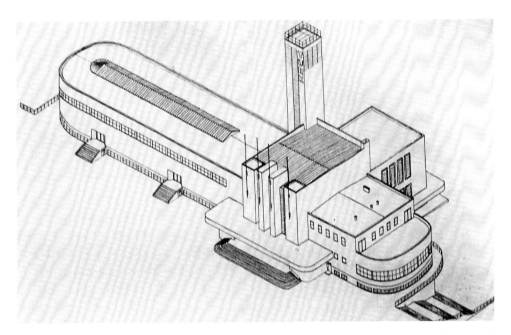

Fig. 3.19. A major architectural and cultural icon of Kemalist Ankara: the Exhibition Hall (1933–1934) by Şevki Balmumcu. **Top:** Axonometric drawing of the competition entry. **Bottom:** A postcard from the mid-1930s showing the new building. Its streamlined form, composition of vertical and horizontal elements, flat roof, band windows, rounded corners, and tower make it a particularly paradigmatic example of 1930s modernism.

lation ducts) within the three vertical elements prominently placed to mark the main entrance. As specified in the brief, the exhibition space was arranged in two levels, taking advantage of the inclined site: the lower level was reserved for bigger objects such as agricultural machinery, cars, and engines, while the upper level was reserved for photographs, graphics, wall panels, and smaller objects. The building's "strong and mature statement of national identity" (clearly referring to the nationality of its Turkish designer rather than to the architecture of the building per se) and its final cost of 310,000 Turkish lira were praised in *Arkitekt*. "The richness of the building's appearance is not the result of the kinds of expensive materials wasted by foreign architects in other buildings of Ankara," said the commentary. "It has to do with the visual effect of the harmonious proportions of the volumes."[67]

From its completion in 1934, the Exhibition Hall became one of the most important public spaces symbolizing the progressive ideals of Kemalism. It was featured extensively in photographs, postcards, and posters of the republic, above all in the pages of *La Turquie Kemaliste*. In 1934, a large exhibition celebrating the five-year industrial plan was held in the recently completed building; it was visited by ninety thousand people in its first seventeen days. "The modern exhibition techniques of large-scale photographs, billboards, graphics, typography, and photomontage were employed,"[68] as one foreign observer described it, to give an educational history of Turkish industry, agriculture, and economy from the late empire to 1934. In 1936, the first major photography exhibition was opened in the Exhibition Hall, with hundreds of black-and-white photographs of republican buildings, construction activities, and urban interventions. Large inscriptions above them declared Ankara to be the "Turkish Construction Symbol" (Ankara Türk İnşa Sembolüdür)[69] The 1937 Industrial Exposition was another spectacular event; the longitudinal space was given to machinery, mining, and metallurgical displays, and the rounded end of the space was covered by a large mural dedicated to coal mining, inscribed with the words, "Coal is civilization's source of speed."[70] After becoming such an important part of republican collective consciousness, not to mention a significant medium for the promotion of a modernist aesthetic at the scale of a large public building, the Exhibition Hall was transformed beyond recognition in the late 1940s by the German architect Paul Bonatz (see fig. 6.31). Today serving as home of the State Opera and Ballet, Bonatz's building is as much a betrayal of the utopian modernist ideals of the republic in its early years as the original building was a celebration of them.

Of equal cultural, pedagogical, and recreational significance was the Izmir International Fair, another quintessentially republican public space for the display of industrial and economic progress in a modernist architectural setting, this time in an economically prosperous, historically significant, and traditionally cosmopolitan west coast city. A song composed by the highly popular Turkish composer Sadettin Kaynak captured the significance of the Izmir fair in the collective consciousness, both as an occasion of national pride to show the progress of the new nation to the world and as a space for public recreation and enjoyment:

Look at beautiful Izmir, look at the golden necklace
The pearl of the Mediterranean, the leader in production
See producers and buyers exchange, let the world watch in astonishment
See the Turkish worker at the top, let the world watch in astonishment
Let the crowds fill the fair, [my sweetheart] let's meet at the fair.[71]

Dating back to the first "Economy Exhibition" (İktisat Sergisi) of 1923 and the "9 September Fairs" (Dokuz Eylül Panayırı) that were held annually after 1927, the Izmir International Fair was institutionalized in 1933. In 1936 it was moved to the new Kültürpark (literally, Culture Park), a site that had been built for the purpose (fig. 3.20), largely owing to the single-minded determination of Behçet Uz, the mayor of Izmir. The architectural significance of the Izmir fairs—the design of mostly modernist pavilions, temporary structures, and exhibition stands by prominent architects and the overall atmosphere of lightness, progress, and optimism expressed by these designs—can be compared to that of other, similar events in Europe and the United States, such as the Stockholm Exhibition of 1930, the Chicago Century of Progress Exhibition of 1933, and the New York World's Fair of 1939. At the same time, the

Fig. 3.20. Kültürpark, site of the Izmir International Fair, under construction in 1936, showing the wide central alley connecting the main entrance (outside the picture on the right) to the elliptical pool and the V-shaped building of the fair's casino-restaurant. Exhibition pavilions are arranged on both sides of this alley.

nationalist motifs of the late 1930s—monumental portals and colonnades, symmetrical façades, and the use of inscriptions, wall reliefs, and sculptures, which dominated the Paris Exposition of 1937—also made their way into the design of the pavilions in the Izmir fairs, especially at the end of the 1930s.

The 1936 Izmır fair, although only nominally "international" with the participation of three other nations (the Soviet Union, Greece, and Egypt), was nonetheless a joyful historic event drawing large crowds to the barely completed Kültürpark. Entrance to the park was through a gateway with eleven pairs of flagpoles, on axis with the main alley leading to the pavilions, a large square with a pool, and a casino. Although the fair's organization committee constructed two hundred standard timber pavilions, it was the individually designed permanent pavilions for major state industries and guest nations that attracted most of the attention.[72] A pavilion combining a modern aesthetic with Pharaonic details represented Egypt; a small doric temple was built for Greece, and a light structure with a tower for the USSR. Among the Turkish pavilions, the State Monopolies pavilion (İnhisarlar Pavyonu) by the architect Emin Necip Uzman, the Sümerbank pavilion by Seyfettin Arkan, and the Turyağ pavilion by Muhendis Aziz were particularly noteworthy. Emin Necip Uzman's project, the result of a competition, consisted of an L-shaped, reinforced concrete main structure surrounded by a temporary colonnade on two sides and marked at the corner by a thirteen-meter-high cylindrical glass tower (fig. 3.21). Arkan's Sümerbank pavilion had a solid, concave façade lifted above a curving colonnade. Apart from those, the Thrace (Trakya) pavilion, with its rounded, "streamlined" form and art deco details, is also representative of the so-called machine-age aesthetic of the 1930s in architectural culture at large (fig 3.21).

The Izmir fairs of 1937 and 1938 firmly established the national significance and international reputation of the event: the number of visitors, 361,527 in 1936, doubled to 608,561 in 1937 and 782,034 in 1938,[73] and many more foreign countries participated, including Italy, Germany, Belgium, the United Kingdom, Romania, and Iran. The significance of Kültürpark as a place of popular public recreation was further strengthened with the addition of a zoo, an artificial lake with an island casino and dancing platform, and an amusement park with a parachute tower, a Ferris wheel, and a shooting pavilion. Among the most significant modern structures of the 1938 fair was the State Monopolies pavilion, with its orthogonal geometric façade subdivisions and its roof terrace. Also significant was the Ministry of Education's "Culture Pavilion" (Kültür Pavyonu), with its rectangular blocks interlocking in a staggered ziggurat-like profile (fig. 3.22); it was designed by Bruno Taut just before his death.[74]

The only exception to the modernist statement of the various pavilions was the Ottoman revivalist structure of the Ministry of Endowments (the Evkaf Pavyonu) (fig. 3.22), the institution responsible for the maintenance and preservation of Ottoman monuments. It was a conspicuously "Ottoman-looking" building, entered through an arched gate flanked by an open kiosk and a clock tower, both capped with Ottoman domes. It contained an interior courtyard surrounded by an arcade. Its seemingly

Fig. 3.21. The 1936 Izmir International Fair. **Top:** The State Monopolies pavilion, designed by Emin Necip Uzman. **Bottom:** The Thrace pavilion, with a streamlined aesthetic popular in the architectural culture of the 1930s.

Fig. 3.22. The 1938 Izmir International Fair. **Top:** The Ministry of Education's "Culture Pavilion," designed by Bruno Taut on the basis of an earlier project he had designed in Berlin in 1910. **Bottom:** The Ministry of Endowments pavilion, designed in the Ottoman revivalist style.

anachronistic style was merely a representational device signifying the institutional identity of the Ministry of Endowments, which in turn signified the Ottoman heritage of the country. The delegation of Ottoman revivalism to a bygone era also meant that this style was now no more than an object of historical interest, preservation, and display. Even in this form, reminiscent of the status of oriental pavilions in European expositions, the building was criticized in the architects' journal for its eclecticism and exuberance, which violated rational design principles. "This small pavilion is stuffed

1 — İnkılâp müzesi	16 — Alman İ.G.F. paviyonu	31 — İzmir vilâyeti	44 — Çocuk Bahçesi
2 — Ziraat »	17 — Belçika »	32 — Trakya pavyonu	45 — Ada gazinosu
3 — Sağlık »	18 — Üzüm Kurumu	33 — Şark Sanayi. Turyağ	46 — Luna Park
4 — Paraşüt kulesi	19 — Hava tehlikesi	Pamuk mensucat, Yün	47 — Atlı spor
5 — Şehir müzesi	20 — Hava gazı	mensucat.	48 — Nebatat Bahçesi
6 — Sümerbank	21 — Romanya P.	34 — Polonya pavyonu	49 — Kır kahvesi
7 — İtalyan paviyonu	22 — Denizli P.	35 — İş Bankası	50 — Helâlar
8 — S. S. C. İ. »	23 — İzmir Ticaret odası	36 — Sigorta pavyonu	51 — 9 Eylûl antresi
9 — Manisa »	24 — Sergi sarayı	37 — İnhisarlar »	52 — Esas antre
10 — Yunan »	25 — Fuar gazinosu	38 — Ser	53 — Antre
11 — Eti Bank	26 — Fransız P.	39 — Gümrük Binası	54 — Gül bahçesi
12 — Vakıflar paviyonu	27 — Kızılay	40 — Tenis Kulübü	55 — Sun'i göl
13 — Ankara Birası	28 — D. Demir Yolları	41 — Atış Poligonu	
14 — Filistin paviyonu	29 — Telefon köşkü	42 — Açık hava tiyatrosu	
15 — Kütahya Çeşmesi	30 — İngiliz P.	43 — Hayvan paviyonları	

Fig. 3.23. Site plan of the completed Kültürpark (1939) showing the addition of pleasure gardens, pools, recreation spaces, and an amusement park to the more formally arranged original fairgrounds.

Fig. 3.24. The 1939 Izmir International Fair: the new entrance gate (**top**) and the exhibition hall (**bottom**), both designed in a distinctly modernist aesthetic by Ferruh Orel, a member of the fair's scientific committee.

with details of old Turkish architecture," said an editorial in *Arkitekt*, "an abundance that evokes feelings of redundancy and excess. Its exterior composition is ill proportioned. It could have been built without this waste of motifs, in a plainer fashion and with more character."[75]

The 1939 fair was the last of the optimistic celebrations of modernity and progress before the specter of war appeared on the international horizon. The building of Kültürpark, with its full infrastructure and landscaping, was now complete (fig. 3.23). A vast park of 360,000 square meters, it combined a more formally planned section for the exhibition pavilions, placed on a grid, with a more "picturesque" landscaped park for the zoo, botanical gardens, and amusement park. The most important structures added to the site in 1939 were a new entrance gateway and, on axis with it at the farthest end, a large exhibition hall, both designed by architect Ferruh Orel and engineer Cahit Çeçen, members of the fair's "scientific committee" (*fen heyeti*). The entrance gateway was a long, curved, two-level structure, "spreading its arms" to receive visitors from the city. Three ticket booths on each end served as structural supports for the floor above, which housed a casino (fig 3.24). The geometric, horizontal arrangement of the block, accentuated with a pattern of vertical glazing and flagposts, a circular window, and metal railings on the upper-level balconies, gave a distinctly modernist aesthetic to this most pivotal structure of the fairgrounds. The exhibition hall, too, was a long, horizontal, rectangular block in its main façade (fig. 3.24), with no openings on that elevation except for the entirely open ground-level colonnade, the composition completed by the vertical rhythm of eight tall columns (flagposts) rising above the entrance canopy. As an abstract composition it was reminiscent of the Florence Railroad Station (1932–1934) of Gruppo Toscana in Italy, again suggesting the existence of a number of aesthetic tropes in the 1930s shared by architects in different countries

In 1939, the pavilions of Romania, the United Kingdom, France, and Italy were designed with symmetrical and classicized elevations, monumental entrance portals or colonnades, and nationalist insignia above the entrances, anticipating the mood of the approaching war years. The Italian pavilion, especially—a symmetrical building with a monumental Roman arch on the entrance—received much praise from Turkish architects for its "size, beauty, and grandeur."[76] A belief in the state as the progressive agent of nationalist modernization underlay most of the architectural and cultural affinities between Italian colonial expositions of the 1930s and the Izmir fairs. In both cases one sees the proud display of "the colonization of the countryside": all the fruits, vegetables, animals and animal products, small industries, and handicrafts of the countryside exhibited in modern new pavilions. As much as they were showcases of nationalist state power, the Izmir fairs nonetheless left an important legacy as a central element of Turkish collective consciousness, national pride, and popular culture in the 1930s, today remaining in postcards, memoirs, and popular songs.

The Question of the Avant-Garde

THE TWO MAJOR CURRENTS among the modernist avant-garde in the early twentieth century—futurism and constructivism—had originated outside the advanced industrial societies of western Europe and the United States, in the more "backward" and agricultural contexts of Italy and Russia, respectively. In these countries, advanced technology and industry were exalted as symbols of a *potential* future, aspired to but not yet accomplished, and machines were sources of aesthetic and poetic inspiration rather than everyday realities as they were in the United States or England.[77] Most importantly, radical artists and intellectuals endowed technology and machine civilization with an apocalyptic power to transform society and to destroy traditional concepts of art. Modern technology and modern industrial society became the "facts"—albeit potential facts and not yet real conditions—in terms of which classical and academic rules were to be fought and ousted. The modernist architectural avant-garde of the 1920s in Europe continued the critical legacy of futurism and constructivism. It embraced modern technology and machine production as a critical standard against which academicism and classicism were declared obsolete.

The poverty of material conditions in postimperial Turkey and the admiration with which Turkish intellectuals viewed modern technology in the 1920s and 1930s can be compared to the experience of Italians and Russians earlier. More significantly, in all three countries the rise of "revolutionary" ideologies (Kemalism, fascism, and socialism) in the aftermath of World War I had prepared fertile ground for a radical break with the past through the aestheticizing of technology. Thus, looking back at the futurist and constructivist experiences, it is tempting to search for a comparable modernist avant-garde in Turkey. The idealization of technological and industrial icons of modernity and the recurrence of avant-garde themes and tropes in republican culture, as discussed in the preceding pages, surely reinforce that expectation.

Indeed, in the favorable "revolutionary" climate of the Kemalist *inkilap,* the references that Turkish artists, architects, and intellectuals made to technology, industry, and the "machine age" often did evoke the aesthetic and theoretical premises of the modernist avant-garde. In poetry, for example, the communist poet Nazım Hikmet wrote odes to machinery in the manner of Vladimir Mayakovski, and after studying film and theater in the Soviet Union, he wrote a screenplay in 1937 with the evocative title "Toward the Sun."[78] In art, a group of young painters and sculptors who had been trained in Paris in the studios of Fernand Leger and Andre Lhote formed the so-called Group D in 1932, introducing a rather belated version of cubism and constructivism to Turkey.[79] In architecture, the "revolutionary" discourse of modernism—especially its use of technological themes and references to the "machine age"—was enthusiastically embraced, celebrating the liberation of architecture from academic and classic traditions. Although there were no major technological fantasies or visionary schemes like those of San't Elia in Italy or Chernikov in Russia, the Corbusean polemics on "machine aesthetic" resonated with young Turkish architects. Paraphrasing Le Corbusier in their journal, they declared that "according to today's conceptions, the building is a habitation machine [*ikamet makinesi*]" waiting to be rationalized and standardized like an automobile.[80] Machines, electricity, airplanes, trains, and ocean liners were presented as the real sources of modern art and architecture.

Beyond a superficial formal and rhetorical level, however, it would be misleading to carry the comparison to futurism, constructivism, and other avant-garde movements too far. Given the nature of the relationship between modernism and the state under the unique circumstances of early republican Turkey, the extent to which these young Turkish artists and architects constituted an "avant-garde" is a contentious issue. Before everything else, a small but crucial time lag separated the Turkish experience from the avant-garde currents of the 1910s and 1920s. By the 1930s, when Turkey was ready to embrace modernism, the critical force of the modernist avant-garde had already been eclipsed in the West. This is not to say that fascination with modern technology and industry waned: rather, ideas of technological mastery and industrial progress got incorporated into the official ideology of many nations as the necessary means by which a modern state could maintain its power, productivity, and efficiency.

In Italy, only traces of futurism survived the First World War, its subversive edge blunted by its embrace of fascism in the 1930s, which turned it into an official art. In Russia, the art of the constructivist avant-garde of the postrevolutionary period was replaced by an officially sanctioned social realism under Stalin. As technology ceased to be a distant dream and began actually to transform Russian society and landscape, the formal experiments of the avant-garde gave way to the productivism of the Soviet state. Especially after the inauguration of the first Five-Year Plan in 1928, the Soviet Union embarked upon gigantic industrial and infrastructural projects, largely by importing American experts, technology, and methods, especially Fordism and Taylorism.[81]

In Germany, the Weimar Republic, which had been the breeding ground of the modernist avant-garde in art and architecture, came to an abrupt end with the Nazis' rise to power in the 1930s. Under National Socialism, modern technology and industry were ideologically recharged as part of a state-sponsored national *kultur*. In what Jeffrey Herf characterizes as the "reactionary modernism" of the Third Reich, the modern idea of technological mastery was accepted while the Enlightenment notion of the autonomous, freethinking individual was rejected.[82] Thus, technology was "liberated" from the principles of individualism, private enterprise, and profit motive that had triggered technological innovation under capitalism and was put into the service of the state. Such a selective appropriation of modern technology, combined with a rejection of the liberalism of modernity—such a recasting of technological *civilization* in the mold of national *culture*—offered a particularly attractive model for Kemalist Turkey, which maintained close ties with Germany throughout the early republican period. It should be noted that even in the United States, where engineering and technology were viewed through technocratic rather than ideological lenses, the federal state assumed an unprecedented role in the aftermath of the Great Depression. Under the auspices of the New Deal, the federal government undertook such gigantic projects of civil (and social) engineering, water management, and regional planning as those carried out by the Tennessee Valley Authority.

Modernism "survived" these historical times by turning into an official doctrine in most countries, thereby losing its critical edge. The scientific and progressive discourse of modern architecture now served and legitimated political power rather than combating it. Kemalist Turkey was no exception. The liberating effect of modern technology and industry upon artists and architects was, to use the insightful terminology of Isaiah Berlin, no longer a form of "negative liberty"—that is, liberty entailing creative freedom without interference from others.[83] Rather, it turned into a form of "positive liberty"—a program that sought to impose its own vision upon the rest of the world. Central to the artistic and architectural culture of the early republic was this notion of "positive liberty," the idea that art and architecture had to have a larger social function and ideology above and beyond individualistic experiments.

The concept of the avant-garde as it emerged historically in the 1910s and 1920s had entailed a radical and subversive challenge to established artistic norms, a challenge that by definition lay "outside" official ideology[84] The avant-garde had exalted the creativity of the freethinking individual, not that of the conformist. It had embraced the abstract and the universal in art, not the figurative and the local. Such a celebration of art as an autonomous, individualistic, often unpopular creative act was anathema to the republican belief in art as an expression of national ideals. It is in this sense that the rhetorical and formal resemblance between Turkish artistic-architectural culture in the 1930s and the early twentieth-century modernist avant-garde in Europe needs to be approached with caution. Modern science, technology, and industry (which had been inspirational to cubism, futurism, constructivism, and other avant-garde currents) were idealized in Kemalist Turkey less as aesthetic, poetic, and fantastic experiences in themselves than as the goals, means, and instruments of a larger national program.

In a 1937 essay in *Yedigün* called "Civilization and Speed"—a title evocative of the futurist preoccupation with speed—the prominent republican author Peyami Safa illustrated this republican predilection for instrumentalizing technology and rationality. Defining speed as the conquest of time and distance by the human capacity to multiply the power of feet to great magnitudes in the form of trains, airplanes, and automobiles, he called for the dedication of this conquest to larger ideals. "To save time is in order to spend it for greater objectives than speed itself," he wrote. "Otherwise, speed would be as unnecessary as stray lightning, and perhaps more destructive."[85] It is well known that prior to World War I, the futurist admiration and aestheticizing of speed had led to a glorification of war.[86] The irony of Safa's point was that he made this observation on the eve of another such war, when the fascination with technology once again unfolded in militaristic terms. Another of his edito-

Fig. 3.25. Cover illustration from *Yedigün*, 25 October 1938, featuring Peyami Safa's essay "Power and Technique."

rials in *Yedigün*, "Power and Technique," written to celebrate "the human soul behind the miracle of technology," was published with a cover illustration of war planes hovering above an armored tank (fig. 3.25).[87] Not surprisingly, the same author would be one of the most vocal critics of modern art and architecture, particularly of cubism. In 1939 he welcomed the eclipse of the avant-garde, celebrating instead the rise of nationalist currents: "Today modern art is distancing itself from its excesses and eccentricities and is coming closer to you. After trying the limits of freedom, it is redefining itself. From aimless individualism, it is returning to the discipline of the society. That is why it is coming close to you. To you, the people! The greatest source!"[88]

Although its intensity increased toward the end of the 1930s, such nationalist criticism of the modernist avant-garde was a familiar undercurrent of the artistic-architectural culture of the republic from its inception. Even at the height of republican fascination with the "new" in art and architecture, many commentaries insisted that art was not an individualistic, self-referential pursuit. The writings of the prominent art critic Ali Sami Boyar in the RPP's journal *Ülkü* are representative of the republican critique of "art for art's sake" and of the basic republican suspicion of the avant-garde in general. Emphasizing the need for a national art (*milli sanat*), Boyar wrote that "before paintings of magnolias and chrysanthemums, we need paintings that will depict our national legends."[89] Whether out of conviction or conformity with the prevailing climate, no artist or architect in early republican Turkey allowed a place for difference, eccentricity, or individualism but instead emphasized the larger, idealized social function of art. The poet Nazım Hikmet, who negated conventional rules of poetry and incorporated machine sounds into his poems like Marinetti before him, was passionately committed to the official socialism of the Soviet Union. The members of Group D, like most other artists of the 1930s, aligned themselves with the cultural program of the RPP and contributed paintings to the *inkilap* exhibitions organized by the state. Channeling their formal and abstract experiments toward the prevailing folkloric and nationalist themes of the 1930s (see fig. 6.3), they produced what one art critic calls "a peasant cubism" (*köylü kübizmi*).[90]

Architects rejected uncommitted individualism even more strongly than did other artists. They perceived modern architecture as both an expression and an instrument of the Kemalist *inkilap*—as an agent of civilization and nation building. Gülsüm Baydar Nalbantoğlu concludes her history of the architectural profession in Turkey with the observation that conformity to ruling political ideologies guaranteed the status of architects as a cultural elite and their unity as professionals, and it prevented the rise of an artistic avant-garde.[91] Herein lies the complexity and the dilemma of Turkish architectural modernism in the 1930s. By identifying themselves so fully with republican ideology, modernist Turkish architects in effect surrendered any possible claims to either artistic autonomy or technocratic detachment from the official ideology of the state. At the same time, it was on the basis of their role as creative artists and competent experts that they sought professional legitimacy. They portrayed themselves as expert professionals, creative artists, and republican ideologues all at once, negating any potential conflict between these realms. Modern architecture became their basis of legitimacy in all three realms: modernism was the expression of a scientifically, aesthetically, and politically "correct" architecture.[92] The next chapter looks more closely at the specific relationship between modernism and the architectural profession in the 1930s.

4

Yeni Mimari

THE MAKING OF A MODERNIST PROFESSION

> In the last couple of years, the New Architecture of this century has been developing in all parts of the world. Young architects are breaking through old mentalities and traditions and are marching toward the truth. We are proud and happy that some of the new construction in Ankara is a manifestation of this architecture. New Architecture has arrived in our country!
> —Newspaper article, *Hakimiyet-i Milliye,* 1930[1]

THE "ARRIVAL" OF the New Architecture (*Yeni Mimari*, as the Modern Movement came to be called in Turkey) was celebrated with a double-page feature article in the official republican daily *Hakimiyet-i Milliye* (National Sovereignty) in 1930.[2] The article hailed recent construction in Ankara as "the new architecture of this century," an expression of "the new truth" that was spreading through all parts of the world. Considering the importance of newspapers in the making of a unified nationalist consciousness, the appearance of a major feature article on modern architecture testifies to the strong ideological significance attached to it by the republican regime. It confirms that, with the construction of Ankara already under way, a newspaper voicing official republican views to the population at large saw modern architecture and urbanism as a matter worthy of general public interest. The article also placed an official stamp on the identification of Ankara with modern architecture—a stamp that would make its imprint on the popular consciousness and contemporary literature of the time.

The *Hakimiyet-i Milliye* article clearly intended to familiarize the public with the basic principles of the Modern Movement as it had evolved in Europe, and it paraphrased extensively from the 1928 La Sarraz declaration of the International Congress of Modern Architecture (CIAM). After explaining how "the Great War radically dissociated architecture from the past," the article emphasized "the needs of the times," "the effect of machines and industry in social life," and "the guiding principles of rationalism and functionalism." The crucial role of *simenarme* (literally, "reinforced cement," a word later replaced by *betonarme,* or "reinforced concrete," still in use in modern Turkish) was highlighted as a major factor informing the principles and aesthetic of the New Architecture. Among the architects "following the new path," the article mentioned Tony Garnier, Auguste Perret, Otto Wagner, Henrik Petrus Berlage, Henry van de Velde, Frank Lloyd Wright, Henri Sauvage, Jacobus Johannes Pieter Oud, Walter Gropius, and Adolf Meyer, with citations of their most important work. The entire scheme of the 1927 Weissenhof Siedlung, the housing exhibition in Stuttgart, was featured, in addition to a photograph of J. J. P. Oud's housing schemes in Rotterdam. Along with these paradigmatic works, a photograph of Ernst Egli's music conservatory in Ankara (see fig. 2.8) was included, confirming the message that "we in Turkey are finally catching up with the zeitgeist of the modern age."

By the time the New Architecture became the trademark of the new republic and was embraced by the emerging modernist profession there, it had already lost its critical edge in Europe. Especially after a series of historical events in the late 1920s, culminating with the 1932 exhibition at the Museum of Modern Art (MOMA) in New York, it had turned into a formal canon and a scientific doctrine under the rubric "international style." The 1927 Weissenhof housing exhibition in Stuttgart and the organizing of CIAM in 1928 as an international body promoting the New Architecture through annual meetings and publications were particularly effective in writing the official history of the Modern Movement. Many publications produced in the 1930s helped to disseminate the Modern Movement as a transnational current based on a seeming unity of scientific and formal concerns, independent of specific locality, and hence as the shared property of all nations. At the same time, it should be noted that this unity of formal and scientific concerns was still framed by national identifiers that were clearly marked. Photographs of modern buildings and projects from different countries were published and identified by their country of origin, yet they signified a much larger discourse that modernist theorists and critics claimed architecture in the twentieth century to be all about—they saw architecture as a sort of counterpart to the League of Nations idea.[3] Among such publications, A. Sartoris's *Gli elementi dell'architettura funzionale* (1931) from Italy, H. R. Hitchcock and P. Johnson's *International Style* (1932), published in conjunction with the MOMA exhibition in New York, and F. R. S. Yorke's *The Modern House* (1934) from England are a few that were well known among Turkish architects in the 1930s.

For the emerging profession in Turkey, to be an architect of the twentieth century was to be part of this international community of architects, which in turn would bring *national* pride. Yet the inward-looking nationalist policies of the early republic largely precluded direct contact with Europe, and Turkish architectural culture remained isolated from the most important developments of modernism in the West. Time-consuming bureaucratic processes were necessary in order to obtain state travel permissions (and allowances) even for short-term participation in international conferences and exhibitions.[4] None of the young Turkish architects who constituted a self-proclaimed modernist elite in Turkey had actually been educated in the Bauhaus or was a member of CIAM during the interwar period. Those educated in Germany, Austria, and Switzerland, mostly in the Technische Hochschule system, such as Seyfi Arkan, Emin Onat, and Arif Hikmet Holtay, were associated with more conservative architects outside the Bauhaus circles. Others often acquired their firsthand experience of major modern buildings during short travels and study trips in Europe. Sedad Hakkı Eldem's travels to Paris and Berlin in 1929–1930 and his association with Hans Poelzig in Berlin, along with Aptullah Ziya's presence in Italy in 1932–1933 and his exposure to Italian rationalist architecture under the Fascist regime, are the best known of these brief encounters.

Although the work that foreign architects did in Turkey was published in Europe, especially in German, Austrian, and Swiss magazines, it would be as late as the end of the 1930s before any modernist work by Turkish architects made an appearance in European publications. The absence of Turkish architects' work in the international media coverage of the Modern Movement in the 1930s had many reasons. One obvious reason was these architects' lack of contact with the Bauhaus and CIAM circles that dominated the modernist discourse of the interwar years and decided what was to be included from each country. It is also possible that given the deeply entrenched orientalism of Europeans, the architecture of countries like Turkey was interesting only insofar as there was something "Turkish" about it. In spite of rhetorical universalistic claims to the contrary, "international style" was in fact a European discourse exported to non-European contexts by European architects. When local architects internalized this export and started designing in the same manner everywhere, they were not nearly so interesting. Only in the 1941 edition of Sartoris's book were two villas by Zeki Sayar and the Yalova Termal Hotel by Sedad Hakkı Eldem included, in a section specifically on Turkey, and none of these buildings followed the formal canons of the Modern Movement. By that time, the term "international style" was already in serious disrepute, and the quest for a national expression was the order of the day in Turkey (see chapter 6).

Without real participation by Turkish architects in the European modernist debates over the new needs of industrial society, machine production, and housing, the New Architecture arrived in Turkey largely as an import for domestic consumption. As we saw in chapter 2, the republican regime promoted it as the most appropriate image of the new Kemalist society it sought to create. The emerging architectural profession in Turkey joined this official program wholeheartedly and adopted the progressive discourse of the New Architecture—especially the doctrines of rationalism and functionalism that legitimated their technocratic claims for power and recognition. James C. Scott observes in his insightful discussion of "high modernism" as an ideology that a utopian modernist worldview is particularly appealing to the bureaucratic intelligentsia, technicians, planners, engineers, and architects. "The position accorded to them is not just one of rule and privilege," he writes, "but also one of responsibility for the great works of nation building and social transformation. Where this intelligentsia conceives of its mission as the dragging of a technically backward, unschooled, subsistence oriented population into the twentieth century, its self-assigned cultural role as educator of its people becomes doubly grandiose."[5] Architects' discourse in Turkey in the 1930s offers a case in point.

It is important to remember that this larger sense of mission was not necessarily inherent in the definition of New Architecture when it emerged in the early twentieth century. "New Architecture" simply designated a questioning of academic design theories and methods in the light of new materials and construction techniques and new social and institutional needs. It entailed a more "functional" approach to a given design problem—that is, a rational arrangement of different components of the program in *plan* (in contrast to the academic emphasis on façade)—and a consideration of site conditions, materials, climate, cost, and so forth, as design factors. The conceptual leap from this definition of the New Architecture to that of an all-encompassing modernist technocratic view is something that needs to be explained historically rather than taken for granted. In the unique circumstances of early republican Turkey, this larger sense of mission was particularly important in lending credibility to the architectural profession as the agent, literally, of nation building. Architects were "technical experts thinking economically and rationally," and they argued that they should be entrusted with the task of giving built form to the Kemalist revolution.

While the "scientific" discourse of the New Architecture became a convenient and compelling argument for professional legitimacy, the distinct "aesthetic" discourse of modern buildings legitimated architects as *artists* giving shape to the new nation. The unresolved tension between the "scientific" and "aesthetic" discourses of modernism is a general phenomenon reaching beyond the Turkish case. The doctrines of rationalism and functionalism that have been the centerpiece of official modernism everywhere were often no more than reductionist clichés incapable of explaining the complex cultural, aesthetic, and personal considerations involved in the making of modern buildings. Modernism in Turkey was no exception. This did not mean that the emphasis on rationalism and functionalism was unimportant. To the contrary, it was this emphasis on the scientific and thoroughly rational nature of the New Architecture that offered the best chance of its earning credibility in a traditional Islamic society aspiring to but still far from the realities of the "machine age" or "advanced industrial civilization." What follows in this chapter is an account of the emergence of a modernist architectural profession in Turkey that sought legitimacy in scientific and rationalist arguments for the New Architecture and at the same time promoted an *image* of that architecture through a specific aesthetic repertoire.

Educational and Professional Setting

IN 1926, THE Academy of Fine Arts (Sanay-i Nefise Mektebi Alisi) was renamed in modern Turkish, the "Güzel Sanatlar Akademisi" and was relocated in one of the old shore palaces along the Bosporus. A prominent painter of the "1914 generation," Namık İsmail (1890–1935), was appointed director. This was the beginning of a radical transformation of this important institution, after which European modernist currents entered Turkish artistic and architectural culture with full force.

Changes in the educational setting were reflected in important developments in the world of practice and in the emerging self-consciousness of architects as a distinct professional body. All the major indicators of a modern profession—specialized education certified by diploma, the establishment of a professional organization and publication of a journal, and the setting of standards for professional competence and conduct—were realized in a short time between 1927 and 1931.[6] The discourse of modernism was adopted and mobilized as an integral part of this process, something that distinguishes the Turkish experience from those of western European countries and the United States. In those countries, the professionalization of architecture had preceded the proliferation of the Modern Movement by many decades, and a robust "architectural culture" (of exhibitions, competitions, organizations, publications, and public debate) had existed at least since the early nineteenth century.[7] In Turkey, the most important institutional developments of professionalization (diploma, association, journal, and codes of competence and conduct) were all compressed into a very short period, coinciding with the making of a new nation under a new regime.

In the architectural section of the Academy of Fine Arts, the reforms after 1926 were truly radical, considering the old traditions of the institution. After the resignation of Giulio Mongeri in 1928 and Vedat Bey in 1930, Ernst Egli (1893–1974) was appointed the new section head, a position he held until 1936, when Bruno Taut (1880–1938) took over. The curriculum was redesigned, replacing the classical beaux-arts model with what came to be known as the rationalist and functionalist principles of European modernism, at the same time that these principles were put into practice during the construction of Ankara as a modern capital. Egli's studio assistant was Arif Hikmet Holtay, who had been educated in the Stuttgart Technische Hochschule in Germany and was therefore familiar with the new developments in Europe. Sedad Hakkı Eldem (1908–1988) and Seyfettin Arkan (1904–1966), both from the class of 1928 at the academy, were also hired as assistants in the early 1930s; they were soon to be the most prominent names of modern Turkish architecture.

It is interesting to observe that the architects whose education overlapped with the switch from the classical beaux-arts model to European modernism (especially those who graduated in 1928) were the most vocal critics of the old system. Having started their education under Vedat Bey and Giulio Mongeri and having experienced the changes after Egli's appointment, they were the first generation to rebel against the teachings of the former and to abandon Ottoman revivalism for good. It was largely this generation that shaped the modernist professional discourse of the 1930s through their writings and their work. From this class of 1928, Zeki Sayar and Abidin Mortaş became the founding editors of the new professional journal *Mimar*, which began publication in 1931. Burhan Arif, the "urbanist architect" (*urbanist mimar*), wrote extensively on new theories and examples of modern urbanism in Europe. Seyfi Arkan and Şevki Balmumcu (1905–1982) designed some of the most canonic modern buildings of the 1930s, buildings comparable to their European counterparts in aesthetic and technical quality. Sedad Hakkı Eldem, arguably the most important architect of modern Turkey, would make his reputation leading the quest for national expression in modernism. As a group, these young architects got together at the Fine Arts Association (Güzel Sanatlar Birliği) in Istanbul, founded in 1928, to begin defining and justifying the new professional identity of the architect and to promote the New Architecture as the appropriate expression of the new Turkey.

The Fine Arts Association was, in essence, an extension of the academy, functioning like an alumni association or a "gentlemen's club," as Gülsum Baydar Nalbantoğlu calls it.[8] Painters and sculptors were also part of the association, and actors, literary figures, and aspiring artists frequented "the club," initially located at the Alay Köşkü (the old military pavilion) near Topkapı Palace. The close relationship between architects and artists testifies to a common "academy culture" that emphasized artistic sensibilities and painterly talent as an essential ingredient in an architect's education. This culture largely accounts for the conspicuous emphasis that was placed on the aesthetic dimension of the New Architecture—an emphasis that members of this generation never totally abandoned, even at the height of their positivist and rationalist convictions. As I elaborate later in this chapter, although Turkish architects did adopt some clichés of the German "*Neue Sachlichkeit*," or "new objectivity," for polemical purposes, its anti-aesthetic excesses found few enthusiastic followers in Turkey so far as actual designs were concerned.[9] Most of the time, however, architects highlighted their "professional" identity and separated themselves from the more "subjective" and "bohemian" connotations of artistic creativity.

Like their architect friends, many young painters challenged the older academic traditions in painting and tried to introduce European modernist currents, especially cubism and constructivism, to the Turkish scene. Whereas the older architects of the Ottoman revivalist national style were contemporaries of the "1914 generation" of impressionist painters (see chapter 1), the young proponents of New Architecture had much in common with the "independent painters" (*müstakiller*) of 1929 and their more "avant-garde" offshoot, Group D, formed in 1932.[10] Around the same time that architects were switching to modern "cubic" forms, members of Group D such as

Sabri Berkel and Zeki Faik Izer were introducing the first abstract paintings to a bewildered and largely skeptical audience. Questions about the extent to which Group D constituted an "avant-garde" and whether there was a truly critical avant-garde movement in Turkey were discussed in the previous chapter. Here it is enough to note that the modernist architects of the 1930s and the painters of Group D shared many of the same dilemmas pertaining to the importation of Western artistic and architectural discourses into a passionately nationalistic climate. Ultimately, both groups were compelled to distance themselves from the abstractions of the avant-garde and turn instead to the forms, motifs, and inspirations of Anatolian folk culture and vernacular architecture (see chapter 6).

A year before the founding of the Fine Arts Association in Istanbul, another professional organization, the Society of Turkish Architects (Türk Mimarlar Cemiyeti), was established in Ankara in 1927. Comprising architects working within the bureaucratic context of the ministries and state institutions in Ankara, this society was more interested in the regulating of practice, the securing of commissions, and the safeguarding of the professional, economic, and legal interests of architects. The same year a law was passed restricting use of the title "architect" to graduates of approved institutions of higher education. In 1935, with intensification of the struggle for state commissions, the Fine Arts Association and the Society of Turkish Architects were consolidated, and a third branch in Izmir was established, starting a long process that would culminate in the organization of the nationwide Turkish Chamber of Architects in the 1950s. During the 1930s, however, it was almost exclusively the Istanbul architects within the Fine Arts Association who were the most prolific designers in practice and the most visible and vocal advocates of the New Architecture in the culture at large. If it is possible to talk about a "Turkish modernism" of the 1930s, it is largely because of these Istanbul architects with their origins in the academy reforms.

In 1931 Celal Esat Arseven (1875–1971), professor of the history of architecture and urbanism at the academy and author of various books on Turkish and Islamic art history, published his important booklet *Yeni Mimari* (New Architecture). It was essentially a synopsis of the French architect Andre Lurcat's *L'Architecture* (1929) with Arseven's own commentaries and additions. The chapters on earlier periods of architectural history that Lurcat had used as a historical precedent to the timeless concerns of architecture such as volume, surface, and color were largely omitted from Arseven's book, which focused on the principles of modern design as it evolved in the 1920s. Arseven explained that he had prepared the booklet primarily for pedagogical purposes, as a contribution to the recent efforts at the academy to educate Turkish architects in conformity with "contemporary mentalities and needs," rather than "stifling their talent in classical curriculums." Joining the prevailing critique of the old system of architectural education at the academy, Arseven wrote:

For some forty or fifty years, students have wasted time drawing Greek temples, the column capitals of the Parthenon, and the acanthus leaves of the Corinthian order. [They have] graduated as draftsmen and decorators rather than architects, drawing ornate pictures of unbuild-able buildings. There was no significant difference between the graduates of the academy and the unschooled builders. No new movement in architecture emerged, and Istanbul got filled with ugly buildings.[12]

The book emphasized how "today new construction methods [are] allowing light and air to penetrate every corner of buildings" and how "both interior plans and exterior forms of buildings now express the function the building is expected to fulfill."[13] Yet Arseven clarified that this rational approach did not mean a negation of aesthetic concerns. He wrote that the new aesthetic realm that was opened up by "the rational arrangement of volumes in space" was one of the defining characteristics of the New Architecture. Given his own background as an aspiring painter (with earlier hesitations between "realists and impressionists" while he was in Paris),[14] this acknowledgment of the aesthetics of the New Architecture was important for Arseven, although the primacy of the scientific discourse was strong. In the rest of the book, he introduced the formal and aesthetic precepts of modernism—flat roofs and terraces, cantilevers and balconies, free façades and horizontal windows, *pilotis* and open plans—discussing them in relation to the "logical criteria" and "contemporary needs" that informed them. He particularly emphasized the role of new materials and techniques that were in the process of "radically transforming the definition of architecture," especially iron and steel, reinforced concrete, laminated wood, and techniques of waterproofing and fireproofing. Arseven declared that the new professional identity of the architect, implied by the principles of New Architecture, departed radically from traditional definitions of the architect's vocation. The architect was no longer an artist or craftsman but an expert with an unprecedentedly broad range of involvement and responsibility in everything from sociological and economic matters to the design of domestic furniture. The booklet was illustrated with photographs of canonic modern buildings from Europe as examples of the New Architecture. The only examples from Turkey were Ernst Egli's recently completed buildings: the music conservatory, the İsmet Paşa Girls' Institute (see fig. 2.8), and the Commercial Lycée, all in Ankara.

In 1931, the same year that *Yeni Mimari* came out, the professional journal of architects, *Mimar,* also started publication under the initiative of Zeki Sayar, Abidin Mortaş, Sedad Hakkı Eldem, Şevki Balmumcu (all 1928 graduates), and Aptullah Ziya (who graduated in 1929). In 1935, the journal was renamed *Arkitekt* as part of a nationalist trend to eliminate words of Arabic origin from the Turkish language; ironically, the new name was another foreign word, this time from the West. As the only specialized publication on architecture until 1941 (when a new journal, *Yapı,* appeared), *Arkitekt* is the primary document testifying to the making of a modernist profession in Turkey. Throughout the 1930s it published projects and articles by the Turkish architects associated with the journal, as well as modern buildings from different parts of Europe and the rest of the world, with a regular "Architecture in Other

Countries" section. It published brief reviews of recent European publications on architecture as well as translations of important theoretical texts by Le Corbusier, Adolf Behne, and Bruno Taut, among others.

The central mission of the journal was to voice Turkish architects' struggle for professional legitimacy and to demonstrate their competence in the New Architecture, "as much as if not more than their foreign teachers and colleagues." They made repeated pleas to the state to organize open competitions for important public buildings, and whenever a competition was held, they published the entries with commentaries. For example, the competition for the Exhibition Hall in Ankara (1933) was extensively covered in the journal, and the winning design by Şevki Balmumcu became an occasion to celebrate Turkish architects' success. Balmumcu's success was of great symbolic significance at a time when Turkish architects were growing increasingly bitter that so many major commissions were going to German and central European architects. When Arseven's *Yeni Mimari* was reviewed in *Mimar,* the absence of examples by Turkish architects in the book was the primary point of criticism in an otherwise favorable review. "We, the young architects of this country," the review said, "are deeply saddened to see that, alas, like many educated people we know, the author of the book too is of the unfortunate opinion that no talented Turkish architects exist."[15]

Among the many European architects who worked in Turkey, Ernst Egli holds the reputation for having introduced the New Architecture to the country, by the example of his own work and, perhaps more significantly, through his seminal role as educator. The published projects of students in Egli's studio demonstrate the primacy and functional organization of the plan and, above all, stripped-down plain façades and a volumetric aesthetic, radically departing from the classical traditions of the school. In the first issue of *Mimar* in 1931, a conspicuously "cubic" villa project by Edip Hikmet, one of Egli's students, was featured as representative of the new direction at the academy (fig. 4.1). The accompanying text said:

In the architectural school you can no longer see the old classical methods. The student prepares his project in response to economic, local, scientific, and constructional criteria *as in real life*. He is a real architect. He sees and studies Roman, classical Greek, and Turkish architectures in history of architecture classes but is not required to imitate their proportions, styles, and constructional norms. He is *an explorer of science and technique* in search of the new Turkish architecture of the future [my emphasis].[16]

The same year, on the occasion of the end-of-year exhibition at the academy, *Mimar* published some of the student projects for an industrial building that Egli had assigned to his studio. Although commending the projects with enthusiasm, the commentary by Faruk Galip also included a brief critical remark that no freehand sketches were included in the exhibition and that the classical curriculum appeared to have been totally discarded, even from architectural history assignments.[17] Such mixed feelings toward the modernist reforms so early on are indicative of the underlying ambivalence of attitudes regarding the importation of a radically abstract European

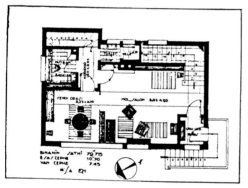 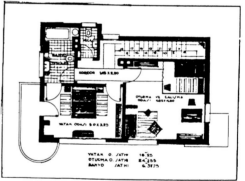

Fig. 4.1. A student project for a single-family house (1930), the work of Edip Hikmet, an architectural student in Ernst Egli's studio at the Academy of Fine Arts. Flat roofs, cantilevers, rounded balconies, horizontal band windows, and an absence of decoration were characteristic features of the "New Architecture" (*Yeni Mimari*), which came to be known in popular parlance as "cubic architecture" (*kübik mimari*).

discourse devoid of the representational power that classical buildings historically possessed. Although the "scientific" and "progressive" connotations of cubic forms were welcomed, many commentators felt the inadequacy of these forms to express the ideals and identity of the Turkish nation. This ambivalence would become increasingly evident in the late 1930s, and the word "cubic" would rapidly acquire negative connotations.

On the other hand, student projects for public buildings (rather than for houses or industrial-utilitarian programs) produced in Egli's studio suggest that the rejection of classical architecture was more a stylistic change, affecting mostly elevations, than a radical conceptual shift in spatial thinking. For example, thesis projects for the Turkish Embassy building in Baghdad prepared by students graduating in 1934 testify to the persistence of classical sensibilities (symmetry, axiality, loggias, and colonnades) in modern disguise (fig. 4.2).[18] They also suggest the strong grip of Egli's influence by the example of his own work. Projecting cubic window bays on the façade, like those in Egli's Court of Financial Appeals building in Ankara (see fig. 4.8), and two-story-high courtyards, tall columns for entrances, and colonnades like those Egli used in his educational buildings in Ankara can easily be identified in these projects. The technical character of the line drawings in these student projects, as well as a contemporaneous photograph of the architectural studios showing neatly arranged desks and clean, well-dressed students (fig. 4.3), suggests a highly professional and "clinical" atmosphere. This is a very different picture from those of the messy, craft-oriented, experimental studios and radical students of the early Bauhaus, reinforcing the argument that when it arrived under the auspices of the republic, modernism in Turkey was already a professional establishment rather than a critical force in architectural education.

In late 1936, after the untimely death of Hans Poelzig, Egli's designated successor as head of the architectural section, Bruno Taut was put in charge of both the school and the architectural office of the Ministry of Education, which was located within the academy. Martin Wagner, Taut's partner and colleague from the GEHAG (Gemeinnutzige Heimstatten- Spar- und Bau-Aktiengesselschaft) cooperative housing program in Berlin, had come to Turkey in 1935 as a consultant to Istanbul Municipality. He was teaching a course at the academy on "Economic and Technical Aspects of Urbanism" and was instrumental in getting Taut (who was in Japan then) invited to Turkey. At the time of Taut's appointment at the academy, the painting section was entrusted to the French painter Leopold Levy and the sculpture section to Rudolph Belling, starting what is often called "a new phase of foreign teachers" at the academy. The sculptor Belling, like Taut, had been a member of the radical Novembergruppe and Arbeitsrat fur Kunst in Germany after the First World War. By 1936, however, for both men, the political radicalism of the Weimar years had long been eclipsed.

Taut's pedagogical program was based on an antiformalist and antistylistic rationalism that can perhaps be characterized as an unorthodox modernism. He

DÍPLOMA KONKUDU PDOJESÍ BAGDATTA TÚRK SEFARETHANESÍ   1838   FERÍDUN

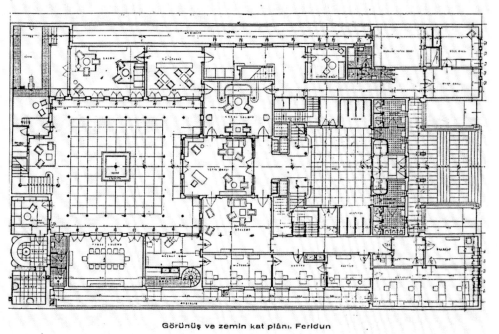

Görünüş ve zemin kat plânı. Feridun

Fig.4.2. Student thesis project for the Turkish Embassy building in Baghdad, from Ernst Egli's studio at the Academy of Fine Arts, 1934. The use of cubic window projections on the façade, the entrance colonnade, the interior courtyard, and the overall "Ankara cubic" aesthetic of such student projects reflect the influence of Egli, who used the same features in his own work in Ankara (see figs. 2.8 and 4.8).

Fig. 4.3. The architectural studios in the Academy of Fine Arts in Istanbul, the oldest school of architecture in Turkey, established in 1882. Photograph circa 1937.

elaborated this position in his textbook *Mimari Bilgisi* (Lectures on Architecture), first published in Turkey in 1938.[19] To this day the book remains one of the most interesting and critical accounts of modern architecture, taking issue with many of the aesthetic clichés and political claims of the Modern Movement. In 1937 Taut assigned his graduating class a housing project for employees of the Directorate of State Monopolies in Ankara—not a hypothetical exercise but a real program requested by the ministry. Turkish architects and architectural students were already familiar with the socialist *Siedlung* (housing) programs of the 1920s in Weimar Germany through articles published in *Mimar* and *Arkitekt*.[20] It was the writings of Martin Wagner and later of Wilhelm Schütte, however, that drew attention to the economics and politics of housing and urbanism.[21] The students in Taut's studio were asked to produce a site plan and floor plans of different house types and detailed specifications for all materials. They were asked to calculate the cost per square foot of construction, workmanship, and infrastructure, including roads, retaining and garden walls, connection to water, electricity, and gas lines, plumbing, and sewage disposal. In the manner of Taut's own work for GEHAG in Berlin,[22] students were also required to calculate the annual rent and conditions of financing for each type, thus exploring the feasibility of their proposals.

Although this studio project remained an isolated exercise and was not implemented, it was published in *Arkitekt* with drawings and descriptions that throw some light on the priorities of the new modernist education.[23] The projects were arranged as combinations of row houses and three-story parallel blocks in which one exterior stairwell served two units on each side (fig. 4.4). Different types of houses were worked out with minimum dimensions and furnishings and with detailed specifications of materials and finishes, down to the cost of pipes, switches, and fittings. No elevations or perspectives were drawn, only plans and a site axonometric. The proposals clearly were not "aesthetic" in either design quality or representation techniques, contrasting with the painterly legacy of the school's beaux-arts tradition. In his *Mimari Bilgisi,* Taut had openly criticized the deceptiveness of elaborate renderings with light and shadow, proposing that students should instead observe and sketch the particular detail of a building through the eyes of an architect, seeing not only the shape but the making of it.[24]

There is no question that Taut's image as studio instructor and practicing architect in Turkey was primarily that of a modernist who taught rational, functional design to Turkish students—something that responded to the republic's urgent expectations for the education of "experts" and "professionals" after European models. Taut's teaching and writing, however, were irreducible to the sterile formulas of the *Neue Sachlichkeit* (new objectivity) in Germany, of which he was always critical. He insistently told his students that rational design thinking did not necessarily or automatically produce "architecture" as such, nor did it determine a particular form or style. Taut's resistance to both the anti-aesthetic posture of the *Neue Sachlichkeit* and the aesthetic canons of modernist orthodoxy after the advent of "international style" fared well in the architectural culture of Turkey in the late 1930s, when architects sought to infuse architecture with feeling and national content. Indeed, as I discuss in chapter 6, the New Architecture as understood and taught by both Egli and Taut entailed a strong "regionalist" message and a deep reverence for the vernacular traditions and Ottoman monuments of Turkey.

As the modernist curricular transformations at the academy shaped the profile of the first republican generation of architects, their repercussions were felt in the Civil Service School of Engineering (Hendese-i Mülkiye Mektebi) as well. Although the classical core of the curriculum was still intact in 1931, some student projects for programs such as houses and schools displayed a modernist aesthetic with flat roofs, simple geometric volumes, rounded corners, and free window arrangements (fig. 4.5). In 1938, more systematic and official modernizing reforms like those of the academy were undertaken through the initiative of Emin Onat (1908–1961). Emin Onat, who graduated from Zurich Federal Polytechnic in 1934 as a student of Otto Salvisberg, was instrumental in institutionalizing the German-Austrian school of modernism at the school of engineering and inviting Clemenz Holzmeister (1886–1983) and Paul Bonatz (1877–1956) to teach there. In 1944 the school was transformed into Istanbul Technical University, and the architectural section became a separate department located in the historic Taşkışla barracks.

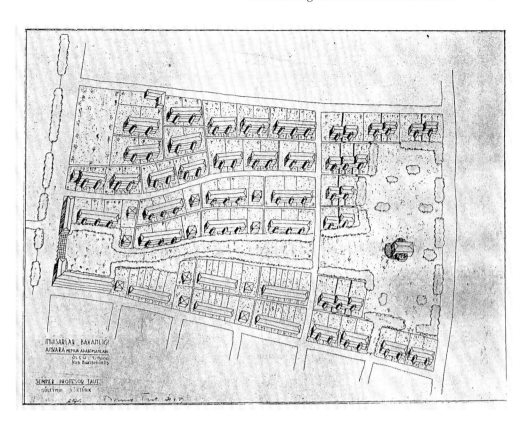

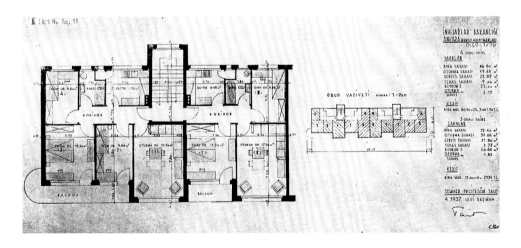

Fig. 4.4. Student projects for Directorate of State Monopolies employee housing assigned by Bruno Taut to his architectural studio at the Academy of Fine Arts in 1937–1938. **Top:** Site axonometric drawing by Süleyman Köktürk. **Bottom:** Plans for three-story *Zeilenbau*-type apartments with two- and three-bedroom variants by Ulvi Başman. Students were asked to provide detailed specifications for materials and to calculate costs for different types of units.

Fig. 4.5. Project for a small elementary school by Zeki Tevfik, a student in the architectural course at the Civil Service School of Engineering, Istanbul. Project circa 1931.

Historically, architects have carried out their struggle for professional legitimacy and power on two interrelated grounds: first, their knowledge and expertise, or their "cognitive capital," and second, their claims to represent the good of society at large—their "professional ideology." In the West, both claims were supported by the writings of turn-of-the-century social theorists such as Thornstein Veblen, who viewed expertise and rationality as the only forces fit to govern society, and Emile Durkheim, who regarded professional groups as the major element of normative regulation in society. Although architects had borrowed extensively from these arguments, their claims to professional status had always been fraught with difficulties, owing to the nature of the discipline. So long as architects worked in traditional patronage relationships with individual clients, who often had particular stylistic preferences and hired architects to execute their wishes, architecture could not be a full-fledged "profession" in the ideal sense. Only with the Modern Movement was this traditional definition of the architect radically transformed along a technocratic and professional model. In countries like Turkey, the historical coincidence of modernism with the professionalization movement was particularly important in empowering architects to use the doctrines of rationalism and functionalism as a basis for their quest for professional recognition.

Rationalism, Functionalism, and Professional Legitimacy

THE 1929 PIECE by Müderris İsmail Hakkı titled "Cubism in Architecture and the Turkish Tradition" is one of the earliest and theoretically most interesting arguments for the New Architecture, written at the height of the Kemalist reforms. Its evolutionary model of architectural history—its identification of particular styles with their corresponding forms of social organization and with the zeitgeist of a particular epoch—was mentioned in chapter 3. From this evolutionary perspective, İsmail Hakkı explained how science became the central institution of contemporary societies and how the tools, principles, and means of these societies, including their cities, buildings, houses, doors, and windows, became "rational" (*makul*), "mathematical" (*riyazi*), and "geometric" (*hendesi*):

In contemporary societies [*muasır cemiyet*] science has replaced religion as the primary social institution. . . . The envelopes of the new life can be neither sacred, nor grandiose, nor dainty. These buildings can only be healthy, comfortable, and rational. The most important feature of contemporary society and its contemporary art is this rationality [*makulluk*]. . . . The tools, principles, and means that, until the intervention of science, received their inspiration from faith and tradition have started to become mathematical [*riyazi*]. As a necessary consequence of this mathematization, cities, streets, sidewalks, houses, doors, windows, tables, paper sheets, and envelopes have become geometric [*hendesi*]. Contemporary civilization [*muasır medeniyet*] is one that covers the world with geometric objects.[26]

His conclusion that "contemporary civilization . . . covers the world with geometric objects" was the most elaborate civilizational argument for "cubic architecture" offered until then. İsmail Hakkı defined geometry as "the manifestation of science in form" (*hendese, ilmin şekillerde tecellisinden başka birşey değildir*) and stated that our affection for geometry was not simply the result of rationalist philosophy as a self-referential system of thought but a profound necessity of *"democratic life"* (my emphasis). Cubism, which he defined as "an art of volumes" and "an abolition of motifs in architecture," was "neither a discovery nor a theory" but "the necessary consequence of new needs pressing upon European societies for a century." It fulfilled a functional purpose (*ameli maksat*), a technical necessity (*teknik zaruret*), and a cultural relationship between form and society (*harsi münasebet*)—a formula evocative of the classic trinity of architectural theory: function, structure, and beauty (*utilitas, firmitas,* and *venustas*).

Thus, the key functionalist and rationalist arguments for form, which would become the main theme of architectural discourse in the 1930s, were eloquently put forward by İsmail Hakkı in this important article. Three years before the first issue of *Mimar,* in which Zeki Sayar, following Le Corbusier's famous dictum, declared a building to be "a habitation machine" (*ikamet makinası*),[27] İsmail Hakkı used a similarly Corbusean expression. He characterized the minarets of Turkish mosques as "tools for calling to prayer," explaining their design as a thoroughly rational process:

Minarets are containers—tools for calling the faithful to prayer—before they are works of art. Their bases are the load-bearing foundations of these tall towers. The *şerefe* is a balcony for the muezzin to go around. The cap is a roof to protect the minaret from rain—the most appropriate roof form for a tall structure. The *arabesk* motifs of the *şerefe* balustrade are not the work of a mind exploring the mystical secrets of geometric shapes; it is the idea of the craftsman who was trying to reduce the load of the masonry balustrade. The stalactites under the *şerefe* are not symbols of stalactite caves, nor the creations of a Romantic mind. They are devised by the mason as the brackets connecting the *şerefe* to the body of the minaret.[28]

Cubic architecture, then, was simply the latest rational form, the most reasonable "container of social life in contemporary society," and the result of contemporary techniques that "combined the strength of cement with the elasticity of iron." İsmail Hakkı went on to declare the discovery of reinforced concrete "the most important revolution of our times," which opened up many new possibilities. He wrote: "It is possible to make large openings in buildings. It is possible to make large horizontal planes without supports, columns, or vaults. It is possible to make large projections or recessions. Rather than building with rows of bricks or stones, it is possible to cast the building as a monolithic object."[29]

The primacy of functional and technical criteria outlined by İsmail Hakkı anticipated the line of rationalist arguments for the New Architecture promoted by *Mimar* and *Arkitekt* throughout the 1930s. Coinciding favorably with the positivist and rationalist biases of the Kemalist project of civilization, the scientific claims of the New Architecture were ideally suited to Turkish architects' professional struggle. The official modernist doctrine that modern form was a thoroughly rational consequence of function and technique and that it had nothing to do with eccentricity or stylistic whim was enthusiastically promoted by Turkish architects. The New Architecture represented, before everything else, "the switch from the realm of forms and aesthetics to that of needs and logic," as Celal Esat Arseven put it.[30] There was a rational—that is, functional and constructional—explanation for every design element in the New Architecture. "New construction methods provide the opportunity to maximize the amount of sunlight admitted to each room and to determine the form and placement of the windows," wrote Arseven. "The walls are liberated from the foundations and the windows from the walls. *Everything has its logical place accordingly* [my emphasis]."[31] Similarly, Behçet Sabri and Bedrettin Hamdi's 1934 article in *Mimar* connected every typical formal element of the New Architecture to a logical constructional or functional explanation:

The twentieth century has given the architect many new means and rational solutions. Instead of the small windows of the past, new construction gives us band windows. We can organize the plan freely without dependence on load-bearing walls. Walls can be the same thickness on every floor because they are no longer load bearing. The purpose of the wall is no longer structural: it is there only to block view, sound, or access. Corner windows are possible. Flat roofs are replacing tile roofs and wood components are giving way to metal. Windows for stairwells can be a large vertical glazed wall. The task of the architect is to find the most logical and most appropriate of these new solutions to formal and constructional matters.[32]

This emphasis on the "logical" nature of modern form was particularly useful in rejecting Ottoman revivalism on *rational* rather than ideological grounds. "Rationalism" and "functionalism," it was argued, had nothing to do with the old stylistic "isms" such as revivalism, eclecticism, and neoclassicism but were signifiers of a new philosophy corresponding to the zeitgeist of the modern age. For example, Zeki Sayar's objection to the prototype schools built according to the stylistic precepts of the National Architecture Renaissance was formulated not as an ideological rejection of Ottoman motifs but as a thoroughly rationalist argument: the idea of a prototype was, by definition, contradictory to rational design thinking, which had to take the specificity of site and program into consideration. Sayar insightfully pointed out that the same building could not be appropriate for different sites, climates, and programs. In an essay titled "Aesthetics in School Design" Sayar explained that classrooms should not distract the student with decoration and should be "plain, well proportioned, well ventilated, and flooded with light." The decorative elements and column capitals of National Architecture Renaissance buildings were "inappropriate" because "dust accumulated in these details," prompting architects to replace them with more hygienic plain surfaces. He wrote: "The old-style prototype schools were built at a time when an architectural theory of school building [*mektep nazariyeti mimarisi*] was nonexistent. They were built all alike, in the absence of technical information and as a result of a simplistic thinking that privileged 'national sentiment' [over scientific criteria]."[33] In another essay, "Economic Considerations in School Design," he emphasized the lower cost of building, wherever appropriate, more stories than the two-story National Architecture Renaissance schools of the 1920s. He emphasized maximizing the ratio of classroom area to total area, rationally placing auxiliary spaces such as the gym and workshops in basements and on ground floors, and optimizing the area for these purposes on the basis of the number of students.[34] In these essays, Zeki Sayar made frequent references to European, especially German, examples, illustrating the first essay with photographs of an elementary school by Martin Elsaesser in Eschersheim, Germany.

A survey of published projects in *Mimar* and *Arkitekt* over the 1930s reveals a consistently "technical" language with which projects were described—a privileging of programmatic, constructional, and economic criteria as determinants of design. Dimensions in plans were explained with respect to intensity and nature of use, choices of materials were discussed with reference to factors such as cost, hygiene, and ease of maintenance, and distances between blocks were explained in terms of angles of the sun, in the way Walter Gropius explained them to the CIAM in 1930. Furthermore, like their contemporaries who were shaping CIAM doctrines, Turkish architects' professional self-definition was not limited to their being experts and technicians. It entailed a much larger social vision. What is particularly remarkable in the professional discourse on the New Architecture is the unequivocal linking of modern forms to societal transformations unleashed by the industrial age—an age that was only an idealized potential in Turkey, not an accomplished fact. "Modern technology and the development of mechanization gave us many new means to do our work and many changes in our construction methods," wrote Samih Saim in a 1931 piece titled "New Elements." "To adapt to this new lifestyle, many elements of our buildings changed their forms or radically renewed their character. Thus hitherto unprecedented forms appeared."[35] These new elements of the New Architecture, adapted from Arseven's book and partly derived from Le Corbusier's five principles, were roof terraces, *pilotis,* horizontal windows (or "logical windows" [*mantıki pencere*], as Samih Saim called them), color, and electricity.

Evoking the same argument about modernism's being a universal and thoroughly rational doctrine, Behçet Ünsal made a similar correlation between social modernization and architectural form. Addressing the public in a radio program in 1939, he explained architects' espousal of the New Architecture in civilizational terms: it was a historical necessity, a mark of contemporariness (*asrilik*), rather than a stylistic choice or fashion:

These terms [functionalism, rationalism] that have just entered our language and these new modes of living that are beginning to effect us are the reflections in our country of a larger universal and social transformation. In *our machine age* [my emphasis], with its changes in mentality and lifestyle, our large wooden houses with spacious *sofas* [halls] are no longer appropriate. That is why the necessity arises for moving to a small home or apartment with corner windows and rounded projections.[36]

The message in Ünsal's words was that modern forms and design principles were rational products of the "machine age," which, although not yet a reality in Turkey, was a universal phenomenon and therefore "our" machine age as much as anybody else's. Although there was no direct causal relationship between the social and technological transformations of the twentieth century and the particular forms of modernism, Behçet Ünsal's rhetorical leap from "changes in mentality and lifestyle" to corner windows and rounded projections was characteristic of the modernist polemic. So were rhetorical leaps from the definition of the architect as a technical expert (who solves design problems under given circumstances) to the idea of architect as an agent of civilization (with a larger mission to transform those circumstances). The former legitimated the latter; rationality and expertise became compelling grounds for discourses of social engineering and technocracy.

Architects exalted this larger role of agent of social transformation and reconstruction, which elevated their stature in the society at large—something particularly important in a country where architecture was traditionally seen as a lesser vocation associated with the non-Muslims of the empire. In their writings they articulated this self-declared mission to teach the people how to live in civilized and contemporary ways in accordance with the Westernizing reforms of the republic. The technocratic discourse of modernism as articulated by Le Corbusier and the CIAM offered them a model. For example, in an article titled "The Architect in the City" in *Yeni Türk Mecmuası* (Journal of the New Turk), architect Faruk Galip explained this new definition of the architect as follows:

Today's architect is no longer the old builder [*kalfa*] whom people hired to prepare plans and build a four-room house. He is a scientist [*ilim adamı*] who delineates the social and economic politics of the country, organizes her civilizational character, builds her cities, and provides the working people of the nation with comfortable and airy spaces of recreation and work. He is an artist whose reputation will transcend national boundaries and will place the imprint upon history, not so much of his own name, but that of his nation.[37]

This dramatically expanded and idealized definition of the profession was the major theme in the inaugural issue of *Mimar* when it appeared in 1931. In an important editorial titled "The Architect Inside the Building," Aptullah Ziya articulated this new professional definition of the architect beyond the boundaries of technical know-how: "The whole world admits today that the architect is not a builder who constructs our houses to shelter us from rain and sun. He is an intellectual leader to guide our social life [*içtimai hayatımıza yol gösteren bir mütefekkir*], a thinker concerned with our comfort, hygiene, and health. He is concerned with the interior design of our homes, as much as, if not more than, the exterior."[38]

As is evident from this passage, the civilizing mission of the architect was a theme especially relevant for residential architecture in the shaping of a new and modern culture of living—a subject I take up in the next chapter. It was also an important theme in designing model villages, "colonizing the countryside," and teaching the peasants "how to sleep on beds, how to use chairs and tables," as covered in chapter 3. In both areas, the quest for professional legitimacy and power was based on a technocratic worldview: it was the rationality of architects, planners, and experts that made them legitimate authorities in prescribing lifestyles. The technocratic overtones of the Modern Movement were epitomized in Europe by the early career of Le Corbusier, who was inspired by Taylorist principles of rationality and efficiency and appealed to industrialists, businessmen, and the state for the implementation of these ideas.[39] Like the great master before them, Turkish architects repeatedly appealed to the state for commissions and tried to expand their involvement in nation building at every level, from the design of homes and public buildings to factories, silos, and cities.

There was no doubt in the minds of Turkish architects that the state was the primary agent of modernization and the primary patron for their expertise, which alone could give built form to the ideals of the republic. They did not hesitate to legitimate the role of the professional architect as an officer of the Kemalist revolution and an agent of its civilizing mission to carry its ideals to the people. Modern architecture was perceived and portrayed as the natural expression of this progressive mission, a powerful instrument of "visible politics," not unlike the way modernist colonial architecture and urbanism were perceived by French and Italian authorities in North Africa at about the same time. For many Turkish modernizers (bureaucrats, planners, architects), words such as "colonization" and "fascism" had unequivocally positive and progressive connotations in the 1930s. They signified the authoritative but enlightened modernization of peoples and lands by strong states. The assumption was that only through the sponsorship of a strong state could modern architecture flourish in a war-torn, poor, and backward country like Turkey in the 1930s.

In their quest for broader professional legitimacy and state commissions, Turkish architects competed primarily against their foreign colleagues and teachers. For the most part, they were faced with the paradox of respecting these prominent foreigners, who had introduced the New Architecture to the country, and at the same time feeling blocked by them from access to important public commissions. One consequence of this paradox was that while constructing their argument for professional legitimacy around scientific criteria (education, expertise, rational thinking), Turkish architects also resorted to the extrascientific factor of nationality, which gave them an edge over their foreign competitors. It was claimed that young Turkish architects "who were born and raised in the Kemalist *inkilap*, living it and loving it," as Aptullah Ziya put it,[40] would be better equipped to give form to the spirit of the revolution. During the construction of new Ankara in the early 1930s, Arif Hikmet Koyunoğlu, the leading architect of the National Architecture Renaissance in republican Ankara, was reprimanded by RPP leaders for writing an article that criticized the commissioning of the entire government complex to the Austrian architect Clemenz Holzmeister. In the article Arif Hikmet had written: "The new Ankara should be built by Turkish artists who know the heroic spirit of the War of Independence. Only Turkish architects can give this city its identity. Architect Holzmeister is a great man and a talented artist. But he is not someone to understand the revolution in our country in order to produce the works worthy of it."[41]

The traditional tendency of Turkish political leaders to prefer foreign architects and planners was a primary grievance of the professional discourse published in the pages of *Mimar* and *Arkitekt*. In another essay, titled "Nationalism in Art," Aptullah Ziya outlined the decline of Turkish art and architecture since the reign of Sultan Abdulaziz in the hands of foreign architects, including the most recent infatuation with foreign experts in the construction of republican Ankara:

Nationalist art is not the work of individuals. It is the work of nations. No national art can be born out of individual talent. From the constitutional period (*meşrutiyet*), we leaped into the republic, thanks to the power of the Gazi. We needed a new art. Yet the new equivalents of Çelebi Mehmet Efendi [an eighteenth-century Ottoman ambassador to Paris who brought in French artistic and architectural influences] still carry the same old mentality and still have the last word in matters of art. Once again they brought foreigners who, instead of baroque and empire styles, this time introduced the New Art. However, since [these foreigners] also tried to look "a little native," their work turned out to be a strange thing, far from reflecting our revolution. These new experts turned out to be no different from the Toma *kalfa* [alluding to Ottoman minority architects] who built Pera in Istanbul, and with their heavy and bulky hands, they shaped the construction of Ankara. We do not want to give the impression that we are negating their rightful role as teachers. We are not talking about art, but "national art."[42]

There are two interesting points in Aptullah Ziya's arguments. The first, also repeated by other Turkish architects, is an acknowledgment of the pedagogical function of the foreign architects in introducing the New Architecture to the country. More interesting is the implication that their modern work was less "revolutionary" than befit the Kemalist ideal. In other words, it was not modern architecture that Turkish architects objected to but the particular modernism of the German-speaking architects. With his admiration for Italian rationalist architects, Aptullah Ziya was particularly vocal in criticizing the heavier modernism of Ankara and casting this in terms of a nationalistic argument to promote the professional power struggle of Turkish architects. Similar sentiments, sometimes bordering on xenophobia, were not uncommon in the generally introverted, nationalistic culture of the early republic.

Making the professional plea for the benefits of a system of competitions that would favor Turkish architects over foreigners, Zeki Sayar, too, cited examples from Italy, where "designers not registered in the Fascist organization of architects were not allowed to participate in national competitions for state buildings." In their paradig-matic essay "The Architecture of the Turkish Revolution," Behçet Sabri and Bedrettin Hamdi also offered a good example of this nationalistic argument, which was at odds with the earlier universalistic and supranational claims of scientific reasoning:

We need to learn from the techniques of European experts. However, the spirit and outlook of the Turk is higher than what they can attain. We must turn to the young generation of Turkish architects who, bearing the blood and talent of the Great Sinan, are now walking along a con-temporary and logical path. The leaders who wrote nationalism and populism into the princi-ples of the republic must commission the architects of the revolution from which *a modern and national* architecture will be born [my emphasis].[44]

The weakness of the logic in most of these arguments is obvious. What relevance could "the blood of the Great Sinan" possibly have for modern architects who, by their own claims, followed "a contemporary and logical path"? If indeed "modern needs [were] the same for everybody in the modern world," as Behçet Ünsal said, paraphrasing Walter Gropius, Hennes Meyer, and other proponents of the *Neue Sachlichkeit* before him, why would the nationality of the architect matter at all? Many such questions remained unresolved in Turkish architects' professional dis-course in the 1930s, with no clear and fixed conceptual boundary for the determinants of modern form. Sometimes modern architecture was discussed as a logical fact deter-mined by function, technique, and the universal needs of modern life. Sometimes priority was placed on national expression. Often, republican architects wanted it both ways.

Aesthetic Discourse of the New Architecture

It was not arbitrary choice or pure semantics that from the very start, Turkish architects insisted on the term "New Architecture" and expressed their dis-taste for the term "international style." It would be misleading, they argued, to char-acterize the New Architecture as international. It was simply an anti-academic architecture and, being the most rational response to site, program, climate, and con-text, was by definition "national." Nor was it a new style. On the contrary, its entire premise was a rejection of stylistic approaches such as the Ottoman revivalist National Architecture Renaissance before it. Moreover, in spite of occasional state-ments reminiscent of *Neue Sachlichkeit* clichés about architecture's being an anti-aesthetic and scientific fact, the radicalism and internationalist spirit of the "new objectivity" was as unpalatable to Turkish architects as the term "international style." There could be many explanations for this. As already mentioned, the European architects teaching and working in Turkey were more conservative Germans and Austrians, outside the mainstream Bauhaus and CIAM circles, often with a classical training informing their austere modernism. Equally important was that the socialist and Marxist views upheld by the radical German architects of the *Neue Sachlichkeit* and the "internationalism" of the left were anathema to the strongly antisocialist, antimaterialist, and nationalist ideological precepts of Kemalism. The prospect of reducing architecture to pure scientific calculation and cold reason meant negating not only aesthetics and taste but also the "national spirit and idealism" that were so dear to republican architects. Finally, it was the aesthetic component of their discipline that legitimated architects as "artists"—as experts in aesthetic matters that could be handled by no one else.

Whatever the reasons, Turkish architects' emphasis on functionalism, rationalism, and scientific expertise and their rejection of stylistic references to modernism did not go so far as negating their preoccupation with form and aesthetics. Rather, they elaborated the remarkably insightful, albeit polemical, formulation that "if a work of architecture fully conforms to its context and its function, then it is beautiful."[45] In other words, they proposed that in the New Architecture, modern form was not really formalism—that is, the geometric masses and volumes of the New Architecture were not a stylistic given but a consequence of rational considerations of the problem at hand. Reminiscent of Le Corbusier's famous statement that "modern decorative art is not decorated,"[46] this formulation allowed the profession to reject the aesthetics of Ottoman revivalism without rejecting the importance of aesthetic concerns. It meant taking artistic creativity on board while leaving stylistic ornamentation out, thus defining the modern architect as distinct from the old "draftsmen and decorators," as Arseven had called them, while still maintaining a creative, artistic edge over engineers as a competing professional group.

That the term "building art" (*yapı sanatı*) was widely used in the 1930s interchangeably with "architecture" is indicative of this desire to legitimate the architect as both a construction expert and a creative artist at the same time. To be sure, such binary oppositions between construction and art, science and aesthetics, logic and feeling were themselves modern constructs, and as modern philosophers have contemplated extensively, it was only after the modern separation of these realms that efforts to recombine them had intensified. In an important piece titled "Feelings and Logic in Architecture," Sami Macaroğlu criticized misrepresentations of the New Architecture as pure logic devoid of feeling—as, for example, in terms then circulating such as "logical windows" and "logical plans." He argued that with the overwhelming domination of social life in the modern world by logical and rational rules, art was the only domain in which feelings could run free, and everyone should acknowledge the value of that:

Recently we have been repeating the same clichés: "I did this because it is rational. This is the form necessitated by construction. This will respond to such-and-such a need." Enough! These logical explanations have no other function than masking the feelings that we refuse to confess even to ourselves. Why not say, "I did it because it is beautiful or because I wanted to express a certain feeling"? In New Architecture, the building must conform to its function. But is the scientific aspect of architecture enough? No. We are always guided by our feelings. If we think about our decisions, we will see that even in those decisions that we consider the most "logical," the role of logic has been no more than that of reinforcing our feelings. How many people are ready to admit this? You must have heard of people talking about the New Architecture in such terms: economical, healthy, rationally constructed—in other words, "logical." An ordinary technician equipped with science can easily make buildings with these qualifications. Reason can take care of all of them. Are we going to call the resulting machine "a work of art"?[47]

This emphasis on the importance of extrascientific factors in design was, in essence, the basis of an undogmatic approach to modernism that both Ernst Egli and Bruno Taut tried to impart to their students at the academy. On the basis of his own method of working out a design problem, Taut explained in his book: "First you come up with a logical diagram in response to site, orientation, landscape, and other such factors. This is truly a diagram: a scientific document, which has nothing to do yet with architecture. It is important to wait until this diagram acquires life and thinking gives way to feeling. Only then is the hand set free to draw."[48] Although the student projects for the Directorate of State Monopolies housing mentioned earlier (see fig. 4.4) show no evidence of having gone much beyond the first, diagrammatic stage, it was important for Taut to restore to building construction the artistic component that had been obscured by the anti-aesthetic excesses of the *Neue Sachlichkeit*. That he published these ideas in Turkish was a particularly important contribution to the architectural culture of the early republic, the significance of which has only recently been appreciated.[49]

As early as 1929, in his important book *Modern Architecture,* Taut had been critical of the tendency to fetishize stripped-down technique and function and had objected to the reduction of modern rational design to "a stylistic zeitgeist," as he called the canonic ocean-liner aesthetic of Le Corbusier. The writings and work of Turkish architects in the 1930s suggest that they had internalized much more of Taut's teaching than they typically acknowledged. In spite of their "functionalist and rationalist" arguments, which fared well with Kemalist positivism, aesthetics had a strong presence in the discourse of the Turkish architects gathered around *Mimar.* They were, however, quite insightfully aware that the best definition of a modernist aesthetic was that it could not be defined beyond generalities such as "geometric," "abstract," and "undecorated." Unlike classical styles, which could be codified into fixed orders and motifs, a modernist aesthetic was one that you knew only when you saw it. In 1933, Behçet Sabri and Bedrettin Hamdi's words captured this basic premise of modernism, connecting it, however, to a larger zeitgeist argument: "Souls have changed, life has changed, and a new era has dawned. This new spirit has left the old repertoire of columns, arches, capitals, pedestals, and entablatures behind and has thrust itself into the world of masses and volumes. The architecture of today, which we call 'modern,' is a harmonious totality of simple, beautiful, geometric shapes dissociated from traditional motifs."[50]

Herein lies the ambiguity of the aesthetic discourse of New Architecture in the Turkish architectural culture of the 1930s. As was emphasized on every occasion, it was supposed to be an aesthetic arising out of rational considerations (of site, program, construction, materials, climate, context, etc.) rather than predetermined stylistic choices. This simply meant that modern architecture was formally indeterminate, irreducible to any a priori form. This was a very insightful position for the 1930s. As architectural historians who have deconstructed the "myths of the Modern Movement" or the "fictions of function" in European modernism have shown in recent years, rational considerations of function and technique are always inadequate as determinants of form.[51] So how is one to account for the "harmonious composition of simple geometric shapes" or the pervasiveness of "the cantilevers, the rounded corners, the circular windows"? An answer that can be tentatively proposed is that there was a certain aesthetic repertoire of modernism in the 1930s that circulated in architectural culture at large and informed the work of Turkish architects as well. Despite their insistence on talking about buildings in strictly technical and functional terms when they wrote in *Mimar,* they could not explain the recurrent aesthetic features so common to the work of the 1930s in those terms alone. This does not mean that wherever these aesthetic features were employed, the designs were not functional or technically sound. It simply means that there is always a margin of indeterminacy between aesthetics and functionalist-rationalist explanations of form. In its eagerness to lend credibility and authority to the New Architecture, the discourse of the 1930s rarely, if ever, addressed that margin.

Let us look at a few of these aesthetic choices. A most immediately recognizable one was a particular composition that combined a long horizontal block or group of horizontal blocks with a prominent vertical element, a clock tower or a chimney. Rounding one or both ends of the horizontal block was an additional feature that enhanced the perceived modernity of the building, perhaps with distant allusions to a ship or ocean liner. Three important and extensively published buildings of the 1930s in Ankara illustrate this particular aesthetic at its most refined expression: the Exhibition Hall (1933), the filter station (*su süzgeci*) of Çubuk Dam (1936), and the casino-restaurant of the new railway station (1937) (fig. 4.6). Three buildings with vastly different functions shared a common aesthetic idiom that made them distinctly "republican" in their iconography. Possible sources of this aesthetic idiom were the numerous contemporary European buildings reproduced in publications, as well as architects' "intertextual" references to each other's recent work. These forms would not have been so successfully imported and circulated, however, if it had not been for their connotations of progress, modernity, and industry (especially through allusions to ships, factory chimneys, and undecorated machine forms) so cherished by republican ideology. Whatever the specific ideas and images in the minds of their

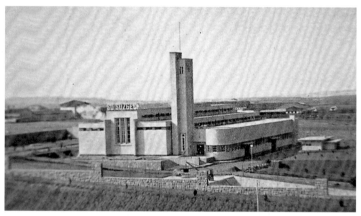

Fig. 4.6. Horizontal blocks with rounded corners juxtaposed with vertical towers: the pervasiveness of a particular formal and aesthetic vocabulary in early republican architecture, often independent of function and program. **Top:** Ankara Exhibition Hall (1933–34). **Middle:** The water filter station of the Çubuk Dam (1935). **Bottom:** The restaurant-casino of the Ankara Railroad Station (1937).

Fig. 4.7. The repetition of a particular formal type: school buildings with rounded corners and corner entrance. **Top:** The Agricultural School in Izmir (1932), designed in the architectural offices of the Ministry of Agriculture. **Bottom:** Gazi Elementary School (1934), also in Izmir, designed by Necmeddin Emre.

Fig. 4.8. The so-called Ankara cubic or Viennese cubic style of Ankara's major public buildings. **Top:** Officers' Club (1929–1933), by Clemenz Holzmeister. **Bottom:** Court of Financial Appeals (1928–1930), by Ernst Egli. The inverted **T**-shaped projections of Holzmeister and the cubic window projections of Egli were distinct leitmotifs of this style.

architects, these buildings clearly embodied richer references and associations than mere responses to the programmatic requirements of exhibition space, water filtration, and public entertainment, respectively.

If the initial sources of some of these aesthetic choices were European, their particular interpretation and repeated use in a particular city or for a particular program suggest that certain formal vocabularies circulated among architects within Turkey as well. For example, a very specific way of entering a building through a rounded corner into a circular space appears to have been a recurring approach for buildings housing official RPP functions and located on corner lots, even with different scales, sites, and constructional constraints. The Yalova RPP Headquarters and People's House (1934) by Sedad Çetintaş and the winning entry for the Sivas RPP Headquarters and People's House competition (1939) by Emin Necip Uzman and Nazif Asal shared this particular formal arrangement in spite of their very different sizes, locations, and budgets (see fig. 2.25). Similarly, the rounded corner entrance of the Agricultural School (Ziraat Mektebi) in Izmir (1932), designed by the office of the Ministry of Agriculture, was repeated in almost identical fashion in the Gazi Elementary School (Gazi İlk Mektebi) in the same city (1934) by Necmeddin Emre (fig. 4.7).[52]

Fig. 4.9. Influence of the "Ankara cubic" on Turkish architects: the Directorate of State Monopolies administration building (1935) in Konya, by Tahir Tuğ, employing Holzmeister's inverted **T** projections. Tahir Tuğ designed for the directorate in other cities as well, employing the same style, as in the case of his State Monopolies administration building in Antalya (1934) with Egli's cubic window projections.

Fig. 4.10. The modernist formal repertoire of villas and rental houses in Istanbul in the 1930s. Flat roofs, rounded corners and projections, wide terraces, cantilevers, and metal railings were the main features. **Top:** Villa in Bebek by Edip Erbilen. **Middle:** Villa in Bağlarbaşı by Münci Tangör. **Bottom:** Rental house in Erenköy by Abidin Mortaş.

On the other hand, many public buildings of the early republic employed the formal language of the so-called Viennese school, or the "Ankara cubic," which had little to do with the canonic aesthetic of the Modern Movement. They showed a characteristic play of cubic and rectangular volumes on the plain façades of otherwise classically conceived, static, axial, and often symmetrical buildings. The spatial "flows," free plans, and free façades championed by the Modern Movement were conspicuously absent in many such "modern" buildings of the 1930s, which were largely influenced by the work of foreign architects in Ankara, Holzmeister and Egli in particular (fig. 4.8). The works of Tahir Tuğ—for example, his Directorate of State Monopolies administration buildings (Tekel İdare Binası) in Antalya (1934) and Konya (1935) (fig. 4.9)—are characteristic examples, with the trademark "inverted T" projections of window bays used extensively by Holzmeister. As I mentioned earlier, many student projects in the academy adopted the cubic projections as well as the "classical" elements such as tall orders, loggias, and colonnades that Ernst Egli introduced at the end of the 1920s (see fig. 4.2). This pervasive "surface modernism" testifies to a unique set of aesthetic considerations—the effects of projections and

Fig. 4.11. A pervasive modernist feature of the 1930s architectural culture at large: apartment buildings in Istanbul with rounded corners. **Left:** Tüten Apartmanı, 1936, by Adil Denktaş. **Right:** Apartment building in Taksim, 1938, by Seyfi Arkan.

recessions on façades, light and shade, proportions, and so forth—that cannot be explained by functional or technical criteria alone, nor exclusively by imported aesthetic notions. Drawing on everything from the individual personalities of the foreign architects who brought these features to Turkey to the distinct textures and colors of Ankara's local stone, this was a modernism particular to republican Ankara.

As will be discussed in more detail in the next chapter, residential architecture was the one domain in which some of the more canonic modern forms and features (such as flat roofs, circular windows, wide terraces, cantilevers, and rounded corners) were most visible (fig. 4.10).[53] Apartment buildings with the 1930s streamlined aesthetic based on the rounded corner became a special trademark of the early republican period; many of them still stand distinctly amid the otherwise eclectic urban fabric of Istanbul (fig. 4.11). With major public commissions typically going to foreign architects, young Turkish architects turned to the design of houses and apartments as their primary field of activity. Wanting to be more "modernist" than their modernist European teachers and colleagues, they often resorted to these formal signifiers of modernity. In their overall effect, these houses and apartments, which combined European influences with local constructional realities, constituted a distinct and recognizable aesthetic that we might call "modernism in the margins." It is an aesthetic similar, for example, to that of the better-publicized residential structures built in eastern Europe or in Tel Aviv during the 1930s.[54] The same flat roofs, rounded corners, continuous balconies, circular windows, and badly aging, plastered surfaces over rather heavy cubic volumes can be observed in houses of the 1930s in Budapest, Ankara, and Tel Aviv alike.

Recurrent formal elements point to the existence of a budding but effective architectural culture in Turkey, with its own aesthetic idioms and formal vocabulary that were reproduced and disseminated through competitions, publications, and emerging professional networks. Although the canonization of "international style" was criticized, the modern forms just mentioned were internalized by the architects who wrote in *Mimar* and *Arkitekt*. Any suggestion that Turkish architects should look not toward these modern forms but toward traditional Turkish elements and motifs was seen as a potential challenge to the modernist consensus and warranted a response. In 1933, for example, at the height of the enthusiasm over the New Architecture, an architect identified as B. O. Celal wrote an essay criticizing the aesthetic canons of "international style" from the point of view of a "national essence." Arguing that "the national essence" refused to melt away despite the increasingly international needs and lifestyles of the times, Celal wrote:

In the decorative and architectural richness of Turkish art, one can certainly find fresh and hitherto untapped sources—elegant, simple, soft motifs. When there are so many rich sources, what kind of logic would copy the deck of an ocean liner or an air control tower or an Assyrian portal stripped of its ornaments? Yes, conservativism does hinder the artist and impede progress, but aimless and unnecessary freedom makes the artist devoid of belief and inspiration.[55]

Although the essay was published in *Mimar,* the editors included a disclaimer that "the position of the journal pertaining to questions of national architecture [is] different from that of the author."

In many built examples of the 1930s, Turkish architects' insistence on functional criteria alone to explain their designs did little justice to the aesthetic qualities of the designs themselves. As we know through more recent critical histories of modernism, "technical determinism" is not a tenable explanation of modern form even in Europe, where industrialization, standardization, and serialized production constituted a real material basis for modernist claims. The unified aesthetic of the Modern Movement (as in the canonic Weissenhof Siedlung, for example) had in fact concealed different methods of construction underneath the surface finishing: some buildings of load-bearing brick, others of reinforced concrete, and yet others of precast concrete panels assembled on site.[56] In Turkey, the conspicuous absence of an industrialized basis for the New Architecture was a further indication that modern forms *preceded* advanced industrial building methods rather than being "logical consequences" of them, as modernist discourse claimed.

For most of the 1930s, the state of the building industry in Turkey was very poor. There were only a few cement factories and no domestic production of iron and steel until 1937. A 1927 law encouraging industrial investments (Teşvik-i Sanayi Kanunu) had offered incentives to private businesses to produce building materials, but it had also allowed the duty-free importation of building materials not produced in Turkey. The primary materials of reinforced concrete construction—cement and steel—were imported. So were the insulation materials for flat roofs (*ruberoid* and *ksilolit,* in particular), major construction equipment and machinery (such as cement mixers), and European finishing materials and fixtures (tiles, kitchen and bathroom fixtures, pipes, boilers, floor finishes, electrical fixtures, etc.) (fig. 4.12). İnci Aslanoğlu writes that "gypsum came from Germany, tiles and pressed brick from France, marble from Italy, lift cabins from Italy and Austria, and parquet flooring from Russia."[57] The high cost of importing building materials and transporting them across the country were major impediments to the proliferation of the New Architecture beyond important public buildings.

Most important of all, there were no major large-scale experiments in rationalized building production and the manufacture of precast, prefabricated building components. These experiments, which modernist architects considered to be a defining feature of the New Architecture everywhere, were at best seriously limited in scope and practical application in Turkey. Leading architects in the profession were aware of these limitations. "The essence of the new spirit and inspiration is serialized building production and standardization," wrote Zeki Sayar in the first issue of

Fig. 4.12. Advertisements from the 1930s for imported building materials, construction equipment, and architectural products. Promotions for the Turkish representatives of Blankenburg radiators, boilers, and heating equipment (**top**), Otto Kaiser concrete mixers (**middle**), and various European and American brands of locks, hardware, and fixtures (**bottom**).

Fig. 4.13. Construction of the Sümerbank building, Ankara (1937). The photograph reflects the primitive conditions of the construction industry even for a building of this size and importance.

Mimar, something that would be possible only "when a strong and well-organized [source of] capital ventures into this task."[58] He explained the benefits and efficiency of industrialized building production that would release the construction process from the constraints of seasonal workers and laborious crafts. Elsewhere in his arguments against prototype designs for school buildings, he reiterated the belief that rather than authorizing standard plans, regulations should standardize industrially produced building materials, components, and fixtures, leaving the designs to the creative intervention of the architect.

Sayar's longing for the establishment of standards for materials and workmanship and for the rationalized organization of the building process remained largely unfulfilled in Turkey until well into the 1950s. The earlier history of modern architecture in the West, especially the important debates and initiatives to reform design education in conformity with the transition from crafts to industrial production, was conspicuously absent in the Turkish context. Various arts and crafts movements in different countries—the *Werkstatte* in Austria and the *Kunstgewerbe* and *Werkbund* in Germany—had no Turkish counterparts, and this has been the single most important handicap of Turkish modernism. Not only were the primary materials of reinforced concrete construction imported, but also skilled workmanship in casting and pouring concrete, assembling imported components and fixtures on site, and using new construction machinery was extremely scarce at best. Construction photographs of Martin Elsaesser's Sümerbank headquarters building in Ankara (1937), one of the major nationalist state monuments of the 1930s, shows how primitive the building process was, even in the case of a major public building of this scale and importance (fig. 4.13).

One highly publicized attempt to remedy the workmanship situation was the establishment of the Building Trade School (Amele Mektebi) in Ankara in 1932.[59] Students were admitted after elementary school and received four-year training in the four major branches of the traditional crafts: masonry (including brick-laying), carpentry (including woodworking), plastering, and stonecutting (fig. 4.14). The curriculum included some theory (math, accounting, and technical subjects), drawing, model making, and full-scale demonstrations. It was conceived as a boarding school with a full range of facilities (dormitories, dining hall, health center, and sports), and there was an emphasis on military discipline and cleanliness. As the director of the school proudly explained in 1938, the graduating young men were in high demand, "alleviating the ongoing dependence on Hungarian and Bulgarian craftsmen, which had been particularly widespread during the construction of Ankara in the early 1930s."[60] However, the dependence on Hungarian and Bulgarian craftsmen was not completely eliminated during the early republican period. In fact, a year after the director of the school gave this interview, a Hungarian craftsman was appointed to the faculty of the school to train Turkish masons and bricklayers.[61]

Builders trained in this school were employed in the construction of important public buildings of the late 1930s, including Bruno Taut's Faculty of Humanities building (1938) (see fig. 2.9). The demonstration exhibition of the Building Trade School was featured in *Arkitekt*, which praised the school's program as an important step toward "responding to the modern architect's need for qualified workmen who can read architects' drawings, understand the details and specifications, and apply them correctly."[62] Ultimately, however, the school was inadequate to meet the growing demand, and its focus on traditional crafts left the problem of workmanship in reinforced concrete and new materials still unaddressed.

The aesthetic discourse of the New Architecture in Turkey is itself a testimony to the limitations of the building industry. In most of the "modern" buildings, the use of reinforced concrete was limited to the structure, the floor slabs, and the cantilevers, with infill walls in brick and sometimes stone. The openings were small, the wooden door and window frames were cumbersome and thick, and the overall formal expression was heavy. Flat roofs were technically problematical (as they were in many other parts of the world in non-Mediterranean climates), and in many cases they were later covered over with a pitched tile roof. Except in some unbuilt projects (see fig. 5.17), the canonic aesthetic of the Modern Movement—large glass walls, long horizontal windows, free plans with lighter and more transparent construction—were simply impossible with the available materials and workmanship. The modern forms of buildings in Turkey in the 1930s were neither simple extensions of the European Modern Movement nor "logical consequences" of the new materials and construction

Fig. 4.14. Training workers in masonry (**top**) and brick-laying (**bottom**) at the newly established Building Trade School in Ankara, which started its program in 1932. Photographs circa 1938.

techniques of the industrial age that were supposed to determine these forms. They were largely *representations* of an imported modernity without the industrial, institutional, and economic transformations of building production that made modern architecture possible and plausible in Europe. Hence, while "looking like" modernist work from European countries, they inevitably embodied local constructional constraints as well as the background, cultural visions, and aesthetic choices of individual designers.

Moreover, by 1939 the initially exalted representational function of modernism had largely fulfilled its "revolutionary" mission, and the New Architecture was becoming increasingly suspect on both pragmatic and ideological grounds. The increased scarcity and speculative high cost of imported building materials due to the effects of World War II aggravated the difficulties of building modern. The import-dependent construction in reinforced concrete was criticized in favor of local materials and traditional construction techniques in wood, brick, and stone. Combined with rising nationalism after Atatürk's death in 1938, the aesthetic discourse of the New Architecture was gradually transformed in ways that will be explored in chapter 6.

Living Modern

CUBIC HOUSES AND APARTMENTS

> Hakkı Bey took the lead in the idea of the house as in any other matter and showed the first example of the cubic. The first house with glass corners, lacquered doors, and punctured ceilings that accommodated hidden electrical installations belonged to him. [He] took a hidden pride in this. Especially on days when he first showed off the rooms and halls, furnished according to the illustrations in the latest exhibition catalogs from Paris or Berlin, he was like a child delighted over his new outfits. Couches like dentists' chairs, seats like operation tables, sofas resembling the interiors of automobiles, octagonal tables, closets like grain storage bins, display windows . . . naked walls, naked floors . . . and a clinical gloss on everything.
> —Yakup Kadri Karaosmanoğlu, *Ankara,* 1934[1]

THE TRANSFORMATION OF upper-class domestic culture and family life along European models predated the Westernizing reforms of the Kemalist republic by at least half a century. European (and more specifically French) culture, table manners, tastes, and bourgeois decorum had penetrated the houses of Istanbul's commercial and bureaucratic elite from the Tanzimat reforms of 1839 onward. The "Europeanization" of educated Ottoman bureaucrats, intellectuals, and officers, and the manifestation of this in the way they lived, dressed, furnished their houses, and appeared in public, has been a major literary and cultural trope of Turkish modernization.[2] In many cases, the interiors of upper-class houses of the late Ottoman Empire were a highly cosmopolitan mix of cultures and tastes. They reflected, for example, the cluttered coexistence of Parisian dressing tables and mirrors with oriental carpets and handcrafted, mother-of-pearl-inlaid and geometrically decorated "Islamic" furniture. Paul Dumont's reconstruction of the daily life of Said Bey, a typical Europeanized Ottoman bureaucrat of the late nineteenth century, through the latter's own documents and notes gives us a vivid picture of the domestic interior in this period. The contents of Said Bey's house in the Aksaray district of Istanbul are described as follows:

The modern and occidental was intimately intermingled in it with the traditional furniture of the Turkish house. For instance, in 1902, Said Bey was in the process of paying for a blue stoneware stove, probably imported from France. But at the same time we note that he is purchasing a brazier (*mangal*) and a kind of little charcoal stove (*maltız*). We also know that his house contained a mass of Turkish style sofas, but simultaneously we find among the purchases made by Said Bey several large *canapés,* armchairs, chairs, a pier-table, a European bed (*karyola*) and also a sewing machine, a phonograph, a telescope, and many other objects such as cases, chandeliers etc. all aiming to give the house a European style. The most prestigious piece of furniture of the family, purchased in 1902, was a piano, a perfect symbol of adherence to Western values.[3]

Deeper and more significant than the acquisition of new tastes, habits, and furnishings, however, were the beginnings of important social and cultural transformations affecting the private sphere. As Cem Behar and Alain Duben have shown in their extensive study of Istanbul households on the eve of the republican period,[4] European concepts of family, marriage, and domesticity had entered upper-class life in Turkey around the turn of the century. Most significantly, an emerging trend had appeared toward the "democratization of the family," with a new emphasis on the conjugal couple as companions and a new interest in the health and upbringing of children. Behar and Duben considered these changes between 1880 and 1940 to have been a major component of the "civilizational shift" in Turkey:

The powerful social forces which transformed a great Islamic empire into a secular republic also reverberated in the rhythms of ordinary family life. The family, marriage, women, children and the mundane, taken-for-granted routines of daily domestic life became focal points in the great drama of political and cultural transformation then taking place. Though the "big stakes" were to be played out in the political arena, it was at home that the revolution was to be lived in all its prosaic glory.[5]

In a situation unique among contemporary Muslim societies, transformations in conceptions of the family and the house, increasing criticism of polygamy and arranged marriages, and new efforts to improve women's education and entry into the workforce were important elements of Turkish modernization even before the republic. By 1923, when the republic was proclaimed, the demise of the traditional extended family in favor of smaller households was already a fact of life in Istanbul (although extended family ties have never completely waned in Turkey). Prevailing concepts of residential space were being revised accordingly, and the traditional gender-based *haremlik-selamlık* (women's and men's quarters) divisions of space were already disappearing from the homes of the better off. The old wooden *konaks* (large,

single-family houses) within gardens—those centuries-old cultural icons of traditional Turkish *Wohnkultur*, or domestic culture—were no longer adequate to represent
the aspirations of a Westernized Istanbul elite in the late empire.

In other words, as Behar and Duben remind us, modernized—that is,
Westernized—lifestyles and small nuclear families did not appear suddenly with the
republican reforms; the reforms merely coincided with societal changes already under
way in Turkey.[6] What distinguished the early republican period from the preceding era
was the radicalness, the totalizing character, and the strong ideological charge of the
Kemalist "civilizational shift" toward a thoroughly Westernized, modern, and secular
society. As I mentioned in chapter 2, the status and image of women were central to
this project, and important institutional changes were initiated on this front. The
1926 civil code established the legal framework for abolishing polygamy and giving
women the right to initiate divorce, inherit property, and seek education and professional careers. Effectively, the 1926 reform extended the Westernizing agenda of the
state into family life and private space. Nilufer Göle argues that Kemalism was unique
among comparable political movements precisely because "it [was] the only one that
interfered with family law, the sphere most resistant to Westernization" and, in the
case of Muslim societies, the sphere symbolized by the veiling and segregation of
women.[7]

Under republican ideology, the new conceptions of family, marriage, and child
rearing that had been spreading since the Young Turk era were articulated in exclusively Westernized formal expressions, claiming a radical break with what preceded
them. Architecture and interior design were, by their nature, integral aspects of this
agenda: the making of a new, modern, and Western domestic culture became a central preoccupation of the 1930s. The very idea of "home" in the larger context of
modern urban life was presented as a republican concept par excellence. One recurrent line of argument was that under the Ottoman Empire, the wars and expeditions
of the sultans deprived the people of stable and settled lives. According to a popular
magazine in 1938, an evidence of this predicament was the ephemerality of the materials used in residential architecture, such as wood in towns and cities and mud brick
in villages. "Having decided to eternally inhabit these lands," the article said with
pride, "the Turkish nation is now building her houses in stone and concrete" and
beginning to learn the idea of what makes a dwelling: "For the European, the house
is a special and private place reflecting his individuality. In our country, the idea of the
house is barely beginning to emerge as a special institution and organization following this higher [European] level of civilization. Like many other good things in life,
the Turkish citizen is getting to know the idea of the house only now, in the republican period."[8]

Throughout the 1930s, the words "modern" (*modern*) and "contemporary" (*asri*)
were used synonymously to designate all the novelty, progressiveness, and desirable
qualities of the new culture of living in modern houses and apartments. As the image
of the small nuclear family (with a working husband and father, an enlightened wife

and mother, and their healthy child or children) was elevated to a national ideal, the physical space of the home, too, was represented in a more unequivocally modern (read Western) expression. This modern *Wohnkultur* was almost invariably juxtaposed with what architects depicted as the contrasting image of the "*konak* and *köşk* life in which mothers, fathers, daughters, and sons-in-law all lived together."[9] As the architect Behçet Ünsal put it, lifestyles were changing, and "our large wooden houses with spacious *sofas* [halls] are no longer appropriate."[10] To be truly modern, Turkey could not be left behind the imperatives of the times, and the transformation had to begin at home.

The private dwelling and daily life of Said Bey, our typical turn-of-the-century Ottoman bureaucrat, displayed a fascinating blend of Western ways with old customs, habits, and domestic objects. By contrast, the new bureaucrat of the 1930s, Hakkı Bey—the character in Yakup Kadri Karaosmanoğlu's classic novel *Ankara* (1934)—epitomized the total Westernization of lifestyles for which modern architecture was both a container and a powerful statement. In the novel, Hakkı Bey commissions one of the first "cubic houses" and furnishes it with abstract, geometric furniture of metal and glass, reflecting the latest trends in European modernism. The difference between Said Bey's domestic setting and Hakkı Bey's symbolically represents the new ideological charge acquired by architecture and interior design in the transition from empire to republic. Architecture was an "agent of civilization" not only in the public space of the nation, as we have seen in previous chapters, but also in the most intimate domestic space of the family.

The emerging architectural profession seized this opportunity with enthusiasm. Through the design of houses and interiors, people's existing habits, lifestyles, and worldviews could be transformed along the precepts of Kemalism, and in the process, the status and legitimacy of architects would be greatly enhanced. While they criticized the commissioning of major public buildings to their European teachers and colleagues, Turkish designers claimed residential architecture as their primary territory. They referred extensively to the modernist discourse on issues of dwelling and housing that dominated European architectural culture in the interwar period. In their writings, they presented the provision of adequate and well-designed housing as the central problem of modern, industrial societies and advocated the rationalization of designs and production methods following European examples.

A big gap existed, however, between imported theory and the realities of early republican Turkey. The poor state of the building industry, the absence of an autonomous bourgeoisie and a strong private sector, and the priority that the state placed on public buildings and nationalist policies rather than on housing and the welfare of individual citizens all contributed to the frustration of architects' ideals. As İhsan Bilgin rightly observes, until the 1950s houses were built in Turkey as a result of either limited, singular architect-client relationships or special state or philanthropic initiatives in response to the housing needs of a specific group, such as government employees.[11] In either case, the dwelling was not an anonymous commodity produced within the market mechanisms of a modern society. In this sense, even when houses had a "modern" appearance and suggested "modern" lifestyles, they did not represent a social and historical "modernity."

The primacy of exterior form was nowhere as evident as in the "cubic house" and "cubic apartment," examples of which proliferated in the 1930s as visual markers of thoroughly transformed, Westernized, and secularized lifestyles until the nationalist criticism of such lifestyles began in the late 1930s. What follows in this chapter is an account of how architects sought to tackle the issue of the modern house within the cultural, professional, and technological context of the Kemalist revolution.

Images of Modern Domestic Life

THE REPUBLICAN DISCOURSE on the modern house was, before everything else, an extension of the nationalist emphasis on the nuclear family, especially on motherhood as a national duty and the family home as the sacred space or "hearth" of national regeneration. Marriage was encouraged and exalted in contemporary publications,[12] and the rearing of healthy, robust children was idealized into a patriotic theme. Parallels between the republican discourse of the 1930s and the "nationalization of women" in Fascist Italy and Nazi Germany are hard to miss.[13] Especially in Italy, which Turkish architects looked upon as a model, the architectural discourse on the modern house went hand in hand with the idealization of marriage and motherhood under fascism.[14] Like their counterparts in Italy, Turkish popular publications presented modern, hygienic, and rationally planned homes as the breeding ground of a youthful, healthy, and patriotic nation. The single-family dwelling became an instrument of the republican project as nationalist publications propagated the idea that "the need for a healthy living and healthy body is not an individualistic concern but a social and national need."[15]

In what is an apparent paradox in the Kemalist claim to having "liberated" Turkish women from the yoke of tradition, the idealized image of the Turkish woman remained that of an enlightened wife, mother, and companion whose world was centered on the home. At the same time that women made their much-publicized and celebrated appearances in public life, public space, and varied professions, many prominent republican intellectuals scorned the idea of a woman's life being centered in the workplace, outside the home. In a series of essays on the ideal "modern Turkish woman," Peyami Safa criticized the overconfident "masculinized" woman for both her appearance and her mentality.[16] Though he emphasized the need "to open wide the windows of the house and the mind of the Turkish girl to the outside, to nature and to society," he nonetheless added:

Some fools talk as if the Turkish revolution intends to move the Turkish girl's center of operation [karargah] from home to the street. They talk as if hatred of family, hatred of marriage,

and hatred of children are the primary features of modern sensibility. . . . From time immemorial, every woman's center of operation has been her home: so will it be for the modern
Turkish girl and woman. Through sun, air, books, and radio, this center, this home, will
be flooded with all the amenities, interests, and excitement of both nature and the society
outside.[17]

Similarly, Hüseyin Cahit Yalçın celebrated the woman as "a homemaker" above
all and lamented the loss of femininity when some women became aggressively com-
petitive with men in professional careers outside the home. At the same time, he
desired the modern Turkish woman to be "a homemaker who is also a socialite, a
friend, companion, and lover for the husband," different from the uneducated and
traditional Ottoman woman of the past.[18] It is important to note that this emphasis on companionship was a new and progressive standard for its time, encouraged
and welcomed by many educated Turkish men and women alike. "Beauty and vanity
should go hand in hand with homemaking," Hüseyin Cahit Yalçın wrote, "and both
are in the service of making the woman a companion and lover for her husband within the family nest. The woman's personality and being can be complete only when she
is *elevated* [my emphasis] to this much-deserved status in family life."[19] This is an
important nuance frequently overlooked in critical commentaries on the otherwise
patriarchal nature of the republican view of modern women and domesticity.

While Kemalist women took pride in their newly acquired legal rights and public
visibility outside the home, there is also evidence that many of them embraced this
new image of the home-bound wife-companion with enthusiasm. That "they volun-
tarily preferred it to working outside the home" probably says more about the views
of male commentators in republican magazines than about the actual preferences of
women themselves.[20] Nonetheless, the concept of woman as homemaker was articulated in terms of the most progressive ideas of the time. The idealized image of the
"family nest" (*aile yuvası*), as it was often called, was that of a beautiful, comfortable,
simple, and practical modern house, tastefully and economically arranged by the
wife's skills as a homemaker. It was a "warm refuge" for the husband who, after coming home from work, "could dine on the terrace with [his] elegant wife and beautiful
child," as it was described in a family magazine featuring a model design (with plan
and perspectives) for a "summer villa" (fig. 5.1).[21]

The education of girls in this direction—the making of young, educated, patriotic Kemalist women who would be enlightened wives and mothers—was one of the
highest priorities of the regime. It gave modern Turkey one of the most paradigmatic
institutions of republican history: the girls' institutes (*kız enstitüleri*) established by
the Ministry of Education in 1928–1929 and mostly housed in buildings with a modernist aesthetic (see chapter 2). The curricula of the girls' institutes combined the
emphasis on "national culture" with a rigorous education in "scientific housework."
They were pioneers in the introduction of Taylorist principles to housework, and in
the preparation of their curricula, Christine Frederick's *The New Housekeeping*

Fig. 5.1. "A Summer Villa," article published in the popular magazine *Yenigün* (1930). Part of the text reads, "Here is a place of happiness: an economical, beautiful, and airy home. The bedroom gets plenty of sunlight, and as is well known, where there is plenty of sunlight there one does not need a doctor. You can dine on the terrace with your elegant wife and beautiful child, and after dinner you can relax on the chaise-longue chatting with your wife."

(1913) was a frequently quoted source. Courses focused on the rational organization of domestic space and on appropriate work schedules to increase household efficiency and productivity.[22] In the familiar "old versus new" format, contrasts were drawn between the "badly arranged kitchens" of traditional homes and the "properly arranged" model kitchens demonstrated to students at the institutes.

This comparison between the inefficiency of the old ways and the enormous savings in time and energy afforded by the rationally organized new kitchen was a central theme in the modernist architectural culture of the interwar period in Europe. In Germany in 1929 it was made into a propaganda film for the New Frankfurt socialist housing schemes of Ernst May, which incorporated the ultra-efficient, laboratory-like "Frankfurter Küche" designed by Margarete Schütte-Lihotzky (1897–1999).[23] Schütte-Lihotzky, who also wrote the paradigmatic *Rationalisierung im Haushalt* and introduced domestic Taylorism to Weimar Germany in the 1920s, was a major link between developments in Germany and the Turkish experiment with girls' institutes. She worked for the Turkish Ministry of Education between 1938 and 1940, designing prototype grade schools for Anatolian villages and an unbuilt project for an extension to the Girls' Lycée in Ankara (see fig. 2.17).[24] Similarly, the prominent German architect Bruno Taut, who dedicated his book *Die Neue Wohnung: Die Frau Als Schöpferin* (1925) to women, worked for the Turkish Ministry of Education from 1936 until his death in 1938. In his book, Taut, too, advocated the rational planning of the house to save women from the endless toil of cooking, cleaning, and washing that took place in traditional homes.[25] Although neither Schütte-Lihotzky nor Taut was acknowledged by name in the popular magazines oriented toward women, their ideas on the efficiency of a rationally planned domestic space made their way into these publications (fig. 5.2).

Unlike the socialist Weimar experiments, however, in which the rationalization of the household was oriented primarily toward liberating women into the workforce, in Turkey the idea of a woman's life being centered on the workplace, outside the home, was still anathema to republican ideology. The task of the girls' institutes was not to question women's primary vocation as homemakers but simply to make this vocation more "scientific" (*fenni*) and "contemporary" (*asri*). It is interesting to observe that in Turkey it was not the architects but women themselves who first popularized the Taylorist ideas that inspired the modernist avant-garde in Europe in the 1920s. In the girls' institutes, an entire generation of urban middle-class women was educated in "rational methods" of cooking, cleaning, washing, ironing, sewing, and child rearing. They made daily, weekly, and monthly schedules and followed meticulous charts and timetables to organize the housework. They followed "precise measurements rather than guesswork" for their recipes, from which they learned how to make European-style fruit pies, cakes, sauces, and soufflés unknown in their mothers' traditional cooking. Following time-and-motion studies, they learned the most efficient movements for dishwashing and ironing, criticizing the dated methods of their mothers. Nowhere is the "old versus new" construct more evident than in the self-perception of

Mutfak, bir ev kadınının salonu demektir. Bu tabirden kadın okuyucularımız'ın gücenmemelerini rica ederiz. Bir ev kadınının mevkii içtimaîsi nekadar mühim ve yüksek olursa olsun evinin mutfağı ile alâkası vardır.

Ayrupada ve bilhassa Amerikada hizmetçi buhranı yüzünden ev hizmeti, ve mutfak işleri kâmilen ev kadınının üzerine düşmüştür. Geçenlerde İngiltereye giden bir Fransız muharriresi İngiliz ricalinden Baldvin'in zevcesini evinin mutfağında görmüş, ve gıpta etmiş. Geçen sayımızda da İsveçli bir prensesin mutfağında çıkarmış bir fotoğrafını dercetmiştik. Demek istiyoruz ki ev kadınının mutfağında iş görmesi pek

tabiî ve lâzım bir şeydir.

Şimdi ev kadınının günün muayyen saatlerini geçirmek mecburiyettnde olduğu mutfağın şeklinden ve taksimatından bahse-

Fig. 5.2. A modern kitchen from the "Home and Furniture" section of the popular republican weekly *Yedigün* (1933). The layout and concept (**top**) display conspicuous similarities to the rationalized, ultra-efficient, laboratory-like kitchen designs produced in Germany by modernist architects, especially the famous "Frankfurt kitchen" of Margarete Schütte-Lihotzky (1929) (**bottom**).

Fig. 5.3. Cover of the first issue of *Muhit,* an "illustrated family magazine" (1928). Such popular publications were instrumental in disseminating images of modern, healthy, Western lifestyles for women and family.

these young women, whose new scientific outlook radically separated them from previous generations. In her study of the girls' institutes, Yael Navaro cites an essay subtitled "Taylorism in Our Homes," by a student at the Izmir Girls' Institute who likened the "disorganized and dirty" kitchens of the old Ottoman home to a "village grocery store rather than a proper kitchen." She contrasted it with the new Turkish home, in which the neatly and rationally arranged kitchen displayed "calorie charts, timetables, and budget boards."[26]

The role of popular family and women's magazines in promoting modern architecture was significant. They were the first to publish illustrated articles on modern concepts of domestic space, household efficiency and hygiene, modern lifestyles, and modern house design, even before *Mimar*, the professional journal of architects, was launched in 1931. These articles and illustrations were often translated and adapted from Western magazines such as *Ladies' Home Journal*, *Women's Home Companion*, and *Scherl's Magazine*, and they appeared along with pages of fashion, recipes, and essays on table manners, scientific home management, and child rearing (fig. 5.3). Through these magazines, architecture and interior design assumed a pedagogical role as teachers of "civilized" lifestyles. Such "illustrated family magazines" (*resimli aile mecmuası*), as they were called, including *Muhit*, *Yedigün*, *Yenigün*, *Modern Türkiye Mecmuası*, and *İnkilap*, often featured a special section on "contemporary homes" in which the quality of contemporariness (*asrilik*) was elevated to a self-justifying and scientific ideal. These sections included descriptions and drawings of model designs with plans and elevations, photographs of real buildings, and instructions on decorating and furnishing a modern home and living "in style." For example, *Muhit*'s architectural editor, Samih Saim, wrote: "Home is one of the most important topics that a family magazine should deal with. At the same time, home is the quintessential topic of this century. Family leaders [*aile reisi*] who dream of a home often lack the necessary technical and esthetical information to realize these dreams. In this new page of our magazine, they will meet the architect every month and learn about beautiful, functional, healthy, and economic houses matching their budgets."[27]

As early as 1929, in the aftermath of the completion of the canonic Villa Savoie, Le Corbusier's work and ideas were popularized through these magazines (fig. 5.4).[28] At about the same time that Müderris İsmail Hakkı made his historical and philosophical arguments for the appropriateness of "cubic architecture" (see chapters 3 and 4), *Muhit* introduced "A Cubic House" in the "Practical, Economical, and Healthy Houses" section of the magazine (fig. 5.4).[29] Featured with the description, photographs, and plans of a house in Frankfurt designed by Otto Haesler, it was presented as "a type of house that will be unfamiliar to the eyes of our readers, a type that we do not yet encounter in our country." The zeitgeist argument was captured in one sentence: "Today architecture has found its true meaning in *cubic*," wrote Samih Saim, "which, while looking simple and plain, represents the entire aesthetic and scientific progress of our age." The "geometric plan" of the house was explained in

 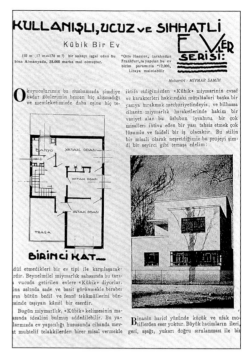

Fig. 5.4. Introduction of the Modern Movement to Turkey through popular publications and illustrated family magazines. **Left:** A Corbusean villa featured as "The Contemporary Villa of Monsieur Jacques" in *Muhit,* 1929. **Right:** "A Cubic House," published in the "Practical, Economical, and Healthy Houses" pages of the same magazine, 1929.

exclusively functionalist and rationalist terms, and its undecorated cubic aesthetic was presented as a manifestation of the character of concrete and steel, "the only building materials suitable for today." The provision of "wide windows, ample light and air, smooth and clean surfaces, [and] the absence of germ- and dust-gathering corners and details" was particularly emphasized to explain the healthy and hygienic character of the building.

"Cubic," however, was by no means the only style promoted in these popular publications. It was only one among a wide range of examples, from colonial American homes and German *heimatstyle* cottages to "Mediterranean-style villas" with arcaded verandahs and loggias, all featured as "modern, healthy, functional, and beautiful homes" (fig. 5.5).[30] About the same time *Muhit* promoted the "cubic house" cited above, it also published a villa in the "French modern style," a house with Queen Anne features, and a number of "American homes" with shingles and wood siding.[31] Even "a classic house"—a Georgian mansion—was published in 1931, showing how "even an old style can accommodate modern comfort and hygiene" (fig. 5.5).[32]

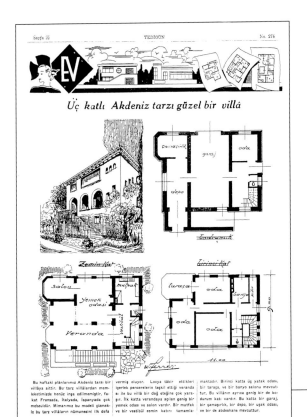

Sayfa 22   YEDİGÜN   No. 276

Üç katlı Akdeniz tarzı güzel bir villâ

Bu haftaki plânlarımız Akdeniz tarzı bir villâya aittir. Bu tarz villâlardan memleketimizde henüz inşa edilmemiştir, fakat Fransada, İtalyada, İspanyada çok mebzuldür. Mimarımız bu modeli çizmekle bu tarz villâların nümunesini ilk defa vermiş oluyor. Locya tâbir ettikleri içerlek pencerelerin teşkil ettiği verandası ile bu villâ bir dağ eteğine çok yaraşır. İlk katta verandaya açılan geniş bir yemek odası ve salon vardır. Bir mutfak ve bir vestibül zemin katını tamamlamaktadır. Birinci katta üç yatak odası, bir taraça, ve bir banyo salonu mevcuttur. Bu villânın ayrıca geniş bir de bodurum katı vardır. Bu katta bir garaj, bir çamaşırlık, bir depo, bir uşak odası, ve bir de abdeshane mevcuttur.

MUHİT

Klasik Bir Ev

Evin ön cebhesi

Birinci katın planı.

Fig. 5.5. Stylistic plurality of model homes published in popular magazines. **Left:** A "beautiful, three-story Mediterranean villa" from *Yedigün*, 1938. **Right:** A "classic house" from *Muhit*, 1931.

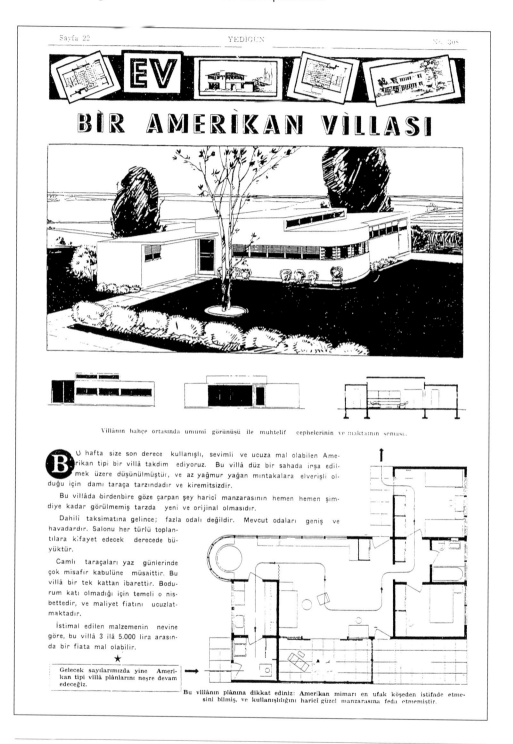

Fig. 5.6. An "American villa" published in *Yedigün* (1939). The openness, horizontally spread-out plan, and lawn suggest an automobile-dependent suburban life.

Collectively these examples suggest that in the late 1920s and early 1930s, it was not so much architectural style but more the connotations of modern, Western-style living that were promoted with these "model homes." Their plurality of styles notwithstanding, they all represented new and Western concepts of family life and domestic culture that the republic idealized. This overt admiration of Western models would become increasingly problematic as nationalist sentiments took over toward the end of the 1930s. Still, the appeal of European and American homes and lifestyles seems never to have diminished for these popular publications. As late as 1938–1939, *Yedigün* featured a series of "model American villas"—the quintessential suburban type of single-story homes with lawns, patios, and garages (fig. 5.6).[33] Without a hint of irony, cost estimates were given for building them out of brick or wood "in the vicinity of Istanbul." Such model designs evoke a utopian vision of Turkey with suburban middle-class lives, single-family dwellings, and access to modern amenities such as cars and household appliances—a vision far removed from the realities of the country.

The highly popular and perhaps most characteristically "republican" magazine, *Yedigün,* consistently published model designs for modern homes throughout the 1930s. Many of these were flat-roofed, boxy designs exhibiting the characteristic features of "cubic style" (*kübik tarz*), a term used descriptively and, for the most part, with positive connotations until the late 1930s. They ranged in size from minimal dwellings like "a charming three-room box house" or a compact two-story "city house" to a "large villa for big families with many guests" or a "five-room but very functional villa" to be built within a large garden.[34] In every case, the estimated cost of the house was given, suggesting that these were indeed intended as models to be emulated by prospective owners. Occasionally, some critical commentary was added, as in the case of a "very modern and cubic villa" that had a large, L-shaped living floor, left open or minimally divided for kitchen, living, dining, study, and music areas (fig. 5.7).[35] According to the magazine's commentary, it "sacrificed the plan to aesthetic considerations," and "while still beautiful and healthy, . . . had too few and rather small rooms." Such comments, coupled with a closer analysis of the actual built examples in Turkey, suggest that although the flat roofs, wide terraces, balconies, and boxy volumes of the "cubic style" were welcomed as expressions of modernity, this understanding of the "modern" was limited to a formal rather than a spatial definition of modern architecture. New concepts of open plan, open kitchen, continuous space, and transparency between layers of space were still undigested by a *Wohnkultur* accustomed to thinking in terms of "rooms" and traditional concepts of privacy.

In 1936, *Yedigün* stated that from then on, in addition to publishing model designs taken from foreign publications, it would also feature designs by Turkish architects. Through 1938, model designs were "commissioned" (*sipariş edildi*) to one unnamed architect,[36] and later they went to Emin Necip Uzman, a prominent republican architect with a successful career mostly in residential design.[37] Their model designs incorporated some features familiar to the lives of Turkish families,

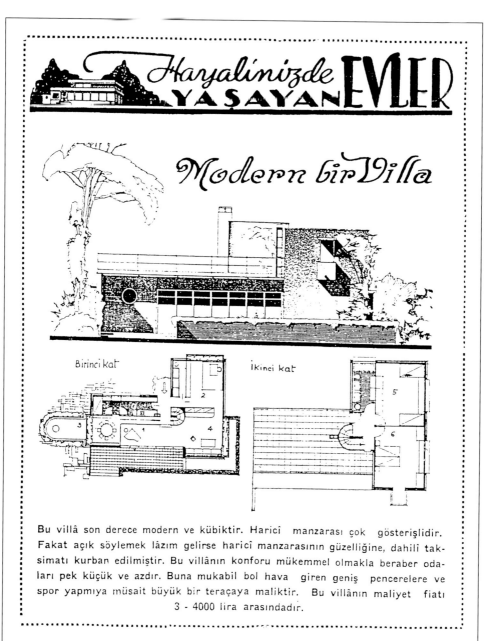

Hayalinizde **YAŞAYAN EVLER**

Modern bir Villa

Birinci kat   İkinci kat

Bu villâ son derece modern ve kübiktir. Haricî manzarası çok gösterişlidir. Fakat açık söylemek lâzım gelirse haricî manzarasının güzelliğine, dahilî taksimatı kurban edilmiştir. Bu villânın konforu mükemmel olmakla beraber odaları pek küçük ve azdır. Buna mukabil bol hava giren geniş pencerelere ve spor yapmıya müsait büyük bir teraçaya maliktir. Bu villânın maliyet fiatı 3 - 4000 lira arasındadır.

Fig. 5.7. A "modern villa" identified as "cubic style" and published in the "Your Dream Houses" section of *Yedigün* (1937). It was praised for "large windows allowing ample ventilation" and the provision of a wide terrace that could be used for "sports and exercise." It was criticized, however, because "there are too few rooms and the interior plan has been sacrificed for the beauty of the exterior."

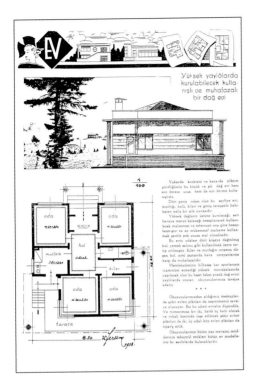 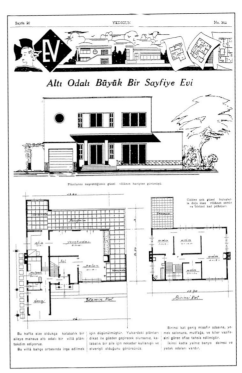

Fig. 5.8. Designs for model homes "commissioned to a Turkish architect" by the popular weekly *Yedigün* in 1938. **Left:** A "mountain house" adapting the traditional central-hall plan type. **Right:** A "large suburban house with six rooms."

mitigating the conspicuous "foreignness" of the earlier examples taken from Western publications. Most noticeable are the addition of a Turkish-style toilet (*alaturka helâ*) separate from the bathroom and the more rigid internal division of the house into separate rooms along a corridor or around a central hall, or *sofa*, in the manner of traditional Turkish houses (fig. 5.8).[38] While the exteriors still displayed the leitmotifs of *cubic*—boxy aesthetic, cantilevers, terraces, often a single circular window (corresponding to the entrance or the bathroom)—the interiors addressed cultural priorities such as privacy, separate kitchen and pantry (*kiler*), and separation of the family living room from the more ceremonial guest room.

An interesting aspect of Emin Necip Uzman's designs for *Yedigün* is their programmatic definition for hypothetical but very specific client profiles and imagined lifestyles. "A four-room farm house," "a five-room mountain retreat," "a four-room village or resort house," "a five-room urban house for an artist," and "a six-room house for those living far from the city" are some examples of these carefully identified designs (fig. 5.9).[39] This emphasis on the individuality of the family and the need for custom-designed homes was one of the major devices architects employed in seeking professional legitimacy. The implicit claim was that each modern family was unique in its needs for domestic space, and like the services of a family doctor, the services of a professional architect could best fulfill those needs. At the same time, the designs published in *Yedigün* reveal a lot about the images of modernity in the minds of the architects. With their hypothetical sites and approximate costs carefully specified, these designs are evocative of a happily transformed modern Turkey in which families built weekend retreats or decided "to move out of the city" to the suburbs (*sayfiye*). The distaste for dense urban life, the idealization of the single-family dwelling within a garden, and the conspicuous absence of higher-density residential types such as apartments, row houses, and multifamily blocks are important clues to the prevailing ideological climate, about which more will be said later.

The reduction of civilization to "civility" and Western lifestyles and the strong pedagogical function of architecture and interior design in inducing these habits and tastes come across strongly in the "contemporary homes" sections of popular magazines. For example, detailed instructions were given on arranging furniture "in the manner of European and American homes," with small side tables for tea or coffee, table lamps, curtains color-coordinated with upholstery, and so forth (fig. 5.10).[40] A

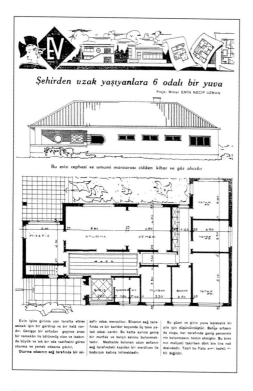
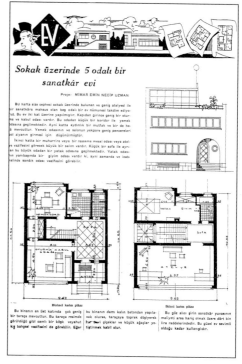

Fig. 5.9. Two model house designs by Emin Necip Uzman published in *Yedigün* in 1938. **Left:** "A six-room house for those living far from the city." **Right:** "A five-room urban house for an artist."

Fig. 5.10. A model interior from the "Interiors of Our Homes" page of *Yedigün* (1937), promoting light, modern, comfortable, and convertible furniture. The caption over the photograph reads: "Novelty in comfort: a room that can serve as living room, dining room, and bedroom."

1938 article in the popular monthly magazine *Modern Türkiye Mecmuası* talked about the importance of individual taste and attention to details like proper lighting above armchairs for reading, covered garbage cans for hygiene, and even "a beautiful bird cage." Emphasizing the need to furnish different parts or rooms of the house with equal "care, affection, and attention to detail," it lamented that "unfortunately, in our country, behind many well-presented guest rooms one can find dirty kitchens, untidy bathrooms, and deplorable bedrooms." It was hoped that these habits would change "with the elevation of the social and civilizational level of the individual."[41] The general consensus was that architecture had a mission to fulfill in transforming the "civilizational level" of Turkish families.

Many of the interiors and furnishing ideas in these publications used the term "cubic furniture" (*kübik eşya*), which designated the desirable qualities of modern movable furniture: practicality, lightness, ease of maintenance, simple geometric designs devoid of ornamentation, and so on. These were contrasted with the bulkiness and superfluousness of period furniture in old houses. Particularly in the early 1930s, at the height of the "civilizing mission" assumed by the profession, some Turkish architects also promoted the idea of "total design," or *Gesamtkunstwerk*. They wanted every object and piece of furniture, from the chair to the pictures on the wall or the flowers in the vase, to be designed and arranged within a coherent modernist vision. In *Yeni Mimari* (1931), Celal Esat Arseven presented this idea about the new expansion of the architect's sphere of involvement and responsibility:

Until now architects neglected spatial needs like a small corner [in which] to have coffee after dinner or a comfortable armchair with adequate reading light. It neglected to offer a place for the housewife to do her sewing and watch the kitchen at the same time and playrooms with small chairs, tables, and furniture scaled down to the size of children. Now all of these are among the concerns of the architect. In addition to being an artist, doctor, economist, and organizer, today's architect is expected to be a furniture designer as well.[42]

Aptullah Ziya's important 1931 editorial in *Mimar*, which voiced the technocratic and social engineering overtones of the professional discourse (see chapter 4), focused particularly on the design of the domestic interior. This was a task at least as important as the design of the exterior of the house, he argued, because it reaffirmed the architect's role as "an intellectual leader to guide our social life . . . a thinker concerned with [our] living in comfort, hygiene, and health."[43] The perspective sketches accompanying Aptullah Ziya's article depicted thoroughly Westernized interiors, geometric furniture designs and Bauhaus-inspired lighting fixtures, and slick, glossy surfaces (fig. 5.11). The piano, that inevitable symbol of Westernization since the nineteenth century, adorned one corner of the living room–study. In reality, few republican interiors matched this image. In many cases, highly eclectic and ornamented furniture crowded the interiors of the most recent "cubic" houses of the 1930s (fig. 5.12). Photographs of interiors from the 1930s suggest that many families were unwilling to dispense with their inherited furniture and family paraphernalia inside the house, even when they moved to the new cubic villas. These interiors are in themselves subjects for rich cultural analysis beyond the scope of this book. As much as they suggest some degree of resistance to the penetration of modern transformations to the interior of the house, they also evoke Adolf Loos's well-known critique of "total design" (*gesamkunstwerk*) as an oppressive and interventionist idea of the architect's that violated the inevitably homely (*heimlich*) character of the domestic interior.

A fairly vivid picture of the Westernized aspirations and domestic ideals of the period can be obtained from a number of recurring themes in the descriptions accompanying model designs in magazines. One of them is an inordinate emphasis on new patterns of mixed-gender entertaining—tea or cocktail parties and especially dancing (fig. 5.13). The significance of ballroom dancing as a symbol of republican modernity is best captured by anecdotes of Atatürk's personal insistence on getting apprehensive Turkish women to dance.[44] Many descriptions of model homes featured in popular magazines of the 1930s designated their spacious halls or salons, their wide terraces, and their flat rooftops as possible dancing floors for appropriate occasions. These practices of mixed-gender dancing, entertaining, and drinking, promoted both socially and architecturally in the early 1930s, would soon become one of the most contentious aspects of republican modernization. They would come under increas-

Fig. 5.11. Sketch for a "modern study" by Aptullah Ziya, illustrating his essay "The Architect Inside the Building," published in the first issue of *Mimar,* the professional journal of Turkish architects (1931). The article promoted architects as design professionals who shaped not just the exteriors of houses but also the interiors, furniture, and details, giving form to modern aspirations and lifestyles. **Fig. 5.12.** Interior of a modern villa in Moda, Istanbul (mid-1930s), designed by Zeki Sayar. The traditional and crowded interior with its period furniture contrasted with the plain and cubic modernist aesthetic of the exterior.

Fig. 5.13. Dancing as a symbol of republican modernity and Westernization. Cover illustration of a 1938 issue of *Yedigün*.

ingly strong attack toward the end of the decade, this time as symbols of corrupt and decadent lives devoid of traditional Turkish values.

The theme of health and hygiene, perhaps the most celebrated qualities of the modern home, constituted another republican obsession. It also underscored the binary opposition set up between a discredited past and an idealized contemporariness (*asrilik*), as discussed in chapter 2. "Whereas moonlight reigned in the old houses," observed a popular magazine in 1930, "the rule of the sun is beginning in the glass-enclosed buildings of today. Our spiritual welfare is intimately connected to a house flooded with light, [equipped with] comfortable chairs and sofas, a garden to rest our tired eyes, and a bathroom devoid of illness-causing germs."[45] The "Beautiful Homes" section of *Yedigün* (see fig. 5.25) featured photographs of recently built examples of modern houses and made abundant references to the Corbusean themes of air, sun, ventilation, and greenery. Some of the captions read, "The purpose of the modern house is ample air and ample light," "All three examples we publish this week are generously sunlit incubators of health," and "Beautiful house means a home penetrated by ample air and light." The paradigmatic republican critique of urban apartments and congested living, in favor of single-family houses within gardens (a critique with broader ideological dimensions that I discuss later), was also formulated in terms of health and hygiene. In an article titled "House without a Garden: Man without Lungs," medical doctor Ali Rıdvan criticized dense urban apartments on health grounds. He advocated building on the green hills of the Bosporus in Istanbul, which were still empty and wooded in the 1930s. He wrote that "to imitate the land-saving dense high-rises of populous Western metropolises in our spacious beautiful city is an unforgivable crime, not just in the name of art, but of health and hygiene. [While] modern families live in apartments in the narrow, dark, and airless center of the city, the green hills of our wonderful Bosporus are looking at each other in puzzlement."[46]

The technical aspects and modern amenities of the house were other comfort-related themes defining the ideal modern home and family life. Amenities such as hot water, heating systems, proper ventilation, electricity for lighting, and household appliances were seen as prestigious symbols of civilization and contemporariness (fig. 5.14). Americans were particularly praised as pioneers in applying the latest technical innovations to everyday lives and domestic settings. Built-in closets "hidden in the wall," thoroughly electrified kitchens already fitted with ovens and refrigerators, and even "electrically heated and illuminated beds," as Aptullah Ziya introduced in *Mimar*, were topics of fascination.[47] The smooth, clean counter surfaces of modern kitchens were likened to those of "surgery rooms and clinics," a clear perception of these as positive qualities rather than as marks of coldness and sterility as would be the case later in the decade. "In these 'Tomorrow's Houses' which already exist in the U.S.," wrote one popular magazine, "electricity is turned into a masterful and docile servant. It sweeps and dusts the rooms, heats and cools the house, runs hot and cold water through the faucets, does the dishes and kitchen work, and illuminates every room with a soft, eye-relaxing light."[48] In short, the modern house was everything its

Fig. 5.14. Technological amenities for a modern and comfortable domestic life: 1930s advertisements in *Yedigün* for electrical appliances (**left**) and refrigerators (**right**).

traditional counterpart was not: scientific, hygienic, economical, and, above all, representative of the spirit of the new "machine age."

Building the Modern House

THE IDEA OF imagining the modern nation through the design of the modern house was highly appealing to Turkish architects, who made this idea the centerpiece of their professional discourse. Without access to larger public commissions, which typically went to German and Austrian architects, they focused their attention almost exclusively on the "architecture of the house" (*mesken mimarisi*), as they called it. Modernist architects such as Seyfettin Arkan, Zeki Sayar, Abidin Mortaş, Aptullah Ziya, and Bekir İhsan (Ünal), among others, made their careers largely with residential work in the 1930s. The republican elite of higher bureaucrats, RPP notables, prominent professionals, and wealthy families of Istanbul and Ankara constituted their primary clientele. Although in practice these privileged clients hired the architects directly in what can be characterized as a traditional patronage relationship, architects' theoretical writings highlighted the professional ideology of serving society at large. Populism being one of the six pillars of the republican regime, the democratic connotation of the modern dwelling was a particularly appropriate theme to lend legitimacy to the profession. In a radio program, "Cubic Building and Comfort," Behçet Ünsal presented the design of the house as "modern architecture" par excellence—the very embodiment of the demands and aspirations of modern life in democratic societies. He said: "The modern architecture of our age will be known in art history as 'the architecture of the house' [*mesken mimarisi*]. This is not an aristocratic architecture. It is a totally democratic architecture. The aim of modern architecture is to turn to the people and to satisfy their need for comfortable, economic, and beautiful houses."[49]

Similarly, "the dwelling is the most important question of today," wrote Abidin Mortaş in 1936. "Until recently, houses were not the subject matter of architecture. Architects neglected the house, instead working on monumental projects like mosques, churches, palaces, banks, and offices. Today's architecture is directly and intimately involved with houses or, in other words, with the real substance of people's lives."[50] Modern architecture, it was argued, with its avoidance of the superfluous, the ornamental, and the exuberant, was the precise expression of these democratic ideals. Its basic principles of rationalism and functionalism were indifferent to and independent of class and wealth. "Modern needs are the same for everyone," said Behçet Ünsal. "Maximum beauty and comfort are as much desired in a worker's house as in a large villa."[51]

Upon closer scrutiny, however, it can be observed that differences of class and wealth were not negated, but rather their visual, symbolic, and ornamental expressions were banished in favor of the unified modernist aesthetic of the exterior. In the same way that the official ideology of Kemalism subordinated class difference and conflict to the homogenizing and unifying ideal of the nation, many projects by republican architects concealed differences of size, budget, and client status behind the unified aesthetic and undecorated simplicity of the "cubic house." In a series of "small house projects" published in *Mimar* in 1933, Bekir İhsan proposed small, two-story, single-family houses for employees of the State Railroads (fig. 5.15).[52] In these projects, the house of a lower-rank employee and that of a supervisor shared similar formal features but differed in size. Two others, identified as the houses of an engineer and a security system supervisor working for the State Railroads in Eskişehir, were variants of the same plan and the same cubic composition of boxes, cantilevers, corner windows, and balconies.

The exterior aesthetics of the cubic boxes and asymmetrical compositions in Bekir İhsan's proposals suggest affinities with Bauhaus experiments in Weimar Germany under Walter Gropius some ten years earlier—especially the standardized building blocks exhibited in 1923. On the other hand, the single-line sketch of the living and dining room interior (fig. 5.15) is reminiscent of the interior sketches of Heinrich Tessenow in Germany, a conservative modern architect and an advocate of

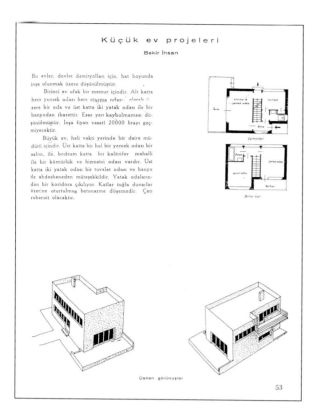

Küçük ev projeleri

Bekir İhsan

Bu evler, devlet demiryolları için, hat boyunda inşa olunmak üzere düşünülmüştür.

Birinci ev ufak bir memur içindir. Alt katta hem yemek odası hem oturma odası olmak üzere bir oda ve üst katta iki yatak odası ile bir banyodan ibarettir. Esas yeri kaybolmaması düşünülmüştür. İnşa fiyatı vasati 20000 lirayı geçmiyecektir.

Büyük ev, hali vakti yerinde bir daire müdürü içindir. Üst katta bir hol bir yemek odası bir salon, ile, bodrum katta bir kalörifer mahalli ile bir kömürlük ve hizmetci odası vardır. Üst katta iki yatak odası bir tuvalet odası ve banyo ile abdeshaneden müteşekkildir. Yatak odalarından bir koridora çıkılıyor. Katlar tuğla duvarlar üzerine oturtulmuş betonarme döşemedir. Çatı ruberoit olacaktır.

Üstten görünüşler

53

Fig. 5.15. "Small house projects" for employees of the State Railroads by Bekir İhsan (1933). Plan and axonometrics of a minimal type (**top**) and sketch of an interior (**bottom**). These undecorated cubic boxes evoke the aesthetic of the German *Neue Sachlichkeit,* while the austerity and simplicity of the interior recall the feeling of Heinrich Tessenow's sketches for simple middle-class homes in small towns.

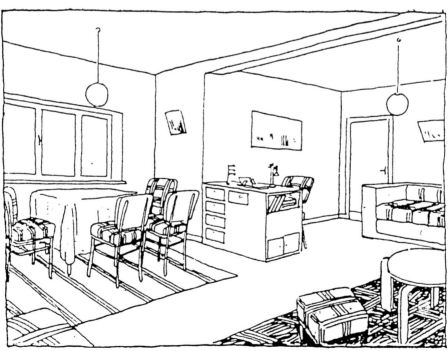

Oturma ve yemek odaları

the middle class as the backbone of the German nation. Like Tessenow's interiors, Bekir İhsan's sketch shows an austere simplicity of bare walls, light modern furniture, and little else. As in the German Heimatschutz movement to which Tessenow belonged, simplicity, modesty, and practicality were made into national virtues in Bekir İhsan's vision.[53] Indeed, throughout the 1930s both the functionality and rationalism of the socialist housing experiments and the antibourgeois sentiments, populism, and middle-class emphasis of the nationalist Heimatschutz housing projects were important sources of inspiration for republican architects. They were interested in and informed about developments in Germany, the Kemalist regime's primary ally in technical matters and national projects from the inception of the republic. As early as 1932, the "urbanist architect" Burhan Arif wrote articles praising Ernst May's work in Frankfurt and in other *Siedlung* programs.[54] Celal Esat Arseven, too, referred to the Frankfurt experiments when he presented the "housing question" as "the question of human society's happiness" (*mesken meselesi cemiyeti beşeriyenin saadeti meselesidir*):

Today the consensus is that every individual in society has the right to live in a sunny, airy, comfortable, hygienic, and economical house, and this is a feasible goal with contemporary means of construction. . . . Many European governments regard the housing question as a matter of government policy. They now understand the relationship between the housing question and the physical and moral health of a nation. Many municipalities have concentrated their activities upon the housing question. For some years now, the city of Frankfurt am Main has been building such healthy dwellings with gardens. The proliferation of such experiments in other countries will, without doubt, increase the well-being of the entire human society.[55]

During the construction of Ankara as a modern capital, there were some small-scale experiments with government housing for employees of the state, such as the 198 detached, single-story houses built on a lot behind the Ministry of Health in 1925. The Bahçelievler Cooperative Housing Scheme (1934–1936) is a more paradigmatic example reflecting the general politics and limitations of the cooperative idea in early republican Turkey.[56] Unlike examples from Weimar Germany and other socialist experiments in Europe, where workers' housing and collective living were the driving ideas, Bahçelievler (literally "houses with gardens") catered to the higher-ranking bureaucrats of the state, providing individual, owner-occupied houses of higher standards and cost. Although the "garden city" concept of Bahçelievler was initially part of Hermann Jansen's master plan for Ankara, his proposal for more uniform rows of small houses along the streets was transformed in favor of detached, single-family villas within gardens. As in other so-called cooperative housing projects in Turkey, the houses became the sole focus of attention, at the expense of communal areas and social facilities. Although some 22 housing cooperatives were established in Ankara between 1935 and 1944, the number of cooperative homes actually built during this period was only 554, and the picture was much worse in other cities.[57]

After 1935, with the arrival of first Martin Wagner and then Bruno Taut a year later as teachers and consultants, Turkey could actually boast of hosting two of the key protagonists of the 1920s Weimar housing programs in Germany. Yet in spite of the presence of these two veterans of the GEHAG cooperative in Berlin, and in spite of architects' emphasis on the democratic potential of the modern dwelling, there were no significant experiments with large-scale, multi-unit housing schemes or with prefabricated, rationalized, and industrialized production processes. The few workers' housing projects produced by Seyfi Arkan in the mid-1930s were exceptions rather than the norm, and even these projects employed rather conventional construction techniques. Arkan's typological study of low-cost workers' houses for the city of Adana, published in *Arkitekt* in 1936, shows a concern for minimal sizes, economy of construction, and appropriateness to the hot climate of this southern city.[58] His most important built work was a large housing project for workers of the coal-mining industry in Kozlu, Zonguldak, in northwestern Turkey (fig. 5.16). The layouts of the housing scheme reflected the rational planning concepts of the German precedents: minimum dimensions for each type and the incorporation of facilities such as a school, a laundry, and a communal kitchen. Arkan's scheme, however, retained the primacy of the architectural object—the individual house—unlike the 1920s *seidlungen* of Frankfurt and Berlin, where the individual units were completely incorporated into the rationality of the assembly. The anonymous housing blocks or rows of attached units in the German examples were replaced in Arkan's scheme by the sublimated aesthetic of the villa, albeit a miniaturized one, and the different sizes of these "villas" (for workers and supervisors) reflected the social hierarchy of the community.

Meanwhile, the architects' own ideals regarding the modern villa remained ambiguous and even contradictory. While the simple, minimal dwelling of the German *Siedlungen* appealed to their republican populism and collectivist ideals, the Corbusean paradigm of the bourgeois villa remained an important source of aesthetic influence on Turklish architects. The cult status of Le Corbusier can easily be observed in projects such as Arif Hikmet's design for a "villa project within a garden" (fig. 5.17) or Emin Necip Uzman's design for a villa in Karşıyaka, Izmir (fig. 5.18), the latter almost replicating the Corbusian aesthetic of Villa Savoie. Almost invariably, an exclusive focus on the architectural object took precedence over larger questions of urbanism. Neither the published writings nor the built works of architects suggest that there was any substantial engagement with issues of urbanism, the very substance of the modernist utopia as it evolved in the West. Unlike the Hilbersheimer slab-block, for example, which was inseparable from Ludwig Hilbersheimer's 1927 vision of the *Grossstadt,* and unlike the Corbusean perimeter block, the meaning of which was incomplete outside of Le Corbusier's 1922 project for the "Ville Contemporaine," the cubic house or apartment in Turkey was an isolated unit existing on its own without any larger urban vision. There were no visionary urban projects for an industrial Turkey or any significant experiments with urban types like perimeter blocks or row housing. A few unbuilt propositions published in *Arkitekt*

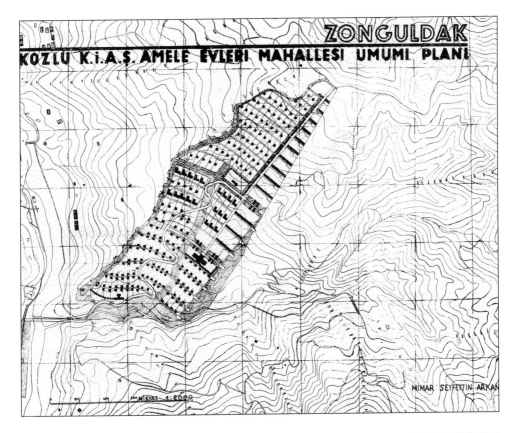

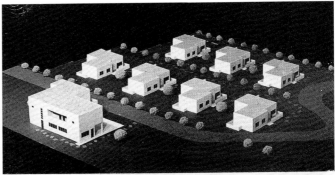

Fig. 5.16. Housing for coal miners in Kozlu, Zonguldak, by Seyfi Arkan (1936). Site plan and photograph of a model of typical workers' units and the supervisor's house.

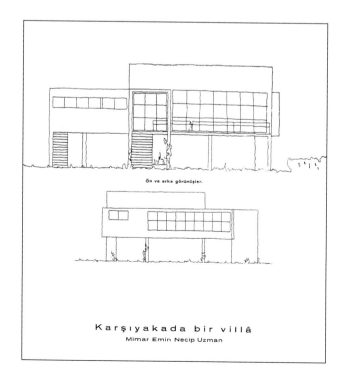

Fig. 5.17. "A villa project within a garden" by Arif Hikmet Holtay (1933), with flat roof, large glazed walls, and cantilevers. **Fig. 5.18.** "A villa in Karşıyaka" in Izmir by Emin Necip Uzman (1936), adopting the purist, modernist aesthetic of Le Corbusier: flat roof, *pilotis,* horizontal band windows, open plans, and free façades.

did offer interesting urbanistic statements, but in small and limited ways. In 1933, for example, Seyfi Arkan designed a series of single-family houses for Ankara unified along the street façade by high garden walls but still retaining their detached character inside the garden (fig. 5.19). In a 1934 proposal for low-income workers' row housing in Unkapanı, Istanbul, the architect Tahir Turan projected a more properly "row-house" scheme adopting the "Ankara cubic" style of Clemenz Holzmeister and repeating it along the street (fig. 5.20). These were isolated design exercises, however, with no significant impact on the predominant building practices of the 1930s.

The reasons for the absence of large-scale rationalized housing production in Turkey rest not only in the inadequacy of the country's material resources and the primitiveness of its building industry (see chapter 4) but also in the priorities, policies, and politics governing its architectural production. Although there were architects and planners within the Ministry of Public Works who published reports on town planning, garden cities, zoning, neighborhood design, and housing examples in Europe and the United States,[59] the government did not act upon these models in any substantial way. Speculative real estate values in major cities, the lack of comprehensive planning and land appropriation policies, and the regime's priority on public buildings, coupled with the nonexistence of a strong private sector to undertake housing developments, were as responsible for inhibiting mass housing as was the lack of advanced technology for serialized production. In the absence of all of these, actual built examples of "modern houses" remained limited to custom-designed and custom-built villas and apartments for a handful of republican elites—the bureaucrats, professionals, and military figures close to the regime. As Martin Wagner observed in 1938, "the new residential buildings constructed in Turkish cities [were] not intended for the needy who constituted the majority of the population but for the wealthy six percent."[60] The actual number of houses built in Turkey in 1928, when a planning office (imar müdürlüğü) was established and the housing shortage was acknowledged, was 7,279.[61] Ten years later, this number had increased only to 14,178—still less than, for example, the 15,000 units built by the city of Frankfurt alone in the 1920s. The total number of houses built in the entire early republican period (1923–1938) was 73,279, while the population of the country increased from 13.6 million in 1927 to 17.8 million in 1940.[62]

The two standard types of early republican residential architecture were the single-family house or villa in a garden and the urban "apartment building." The term "apartment" needs further qualification; it had a very different meaning in the early republican period from what it came to signify after the "flat ownership," or condominium, legislation of 1965 (kat mülkiyeti kanunu), which marked the real boom in speculative apartment building in Turkey.[63] The more commonly used term in the 1930s was "rental house" (kira evi), which designated a multi-unit residential building with a single owner who rented out the units for revenue. Rental houses ranged in size from what was essentially a large house comprising a few separate residential units to higher-rise urban apartments for which the term "apartment building" is more appro-

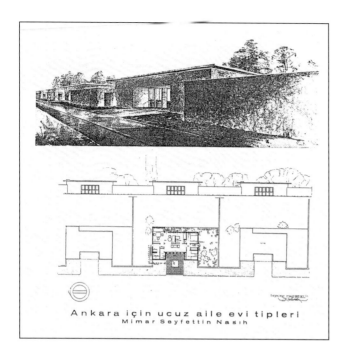

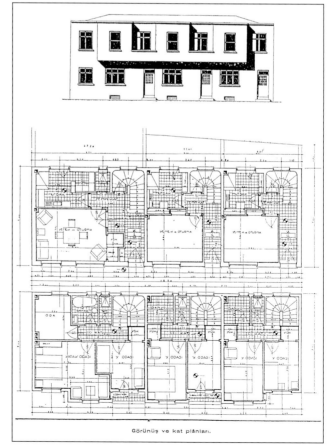

Fig. 5.19. Project for "economical prototype family houses for Ankara" by Seyfi Arkan (1933). **Fig. 5.20.** Project for row houses by Tahir Turan (1934) showing the influence of "Ankara cubic" on the façade articulation (see fig. 4.8).

priate. In most cases, these rental houses or apartments were commissioned to prominent architects, and the quality of design and construction was an important source
of pride and prestige for the owner, whose name was typically given to the building.
As a stylistic signifier, the term "cubic" was equally applicable to the single-family
houses or villas and to the rental houses or urban apartments of the 1930s, most of
them designed by modernist Turkish architects. Nevertheless, the ideal type or paradigm of the "cubic house" was always the detached, single-family house or villa,
which was celebrated for its closeness to nature, sunlight, and healthy living—the
qualities cherished in the modernist discourse of the 1930s.

During the construction of Ankara as a modern capital, many modern villas were
built in the new districts of Yenişehir and Çankaya for republican leaders close to
the inner circle of Atatürk, who himself resided in the presidential residence on Çankaya Hill (fig 5.21). The presidential residence, designed in 1930–1932 by Clemenz
Holzmeister, and the first foreign embassy residences to be built in prime locations
between the presidential residence and the government complex below the hill came
to define the ideals of modern residential architecture of the time. In 1933–1934, Seyfi
Arkan won the competition for a highly prestigious commission to design the
Ministry of Foreign Affairs residence, a major boost for the Turkish architects competing with their German and Austrian colleagues. Though inevitably larger than the
typical single-family house, Arkan's building can be seen as the paradigm of the modern villa (fig. 5.22). Its wide, cantilevered roof above a wide terrace on the upper level,
its cantilevered entrance canopy, covered colonnade, and plain rectangular façade
compositions, and, on the interior, its large glazed surfaces and double-height spaces
are particularly strong modernist features. Arkan designed most of the interior finishing, details, and furniture as well, in high-quality materials and with utmost care,
in what was essentially one of the few opportunities to demonstrate the architects'
commitment to the idea of *Gesamkunstwerk*. Collectively, the presidential residence,
embassy residences, and other Çankaya villas for republican dignitaries constituted
the highest end of modern residential construction, made possible by the specific political circumstances of legitimating Ankara as a modern capital on a par with
its Western counterparts. In June 1939, these "modern villas" were featured in a
photo essay in *La Turquie Kemaliste* as testimony to the modernity of the new nation
(fig. 5.23).

In Istanbul it was primarily a wealthy private clientele—professionals, businessmen, and bureaucrats—that served as patrons of modern residential construction. In
two areas of the city, the fashionable villages along the Bosporus (Bebek and
Arnavutköy in particular) and the newly developing suburbs on the Anatolian shores
of the Marmara Sea (Moda, Göztepe, Suadiye, and Erenköy in particular), modern
villas proliferated in the 1930s. A pioneering example and the only significant residential work by a foreign architect was the Devres villa in Bebek by Ernst Egli (fig.
5.24). A boom in the construction of modern villas followed this two-story white
cubic villa with a flat roof and a wide terrace with metal balcony railings overlooking

Fig. 5.21. The presidential residence on Çankaya Hill in Ankara (1930–1932), by Clemenz Holzmeister. **Fig. 5.22.** The Ministry of Foreign Affairs residence, Ankara (1933–1934), by Seyfi Arkan

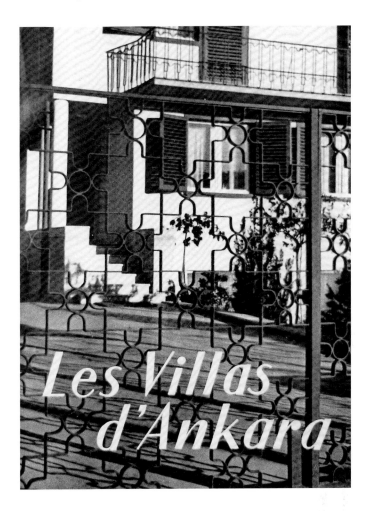

Fig. 5.23. "The Villas of Ankara," a photo essay in *La Turquie Kemaliste* (1939) in praise of the new "garden city" houses built in the southern extension of the national capital.

the Bosporus. In 1936 *Yedigün* introduced a "Beautiful Houses" (*güzel evler*) section, publishing photographs of recently built examples, most of them in Istanbul (fig. 5.25). They were promoted as models of modern, healthy, Westernized living, in the hope that "they will not remain limited to Istanbul [and] such beautiful homes will proliferate in every corner of our country."[64] Many of these single-family villas within gardens displayed *cubic* features: the geometric, often asymmetrical composition of boxes, continuous window sills, wide balconies, and terraces with cantilevered canopies over them, many with flat roofs and some with a rounded corner (see fig. 4.10). Documented only in the 1930s issues of *Arkitekt,* most of these buildings were demolished in the 1950s and 1960s to make room for higher-rise speculative apartments.

The rental-house type (*kira evi*) was particularly suited to the specific historical circumstances of Ankara. In the first few years after Ankara was declared the seat of the new nationalist government, it was faced with a dramatic housing shortage, which has been the topic of numerous novels, contemporary accounts, and foreign reports. For many of the new bureaucrats, civil servants, and staff of foreign embassies and

Fig. 5.24. Top: Villa for Ragıp Devres on the Bosporus, Bebek, Istanbul (1934), by Ernst Egli, as published in *Der Baumeister,* 1936. **Bottom:** A 1990s view of the villa.

Yurdumuzun her köşesini böyle güzel yuvalarla dolu görmek istiyoruz.

Birkaç haftadanberi neşretmekte olduğumuz İstanbul ve civarının güzel ev fotoğrafları her tarafta alâka uyandırdı. Bunu bize gelen mektuplardan anlıyoruz ve halkımızın modern inşaata karşı gösterdiği alâkayı da öğrenmiş oluyoruz. Şunu da söyliyelim ki bu nümuneler yalnız İstanbul evlerine inhisar etmiyecektir. Güzel yurdumuzun her köşesinden elde ettiğimiz yeni ve modern ev nümunelerini bu sayfada neşre devam edeceğiz. Bu münasebetle okuyucularımızdan yeni ev yaptıranlardan bu sayfada neşredilmek üzere evlerinin resimlerini göndermelerini dileyoruz.

Fig. 5.25. "Beautiful Houses," a weekly page in *Yedigün* featuring photographs of new houses built in and around Istanbul. The caption on this example from 1936 reads, "We want to see such beautiful homes proliferate in every corner of our country."

Fig. 5.26. Example of a small rental house (*kira evi*) in Ankara by Bekir İhsan (late 1930s).

missions moving to Ankara in the late 1920s, accommodation had been a serious problem. Initially, their choices were limited to the houses of local residents in the "old city" around the citadel, some old-fashioned inns, and the historical Taşhan, the only decent hotel in early Ankara. After 1931, however, the construction of rental houses in the newer sections of the city gained momentum, especially around the prestige axis, Atatürk Boulevard, and close to the ministries and government offices. The most prolific architect working in Ankara was Bekir İhsan, although Zeki Sayar, Seyfi Arkan, and other Istanbul architects also built rental houses there. As is seen in an example designed by Bekir İhsan (fig. 5.26), many were three-story buildings with one or two units on each floor. In spite of their modest scale, features such as separate service entrances, maids' rooms, garages, and landscaped gardens suggest a particular income level and modern lifestyle for the tenants of these rental houses.

Other revenue-generating urban rental houses owned by private clients or by institutions such as the Children's Protection Fund (Çocuk Esirgeme Kurumu) typically had shops on the ground floor and a larger number of smaller units in four- or five-story buildings. Two published examples from Ankara—the Mühendis Ragıp rental house by Bekir İhsan and a rental house for the Children's Protection Fund (fig. 5.27)—illustrate this type of mixed use. Their characteristic modernist formal features were flat roofs, balconies with rounded corners, compositions of cubic volumes, differentiation of vertical circulation spaces on the exterior, and plain façades with

continuous bands of windows and/or corner windows. In 1934, in an unusual practice, a competition was held for the Celal Bey apartment building in Yenişehir, and the entries, by many of the prominent Turkish architects, were published in *Mimar*.[65] The winning design, by Bekir İhsan, placed shops, a café, and a restaurant on the ground floor and arranged six units per floor in what was described as "an efficient use of space, minimizing corridors and maximizing light" (fig. 5.28).

Fig. 5.27. Rental house for the Children's Protection Fund by H. Hüsnü (mid-1930s). The ground floor was reserved for shops and businesses for revenue generation.

In contrast with the novelty of apartments for Ankara, dense apartment living had been a familiar feature of urban life in Istanbul since at least the late nineteenth century, especially in the more Europeanized, cosmopolitan, and commercial districts of Galata, Pera, Taksim, and Şişli. Turn-of-the-century examples, often the work of Greek, Armenian, and Levantine architects, displayed the characteristic cosmopolitanism, stylistic eclecticism, and richness of the time, ranging from neoclassic to art nouveau. With their strong associations with the empire, however, Istanbul apartments became targets of ideological attacks by many republican intellectuals who glorified the small, single-family house as a national ideal against the corruption, cosmopolitanism, and unhealthiness of apartment living. Many authors wrote about the malaise of greed, profit motive, and land speculation as having given rise to apartment construction in Istanbul.[66] In the context of the ideological confrontation between Istanbul and Ankara (see chapter 2), the latter was praised as "a pleasant new city consisting of small modern houses inside gardens" that, the nationalists argued, should serve as a model for "salvaging Istanbul from the malaise of apartments."[67]

Birinci mükâfat. Ön ve yan görünüşler.

Birinci mükâfat. Kat plânları.

Fig. 5.28. Competition project for a large apartment block in Ankara (1934) by Bekir İhsan. Drawings of front and side elevations, ground floor with shops, and a typical floor plan with residential units.

A substantial number of "cubic apartments" were added to the eclectic repertoire of Istanbul apartment buildings in the 1930s. Next to art nouveau or neoclassical façades, one could see the recognizable modernist aesthetic of rounded corners, horizontal lines of balconies and window sills, and, occasionally, circular windows as a leitmotif of 1930s modernism (fig. 5.29; also see fig. 4.11). Still known by the names of their original owners, these apartments were among the most significant work of modernist Turkish architects who considered themselves pioneers in transforming the prevailing concepts of residential architecture as well as the lifestyles contained by it. Most of the descriptions accompanying their published designs talked about the rational planning of the modern dwelling, the functional arrangement of the rooms, the structural possibilities and constraints of reinforced concrete, the rational considerations of budget, materials, maintenance, and program, and so forth. Collectively, however, these buildings represented a powerful *aesthetic* discourse with recurring formal features that bore testimony to the inadequacies of reducing form to functional and rational criteria, as I discussed in chapter 4. Rounded corners, typically attributed to the inspiration of the German architect Eric Mendelsohn, were an especially pervasive aesthetic symbol of modernity.

Although Istanbul and Ankara remained the primary sites of cubic houses and apartments in the 1930s, other cities, such as Izmir, Adana, Kütahya, and Eskişehir, had their share of these new buildings (fig. 5.30). But in the absence of any large-scale public housing schemes or of an autonomous bourgeoisie to compose a large private

Fig. 5.29. Small apartment building in Istanbul with the characteristic modern aesthetic of the 1930s: rounded balconies, continuous window sills, and an asymmetrical entrance. **Fig. 5. 30.** Proliferation of "cubic apartments" outside Ankara and Istanbul in the 1930s: an anonymous example from Kütahya in west-central Anatolia. Photograph from the 1990s.

clientele for architecture, cubic houses and apartments constituted a very small residential output relative to the size and population of the country. More significant was their symbolic charge—their direct association with republican ideology and modern lifestyles that, outside the republican circles of Ankara and the emerging national bourgeoisie in a few other cities, remained alien to the vast majority of the traditional population. The prolific republican discourse and imagery on the cubic house and the modern lifestyle housed in it should be viewed less as the expression of an accomplished reality than as a statement about elite aspirations of the 1930s. By the late 1930s, the fortunes of the term "cubic" were dramatically reversed in an increasingly nationalist climate, parallel to nationalist attacks on the modernist avant-garde in Germany and other places. The term "cubic," which had been simply a stylistic signifier in the early 1930s, acquired a negative connotation, and many modernist architects were put on the defensive, dissociating themselves from the term.

The "Cubic" Controversy

THE KEMALIST PROJECT of modernity had been profoundly ambiguous from its inception. Republican leaders wanted to import Western forms, institutions, and lifestyles without importing the feelings of "alienation" and individual subjectivity that are central to the experience of modernity. The idea of extending Westernizing and secularizing reforms into the private sphere—into family law and the physical space of the home—was a particularly bold move and, by the same token, the most controversial one. The "cubic house," as a signifier of a modern, Western, secular lifestyle, was at the center of such mixed feelings and heated debates even at the heyday of the Kemalist reforms. Perhaps the best-known literary representation of these ambiguous sentiments is Yakup Kadri Karaosmanoğlu's description of a modern cubic interior in his 1934 novel *Ankara,* quoted at the opening of this chapter. What is most striking in that passage is how the same architectural qualities of shiny, hygienic surfaces and modern furniture ("couches like dentists' chairs, seats like operation tables," "a clinical gloss on everything") could be read as the indicators of progress and contemporariness idealized by Kemalism and simultaneously as the symptoms of alienation, coldness, and sterility characterizing cosmopolitan modernity in its most negative sense. Indeed, for the most part, republican ideology was willing to take modernism (and "cubic" as its stylistic expression) on board for its scientific and progressive connotations but was deeply uneasy with its urban, cosmopolitan, and "international" signifiers.

As captured by theorists of modernity from Georg Simmel to Marshall Berman,[68] the experience of modernity and modernist abstraction in art and architecture by definition signifies an alienated consciousness, a detachment of the individual from tradition, community, or nation, and a heightening of his sense of individuality. Therefore, despite all its rhetorical emphasis on modernity, by placing the nation

Fig. 5.31. A late 1930s cartoon ridiculing "cubic architecture" and associating it with greedy and untrustworthy character. The caption reads: "Did you hide the entrance of your building to make it 'cubic'? No, I did it so that my creditors would not be able to find it."

— Apartımanın kapısını kübik olsun diye mi gizli yaptırdın?

— Hayır, alacaklılar bulamasınlar diye!...

above the individual and the single-family home above the anonymity of apartment life in the modern metropolis, republican ideology was in essence profoundly antimodern and antiurban. The "cubic apartments" of Istanbul came especially to represent alienated, unpatriotic, and foreign lifestyles—the despised "other" of the simplicity, nationalism, and idealism of Anatolian towns. It is fascinating to observe that in the later part of the 1930s, the same magazines that published model designs for cubic houses and furniture also published highly critical assessments of the values and lifestyles that this term came to represent. Cartoons and editorials drew explicit associations between "cubic architecture" and corrupt lifestyles directed by greed and profit motive that were deemed to be un-Turkish (fig. 5.31).

In 1939, Halide Edip Adıvar's "great nationalist novel" *Tatarcık* was serialized *Yedigün*. In the novel, a certain "cubic villa" (*kübik palas*), which was illustrated for the magazine in a sketch by Münip Fehim (fig. 5.32), was described as follows: "This new building is the *yalı* of Mr. Sungur Balta. Built along the water's edge, Kübik Palas attracts the eye and, according to some, disturbs it. Its style, as evident from the name, is cubic. . . . It has all sorts of arbitrary shapes, projections, and setbacks, and in the most unexpected places, strange balconies covered with glass. One gets the impression that the architect conceived this building during a fit of malaria."[69]

The last sentence, suggesting "cubic" to be a pathological phenomenon, came close to the nationalist attacks on avant-garde art in Germany at the time. It should be remembered that in the later half of the 1930s there were many Nazi sympathizers

Fig. 5.32. The notorious cubic villa (*kübik palas*) in Halide Edip Adıvar's "nationalist novel" *Tatarcık*—a building associated with the book's corrupt, cosmopolitan, and unpatriotic characters. Illustration by the graphic artist Münip Fehim for *Yedigün* (1939), which serialized the novel for its readers.

in Turkey, and ultranationalist publications like *Milli İnkilap*, edited by Cevat Rifat, published praise of the German National Socialists along with anti-Semitic editorials and cartoons.[70] References to cubism as "a distorted art" (*çarpık sanat*) became increasingly common in popular publications,[71] along with commentaries questioning whether it qualified as art at all: "Cubism, which is a strange and ridiculous trend in art, has succeeded in proliferating in architecture. Aren't cubic apartments and cubic furniture like an epidemic in our country for the last ten or fifteen years? The explanation for the spread of this style rests in considerations of cheapness and practicality rather than any indication of higher taste. Therefore the [cubic] issue has no relationship to Fine Arts."[72]

Especially after the notorious exhibition by the Nazis ridiculing and condemning the modernist avant-garde as makers of "degenerate art" (*Entartete Kunst*, an exhibition opened in Munich in 1937), echoes of similar sentiments could be found in Turkish publications. Even more mainstream nationalist republican intellectuals such as Peyami Safa published criticisms of cubic art and architecture, condemning the individualistic excesses of the modernist avant-garde. In an editorial in *Yedigün* titled "Cubic in Turkey and Abroad," he characterized "cubic" in painting and architecture as "an aggressive countercultural tendency, born out of postwar hysteria and cut off from any ties to habit and tradition," adding, however, that it had already been left behind in Europe.[73] In Turkey, he lamented, it was still "a disease" more destructive than the fires to which the wooden houses of Istanbul had succumbed in the past. What is interesting in his criticism of the cubic apartment is his negative assessment of qualities such as minimal size, the flat roof, and ample sunlight, which were precisely the same qualities hailed in architectural discourse as expressions of progress and efficiency. Peyami Safa wrote: "In Turkey, cubic is the name of the squat, flat, formless apartment building with tiny rooms and low ceilings, constructed with cheap mortar, its wooden parts damaged by an uncontrolled and uncalculated amount of excess sunlight."[74]

The editorials of Hüseyin Cahit Yalçın in the same magazine were less despairing about the architectural properties of "cubic" than about the larger and more profound "homelessness" of modern living. Especially critical of apartments, he lamented that "we left behind our old houses, the repository of our family histories and memories, in exchange for the conveniences of modern living afforded by apartments."[75] In 1937, in a nostalgic piece about old Istanbul, he observed: "Now we are building cubic apartments and furnishing truly *alafranga salons.* But none of these reflect a spirit or taste that is authentically ours, and the noble taste of the past is watching us with a broken heart from behind our old monuments and our old houses within gardens."[76]

In another 1938 editorial, "House and Apartment," he expressed the same sentiments in what can be seen as a profound philosophical critique of modernity, alienation, and placelessness within the confines of an illustrated popular magazine. "A society is not a machine and cannot be reduced to sheer materialism," he wrote. "We are destined to be miserable in those [new] apartments. In this contemporary civilization, apartments have turned us into nomads without home and hearth."[77] Once again, reproducing the prevailing republican ideological construct, he viewed the apartment as an emblem of materialism and individualism, the antithesis of the small, single-family home—the idealized residential type, connected to the earth and associated with nationalism.

In this climate, modernist Turkish architects were placed on the defensive, and they justifed themselves by arguing on two grounds. At the more immediate level, they acknowledged the *technical and architectural* deficiencies of some new buildings, which, they claimed, gave a bad name to "cubic" in the hands of incompetent builders. Reiterating their arguments for professional legitimacy and the importance of employing an architect for residential work at all scales, they offered examples of rationally and functionally designed cubic houses elsewhere in Europe. In his 1939 radio address, for example, after explaining how cubic was a product of "our machine age with its changes in mentality and lifestyle," Behçet Ünsal said: "But alas, our cubic buildings do not look like contemporary examples elsewhere, which reflect the social changes of the new age. Our cubic buildings are merely caricatures resulting from the collaboration of mediocre builders with tasteless and profit-driven clients."[78] In other words, the problem lay not in "cubic houses and apartments" but in how and by whom they were designed.

At a deeper theoretical level, they tried to dissociate modern architecture from the now discredited term "cubic," the stylistic connotations of which had always made them uneasy. They explained how it was a mistake to equate "cubic" with a style and not see the major social and technological transformations in society that prepared its emergence. "The purpose of the New Architecture is not cubism but rationalism," wrote Behçet Ünsal in 1935, arguing that rationalism was a design principle or approach that did not prescribe particular forms.[79] In his 1936 essay "Our Houses," Abidin Mortaş wrote that "modern architecture does not mean horizontal windows, flat surfaces, and wide terraces. It is the most logical and aesthetically sophisticated solution to modern psychological and sociological needs."[80] In an important passage he suggested that modern architecture was formally indeterminate, acquiring shape only in the specific circumstances at hand, thereby effectively negating the stylistic uniformity claimed by a more doctrinaire and canonic Modern Movement. "Examining its best examples from different countries, one cannot doubt that the New Architecture displays different forms and qualities depending on the specific climate, traditions, lifestyles, and worldviews of the country. The unity of technique and materials cannot, in itself, be a basis for the creation of an 'international' architecture. You cannot comfortably accommodate a German family in a Japanese house, or an Englishman in a Hungarian house."[81]

This was, in essence, the primary argument upon which modernist Turkish architects tried to reconcile modernism with nationalist cultural politics. In this task they found invaluable support in the teachings and outlook of their more conservative German and central European teachers and colleagues, who stood largely outside the official circles of CIAM and "international style." Bruno Taut, for example, compellingly argued that the idea of the modern Turkish house should be dissociated from "cubic" and allowed to follow its own natural evolution. In 1938 he wrote, "The new 'Turkish house' will be born only when your architects free themselves from the fashion of 'cubic architecture' that has become a mainstream style everywhere. Only then will the progressive aspects of modern technique be applied with an open mind; climate will be considered before everything else, and in this way, without any self-conscious and contrived effort, some characteristics of the old Turkish houses will be recaptured."[82]

By the end of the 1930s there was much less talk of "harmonious composition of cubic volumes" or of flat roofs and rounded corners. Turkish architects (sometimes the same ones who used these formal elements in their built work) deemphasized the stylistic dimension of modernism, focusing instead on its rationality and, by extension, its inevitable compatibility with the Turkish quest for national expression. They argued that "modern architecture" was naturally and by definition a *national* architecture because it demanded the most rational response to the specific site, program, climate, and lifestyle of particular people in a particular locale. The larger political and ideological context within which architects tried to "nationalize the modern," and the different ways in which they approached this question, is the topic of the next chapter.

6

Milli Mimari

NATIONALIZING THE MODERN

> In today's architecture, the trend is toward nationalism rather than interna-
> tionalism. Although the same new constructional concepts and elements
> are adopted by many different nations, when it comes to ideals, they all
> look for ways of maintaining, developing, and expressing their own identi-
> ties. Modern architecture in Germany is different from modern architecture
> in Italy, France, or the northern countries. . . . During the initial construc-
> tion of Ankara by foreign architects, the urgency of the task left no time to
> contemplate matters of style. It is now time to focus on the need for a
> "national architecture" [*milli mimari*] in Turkey.
>
> —Sedad Hakkı Eldem, "Milli Mimari Meselesi," 1939[1]

THE CRITIQUE OF cubic apartments and the Westernized lifestyles
associated with them was just one manifestation of a larger ideological perspective to
which the leaders of the RPP and most republican intellectuals came to be fully committed—namely, a nationalist view based on a double negation. As much as they
rejected the country's Ottoman and Islamic past as the "civilizational other" of the
new nation, the image of a liberal, cosmopolitan, and individualistic Western society
was equally threatening to their conception of a patriotic and homogeneous Turkish
nation. Especially under the circumstances of the late 1930s—with nationalism ram-
pant everywhere in Europe and war looming on the horizon—the emphasis on nationalism became strong in all aspects of life and culture in Turkey. The same popular
publications and illustrated family magazines that published images of modern
women and lifestyles on their covers came out with conspicuously more nationalistic
and militaristic images in the late 1930s. As republican political discourse emphasized
the difference (and superiority) of Kemalism from the ills of both capitalism and

socialism, republican cultural politics drew closer to the examples set by the National Socialists in Germany and the Fascists in Italy. In this climate, nationalist publications intensified their attacks on avant-garde, modernist, and internationalist currents in art, often with explicit admiration for the cultural politics of the National Socialists and Fascists. A heavy emphasis on the need for "Turkishness" in art and architecture replaced earlier preoccupations with modernity and progress.

The question of a "national architecture" (*milli mimari*) was a complex and difficult one, with no obvious stylistic answer. The very posing of this question and its centrality in the architectural discourse of the late 1930s represent the end of what we might call "the heroic period of early republican modernism"—a closure symbolically marked by the death of Atatürk in 1938. This does not mean that architects abandoned the rationalist and functionalist principles of modernism or that they were any less influenced by what was going on in the architectural culture at large in Europe and the United States. Rather, at a time when nationalist sentiments and statist policies were strong everywhere, they embarked upon a program of "nationalizing the modern," which meant showing the compatibility between Turkish building traditions and the rationalist precepts of modern architecture. Aesthetic canons of cubic modernism were rejected in favor of either more "regionalist" or more monumental and classicized forms. In architectural terms, this nationalism-driven interest in vernacular traditions and historical references resulted in highly original and ultimately more enduring individual works (such as the buildings and projects of Sedad Hakkı Eldem), the significance of which has been fully appreciated only recently. In larger ideological terms, however, Turkish architects collectively contributed to the identification of "national architecture" with the *nationalist ideology* of a powerful and authoritarian state. In the same way that they had embraced the "New Architecture" (*Yeni Mimari*) as an expression of the Kemalist revolution, they now called for a "national architecture" (*milli mimari*) capable of representing the Kemalist program of tracing the historical roots of the Turks. The former embodied the future-oriented aspirations of the new nation; the latter emerged out of a desire to construct for it a deep-rooted historical identity.

If fascination with the technological and industrial icons of modernity constituted the futuristic and utopian dimension of the Kemalist revolution, equally important was an archaic dimension through which Kemalism sought to legitimate the idea of a unified Turkish nation. Many historians and scholars of nationalism talk about the need for all nationalist claims to ground themselves in some preexisting, pure, and timeless identity—a mythical origin in a remote past. "If nation-states are widely conceded to be 'new' and 'historical,'" writes Benedict Anderson, "the nations to which they give political expression always loom out of an immemorial past and still more important, glide into a limitless future."[2] In the same vein, Eric Hobsbawm points out how all nationalisms, which are relatively new constructs in the long history of human society, nonetheless present themselves as ancient and timeless.[3] Whereas Hobsbawm considers nations and their associated rituals to be "invented traditions," a term that suggests a process of simple fabrication, Anderson's evocative term "imagined communities" suggests a more creative process that accounts for the durability and power of nationalisms. Early republican history in Turkey offers ample evidence of the creative zeal with which republican leaders, intellectuals, and artists imagined the nation through symbols, rituals, and spatial practices, including architecture. The message, to be conveyed through art, architecture, and ritual, was that the Turkish nation had existed from time immemorial, albeit in a latent state, and that the new republic was the political expression of this "national essence," coming into self-consciousness under the leadership of Mustafa Kemal and the Republican People's Party.

Having dissociated the country from its more recent Ottoman past, republican leaders focused on two alternative sources for Turkish identity and national essence. The first source was the early civilizations of Central Asia and pre-islamic Anatolia, where the archaic roots of the Turkic peoples and tribes before their assimilation into Islam were located. The second source was the vernacular language and culture of Asia Minor, the Anatolian heartland now seen as the repository of a timeless and authentic Turkish identity from which a national culture could be born. In this way, an unbroken historical continuity of the Turkish "race" was established between prehistory and the present, spanning many empires, states, and geographical regions and culminating with the new republic in Anatolia. To this day, heroic figures in succession from Attila the Hun and Tamerlane to the Ottoman sultans of the early and classic periods are honored as "the ancestors of the Turks" with their pictures in schoolbooks and their busts in public parks.

On these ideological premises, the RPP undertook an active program of "imagining" the Turkish nation, tracing its origins in the remote past and delineating the timeless features that had survived in the present. This task was assigned to the three primary institutional extensions of the RPP: the People's Houses (*Halkevleri*), the Turkish Historical Society (Türk Tarih Kurumu), and the Turkish Language Society (Türk Dil Kurumu).[4] While the People's Houses focused on the folk culture and vernacular traditions of Anatolia, the historical society and the language society started a rigorous program of rewriting national history and, in most cases, propagating its originary myths. Art and architecture were once again important components of this monumental enterprise. Many of the classic studies addressing the question of what constitutes "Turkish art" and "Turkish architecture" were produced in the early republican period, setting the tone for subsequent scholarship. It would not be too far-fetched to suggest that the emergence of Turkish scholars on the scene and the establishment of the history of art and architecture as a distinct discipline in Turkish academia were intimately connected to this republican project of mobilizing historiography for purposes of nation building. This is a vast topic in itself, beyond the scope of this book. The basic outlines of the project, however, are addressed in the first part of this chapter because without this cultural and ideological context, it is impossible to situate the stylistic shifts in architecture in search of a national expression.

Writing Nationalist History and Culture

ALTHOUGH DISCREDITED BY subsequent scholarship, the ideologically motivated "Turkish history thesis" (1932) and "sun language theory" (1936) proposed by the Türk Tarih Kurumu (TTK) and the Türk Dil Kurumu (TDK), respectively, had a major impact on official views of history, culture, and archaeology in the 1930s. Inspired by some eastern European ethnographers, linguists, and archaeologists, the Turkish history thesis proposed that as a consequence of droughts and wars in prehistoric times, Turks had migrated to India, China, Mesopotamia, Anatolia, and, crossing the Ural Mountains, into Europe, carrying their civilization and disseminating it to diverse peoples. Thus, for example, it was postulated that the first indigenous people of Anatolia, the Hittites, were in fact ancestors of Turks. Needless to say, this postulate conveniently reinforced Turkish claims to the land of Anatolia and made Turks the rightful inheritors of an ancient and advanced civilization. Similarly, the sun language theory, which was launched during the First Turkish Language Congress in 1932, sought to establish pure Turkish as the primordial language from which all other languages emerged. The affinities of Turkish to Sumerian and other prehistoric Anatolian and Mesopotamian languages, as well as to other Ural-Altaic languages such as Finnish and Hungarian, were put forth in support of the theory. Collectively, by locating the origin of all civilization and of the white race in Central Asia, these theories not only traced the roots of the Turkish nation to an ancient cradle of civilization but also sought to establish a common ancestry between the Turks and Western civilization.

From one angle, these theories, which sought to provide "scientific" grounds for Turkish claims to be part of Europe and Western civilization, are interesting and illuminating testimonies to the republic's desire to contest Eurocentric and racist theories produced in the West. For example, it is a fact that until recently challenged by a younger generation of critical historians, traditional histories of the Ottoman Empire produced in Europe indeed portrayed "Turks" as complete "outsiders" to Western civilization and largely overlooked the real history of cultural intermixing over centuries.[5] At the same time, however, real historical complexity and cultural overlays were as absent from these nationalist republican theories as they were from the Eurocentric accounts of Western civilization. In a reverse form of racism (this time to demonstrate the superiority of the Turkic race), historical accuracy was subordinated to the ultimate ideological mission of establishing a remote ancestry for the Turkish people. Such a genealogy of Turks was used to legitimate their claims to nationhood in the twentieth century and to enhance their sense of pride and belonging in the Anatolian heartland.

Not unlike other nationalisms that have mobilized archaeology, philology, and museology in support of narrating and imagining the nation, the republican regime actively promoted archaeological excavations and the establishment of museums, claiming the prehistoric and pre-islamic heritage of Anatolia as national treasures.

Archaeological remains, ruins, wall reliefs, and artifacts dating from the Hittite, Urartu, Phrigian, and Lydian civilizations were exhibited in museums, published extensively in the pages of *La Turquie Kemaliste,* and disseminated in postcards and other official propaganda material (fig. 6.1). Many of these archaeological motifs, such as lions, double-headed eagles, and Hittite sun courses, made their way into architecture and sculpture during the 1930s and afterward. Prehistoric Hittite emblems became the official municipal symbols of republican Ankara, today a point of controversy between their Kemalist defenders and a growing Islamic movement that would prefer to replace these "pagan symbols" with religious Muslim ones such as the crescent and the dome.

The most significant outcome of this nationalist climate was the emergence of new perspectives, interpretations, and scholarship in the historiography of Turkish art and architecture. Extending the roots of Turkish art and architecture to prehistoric Central Asia and to other regions of Turkic presence, art historians adopted a much larger temporal and geographical continuum within which the Ottoman period was only one episode rather than the paradigm. They elaborated two basic and interrelated arguments that to this day constitute the hard core of republican historiography in Turkish art and architecture. The first was the argument that Turkish art and architecture had a unique, innovative, and evolving character distinct from other oriental and Islamic arts, and this unique character had been overlooked by orientalist European scholars. The second argument, following from the first, was that in terms of their structure, rationality, and capacity for historical evolution, Turkish art and architecture were closer to the evolution of Western art and architecture, the two traditions connected by threads of common ancestry. While these arguments had their own nationalistic and essentialist biases, they nonetheless posed a challenge to the orientalist and Eurocentric biases of art historiography in the West. They contended that the growth of knowledge, documentation, and evidence on Turkish art and architecture would eventually refute the orientalist-Eurocentric view of all non-Western traditions as "frozen" and incapable of historical evolution. With a much broader historical scope and theoretical boldness than their predecessors in the late empire (see chapter 1), republican architects and architectural historians sought a niche for Turkish art and architecture within the larger schema of world architecture, tracing their historical evolution and comparing them with other artistic and architectural traditions.

Its nationalistic premises notwithstanding, the outcome of this quest was one of prolific scholarly research, archaeological work, and intense debate, the legacy of which is still strong in Turkey. Many prominent art and architectural historians, Turkish and foreign, who taught at the Academy of Fine Arts contributed to this scholarship and debate throughout the 1930s and 1940s. The Austrian art historian Heinrich Gluck (1889–1930) traced Seljuk and Ottoman art in Anatolia to certain Central Asian motifs and monuments. Albert Gabriel (1883–1972) focused on the rationality, innovativeness, and formal purity of Ottoman-Turkish architecture, which

Fig. 6.1. The nationalist search for prehistoric roots in Anatolia: reclaiming the Hittite civilization.
Top: Hittite statues in the Antiquities Museum in Istanbul (Ministry of Interior Press Office postcard, 1930s). **Bottom:** the Hittite monument in Ankara, at the busiest intersection of Atatürk Boulevard (1990s photograph).

was "unique among other Islamic traditions."[6] Gabriel's writings on the rationality and functionality of the Ottoman-Turkish house were also of great interest to Turkish architects in their efforts to nationalize modern architecture. The first prominent Turkish scholar to present Turkish art and architecture within a vast historical continuum and to draw attention to its rational, formally pure, and evolutionary character was Celal Esat Arseven (1875–1971), artist, public figure, and professor of architectural history at the Academy of Fine Arts. That Arseven was the author of the booklet *Yeni Mimari* (New Architecture, 1931), the publicity document for European modernism (see chapter 4), also suggests something about the Kemalists' desire to see Turkish architecture as a rational evolution from prehistory to the "New Architecture" of the twentieth century.

Arseven's construction of a genealogy and evolutionary history for Turkish art and architecture was a result of his participation in the larger effort by the TTK and TDK, as a member of the scientific committee to research the origins of Turkish history and culture.[7] Echoing the Turkish history thesis, he authored monumental works that sought to establish central Asian and Anatolian civilizations of prehistoric times as the birthplaces of Turkish art and architecture, the influences of which were disseminated to diverse regions and cultures from India to Europe. For example, citing the Hittites as the earliest "Turks" who came from Central Asia to Anatolia, he wrote about the similarities and continuities between Hittite building techniques (adobe walls plastered with mud, wooden posts, flat earthen roofs, etc.) and the contemporary building practices of Anatolian peasants.[8] He pointed to continuities between the tomb forms and monumental portals found in central Asia and those of the Anatolian Seljuks. He traced decorative motifs like the double-headed eagle from Hittites to Anatolian Seljuks to European Crusaders who, he argued, carried them over into Romanesque and Gothic styles.[9] He summarized these continuities metaphorically: "Turks are like a large river that, departing from its remote origins, follows the lands and valleys that it encounters on the way, sometimes wandering into far-away lands only to return closer to its source again and sometimes joining, among sandy deserts, with other tributaries, once part of itself. [It is] a river known by a different name each time it crosses a new place."[10]

The departure point for Arseven's work was a critique of orientalist art historians who, he argued, ignored the uniqueness of Turkish art and architecture and classified them indiscriminately under a single "Islamic" category. In the preface to his monumental *History of Turkish Art,* he offered what can be seen as one of the earliest criticisms directed at orientalism and oriental pavilions in the great expositions, long before Edward Said's work in the late 1970s. Arseven wrote:

Today, with the exception of those closely engaged with art and architecture, Europeans cannot see the differences between the characters of various domes and minarets of the orient and the world of Islam. In their minds, there is *an imaginary orient* [my emphasis] composed of Iranian minarets, Syrian domes, Magribi arches, and Egyptian decoration. In the recent exhibition pavilions in Europe and America, it is possible to see an Egyptian *masharabbiya* on a Turkish house, or an Iranian minaret next to a Moroccan dome. It is not unusual to see the decorative motifs of Islamic countries all jumbled together, such as the geometric decoration of the Arab next to the *Rumi* and *Hatayi* motifs of the Turk.[11]

Immediately after this general critique of European orientalism, the nationalist premises of his analysis emerged, with their emphasis not only on the difference of Turkish art from other oriental and Islamic traditions but also on its superior qualities:

Turkish art is completely different from these examples [Indian, Iranian, Arab] in the simplicity of its composition, its restraint from exaggeration, and the harmony and logic of its forms. . . . It is a grave mistake of Europeans to classify Turkish art as a small branch of Islamic art. No other art among the arts of Islamic countries are as noble as Turkish art. As in the history of civilization, in the history of art as well, Turks have been denied their rightful place for so long.[12]

It should be noted that the historiography promoted by Arseven and by other republican historians after him did acknowledge exchanges, mutations, and cross-fertilizations with other traditions while maintaining, however, the uniqueness of the "Turkish character." In response to those who claimed that Turkish art was not "original," Arseven wrote:

It is important not to misunderstand the term "originality." There is no art that is born out of itself alone and is completely unique. We know that Renaissance art, which is considered a unique style, was born out of the inspiration of Greek and Roman art and that Romanesque and Gothic art assimilated numerous influences from the Orient. Undoubtedly, Turkish art, too, bears certain elements and influences of others. Yet in its evolution it has never lost the Turkish character of its origins.[13]

This explanation neatly sums up the major thrust of art historiography in the republican period, and many other scholars have repeated similar arguments. As Arseven stated explicitly on many occasions, the tasks of producing scholarship, informing the world about Turkish art and architecture, and correcting misconceptions were elevated to the status of national duty. Among the slightly younger generation of scholars, Oktay Aslanapa was one who followed in Arseven's footsteps. Drawing attention to recent research and excavations in Central Asia, Iran, Afghanistan, and Anatolia, he traced the evolution of Turkish art and architecture from prehistoric Central Asia to the late Ottoman period. Like Arseven, he admitted the cross-fertilization of Turkish art with influences from Sassanid, Abbasid, and other sources, but he argued that "in all monuments of Turkish art, in whatever geographical region they may be, one is immediately struck by a characteristic style that clearly distinguishes them from any other artistic tradition."[14]

Behçet Ünsal, the prolific republican architect and educator who wrote about modernism and "cubic architecture" in *Arkitekt,* also made similar arguments about the uniqueness of Turkish architecture and compared it with Arab and Persian architecture. He argued that to negate their "unmistakable differences of character" would be the same thing as lumping French and English Gothic or English and Italian Renaissance art under the label "Christian art."[15] His was not a neutral comparison, however. For example, Turkish architecture had "modest harmonious proportions," compared with the "irregular proportions" of Arab or the "disproportion" of Persian architecture. The conception of Turkish architecture was "simple and clear" in comparison with the "intricate geometrical conception" of Arab and the "fantastic and poetical conception" of Persian architecture. In Turkish architecture, "character was appropriate to the nature of the material," unlike in Arab architecture. "Moderation in ornament, effects of light and shade" distinguished Turkish architecture from the decorative extravaganza and crowded ornamentation of Arab and Persian examples. In other words, Turkish architecture already possessed many qualities exalted by modern architects in the West, whereas other Islamic architectures were "oriental."

In the context of this new nationalist historiography in the early republic, the status of Ottoman art and architecture is particularly interesting and ambivalent. On the one hand, as discussed in chapters 1 and 2, republican architects had already abandoned Ottoman revivalism in favor of European modernism, and the country's Ottoman past was cast aside as the "civilizational other" of the Kemalist revolution. A sharp and ideologically charged binary opposition between the old (Ottoman) and the new (republican) was built into the official discourse and revolutionary rhetoric of the RPP. At the same time, however, once stripped of their Islamic and cosmopolitan aspects, the six hundred years of Ottoman dynastic history and culture were reincorporated into the larger history of Turks and Turkish culture as one of its most powerful and victorious epochs. Republican discourse on the art, architecture, and culture of the Ottoman period was devoted almost exclusively to identifying the "Turkish character" of Ottoman heritage and reclaiming it for the nationalist narrative.[16] Seljuk monuments, along with early and classical Ottoman heritage, were promoted in official publications and postcards as national treasures (fig. 6.2). One particularly significant event was an exhibition of the drawings and photographs of "Turkish architectural monuments of the Ottoman period" by the republican architect Sedad Çetintaş, head of the Directorate of Historical Monuments and Museums Survey Office and a modernist in his own work.

Rather than completely abandoning Ottoman architecture, this nationalist reclamation of Ottoman heritage became an important theme in the writings of republican architects and architectural historians from the late 1930s onward. The point they made on every occasion was that Ottoman architecture was only *one* historical manifestation of Turkish character in architecture—a character the Turks had possessed long before the Ottoman Empire was established and would continue to possess long after it was replaced by the republic. For example, they argued that the domed system

Fig. 6.2. Official postcards of Seljuk and Ottoman monuments intended to illustrate the historical continuity of the Turkish nation. Published by the Ministry of Interior Press Office, late 1930s.

of Ottoman mosque architecture was *not* a derivative of Byzantine architecture, as many European scholars claimed, but a unique contribution of Turks dating back to their earlier history—something that "Byzantium had actually borrowed from Mesopotamia and from the Sassanians."[18] More significantly, like Behçet Ünsal, many others claimed that it was the "Turkish character" of Ottoman mosques and monuments that explained their formal purity, their rationality, and their simplicity, qualities unmatched by other Islamic traditions. In 1934, the republican architect Aptullah Ziya located this "Turkish character" in the classical period of Ottoman architecture, prior to its contamination and "enslaving" by Arab and Persian culture (*Arap ve Acem kültürü esareti*).[19] The same year, in an article titled "Architecture and Turkishness," Behçet Sabri and Bedrettin Hamdi juxtaposed a photograph of an Ottoman mosque with one of an Arab mosque, making a clear value judgment in favor of the former. The captions read "Perfection in architectural taste: a Turkish mosque in Istanbul" versus "Primitiveness in architectural taste: an Arab mosque in Baghdad."[20] Celal Esat Arseven exhibited similar biases in his history of Turkish art, in which the pattern of a tile decoration from a classical Ottoman monument was captioned as the paradigm of "purity and simplicity," whereas the plaster ornament from the walls of the Alhambra Palace was labeled "overcrowded and exaggerated complexity."[21]

In general, echoing the same orientalist biases that Europeans typically displayed toward Islamic architecture, most republican architects and art historians celebrated the rational and tectonic character of the Turkish mosque against the "decorative excesses" of Arab architecture. What is particularly important in this overemphasis on the rationality, simplicity, tectonic character, and evolutionary capacity of the Ottoman—that is, *Turkish*—mosque is that these were precisely the qualities art historians had traditionally attributed to European architecture from classical antiquity to modernism. Hence, this particular reading of Turkish art legitimated republican claims to be part of Western civilization without negating heritage and history, and it allowed Turkish architects to claim modernism as an idea already implied in "national" architecture. The appreciation of classical Ottoman architecture for its rationality, structural logic, and tectonic quality was not limited to nationalist Turkish architects but was also strong among their German-speaking teachers and colleagues. Ernst Egli made extensive studies of Sinan's classical mosques and later published a book on Sinan.[22] Bruno Taut so deeply admired Sinan's masterpieces that while working on an urban scheme for the Istanbul University area, he proposed a terrace-platform from which the magnificence of the Suleymaniye Mosque could be viewed.[23]

Many scholars point out that although nationalist theories about Central Asian Turks being the fountainhead of all civilization were later abandoned, "a milder synthesis" based on the idea of "recuperating the soul of the folk" proved to be a more enduring constituent of Turkish nationalism.[24] Anatolia was the geographic heartland of this folk nationalism. Having rejected earlier ideologies of Ottomanism, Islamism, and pan-Turkism, all three of which extended beyond the geographical boundaries of Anatolia, Kemalist nationalism focused its attention on the land within the borders of the National Pact (Misak-ı Milli). These borders, which corresponded roughly to the borders of present-day Turkey, were secured by the heroic War of Independence and the Lausanne Treaty (1923) and were therefore highly charged with the symbolism of the birth of the nation. While the prehistoric civilizations of Anatolia provided the archaic roots of national culture, the folk culture and peasant life of Anatolia were seen as the repository within which the survival of that culture into the present was maintained.

Throughout the 1930s, the romantic populism of the republic was nurtured by this myth of Anatolia—the locus of patriotism, idealism, and purity, separate from and contrasting with cosmopolitan and imperial Istanbul. The departure of Mustafa Kemal Atatürk from Istanbul and his setting foot on Anatolian shores in 1919 have been elevated to mythical status by the Turkish nationalist narrative as the onset of the War of Independence. In this narrative, the real heroes of the war were the nameless peasants of Anatolia, and the birth of the nation was set upon the barren land, battlegrounds, and poverty-stricken villages of this heartland. It was in the peasant life, vernacular language, and folk culture of Anatolia, therefore, that the source of an authentic, uncontaminated, and timeless Turkish identity could be located. At the same time that Western civilization, science, and progress were presented as pillars of the Kemalist revolution, it was also postulated that these had to be carried into Anatolia to be nationalized and authenticized there. The prominent novelist and republican intellectual Yakup Kadri Karaosmanoğlu put it this way: "For the nationalist Turkish Westernist [*garpçı*], the most characteristic attribute of his Westernism [*garpçılık*] should be to stamp it with a Turkish style. The hat should not be our master, but we should be mastering the hat. Westernization is a particular principle of life. Only in the service of a national will, a national culture, and, most significantly, a national morality can this principle fulfill its creative and constructive role."[25]

It was proposed that national culture could be born only from the synthesis of the timeless "national essence" located in Anatolia with the norms of contemporary— that is, Western—civilization. The entire cultural politics of the republic was construed around this formula, best expressed in the 1935 "program" published by the RPP as the desirability of an art or culture that was "international in technique and method, Turkish in spirit and style" (*teknik beynelmilel, ruh Türk; usul beynelmilel, üslup Türk*).[26]

One particularly illustrative expression of this official cultural policy was the attempt to create a polyphonic Turkish music after Western models but inspired by the folk tunes of Anatolia. After rejecting Ottoman court music and the music of religious orders, the republic looked in two directions: toward Western polyphonic classical music and toward the folk music of Anatolian villages. In 1935, the German composer Paul Hindemith was appointed to reform Turkish music education along European lines and to establish the State Conservatory of Music in Ankara, "the prize institution and the privileged offspring of the republic."[27] A year later, the RPP People's House in Ankara invited the Hungarian composer Bela Bartok to advise officials on "how a Turkish national music should be developed from Turkish folk music."[28] Bartok had already made a reputation with his ethnographic music research in Hungary and had written extensively on the relationship between folk music research and nationalism. In a 1929 essay on Hungarian folk music, Bartok had defined folk music as "a separate type of melodic creativity, which, by reason of its being a part of the peasant environment, reflects a certain uniform emotional pattern and has its own specific style."[29] He had argued that peasant music was the outcome of "a natural force whose operation is unconscious in men who are not influenced by urban culture" and that "peasantlike" and "primitive" were not derogatory terms but designated "a concept of ideal simplicity devoid of trashiness."[30] In a series of essays in the late 1930s and early 1940s he gave detailed instructions concerning the collection of folk music as ethnographic specimens from the villages farthest removed from urban culture, to be obtained from informants untainted by education and urban influences.[31] Most significantly, he made comparisons between linguistic research and ethnographic music research and warned against "ultra-nationalism in musical folklore"—that is, the myth of "race purity in music," which ignores the continuous give and take of melodies between different peoples over long periods of encounters, exchange, migrations, and conquests.[32]

Bartok came to Turkey in October 1936 and, following three lectures and a concert in Ankara, set off to collect folk tunes and songs from nomadic Yürük tribes and villages in southern Anatolia around Adana. Accompanied by his European-educated Turkish colleagues from the State Conservatory, Ahmed Adnan Saygun, Necil Kazım Akses, and Ulvi Cemal Erkin, Bartok made recordings and notations that became the basis for many classical compositions in the Western genre. The systematic collecting, classifying, and archiving of tunes continued thereafter, and to this day these songs have been preserved in the official archives of the State Conservatory and the State Radio. More significantly, Bartok's own words regarding the similarities between Hungarian and Turkish folk music lent support to the nationalist history and language theses proposed at the same time. Echoing the way these theories traced the origins of Turks to the waves of migrations of Turkic tribes from Central Asia toward Europe and Asia Minor, Bartok wrote:

No such tunes can be found among the Yugoslavs, the Slovaks of the West and North, or the Greeks, and even among the Bulgarians they are only occasional. If we take into account the fact that such tunes can be found only among Hungarians, among the Transylvanian and Moldavian Rumanians, and the Cheremiss [a Finno-Ugric people living in the Volga region] and Northern Turkish peoples, then it seems likely that this music is the remains of an antique, thousand-year-old Turkish musical style.[33]

The example of music offers the paradigm of official republican cultural politics in the 1930s. Literature, drama, painting, and sculpture followed similar lines under the nationwide guidance of the People's Houses, and in every branch of the arts,

Western genres and techniques were applied to Anatolian subject matters. At the same time that the RPP embarked upon its "civilizing mission" for the colonization of the countryside (see chapter 3), and at the same time that model villages and new infrastructure were proposed to transform Anatolia, the primitive beauty of the countryside and its peasants became an artistic trope. Folk arts and artifacts—the kilims, baskets, copper utensils, primitive tools, colorful dresses, songs, and dances of the peasants—were now objects of artistic inspiration as well as ethnographic study, systematic preservation, and public display.

The predominance of Anatolian themes and folk culture in painting was conspicuous in the cultural scene of the 1930s, setting apart the "nationalist school" from the more urban, cosmopolitan, and academic schools of painting located in Istanbul. In 1932, the art department of Gazi Teachers' College was established in Ankara, ending the monopoly of the Istanbul Academy of Fine Arts upon art education and soon becoming an important center in the proliferation of "Anatolian themes" in Turkish art. In 1937, a travel program for artists was established by the RPP under the auspices of the People's Houses. Analogous to the efforts of Bela Bartok, this program was intended to encourage artists to travel in Anatolia and paint the landscapes, villages, peasants, and folkloric characteristics of its rural settings. In tandem with the nationalist attacks on avant-garde art, many Turkish artists distanced themselves from abstract, formalist, and individualist conceptions of modern art, instead seeking to represent the collective national essence believed to be rooted in Anatolia.

Particularly illustrative is the case of Group D, the first "avant-garde" group of young Turkish painters who, after introducing modernist trends such as cubism, expressionism, and constructivism to Turkey (see chapter 4), aligned themselves with the official ideology and produced what one art critic calls "a peasant cubism."[34] Of the most prominent members of the group, Bedri Rahmi Eyüboğlu, Nurullah Berk, and Cemal Tollu were especially prolific in adapting cubist abstraction techniques to folkloric motifs, peasant women, and Anatolian landscapes (fig. 6.3). They also incorporated inspirations from archaeological findings, Hittite figures, and other motifs from pre-islamic Anatolian civilizations. The work of Turgut Zaim in the late 1930s and early 1940s epitomizes the Turkish "naïve" genre, with highly stylized and idealized paintings of peasant women and children, barren Anatolian landscapes with mud-brick houses and poplar trees, folk arts, crafts, kilims, and copper pots. It should be noted that Zaim also designed stage sets for productions of the National Theater, the State Opera and Ballet, and the State Symphony Orchestra, where the work of Bartok's colleagues, the new Turkish composers inspired by Anatolian folk tunes, was performed. Collectively, such artistic and cultural production of the 1930s set the foundation for what became Turkey's official, state-sponsored art and culture—an official art and culture challenged today by many alternative expressions.[35]

Architectural culture was inevitably informed by these attempts at rewriting nationalist history and by the prevailing nationalist sentiments centered on Anatolian themes. The initial enthusiasm for the New Architecture when it was introduced in

Fig. 6.3. Anatolian folk motifs in Turkish painting: "peasant cubism" of the 1930s. **Top:** "Woman ironing" by Nurullah Berk. **Bottom:** "Composition" by Bedri Rahmi Eyüboğlu. Both artists were members of the "avant-garde" Group D, which was influenced by cubism and constructivism.

the late 1920s and early 1930s was toned down, and an increasingly intensified plea for "national architecture" (*milli mimari*) became the order of the day. Parallel to the developments in historiography, archaeology, and ethnography already mentioned, a renewed interest in vernacular building traditions as well as those of the pre-islamic civilizations of Anatolia rapidly became architects' version of participating in this effort. The challenge was to reconcile this interest with the inviolable core of architects' professional discourse, namely, the rationalist, functionalist principles of modernism and the notion of progress upon which modernist doctrines were predicated. It is possible to identify a range of positions on the question of "nationalizing the modern"—positions overlapping in certain respects, contradictory in others, but always in search of a modern *and* national Turkish architecture. The basic consensus among Turkish architects on exactly how the modern could be nationalized was that they should turn their attention to the country's own vernacular building traditions spread over the Anatolian landscape.[36]

Appropriating Vernacular Traditions

VERNACULAR ARCHITECTURE WAS neither "Western"/cosmopolitan nor "Ottoman"/imperial, both of which were rejected by Kemalist nationalism. As a product of the country's native soil, it embodied "the essential core of the nation" and "the soul of its peasant folk"—important themes in the nationalist narrative of the 1930s. More significantly, vernacular architecture represented a particular wisdom of building distilled over centuries and admired by rationalist architects everywhere. Buildings of the common folk were seen as perfect expressions of utility, practicality, simplicity, constructional honesty, and conformity to local materials, climate, and resources: that is, the same basic qualities and criteria that modern architecture sought after. Modern architecture, after all, had emerged as a critical discourse by those wishing to replace the fixed stylistic norms of classicism and academicism with an empirical approach to design that had to be, by definition, responsive to local conditions. Form would not be an a priori stylistic choice but a consequence of rational considerations of program, site, soil, climate, budget, and materials, just as it had always been with vernacular buildings or folk architecture.[37] Therefore, in its true spirit, modern architecture could not possibly be an "international style": integral to its very conception was a profound contextualist and regionalist sensibility.

This understanding of modern architecture as a context-sensitive, rational approach to building constituted the hard core of Turkish architectural discourse in the 1930s, according to which the truism "modern equals national" was construed. In other words, if modern buildings were the most rational and appropriate responses to the climatic, topographical, cultural, social, and economic conditions of a particular place, then they could not be anything but "national." The ideals of modern architecture and vernacular building were one and the same, and therefore architects had much to learn from the lessons of the vernacular, which, it was argued, gave superb examples of rationality. That European modernism was itself inspired by vernacular traditions from Japan to the Mediterranean further strengthened this belief. In 1934, Behçet Sabri and Bedrettin Hamdi wrote that given the poverty of the building industry in Turkey at the time, vernacular architecture showed the only viable solution:

If we cannot use flat roofs or metal windows or if we are limited to building in concrete, stone, and wood in the absence of feasible steel construction, it does not mean that our works are not "modern." In traditional Turkish architecture, all the elements and materials were appropriately used, logical and functional, offering a source of inspiration to European thought and architecture. The new works of young Turkish architects should be viewed in the same way that traditional [vernacular] Turkish architecture was viewed.[38]

This contextualist and regionalist message constituted a central theme in the teachings of the European architects who educated the entire first generation of republican architects. From Ernst Egli and Clemenz Holzmeister in the early 1930s to Bruno Taut and Paul Bonatz in the late 1930s and the 1940s, they all encouraged the study of vernacular traditions. In 1930, in an important article titled "Architectural Context" published in *Türk Yurdu* (National Homeland), Ernst Egli introduced the inherent connection between modern architecture and nationalist passion for the homeland. "Architectural context (or locality)," he wrote, "is the overall character of light, air, sun, wind, topography, terrain, water, vegetation, the harshness or mildness of nature, the distinct quality of the night, and the mysterious music of dusk. Modern architecture calls for the cross-fertilization of the international seeds of modern architectural progress with the specific forms of architectural contexts. It is my opinion that Anatolia can play a major role in modern architecture."[39] Egli then praised the introverted character of the traditional Anatolian house with its cool and shady courtyards "open to starry skies above" and "closed to the dust of the streets." He concluded that "if designed with modern means for modern lifestyles, this could be a model house for Anatolian towns."[40]

Egli's use of courtyards, shaded porticos, slender columns, and cubic window projections in his own work for public buildings in Ankara can be seen as a subtle reflection of these sensibilities. Although the work of Egli and Holzmeister, commonly known as "Ankara cubic" or "Viennese cubic," became the target of nationalist architectural discourse in the later half of the 1930s, to their architects and contemporaries these buildings *were* responsive to their context. They drew upon the idealized qualities of simplicity, austerity, and modesty that were regarded as appropriate for the making of a capital city out of scratch in the middle of the Anatolian plain. Holzmeister's presidential residence for Atatürk (1930–1932), for example (see fig. 5.21), was celebrated in contemporary publications for its modest scale, undecorated simplicity, and modern aesthetic, in the spirit of Ankara's humble but heroic emergence on the scene. Not unlike the efforts to create a polyphonic Western music out of Anatolian folk tunes or the cubic paintings of peasant life, this building was

Fig. 6.4. Two color drawings by Sedad Hakkı Eldem (1928) capturing the atmosphere of the central Anatolian plain. **Top:** Mud-brick houses of central Anatolian villages. **Bottom:** An unidentified perspective evoking an arid climate and a barren land. The ceiling of the portico is decorated with kilim motifs of the region.

praised for "skillfully combining the latest building techniques of the West with *the cubic tradition of the Anatolian plain* [my emphasis]."[41]

Through the late 1920s and early 1930s, as the building of Ankara was turned into a national saga, the arid climate, barren landscape, and "noble" poverty of central Anatolia were idealized, and architects were inspired to explore a purist aesthetic in the spirit of the central Anatolian vernacular. For modernist architects, the cubic forms, plain surfaces, and flat roofs of the New Architecture found romantic justification in the poorer mud-brick traditions as well as in prehistoric Hittite settlements of the central Anatolian plain. Even Sedad Hakkı Eldem, who championed a different kind of timber vernacular building tradition as the source of Turkish identity, observed in his early sketches the beauty of plain adobe walls, flattened earth roofs, courtyards, and shaded porticos in a dry, barren landscape (fig. 6.4).

The efforts to postrationalize modern forms (cubic volumes, wide terraces and balconies, flat roofs, etc.) by reference to vernacular precedents in Anatolia conflicted conspicuously with the equally strong claim that modern form was a logical response to the new requirements and possibilities of the industrial age. Modernist Turkish architects such as Behçet Ünsal, Aptullah Ziya, Abidin Mortaş, Zeki Sayar, and Behçet Sabri and Bedrettin Hamdi who wrote in *Mimar* and *Arkitekt* wanted modern form to be the expression of progress and revolution and, at the same time, of a "contextual" and therefore "national" architecture. Canonic buildings of the Modern Movement, even the most paradigmatic examples of "international style," were presented, with no hint of irony, as contextual and responsive to local conditions. For example, according to Behçet Sabri and Bedrettin Hamdi, the unity of technique and materials was not enough to create an "international style"; there was no such thing as a universal "concrete architecture" or "cubic architecture." "Context" was the most important factor. In an article titled "Architecture and Turkishness," they wrote: "The mother of all architecture is context [*muhit*]. Our country needs serious works that respond to its soil, its water, its air, and its nature—works that connect with the context and revitalize local feelings in the contemporary world. . . . Local art is both rational [*rasyonel*] and national [*milli*]. Today a national architecture [*milli mimari*] can be born only out of rational Turkish works responsive to the locale [*mahal*]."[42]

Yet when it came to illustrating this article, they used a photograph of Mies van der Rohe's Tugendaht House (1928–1930), a modernist glass box, as an example of "responsiveness to light, nature, and context." After declaring that "only local works can give birth to a national/rational architecture," they added: "However, there is no room for tradition and old forms in rational architecture. . . . National architecture is not the art of traditions and motifs. It cannot be assembled and pieced together; it can only be created anew."[43] Even more strikingly, in Aptullah Ziya's essay "Nationalism in Art," two of the most canonic, geometrically conceived concrete and glass buildings of the Modern Movement were identified as examples of "national architecture." Aptullah Ziya characterized Le Corbusier's villa for the Weissenhof Siedlung exhibition in Stuttgart—a building epitomizing the canon of "international style" in the architectural culture at large—as "a work reflecting its *national* character" (my emphasis). Similarly, he described Ilya Goloshov's constructivist building for a workers' club in Moscow as expressive of "Russian character."[44]

These examples suggest that for modernist architects, appropriateness to context (*muhite uygunluk*) often meant response to *physical* context—climate, terrain, vegetation, and so forth—ultimately reducing "culture" to "nature." Bruno Taut, Egli's successor at the academy, also identified culture with nature but elaborated a more sophisticated understanding of the term "nature." In his collected lectures, *Mimari Bilgisi,* published in Turkish in 1938, he talked about "nature" (*tabiat* in Turkish) in the double meaning of the term and with strong evocations of the "nation." "Nature" signified both the "elements" of the locality (rain, fog, sun, wind, light, etc.) and the "character" of its people: "Nations have adapted to climate, and many different characters have resulted from it. . . . Architecture is a mirror reflecting the character and nature of nations. It is this mirroring aspect that largely determines whether it is light or heavy, lively or serene, diffused or concentrated, elegant or systematic."[45]

This understanding of architecture that Taut sought to impart to his students was an expression of his basic critical modernist position and his distaste for "international style"—or, for that matter, any stylistic orthodoxy that claimed universal validity.[46] He criticized the Modern Movement's fetishizing of stripped-down technique, construction, and function and lamented the reduction of architecture to "objects of use or means of traffic" that imitated the aesthetic of ocean liners, cars, airplanes, and grain elevators.[47] According to him, architecture was irreducible to the technological icons of modern transportation that had unfortunately become a fashionable "stylistic zeitgeist" for the modernist avant-garde and their followers in Turkey. Unlike engineering design, architecture was inseparable from the particularities of locality. He argued, for example, that the beauty of the Japanese temple, born out of humid summers and cold winters, would have been "dead like a fish out of water in the bright sun and transparent air of Greece." Conversely, the classical columns of the Greek temple, which could survive only in this bright sun, would be condemned to death when taken to distant lands "as if they were cars or trains, suffocating them in the fog and the humidity of the north."[48] Insightfully avoiding the term "international style," Taut talked about the "international art of construction" (*yapı sanatı* in Turkish), a universal creative spirit of construction, proportion, and quality that acquired form only through the specifics of locality and "national character."[49] His deep reverence for the Ottoman high tradition, epitomized by the work of Sinan, as well as for vernacular traditions of house building, was a reflection of his divergence from the orthodoxy of the Modern Movement.

Although the "cubic tradition" of mud-brick and stone houses in Anatolia offered a convenient justification for modern form, Sedad Hakkı Eldem, arguably the most important figure of modern Turkish architecture, championed a very different kind of vernacular. He devoted his life and career to studying, documenting, and adapting to modern design the old wooden houses with pitched tile roofs—the

Fig. 6.5. A traditional wood frame "Turkish house" from Safranbolu, a Black Sea town in northern Turkey.

archetypal "Turkish house" spanning the vast territories of the Ottoman Empire from the Balkans to Istanbul and northern Anatolia (fig. 6.5). As the leading figure of the "national architecture" movement (*milli mimari hareketi*), Eldem was "doubly rebellious" against both the Ottoman revivalist national style that he had been taught at the academy by Vedat Bey and Mongeri and the "Ankara cubic" of Egli and Holzmeister.[50] He was brought up in an elite Ottoman family—both his grandfather Osman Hamdi Bey and his great-grandfather İbrahim Edhem Paşa had been important figures in late Ottoman artistic and cultural life—and had spent his childhood and youth in Germany, where his father was posted as ambassador. Thus he was thoroughly familiar with both the Ottoman building tradition and the German modern architecture of the interwar years. As an architectural student at the academy on the eve of the modernist reforms, he had lovingly sketched the old wooden houses of Istanbul, and he saw in them a particular "type" that could be appropriated as the basis of a modern and national Turkish architecture.

Like that of many of his colleagues, Eldem's appreciation of the vernacular was motivated by a distinctly modernist agenda. However, as an almost tautological corollary to their argument that modern architecture was "by definition national" (because it was the most appropriate response to context), he proposed that the traditional

Turkish house was "already modern" (because it embodied precisely the same qualities that modernism sought after). In a much-quoted passage he said:

The traditional Turkish house is remarkably similar to today's conceptions of the modern house. Ample windows and light, free plan, the emphasis on comfort over ostentatious display, conformity to the nature of materials, generous supply of terraces, garden and courtyard intimately linking the house with nature. Aren't these the same characteristics that we look for in modern houses? We find them all in the traditional Turkish house. . . . The leading figure of modern architecture, Le Corbusier, is profoundly inspired by the Turkish house. He lifts his houses upon stilts, reserving the ground for services, garage, etc., just like our storages, *arabalık* and *taşlık*s. . . . He uses wide terraces above the ground, just like our *hayat*s, directly connected to the garden or the courtyard. His windows are oriented toward the line of the view and the horizon, just like our rows of windows.[51]

In fact, Eldem admitted to having "discovered" the Turkish house *in Europe* during the two years he spent in Paris and Berlin after his graduation from the academy in Istanbul. He cited three specific sources for this "discovery."[52] First, as expressed in the foregoing quotation, Le Corbusier's ideas about the lightness of the house lifted above ground level matched the form and organization of Turkish houses. Second, Auguste Perret's use of reinforced concrete was inspirational for Eldem, who wished to translate the constructional logic of the traditional timber frame into reinforced concrete—the material to which he expressed his devotion on every occasion.[53] Perhaps most important of all was Eldem's discovery of Frank Lloyd Wright's prairie houses through the Wasmuth publications that he saw in Germany. "In these houses, I found the characteristics of the Turkish houses of the future," Eldem said. "Flat, horizontal lines, rows of windows, wide overhangs, and pitched roofs were very close to the ideal Turkish house I had in mind."[54] The "romanticism, closeness to nature, and honest use of wood and natural stone in these houses" were more appealing to Eldem than the cubist/purist boxes of Le Corbusier.

Under the influence of Frank Lloyd Wright, and preoccupied with the idea of a national modern architecture, Eldem prepared a series of drawings that he titled "Anatolian Houses" and exhibited in Paris and Turkey in 1928 (fig. 6.6). These beautifully rendered sketches projected modern, single-family dwellings with pitched roofs and rows of windows above solid walls, all set in idyllic landscapes. In spite of the title, these hypothetical countrysides bore no resemblance to the barren Anatolian landscape or to any other particular location; the buildings were as "acontextual" as, for example, the minimal cubic houses that Bekir İhsan proposed for middle-class families in Anatolian towns (see fig. 5.15). There is a certain romantic and utopian dimension to Eldem's "Anatolian Houses," reminiscent of the conservative utopias of Heinrich Tessenow and the Heimatschutz movement in Germany, with which Eldem was thoroughly familiar. Admittedly, important ideological differences separated the two architects. Eldem was an elite urbanite whose interest in the vernacular had little

Fig. 6.6. Sedad Hakkı Eldem's modern reconstruction of the traditional "Turkish house": an example from his "Anatolian Houses" series (1929). This was a beautifully rendered set of color perspectives showing single-family villas set in idyllic countrysides and inspired by traditional wood-frame houses (especially window modulations and tile roofs).

to do with Tessenow's glorification of the simplicity of the peasant and the morality of the small town against the alienation and excess wrought by modernity. Advanced industrial civilization, the object of Heimatschutz critique, was the very ideal of progress that Kemalist Turkey struggled to reach. Eldem's "Anatolian Houses" included not only romantic dwellings in the forest but also large modern homes with cars parked in front of them in imagined suburban settings, and even urban apartments. Yet Eldem's preoccupation with the "Turkish house" as the embodiment of a culture of building and living (*Baukunst* and *Wohnkultur*) informed by "national character" does bring to mind some of Tessenow's ideas on the "German house." Rejecting the term "international style," Eldem adopted the premise that "as long as there is a difference between the characters and moods of nations, there will be a difference in the culture of living and, in turn, in the form and concept of the house."[55]

Eldem's appreciation of the traditional Turkish *Wohnkultur* was also filtered through his modernist sensibilities. He argued that the elements that distinguished the traditional interior of a Turkish house were in fact embodiments of modernist criteria such as comfort, hygiene, flexibility, and the use of built-in furniture. In his interior studies dating from 1928–1929, he incorporated highly rationalized and stylized versions of traditional elements such as the hearth and the built-in low seat, also displaying the modernist penchant for simplicity, lightness, geometric patterns, and natural materials (fig. 6.7). In the same way that he argued for the "modernity" of the traditional Turkish house, he argued for the "modernity" of its interior:

The built-in furniture of today's modern houses has always existed in our old houses with their built-in closets, shelves, lamp niches, etc., all incorporated into the wall. Aren't the European convertible bed and the American mechanical beds that disappear into the wall only contemporary versions of our low seats (*sedir*), which transformed into beds at night? Isn't the fireplace the equivalent of our traditional hearths (*ocak*)? What about hygiene? While Europe used chamber pots until the last century, our *hamam*s had hot-and-cold running water. How can one miss the similarities between the secret *gusülhane*s hidden in the closets of our old houses and the shower/sink cabinets of most modern houses and hotels of Europe? Aren't all these features, which Europe has discovered only recently, a testimony to the superiority of our nation?[56]

In the 1930s Sedad Eldem assumed the leadership of the so-called national architecture movement (*milli mimari hareketi*) to combat the "Ankara cubic" of Egli and Holzmeister. Under his leadership a national architecture seminar was established at the academy in 1934. Over the years, this seminar turned into a monumental enterprise to study and document the surviving examples of traditional wooden houses. Many architects, preservationists, and officials wrote about the importance of this residential heritage as the repository of both a timeless "national character" and the most desirable modern qualities of contemporary living. Writing in *Arkitekt* in 1936, an official of the Ministry of Endowments presented two examples—the *konak* of Çakırağa in Birgi and the house of Emine Kadın in Tire—as "comfortable, hygienic, sunny, and ventilated houses reflecting and responding to the local context and the

Fig. 6.7. Sedad Hakkı Eldem's studies of modern interiors inspired by traditional Turkish elements: built-in low seats, fireplaces, stylized folkloric motifs on the walls, and Turkish kilims and carpets on the floors.

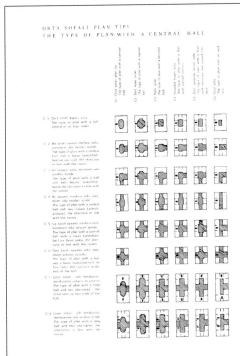

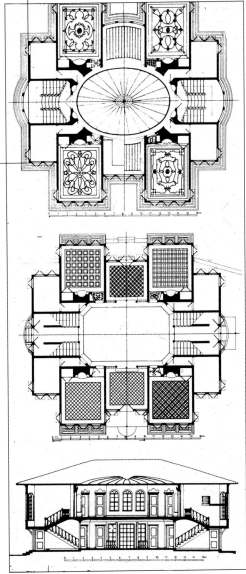

Fig. 6.8. Sedad Hakkı Eldem's codification of the plan types of traditional "Turkish houses" based on the location and configuration of the hall (*sofa*). **Left:** A page from his monumental *Türk Evi*, volume 1, showing the typological matrix of "central hall plan type" (*orta sofalı plan tipi*). **Right:** An example of this plan type: Sadullah Paşa Yalısı, Çengelköy, Istanbul, eighteenth century.

needs of its inhabitants."[57] Eldem himself studied a number of examples in Istanbul and wrote monographs on them, as well as producing, later in his life, his monumental three-volume *Türk Evi*, based on the research started in the national architecture seminar (fig. 6.8).[58] Throughout the late 1930s and the 1940s, many architectural students studied, produced measured drawings, and wrote theses on the traditional houses of different Anatolian towns. The teachings and writings of Professor Albert Gabriel also promoted Eldem's agenda and urged young architects to study the plan types and "modern character" of traditional houses as invaluable lessons:

It is impossible not to fall in love with the "modern character" of some old Istanbul houses. By translating the exterior form and wooden construction of these houses into concrete, it is possible to obtain results much more reasonable and aesthetically pleasing than today's monotonous "cubic." For example, although it is built of a perishable material, the *yalı* [a house along the edge of the Bosporus] of the Köprülü family stands today as a perfect lesson in architecture. To study the sources of this perfection and to analyze its elements are far more useful for a modern architect than studying standardized house types developed for foreign countries.[59]

It should be pointed out that the late-seventeenth-century *yalı* of Amcazade Köprülü Hüseyin Paşa, which Gabriel mentions in this passage, was one of the oldest surviving examples to which Sedad Eldem looked as a model. Eldem's paradigmatic Taşlık Coffee House of 1948 was a reinforced concrete replica of the seventeenth-century wooden precedent and a built manifesto of Eldem's program for a "national architecture" based on the traditional Turkish house (fig. 6.9). Many of the examples Eldem focused on in his own research, scholarship, and career as an architect were the most elaborate and refined *yalı*s and *konak*s of the Ottoman notables. His monumental work *Türk Evi* was an elaborate typological matrix of house plans based on the shape, configuration, or location of the *sofa*, or central hall (see fig. 6.8). His architectural theory and methods were systematic, analytical, and "rationalist" in the sense of beginning from culturally and historically established a priori "types" whose validity, he argued, persisted over time. It was this typological approach based on precedents that separated Eldem from the empiricists, with their approach of true modernist contextualism that would have deplored the idea of fixed types and a priori cultural constructs. It also gave his work its characteristic uniformity in what continued to be his signature style throughout his long career, even after nationalism lost its grip upon architects' discourse (fig. 6.10).

In the late 1930s, Bruno Taut and Sedad Eldem held something in common: a shared reverence for traditional Turkish houses and classical Ottoman monuments and a shared criticism of the "cubic" architecture that had become the trademark of the new regime in Ankara. Taut's appointment as head of the architectural section at the academy in 1936 was announced in the academy brochure as follows: "Under the direction of the prominent and experienced German architect Professor Taut, the students of architecture are preparing to combat the nondescript style, totally devoid of identity, that has been invading Istanbul, Ankara, and other cities of the nation under

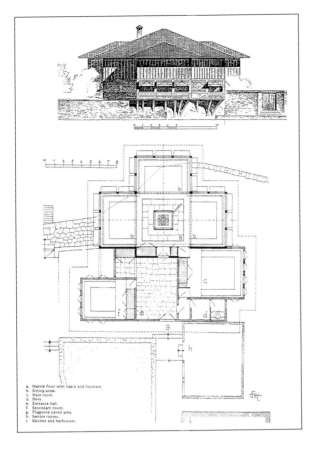

a. Marble floor with basin and fountain.
b. Sitting areas.
c. Main room.
d. Privy.
e. Entrance hall.
f. Secondary room.
g. Flagstone paved area.
h. Service rooms.
i. Kitchen and bathroom.

Fig. 6.9. Top: Sedad Hakkı Eldem's paradigm of the traditional "Turkish house": the *yalı* of Amcazade Köprülü Hüseyin Paşa, Istanbul, end of the seventeenth century. Drawings of the plan and front elevation by Eldem. **Bottom:** A reinforced concrete replica of this building was Sedad Hakkı Eldem's signature work: Taşlık Coffee House (1948) overlooking the Bosporus.

Fig. 6.10. Sedad Hakkı Eldem's residential work in Istanbul in the 1930s, showing his appropriation of the formal language and plan types of traditional wooden houses for modern villas, mostly along the shores of the Bosporus. Ayaşlı Yalısı, Beylerbeyi (**top**), and Tahsin Günel Yalısı, Yeniköy (**bottom**), both from 1938.

Fig. 6.11. Detail of the Faculty of Humanities, Ankara (1937), by Bruno Taut (see also fig. 2.9). The alternating courses of stone and brick are used in the manner of traditional Ottoman walling techniques.

the rubric of 'modern.' There is no doubt that the new Turkish architecture will be born out of this combat."[60]

Indeed, while he assigned his own students housing projects along the rationalist and functionalist precepts of modernism (see chapter 5), Taut lent his full support to the national architecture seminar for pedagogical reasons. As an ardent critic of modernist orthodoxy and "international style," Taut believed that "the traditional Turkish house embodied many elements that will always remain modern in their rationality."[61] Among such rational elements, he cited wide overhanging eaves for shading, high ceilings with a lower row of windows for view and an upper row for diffused light, and interior halls protected from exposure to sun and wind. Most significantly, he admired the overall urbanistic quality of narrow streets and silhouettes as viewed from the sea. In his own work for the Ministry of Education, he incorporated some of these ideas into his otherwise modernist school buildings, making subtle references, for example, to traditional roofs and traditional composite wall techniques with alternating layers of brick and stone (fig. 6.11).

Beyond these premises, however, Taut and Eldem could not have been more different in philosophy, methodology, and political position. As much as Taut believed in "local" and "national" adaptations of what he saw as the transnational creative spirit of construction, he was also insistent that "national character" should not be a self-conscious determinant or stylistic formula in design. Like most critical and contextual modernists, he believed in the inevitably and unselfconsciously "national" character of modern architecture but objected strongly to the self-conscious employment of architecture for nationalist politics. He wrote: "It is important to avoid a superficial imitation [of tradition]. Otherwise, this tendency can lead to a sentimental romanticism and a misunderstood nationalism resulting in kitsch. The more fervor with which a misunderstood nationalism is pursued, the worse will be the result. . . . *All nationalist architecture is bad but all good architecture is national* [my emphasis]."[62]

It was precisely the kind of codified, repeatable, recognizable, and officially sanctioned "national architecture" Taut deplored that Sedad Hakkı Eldem sought to establish in the 1930s, with increasing advocacy of strong state sponsorship. Defying the inevitable formal indeterminacy of a truly critical modern architecture, he wanted to codify a national architecture *movement,* an alternative to the Modern Movement but, as implied by the word "movement," equally formalist and ideologically charged. Against Taut's reminder of "the wisdom of studying not what old masters did but what they were after,"[63] he saw the formal purity and rationality of the timber-frame Turkish house as a license to replicate it under the rubric of "national architecture." Furthermore, Eldem's interest in the Turkish house was confined to the individual house without much attention to the qualities of urban fabric—the streets and the relationships of houses to each other that Taut so deeply admired. Eldem's "Turkish house" was ultimately an "object-type" complete in its own rationality and its specific message—not unlike the individual cubic villas he criticized. It transcended any urban, local, or regional sensibility in favor of a larger and more abstract statement of "Turkishness."[64]

It is important to emphasize that whether they tried to justify modern forms through the "cubic traditions" of Anatolian vernacular or promoted the wooden Turkish house, Turkish architects of the early republic almost invariably preferred the term "national" to "regional." They frequently paraphrased their German-speaking teachers on the importance of "architectural context" (*muhit*), and they put forth insightful regionalist arguments such as Zeki Sayar's criticism of building prototype schools for the entire country (see chapter 2). Yet "regionalism" was an inherently problematic term at the height of nation building under a unitary state. Regionalism, before everything else, is about *diversity* of expression, especially in a country like Turkey, which has at least five different "regions" with particularities of climate, terrain, local materials, and building traditions, not to mention ethnic and religious diversity. Under the unique historical circumstances of Kemalist nation building, however, the emphasis was on *uniformity* rather than diversity. Hence, the local and "subnational" affiliations implied in a regionalist sensibility were as ideologically problematical as the supranational connotations of "international style." The nation-state wished to erase such subnational affiliations and homogenize them into a unified ideal. Most Turkish architects assumed this larger-than-life mission of fixing and representing the identity of an entire nation in recognizable architectural forms. Sedad Eldem expressed it by writing that "local architecture is not necessarily national architecture. People of a nation may be living in different regions and consequently building different houses, but this does not make all of them national architecture."[65] Ultimately, however, it was public buildings, not houses, in which the republic placed its priorities; something as humble as the traditional house was incapable of representing the imposing character of state power. Unlike the pervasiveness of the New Architecture in the early 1930s, Sedad Eldem's "Turkish house" idea remained his personal theoretical agenda with little following and no large-scale impact on actual construction. Instead, his ideas for a state-sponsored "national expression" in public buildings took off in the early 1940s.

Nationalist State Monuments

WITH THE DEATH of Mustafa Kemal Atatürk in 1938, on the eve of the approaching world war, the revolutionary period of the republic came to an end. As Atatürk was rapidly transformed into a near deity, the nationalist component of Kemalism hardened into the dominant doctrine of the republic, which saw no liberalization or democratization of its regime until 1945. Within a month of Atatürk's death, and after having designed the national hero's catafalque, Bruno Taut, too, died unexpectedly—a symbolic and ominous event considering Taut's critical position with respect to both the doctrinaire Modern Movement of the West and the doctrinaire nationalism of the country that had hosted him since 1936.

Architectural culture became increasingly nationalistic during this period, and the representation of state power and ideology took precedence over all other architectural questions and debates. Monumental public buildings of overpowering scale, stone façades, and an official, stripped-down classicism dominated the building scene in what Sedad Eldem retrospectively called "the stone age." In spite of Turkey's eventually remaining "neutral" and uninvolved in the Second World War, its arts, sculpture, and architecture at the end of the 1930s and beginning of the 1940s testified to close ties with Nazi Germany and Fascist Italy. Both countries participated in the Izmir International Fairs of the late 1930s with imposing pavilions (see chapter 3), and commentaries praising their endeavors in art and culture appeared in many popular publications. The culmination of this admiration was the opening of the New German Architecture (Yeni Alman Mimarisi) exhibition in Ankara in 1943 (fig. 6.12), which was brought to Turkey by Paul Bonatz (1877–1956). Bonatz then remained to work in Turkey as an educator, consultant, and architect.[66] The exhibition made a big impression on Turkish architects and on the official state architecture of the 1940s. Bonatz,

Fig. 6.12. Poster for the "New German Architecture" exhibition in Ankara, January–February 1943.

who was invited to teach in the newly independent school of architecture within the old engineering school (Hendese-i Mülkiye Mektebi), now renamed Istanbul Technical University, left his mark on architectural education for the next decade.

At the end of the 1930s, Eldem wrote a number of particularly important articles calling for the intervention of a strong state to sponsor the national architecture movement, which, he argued, could be achieved only by native architects and builders, with native materials, and, above all, in conformity with the "native spirit."[67] Most significantly, he affirmed the role of architecture as an instrument of the nationalist regime, in the service of its ideological agenda: "For an architectural style to be "national" [*milli*], it must represent the ideals and lifestyles of that nation. If the nation does not have such an ideal, it can be given [to the nation]. Today, people have acquired many new ideals that they did not know before. They can do the same in matters of art and architecture. Until the [desired] ideal becomes the ideal of the nation, it can be the ideal of the leaders of the nation who show the way. The result is the same."[68]

Eldem's portrayal of national architecture as a matter of strong regime and state sponsorship had been a major sore point in his relationship with Bruno Taut before Taut's death. According to Taut, who always objected to the employment of architecture for nationalist politics, "those who were looking for a particular party line in architecture have never been able to go beyond formal issues."[69] Eldem's search for

Fig. 6.13. Saraçoğlu Housing for government employees, Ankara (1944–1947), by Paul Bonatz. The scheme bears the mark of Sedad Hakkı Eldem's "Turkish house" paradigm. **Fig. 6.14.** Faculty of Sciences and Letters, Istanbul University (1942–1943), by Sedad Hakkı Eldem. The lower structure of the building makes references to the Stuttgart Railway Station (1912–1928) by Paul Bonatz.

a "party line" through his campaign for a national architecture movement did not accord well with Taut's convictions but after 1943 found a receptive partner in Paul Bonatz. The close collaboration and reciprocal influences between the two men can be detected in their work of the early 1940s. Bonatz's Saraçoğlu Housing for state employees in Ankara (1944–1947) bears the mark of Eldem's "Turkish house" paradigm on the exterior (wide eaves, window modulations and projections, etc.), adapted to blocks of three- and four-story, multiunit dwellings (fig. 6.13). Correspondingly, Eldem's Faculty of Sciences and Letters building for Istanbul University (1942–1944, in partnership with Emin Onat) enlarges the Turkish house idea to the scale of a large public building, perching it on top of a colonnaded lower level with conspicuous affinities to Bonatz's railroad station in Stuttgart (fig. 6.14). As one of the paradigmatic examples of the national architecture movement, this building appropriates traditional elements and incorporates them into a monumental and classicized modern design. Some of these elements are the composite walling techniques in the classical Ottoman tradition and the open pavilions with tall slender columns—a motif that can be traced back to a wide range of precedents from Iran and Central Asia to Ottoman imperial kiosks and pavilions.

A few other projects by Sedad Eldem in this period, such as his competition entry for the Adana Municipal Palace (fig. 6.15), demonstrate that it was not just the wooden houses but also the more monumental stone architecture of the Seljuks and Ottomans that Eldem studied for inspiration. In the Faculty of Sciences building of Ankara University, designed in collaboration with Paul Bonatz, he accentuated the axial layout of the campus with a symmetrical arrangement of imposing, stone-clad buildings. The monumental entrance porticos supported by tall columns, along with the use of Seljuk and Ottoman details such as the "porcupine cornice" and stalactite column capitals, epitomize the national architecture movement (fig. 6.16).

Largely the legacy of these three architects—Eldem, Onat, and Bonatz—the switch to a heavier, classical, monumental expression and to the incorporation of historical motifs in detailing was particularly pervasive in Ankara, where architecture came to be identified with the power of the state. The new trend manifested itself first in the design of the new railroad station (1935–1937), a building of great symbolic significance as the primary point of entry to the capital. It was designed by Şekip Akalın, an architect in the Ministry of Public Works and a graduate of the engineering school in Istanbul, which was now an important contender in an architectural scene long dominated by the academy. Behind the imposing symmetrical entrance with tall colonnades flanked by rounded projections on each side, a spacious passenger hall, lit by a large glazed façade, led to the tracks beyond. To one side of the main building sat the station casino (*gar gazinosu*), a restaurant-café, illustrating the paradigmatic modernist formal composition of the time: a horizontal block balanced by a vertical clock tower (see fig. 4.6). The main hall is a superb example of this classicized modern architecture, meticulously detailed in marble, brass, and wood and lit by the diffused light filtering through the roof truss (fig. 6.17).[70] Photographs of the opening

Fig. 6.15. Competition entry for the Adana Municipal Palace (1944) by Sedad Hakkı Eldem in collaboration with Samim Oktay and Demirtaş Kamçıl, showing Eldem's heavy, classicized, stone-clad architecture of the early 1940s.

Fig. 6.16. Detail of the entrance portal of Ankara University's Faculty of Sciences (1943), by Sedad Hakkı Eldem. Seljuk and Ottoman motifs are incorpo-rated into the monu-mental stone portal, especially the *muqarnas* details, relieving arches, and the "porcupine cornice."

Fig. 6.17. Ankara Railroad Station (1935–1937). Photographs from the official album showing the transparency of the elevation facing the tracks (**top**) and a view of the roof trusses above the central hall (**bottom**).

ceremony of the station are particularly illustrative of the mood of the period, when official ceremonies became quasi-religious rituals displaying the power of the state in the public realm (fig. 6.18). They show the prime minister, Celal Bayar, inaugurating the building while the minister of public works, Ali Çetinkaya, and other republican leaders, all wearing hats, look on. Police and army officers and spectators watch from across the road,

Fig. 6.18. Ankara Railroad Station (1935–1937), by Şekip Akalın. An official photograph of the opening ceremony in 1937.

cars are ceremonially parked in the plaza, speeches are made, and flags flutter.[71] A few years after the opening of the new station, Bedri Uçar's State Railroads directorate building was completed adjacent to the station (1941), carrying this austere official style associated with the state to an even heavier and more monumental expression (fig. 6.19). The four-story-tall colonnaded entry of the stone-clad building is topped by the winged emblem of the State Railroads, completing the overall feeling of affinity to Nazi architecture of the same period.

In 1943, the New German Architecture exhibition was featured in *Arkitekt* with photographs of Albert Speer's work in Berlin and of the viaducts of Paul Bonatz.[72] While the commentary, by Abidin Mortaş, was cautious and largely descriptive, the text of Bonatz's opening talk, published in full, offered to Turkish architects one of the major attacks on avant-garde modernism in favor of a modern interpretation of the classical. Embellishing his talk with quotations from Adolf Hitler, Bonatz criti-

Fig. 6.19. Monumental classicism and the use of giant orders in the early 1940s: elevation drawing of the State Railroads headquarters building (1941), by Bedri Uçar.

cized both expressionism and the "new objectivity" (i.e., the Bauhaus) as "individualistic experiments" of the chaotic period after the First World War. Celebrating the recent birth of a new architectural ideal in Germany, he presented the classical as the antidote to the ills of individualism, pluralism, experimentation, and open-endedness in art and architecture: "For us, classical means the will to attain the final and the absolute. In other words, it means a distance from the fashions of the day and the whims of the individual. As in the great periods of antiquity, the individual will not represent his or her self but will conform to the common will of the public. The art of construction will be carried out in the same way as politics. Not a multitude of meanings but one singular meaning will be expressed."[73]

It is important to note that Bonatz carefully differentiated between this ideal and a mere imitation of the classical architecture of the Greeks and Romans. Classicism was not a "period style" but a timeless principle that had to be internalized and "made into the contemporary expression of our own time." That is why, he argued, as much as a return to the traditional techniques of each nation's own soil was a necessary foundation, there was also a need to master modern techniques and turn bridges, viaducts, dams, and power plants into cultural monuments.[74] The desired new "national classic art" could not be derived by replicating historical styles or copying their motifs.

It was this idea of classicism as perfectly compatible with the search for a modern and national Turkish architecture that appealed to Turkish architects, Sedad Eldem in particular. At the end of his talk, Bonatz referred to the commonality of ideals between Germany and republican Turkey, implicitly proposing the classical ideal as an appropriate path for Turkish architects: "Ankara offers a good example of what a nation can accomplish in less than twenty years, under the leadership of a strong statesman. Great waves of construction do not always and necessarily follow great political upheavals. Yet when these two coincide, as in the rise of modern Turkey and in today's Germany, and if all the forces are directed toward a great singular goal, extraordinary things can be accomplished."[75]

Even without Bontaz's endorsement, Turkish architects had many reasons to be attracted to the classical ideal in architecture. First, in the light of the new nationalist theories of Turkish history and language mentioned earlier, the classical heritage of Anatolia (its Greek, Hellenistic, and Roman heritage) was as much a part of the common ancestry to which Turkish roots extended as was the heritage of the Hittites and Sumerians. Second, many of these first-generation republican architects had been trained in the classical academic tradition of the Academy of Fine Arts before the complete dismantling of that tradition in the 1930s, and hence they were familiar with the precepts of classicism. Most importantly, the idea of the classic not as a style but as a transhistorical model of rational architecture was a powerful formulation that would allow them to be "classical" and "modern" at the same time. The fact that in Europe and the United States, architecture showed similar tendencies to classicize modern buildings into a more official and monumental expression further strengthened Turkish architects' sense of being part of the international community in architecture, albeit with each country championing its own state. In that sense, the architectural historian Bernd Nicolai's seemingly paradoxical designation of this period in modern Turkish architecture as one of "international national style" is highly convincing.[76] By contrast, Turkish architectural historians' more typical characterization of the period as one of a "second national style" following the international style of the early 1930s (which had, in turn, followed the "first national style" of Ottoman revivalism) is problematical.[77] Sharp binary oppositions between "international" and "national," "modern" and "historicist" do not do justice to the fact that throughout the 1930s the picture was far more blurred. Whether they worked with the "cubic" modern forms of the New Architecture or with the classicized, stripped-down official buildings of the 1940s, Turkish architects wanted to be "modern" yet grounded in tradition, "national" yet simultaneously part of Western civilization.

A major event representative of the Turkish architectural culture of the period in all its aesthetic, symbolic, and political dimensions was the international competition for the Grand National Assembly building in 1937. Out of fourteen entries, three were awarded first prize by an international jury that included Willem M. Dudok from Holland, Ivar Tengbom from Sweden, and Howard Robertson from England. These projects, by the Austrian Clemenz Holzmeister, the Frenchman Albert Laprade, and the Hungarian Alois Mezara, all had monumental, classical façades with tall colonnades and were made even more imposing in the perspective renderings with sharp shadows, statues, flags, inscriptions, and wall reliefs (fig. 6.20). Of the three first prize-winners, the project by Holzmeister was eventually built, its completion extending into the 1950s (fig. 6.21). Turkish architects participated with similarly imposing monumental buildings that, in their gargantuan scales, dwarfed the individual before the overpowering presence of the state. Even a modernist architect like Seyfi Arkan,

Fig. 6.20. Two entries for the Grand National Assembly competition, Ankara (1937). Perspective drawings of projects by Albert Laprade (top) and Alois Mezara (bottom).

Fig. 6.21. Top: Winning project for the Grand National Assembly competition (1937) by Clemenz Holzmeister. **Bottom:** A 1950s postcard of the completed building.

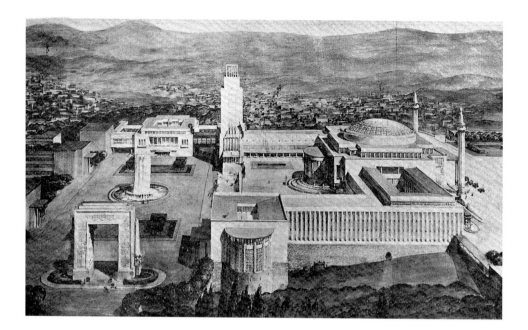

designer of many "cubic" buildings of the New Architecture, produced an enormous classical building approached by monumental stairs and marked by an
oversized statue of Atatürk on the axis of symmetry.
Only one entry chose to make allusions to the mosque
form, with a domed assembly hall and two minaret-like
towers (fig. 6.22); the jury characterized this project as a
"fantasy that lacked an overall coherence."[78]

Bruno Taut, just months before his death, produced
a sketch design for the Grand National Assembly without officially entering the competition (fig. 6.23). It was
a "conceptual exercise" that to a certain extent also

Fig. 6.22. Project for the
Grand National Assembly
competition (1937) by
Joseph Vago. The incor-
poration of dome and
minaret forms into the
classical design was con-
sidered inappropriate for
the secular nationalism
of the republic.

catered to the prevailing nationalist sentiments. Crowning the top of the hill overlooking Ankara's government complex, Taut's project carried reminiscences of his
expressionistic *Stadtkrone* projects of 1919. The project description accompanying
the sketches combined the quasi-religious and spiritual overtones of expressionism
with the democratic ideals of the nation-state and resorted to classical analogies:
"The National Assembly Complex will rise on a hill dominating the city like some
kind of Acropolis. But this is not an Acropolis for the temples of gods as in Athens,
but a complex for governing the country and making its laws. This will be a unique
location, symbolizing for future generations the heights of civilization attained by the
young Kemalist Turkey."[79]

The ultimate nationalist state monument of the republic, however, is Anıt-Kabir
(literally, "monument-tomb"), the mausoleum of Atatürk and still the "holiest" site
of modern Turkey. An international competition was held for it in 1942, and the final

building was completed in 1955. The transformation of Atatürk into a cult hero personifying the nation had already begun in his lifetime. Public spaces, squares, schoolyards, and parks throughout the country were rapidly filled with statues of Atatürk sitting, standing, on horseback, in military outfits, or in civilian clothes, and every public building displayed busts and portraits of the national hero (fig. 6.24). It can be said that the production of Atatürk imagery has been a major industry in modern Turkey, not unlike the production of religious icons in Catholic and Orthodox communities. To this day, his image on posters, banners, and lapel pins and in photographs reproduced for mass consumption is used by Kemalist and secularist groups in Turkey to make statements against other groups, Islamists in particular.

Fig. 6.23. Project for the Grand National Assembly competition (1937) by Bruno Taut alluding to his earlier ideas of "crowning the city" (*Stadtkrone*).

As in architecture, so in sculpture, German and other European artists played a major role both as educators and as creators of republican monuments and Atatürk statues.[80] Some of the earliest ones, such as the equestrian statues of Atatürk in front of the Ethnography Museum in Ankara (1927) and the Atatürk Monument in Izmir

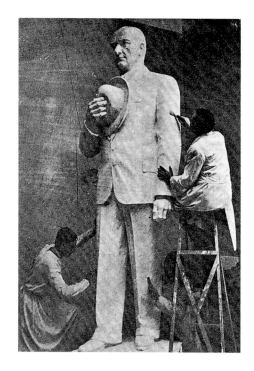

Fig. 6.24. The transformation of Atatürk into a near deity and the proliferation of Atatürk statues, monuments, and busts: the making of the Atatürk Monument in Çankırı (1944).

(1932), were commissioned to the Italian sculptor Pietro Canonica (fig. 6.25). The Victory Monument in Ulus Square, Ankara (1927), and another of the same name in Afyon (1935), the equestrian statue of Atatürk in Samsun (1931), and the standing statue of Atatürk in Konya (1926) were the work of the Austrian sculptor Heinrich Krippel, one of the most prolific artists who worked in Turkey (fig. 6.25). In 1937, Rudolph Belling, a former member of the Novembergruppe in Berlin, was appointed head of the sculpture section at the Academy of Fine Arts at the same time that Bruno Taut was brought into the architecture section. Along with his role as an educator, Belling worked on a monument to Ismet Inönü, the next president after Atatürk's death, sat as a jury member for the Anıt-Kabir competition, and directed and advised the tomb's sculpture program during its construction. Perhaps the most paradigmatic monument of this nationalist period is the *Güven* (Trust) Monument in Kızılay Square, Ankara (1935), by Anton Hanak and Joseph Thorak—a monument epitomizing the influences of Nazi art (fig. 6.26).[81] Placed in the heart of new Ankara, this monument consisted of a granite wall showing, in bas-relief on one side, Atatürk flanked by four naked youths. On the other side of the granite wall were placed two freestanding figures with austere expressions and a heavy, monumental feel. The entire monument rests atop a granite pedestal with allegorical human figures in relief, the date inscribed in Roman numerals on one side, and the words of Atatürk—"Turk, be proud, work hard, and trust!" (*Türk, öğün, çalış, güven!*)—on the other.

After his death on 10 November 1938, the national day of mourning, Atatürk's elevation to the status of "deity" was complete. Thereafter his image watched over the entire nation from every corner. He was given the title "eternal leader" (*ebedi sef*), and

Fig. 6.25. Two of the most famous equestrian statues of Atatürk, made by European sculptors in the early republican period. **Left:** Victory Monument in Ulus Square, Ankara (1927), by Heinrich Krippel, with War of Independence scenes carved on the pedestal and free-standing figures of soldiers and women in the war placed at its base. **Right:** Atatürk Monument in Izmir (1932), by Pietro Canonica, also with an allegorical representation of the War of Independence in high relief on the pedestal.

Fig. 6.26. The "Trust Monument" in Kızılay, Ankara (1935), by Anton Hanak and Joseph Thorak. The other side of the monument has two free-standing figures and the inscription "Turk, be proud, work hard, and trust!"

the international competition was held for the design of his mausoleum, which, according to one architectural historian, would be "a design beyond style and outside time."[82] The competition brief stated that it would be a place for paying respects to Atatürk, "in whose person the entire nation is symbolized." It should commemorate Atatürk "as soldier, president, statesman, scientist, intellectual, and great creative genius" and should evoke feelings of "respect, dignity, and immortality."[83] From its conception, Anıt-Kabir, located on top of Rasattepe Hill, was the ultimate monument to the casting of the nation as secular religion, the nationalist substitute for a space of religious ritual, prayer, and spirituality.[84]

Out of forty-nine entries, eight projects (three of them by Turkish architects, three by Italians, one German, and one Swiss) were short-listed. Collectively the entries demonstrated a fascinating mix of historical precedents and nationalist references. There were many pure solids in the spirit of Boulee and Ledoux: monumental pyramids (Giovanni Muzio), bulbous objects upon circular plans (Clemenz Holzmeister), and Roman "pantheons" with frescoes and gold mosaics (Arnoldo Foschini) (fig. 6.27). Among the Turkish architects' entries there were references to Seljuk tombs with pyramidal roofs (Kemali Söylemezoğlu, Kemal Ahmet Aru, and Recai Akçay), to Central Asian Turkish tombs with cylindrical forms and circular

Fig. 6.27. "Anıt-Kabir," a competition entry for Atatürk's mausoleum, Ankara (1942), by Arnoldo Foschini.

Fig. 6.28. Three projects by Turkish architects in the competition for Atatürk's mausoleum, Anıt
Kabir (1942), showing the use of forms from Central Asian, prehistoric Anatolian, and Seljuk
sources. Entries by the team of Kemali Söylemezoğlu, Kemal Ahmet Aru, and Recai Akçay (**top**),
Sedad Hakkı Eldem (**middle**), and Necmi Ateş (**bottom**).

plans (Sedad Hakkı Eldem), and to Egyptian temples mixed with Hittite symbols (Necmi Ateş) (fig. 6.28). The winning scheme, by Emin Onat and Orhan Arda, implemented with major revisions and taking fifteen years in construction, was a monumentalized and abstract version of the classical temple incorporating numerous prehistoric Anatolian references in its decorative program (figs. 6.29 and 6.30).[85] As its architects stated in their explanation of the design, it was a built manifesto to the prevailing nationalist history theories that connected the history of Mediterranean and world civilization to the history of the Turkic peoples:

Fig. 6.29. Winning design in the competition for Anıt-Kabir, Atatürk's mausoleum (1942), by Emin Onat and Orhan Arda. Construction of the mausoleum was completed in 1955.

Our past, like that of all Mediterranean civilizations, goes back thousands of years. It starts with Sumerians and Hittites and merges with the life of many civilizations from Central Asia to the depths of Europe, thus forming one of the main roots of the classical heritage. Atatürk, rescuing us from the Middle Ages, widened our horizons and showed us that our real history resides not in the Middle Ages but in the common sources of the classical world. In a monument for the leader of our revolution and our savior from the Middle Ages, we wanted to reflect this new consciousness. Hence we decided to construct our design philosophy along the rational lines of a seven-thousand-year-old classical civilization rather than associating it with the tomb of a sultan or a saint.[86]

The site plan of Anıt-Kabir is laid out along two perpendicular axes loaded with allegoric significance. The axis of the mausoleum proper culminates on the citadel in the distance, symbolizing Ankara's "old city" as the heart of the heroic years during the War of Independence. The other axis—the "processional alley"— corresponding to the main approach, visually extends toward the Grand National Assembly and the Çankaya Hills, symbolizing the new seat of the modern, secular republic. The pro-

Fig. 6.30. Typical postcard of Ankara showing Anıt-Kabir and the Victory Monument

cessional alley is lined on both sides with Hittite lion figures, and the two groups of statues marking the entrance to the alley (a male youth, peasant, and soldier on one side, three grieving women on the other) bear stylistic affinities to Mesopotamian sculptures (fig. 6.31). Both the lions and the human figures were the work of Hüseyin Özkan, a student of Rudolph Bel-ling's. The monumental stairs leading to the mausoleum are flanked by two major groups of wall reliefs telling the saga of the War of Independence—"Sakarya Battle" to the right, by İlhan Koman, and "The Final Battle" to the left, by Zühtü Müridoğlu—again executed in the genre of prehistoric wall reliefs. On the ceiling of the colonnaded entrance portico, Anatolian kilim motifs are inscribed in colored and gold mosaic, classicizing folk art into high art.

Monumentality, national symbolism, and power constituted the primary preoccupations in the architectural discourse of the early 1940s. The Anıt-Kabir competition was followed in 1944 by a national competition for the Victory and Unknown Soldier monuments in Çanakkale, commemorating the battle of Gallipoli during the First World War.[87] Many prominent Turkish architects participated with imposing stone and brick monuments, again alluding to a range of historic and prehistoric precedents, tomb forms, and monumental arcades.

By the mid-1940s, the enthusiasm with which the New Architecture was welcomed in 1930 had been irretrievably lost, along with references to the modernist avant-garde, the machine age, and the revolutionary spirit. This closing of the long 1930s with its modernist legacy is best captured by a highly symbolic event. Between

Fig. 6.31. References to prehistoric and folk sources of Anatolia in Anıt-Kabir (1942–1955). **Top:** Hittite lions along the processional alley. **Bottom left:** Figures representing youth, peasant, and soldier, by the Turkish sculptor Hüseyin Özkan. **Bottom right:** The ceiling of the colonnade around the mausoleum, showing it decorated with kilim motifs in gold mosaic.

Fig. 6.32. The eclipse of the "New Architecture" in republican Ankara. Conversion of the Ankara Exhibition Hall, a modernist icon of the early 1930s, into the State Opera and Ballet (1948) by Paul Bonatz (**bottom,** 1990s photograph). The flat roof, horizontal band windows, and tower of the original building were eliminated, and a classical "diamond-order" colonnade was added to the front of the now heavier-looking building (**right**).

1944 and 1948, the Ankara Exhibition Hall (1933), one of the most paradigmatic buildings of the New Architecture, designed by Şevki Balmumcu and an icon of Kemalist public space for fifteen years, was transformed into the State Opera and Ballet by Paul Bonatz. The modernist aesthetic and constructivist composition of the original building were irreversibly demolished—its horizontal band windows filled in, its vertical tower eliminated, and its façade remodeled with a classical colonnade of Seljuk-Ottoman orders and details (fig. 6.32). With this conversion, an architectural culture initially mobilized by ideals of modernity, progress, free expression, and contemporary construction was defeated by one of classicism, nationalism, and state power— as in many other places from Germany and Italy to Russia and the United States. Ironically, as this conversion was under way, the single-party regime of the RPP was drawing to an end, and the new Democrat Party was extending its power base with more liberal policies and politics. Within a few years, the 1950 elections would carry the Democrat Party to power, concluding three decades of early republican history.

Conclusion

All nationalist architecture is bad but all good architecture is national.
—Bruno Taut, *Mimari Bilgisi,* 1938[1]

In visual terms, the architectural history of the early republican period in Turkey was primarily a succession of stylistic experiments: first Ottoman revivalism, then the modern forms of "New Architecture," and not long after that the resort to vernacular and historical references. From about the time of the Young Turk revolution of 1908 to the end of the RPP's single-party regime in 1950, every important shift in the cultural politics of the state unfolded in the form of a different architectural vocabulary, each one critical of what preceded it. What gives this period its coherence, its "deep structure" under the surface of visible stylistic shifts, is the strong political and ideological charge of architecture in the service of nation building. During this period, "style" was not an autonomous aesthetic realm or simply a technical matter internal to the discipline of architecture. It was a powerful vehicle through which political leaders and professional architects sought to "imagine" the nation where it did not exist. This is a point frequently missed by architectural historians, who tend to divide the early republican period into three stylistically defined phases: "the first national style" (Ottoman revivalism), the "international style" (the New Architecture), and the "second national style" (vernacular and classical references). These terms, which suggest a switching back and forth between the poles of a national-versus-international dichotomy, obscure the fact that regardless of changes in formal expression, *nationalism* was the driving force of Turkish architectural culture between 1908 and 1950.

The position of modernism (or *Yeni Mimari,* the New Architecture) within this larger search for national expression is a particularly intriguing topic that I have tackled in this book from different angles. By the time modernism "arrived" in Turkey under the rubric of the New Architecture, it had already lost its critical edge in the West and had become an aesthetic formula certified by the term "international style." This label amounted to a tacit admission that the rationalist and functionalist doctrines could not offer an adequate basis for formal articulation and that modernism was, before everything else, a "style." Although many modernist architects continued to follow this aesthetic formula as a deliberate *stylistic choice,* others, including Le Corbusier himself, had already started experimenting with new regionalist aesthetic sensibilities.[2] The unifying claims of "international style" could no longer conceal the fact that the modernist canon of abstract, geometric forms, flat roofs, cantilevers, and curves was only one among many possible ways of articulating modern form during the interwar years. While the celebrity figures of modernism such as Le Corbuier, Walter Gropius, and Mies van der Rohe perfected this aesthetic canon, many other modern architects were quietly working outside the canon and producing works the true significance of which would be appreciated much later, often posthumously. Notably, Alvar Aalto of Finland, Bruno Taut, who left Germany for Japan and Turkey, Dimitris Pikionis in Greece, and Sedad Hakkı Eldem in Turkey represented such departures from the dominant canon.

Nevertheless, in the 1930s the doctrines of rationalism and functionalism were still powerful arguments against the old order in architecture (classicism, academicism, and beaux-arts), and the progressive connotations of these doctrines remained highly appealing to revolutionary or reformist ideologies everywhere, including Kemalism in Turkey. Polemicists for modernism, both in Turkey and abroad, continued to portray abstract, geometric forms as the most rational and historically inevitable expressions of the modern zeitgeist—that is, of the new materials, construction techniques, and lifestyles of the so-called "machine age."[3] The abstract and universalistic formal language of modernism may seem an unlikely choice for *national* expression, but it was certain heroic attributes associated with these forms (i.e., revolutionary, scientific, and progressive) that resonated so well with the spirit of the Kemalist revolution. There is no doubt that these modern forms fulfilled an important role in boosting national morale, giving visual expression to the new regime's aspirations of joining twentieth-century industrial civilization. For a brief period in the early 1930s, modernism was the "national style" of Kemalist Turkey, precisely when in Europe and the United States the term "international style" was attached to it.

Whereas arguments about the "machine age" at least had some real historical basis in western Europe and the United States, they were seriously out of place in the Turkey of the 1930s, a war-torn, poor, and predominantly agricultural society. The new methods of industrial building production (prefabrication and serialized production of construction materials and components in concrete, steel, plate glass, and new synthetic materials) that were claimed to be the raison d'être of modern forms were largely nonexistent in Turkey throughout the early republican period. Flat roofs were neither "logical" nor "economical" given the state of the building industry and the unavailability of advanced insulation techniques, not to mention the climatic conditions of northern regions including Ankara and Istanbul. Large openings and wide cantilevers were far from being "rational" when the prevailing mode of building was still largely limited to traditional load-bearing construction in brick or stone. In the end, the celebrated modern buildings that gave the early republican era its distinct architectural character were often built as formal compromises with respect to the aesthetic canons of "international-style" modernism. In many cases they were hybrids of modern forms (terraces, cantilevers, rounded corners, continuous window sills) and traditional materials, traditional construction methods, and traditional conceptions of symmetry and proportion.

Also nonexistent in early republican Turkey were an effective civil society, a modernist mass culture, and an autonomous bourgeoisie that could nurture architecture outside the official domain of the state.[4] When one looks at the history of early modernism in Europe and the United States, one sees that the most innovative and enduring ideas in modern architecture were produced on the initiative of individual industrialists and manufacturers, local governments, and independent organizations for reforming crafts and design education. In these industrialized countries, questions of production, housing, and urbanism were central to the definition of modernism, and the transformation of architecture into a commodity for mass production and mass consumption was a basic precondition for the modernist vision of a more democratic society. In Turkey, although the aesthetic canons of modernism were quickly internalized, this "democratization of architecture" was not accomplished, nor was its absence debated in a rigorous way. Architecture remained an elite profession as it always had been, no longer connected to the imperial court but now tied almost exclusively to state patronage.

Ultimately, in the absence of the industrial and socioeconomic conditions within which modernism emerged in the West, what republican architects imported from Europe remained, in essence, "a style"—a particular way of formally articulating republican buildings so that they would *look* modern and not "Ottoman." The *representational* function of buildings—their capacity to visually communicate the character and ideals of the new nation—took precedence over other important but visually less spectacular issues such as materials, construction, financing, landscape, housing, urbanism, and the use and maintenance of buildings. These issues were regarded as purely technical matters, perhaps of interest to the professional community but secondary to the larger cultural and ideological significance of exterior form. To use the terminology of Jürgen Habermas, "aesthetic modernism" was imported before "societal modernity" was accomplished.[5] This is not to say that societal modernity could possibly have been "accomplished" in the image of the Western model, given the nature of the Turkish state, but that does not alter the point. Until the 1950s, modern architecture in Turkey was a contrived *representation* of a desired but nonexistent modernity, not the natural outcome of the country's transformation into a modern society by its own internal dynamics.

On the other hand, it needs to be reemphasized in the strongest possible terms that even in the industrialized West, modern form was never exactly a "natural" outcome of modern industrial society and that architecture can never separate itself from its representational function. There was always a margin of indeterminacy between the forces of modern society (new functions, new materials, new construction techniques, etc) and the canonic architectural forms of the Modern Movement. As many architectural historians observe today, contrary to the claims of the official modernist discourse, modern forms did not arise out of logical considerations of program, site, materials, and construction alone, although these are important and necessary considerations for any good architecture, not just modernism. Something else was at stake with modernism: the aesthetic preferences of individual architects and the progressiveness associated with these new abstract forms were often the real reasons for their pervasiveness. In Turkey, the formal repertoire of simple volumes, undecorated surfaces, curves, and cantilevers captured the architectural imagination so effectively not because these were the only "rational" and "functional" forms possible but because they represented an obvious break with the Ottoman dynastic past and produced buildings that *looked like* contemporary buildings in Europe. By the late 1930s, when the republican regime was fully consolidated in Turkey and overt references to the Ottoman past were effectively erased, the stylistic repertoire of the modernist canon had largely fulfilled its initial mission. The abstract geometric formalism of the New Architecture was no longer capable of fulfilling the desire for national expression, and efforts to "nationalize the modern" began to intensify.

If one looks beyond their polemical statements and "cubic" designs, there is evidence that the proponents of modernism in early republican Turkey were at least theoretically aware of the pluralism inherent in a truly rational (not *rationalist*) approach to architectural design. That is why they were so much opposed to stylistic identifiers such as "cubic" and "international style" and often talked about the "architecture of the Kemalist revolution" (*inkilap mimarisi*) as an ideal that was still formless, still in process. What they did not entertain was the idea that it is precisely this formlessness and open-endedness—that is, an implied resistance to efforts to turn modernism into a stylistic orthodoxy—that a critical modern architecture is all about. In most of their writings, they rightly declared that there was no single and universally valid "international style," but many different approaches to modern architecture. They argued that the qualifier "modern" was not the monopoly of "cubic architecture" alone, nor did it exclude responsiveness to culture and context. Their critique of "cubic architecture," however, fell short of opening up a critical, nonideological understanding of modern architecture. Even when they were critical of the reduction of modern architecture to "cubic," what they were really after was to replace the pervasiveness of cubic forms with the pervasiveness of an alternative formula that could better represent the nation. As Bruno Taut cogently captured the idea in 1938, a regionalist sensitivity to culture and context (resulting from a critique of abstract modern forms) need not be collapsed into a "nationalist" agenda. But this is largely what happened in Turkey in the aftermath of the critique of "cubic architecture." Whereas a regionalist concern for local materials, climate, topography, and culture imply diversity, difference, and plurality, a nationalist agenda seeks, above all, a unified image representative of a unified nation. In the historical circumstances of nation building in Turkey, the plurality and diversity inherent in a critical understanding of modern architecture did not fit the homogenizing nationalist agenda of the republican regime.

The historical coupling of modern architecture with nation building in the 1930s has been a mixed blessing for Turkish architectural culture. On one hand, the alliance of modernism with the official ideology of the state gave the architectural profession an unprecedented importance, forcefulness, and larger sense of mission, unlike the feeling of impotence architects have experienced in later periods of modern Turkish history. By the same token, however, this alliance instrumentalized architecture as a form of visual politics, blunting the critical edge of modernism and compromising the autonomy of the discipline with respect to the state. If modernism is defined as a critical discourse that is not only against established stylistic canons but also against authority in general, then modernism in Turkey was flawed from the moment of its arrival in the country under the sponsorship of an authoritarian state. And if modernity, the very ideal that modernism claimed to represent visually, is defined as "a culture out-of-bounds," using the words of Susan Buck-Morss,[6] then it cannot be confined within the boundaries of a nationalism—or of any other particularistic definition of identity, for that matter. In this sense, "a modern and national" architecture, the exalted ideal of republican architects, was a contradiction in terms, unless one uses the term "national" (*not* "nationalist") in the way Bruno Taut used it, simply to designate an architecture responsive to history, context, and culture in an *unselfconscious* manner.

Retrospectively speaking, independent of the particular stylistic choices that prevailed from about 1908 to 1950, the fundamental flaw of Turkish architectural culture in the early republican period was the charging of architecture with larger political and ideological meanings. Especially after the proclamation of the republic, architecture assumed a larger-than-life mission in Turkish nation building, not just literally but also symbolically. The public buildings of the new republic were identified with

the republic itself (fig. C.1). This is by no means a commentary on the *architectural* quality or significance of individual works. Many "cubic" buildings produced in the 1930s were superb examples of modern architecture in terms of their formal articulation and aesthetic composition. Others, which tried to "nationalize the modern" by incorporating historical and vernacular sensibilities, anticipated by decades the "regionalist" and "contextualist" trends that became popular in architectural theory and practice only after the 1960s. The fundamental flaw of Turkish architectural culture had to do not with the individual works but with the larger role architecture assumed in transforming society according to the official ideology of the regime. Ultimately, its legacy has largely been an austere and official-looking architecture associated with the state—a top-to-bottom "civilizing mission" that, for technical and cultural reasons, failed to effectively penetrate the society at large and change the lives and outlooks of ordinary people in any substantial way.

Fig. C.1. The identification of early republican architecture with nation building: "The Living Works of the Republic," a collage published in *Yedigün* (1939).

This book was written as an account of this top-to-bottom mission. It has relied largely on cultural evidence (texts and images in official, professional, and popular publications) that inevitably represent the views of republican elites: political leaders, intellectuals, leading architects, artists, and journalists who aligned themselves with the Kemalist vision. To what extent ordinary people accepted their vision and to what extent they resisted it is still an issue of contentious and lively debate in Turkey. In architecture, as in all other areas of cultural production, many more studies are needed to uncover the dissenting voices or simply the "silences"—how people accepted, contested, resisted, or transformed the official models presented to them.[7] A very visible case of how these "silences" are finally erupting into a cacophony of voices is the predicament of mosque construction in Turkey. Having been totally neglected by early republican architectural culture (or occasionally interpreted in abstract modernist designs far removed from traditional precedents), mosque construction has come back with a vengeance since the 1980s. The sheer quantity, poor quality, and stylistic pastiche (domes, minarets, and other traditional markers in cheap materials) of many recent mosques would be enough to make early republican architects turn in their graves. Another example is the case of standard apartment life in mid- to high-rise concrete blocks, which has become the residential norm in Turkey, especially after the 1950s. Both the designs of the apartments and the manner in which they are inhabited often show little resemblance to the thoroughly Westernized models that the 1930s "cubic apartments" displayed. Many aspects of traditional domestic life (such as a separate ceremonial guest room, family eating in the kitchen, or a Turkish-style toilet in addition to a Western-style bathroom) are incorporated (sometimes forced) into these modern apartments.[8] Rather than modern architecture transforming its inhabitants into Westernized citizens, it was often the inhabitants who transformed modern architecture into hybrid expressions defying the early republican belief in the social engineering power of architecture.

Looking back from the 1990s, it is not difficult to conclude that the social engineering mission of the 1930s failed dramatically in its effort to mold Turkey into a modern, secular, and thoroughly Westernized society. The presence of Islam in society, as well as an interest in Ottoman culture, is on the rise there. The official culture of the Kemalist republic is incapable of expressing the self-image, tastes, and aspirations of an increasingly vocal and visible civil society. The West itself seems less appreciative of the cultural production of Kemalist Westernization (including its architecture) than many Kemalist Turks had hoped. While students of architecture from Europe and the United States make pilgrimages to see the classical Ottoman architecture of Istanbul, the "New Architecture" in Ankara is rarely more than an uninteresting footnote in their itineraries. Classical Ottoman music and performances by Sufi religious orders attract huge audiences in major Western cities, while the work of early republican Turkish composers following the norms of Western classical music remain unknown to most Westerners. It would be easy to explain this away as another instance of Western "orientalism" if it were not for the fact that a majority of Turks feels the same way about, say, the government buildings in Ankara or a classical composition by the Turkish composer Adnan Saygun. Yet to this day the strong identification of the buildings, music, or other cultural production of the 1930s with the near-sacred legacy of Atatürk has kept them beyond criticism, and any such criticism could easily be regarded as a threat to the republic itself. This is an unfortunate rigidity, because the hybrid cultural expressions of the 1990s reveal that although the Kemalist revolution may have failed to impose its own Western models, it succeeded in undoing the cultural, artistic, and architectural norms of a traditional Muslim society in a unique and irreversible way.

In spite of the powerful visual culture, or what we might call the "spectacle" of modernism, in the early republican period, it is only after the 1950s that one can talk about "modern architecture" as a real force in Turkish society. The rapid modernization of the economy and the phenomenal urbanization unleashed by massive migration from rural areas to major cities dramatically transformed the architecture and urbanscape of Turkey at a scale far greater than that of any of the early republican interventions outlined in this book. As Turkish society faced the real historical conditions of modernity as well as its real problems, architecture lost its ideological charge in the service of the state. While many successful architects turned to private patronage, the professional association of architects (the Turkish Chamber of Architects) assumed an oppositional voice in the political arena, especially after 1960. Since the 1980s an even more powerful popular reaction to the official cultural norms of the early republic has been under way, to the extent that many people openly talk about a "post-Kemalist" Turkey or a "second republic." The present moment is ambiguous at best.[9] On one hand, an invigorated polarization of culture between "Kemalists" and "Islamists" frustrates hopes for a much-desired reconciliation between the Western and traditional elements that make up Turkish culture and society today. It frustrates hopes of a pluralistic artistic and architectural climate where there is room for all expressions: Western imports, traditional precedents, and creative mixtures. On the other hand, there is something liberating about this critical moment. As the country makes peace with its Ottoman and Islamic past, and as the ideological nature of modernism in the 1930s gets exposed, it may be possible to look at architecture *as architecture* rather than as the bearer of some larger message such as national identity. Only then can the architectural culture of the early republican period be restored to its place in history and early republican buildings, once liberated from exclusive identification with Kemalism, be physically preserved as part of the country's architectural heritage.

An important first step in this direction could be the establishment of a Turkish chapter of DOCOMOMO, the growing international organization for the "documentation and conservation of the Modern Movement" established in 1990. The very existence of such an organization testifies to the realization that modernism is no longer a universal ideology or a scientific doctrine but a historical period in architecture like baroque or Gothic and deserves to be treated as such. Today in Turkey there is something extremely sad about the built legacy of the 1930s. Many of the buildings mentioned in this book have already been torn down; others are transformed beyond

Fig. C.2. "Ruins of modernity": the restaurant-casino of Çubuk Dam in the 1990s, dramatically transformed from its original pristine modernist aesthetic (see fig. 2.12) and abandoned next to the dried-out reservoir. **Fig C.3.** One of the few remaining examples of the "cubic villas" of the 1930s, standing empty and dilapidated in the 1990s, Göztepe, Istanbul.

recognition or simply forgotten in the postmodern building boom—including some that were major cultural icons in the early republican period. To give but one example, a short trip to the Çubuk Dam and public garden outside Ankara is adequate. The restaurant-casino with its "ocean-liner aesthetic" built in 1936 (see chapter 2), that legendary republican icon where once elegant ladies and their impeccably dressed companions dined and danced, stands in a pathetic condition, overlooking an equally pathetic dried-out reservoir (fig. C.2). Cheaply built additions have destroyed its original modernist formal composition, a condition exaggerated by new pink paint, and the park around it is littered with the waste of picnicking crowds from the poorer urban fringes of Ankara. As for private houses and "cubic villas" of the 1930s, most of them have been demolished and replaced by high-rise apartment buildings of inferior design and construction. A few that are still standing are in dilapidated condition, waiting for the highest-bidding developer (fig. C.3).

The predicament of these "ruins of modernity" invites us to reflect on the ultimately historical nature of all architecture and the need to preserve a sense of history against the latest attempts to erase it.[10] Turkish architectural culture has already gone through too many experiments depending on shifts in cultural politics, sticking with none for long. If there is any consensus on the value of historical consciousness and cultural continuity, then post-Kemalist Turkey cannot afford to reject the architecture of the 1930s in the same way that the architectural culture of the 1930s rejected its Ottoman precedents.

Notes

Introduction

1. Le Corbusier, *L'art decoratif d'aujourd'hui* (1925), published in English as *The Decorative Arts of Today* (Cambridge, Mass.: MIT Press, 1987), 190.

2. C. E. Jeannaret, *Voyage d'Orient* (1911), published in English as *Journey to the East,* ed. I. Žaknić (Cambridge, Mass.: MIT Press, 1987).

3. For example, the prominent historian Arnold Toynbee, writing in 1922 at the height of the Turkish War of Independence, pointed out the disastrous consequences of nationalism for Middle Eastern civilizations while regarding nationalism and other Western influences, however, as "a necessary evil." He wrote: "This infusion of western life, which was essential to the peoples that experienced it and was welcomed and brought about by these peoples deliberately because they recognized that it was the alternative to going under, has worked havoc with their lives. It has been new wine poured suddenly and clumsily into old bottles." A. Toynbee, *The Western Question in Greece and Turkey* (Boston: Houghton Mifflin, 1922), 15.

4. See F. Passanti, "The Vernacular, Modernism and Le Corbusier," *Journal of the Society of Architectural Historians* 56, no. 4 (December 1997): 438–451. Also see A. Max-Vogt, *Le Corbusier: The Noble Savage* (Cambridge, Mass.: MIT Press, 1998).

5. The shared high modernist vision that has informed most of the designed capital cities in the twentieth century—among them Ankara, Chandigarh, and Brasilia—is the topic of L. Vale's *Architecture, Power, National Identity* (New Haven, Conn.: Yale University Press, 1992).

6. James C. Scott, *Seeing Like a State: How Certain Schemes to Improve the Human Condition Have Failed* (New Haven, Conn.: Yale University Press, 1998), 90.

7. Ibid., 97.

8. Ibid., 5.

9. For fruitful discussions regarding the analogies between Turkish and Italian cases during the 1930s, I am thankful to Brian McLaren's work. See his *Mediterraneita and Modernita: Architecture and Culture during The Italian Colonization of North Africa* (Ph.D. diss., MIT, History Theory Criticism Program, 2000). Also inspiring were A. Hewitt's *Fascist Modernism: Aesthetics, Politics and the Avant-Garde* (Stanford University Press, 1993) and S. Falasca-

Zamponi's *Fascist Spectacle: The Aesthetics of Power in Mussolini's Italy* (Berkeley: University of California Press, 1997).

10. Scott, *Seeing Like a State*, 93.

11. I use "orientalist" in the ideologically charged sense of the term that became common parlance after Edward Said's seminal work, *Orientalism* (New York: Vintage Books, 1978). The implication of an entire field of scholarship with imperialism and colonialism is fraught with problems, as Said's critics have argued on many occasions. Nonetheless, I consider Said's work to be groundbreaking and inspirational in terms of exposing the political nature of knowledge and representation, an issue of great relevance for the history of architecture and urbanism.

12. On the architectural history of the early republican period in Turkey, although there are numerous works in Turkish, there is still a dearth of English and European language sources, with two significant exceptions. The first is a collection of essays written by Turkish historians and edited by A. Evin and R. Holod, *Modern Turkish Architecture* (Philadelphia: University of Pennsylvania Press, 1983). The other is Bernd Nicolai's more recent *Moderne und Exil: Deutschsprachige Architekten in der Turkei 1925–1955* (Berlin: Verlag fur Bauwesen, 1998), which focuses primarily on the work of German-speaking architects in Turkey.

13. Especially important was the publication of Said's *Orientalism*. The first important art historical application of Said's arguments in a critical discussion of orientalist painting was that by L. Nochlin, "The Imaginary Orient," *Art in America* (May 1983): 119–129, 187–191.

14. Among the first significant publications on these topics, one can cite T. Metcalf, *An Imperial Vision: Indian Architecture and Britain's Raj* (Berkeley: University of California Press, 1989), G. Wright, *The Politics of Design in French Colonial Urbanism* (Chicago: University of Chicago Press, 1991), N. AlSayyad, ed., *Forms of Dominance on the Architecture and Urbanism of the Colonial Enterprise* (Aldershot, UK: Avebury, 1992), L. Vale, *Architecture, Power and National Identity* (New Haven, Conn.: Yale University Press, 1992), G. Gresleri et. al., eds., *Architettura italiana d'oltremare* 1870–1940 (Venice: Marsilio, 1993), M. Crinson, *Empire Building: Orientalism and Victorian Architecture* (London: Routledge, 1996), and Z. Çelik, *Urban Forms and Colonial Confrontations: Algiers under French Rule* (Berkeley: University of California Press, 1997).

15. I use "great transformation" in the way that is discussed in Karl Polanyi's classic *The Great Transformation* (Boston: Beacon Press, 1957).

16. Jane Jacobs, *The Death and Life of Great American Cities* (New York: Vintage Books, 1961).

17. Among them, I wish to acknowledge Inci Aslanoğlu for her pioneering study *Erken Cumhuriyet Dönemi Mimarlığı* [Early republican architecture] (Ankara: ODTÜ Yayınları, 1980). Others who have written the standard Turkish references on the topic are Üstün Alsaç, *Türkiye'deki Mimarlık Düşüncesinin Cumhuriyet Dönemindeki Evrimi* [The evolution of architectural thought in Turkey in the republican period] (Trabzon: KTÜ Yayınları, 1976); Metin Sözen, *Cumhuriyet Dönemi Türk Mimarlığı 1923–1983* [Turkish architecture of the republican period 1923–1983] (Istanbul: Turkiye İş Bankası Kültür Yayınları, 1984); and the authors of the essays in Evin and Holod, *Modern Turkish Architecture*.

18. It was such a critical and revisionist perspective that informed our interdisciplinary discussion in S. Bozdoğan and R. Kasaba, eds., *Rethinking Modernity and National Identity in Turkey* (Seattle: University of Washington Press, 1997).

19. Among these, I have learned a great deal from Zeynep Kezer's Ph.D. work on early republican Ankara, and I am grateful to Neşe Gürallar Yeşilkaya and Zeynep Yürekli for sharing their Master's theses with me. See Z. Kezer, "The Making of a National Capital: Ideology, Modernity, and Socio-Spatial Practices in Early Republican Ankara" (Ph.D. diss., University of California, Berkeley, 1998); Z. Yürekli, "Modernleştirici Devrimlerde Geçici Mimarlık ve 1930'larda Türkiye Örneği" [Temporary architectural structures in modernizing revolutions and the case of Turkey in the 1930s] (Master's thesis, Istanbul Technical University, 1995); and N. G. Yeşilkaya, *Halkevleri, İdeoloji ve Mimarlık* [People's houses, ideology and architecture] (Istanbul: İletişim Yayınları, 1999). Other graduate theses are being prepared from similar perspectives, and interest in republican architecture is growing conspicuously among Turkish students of architectural history. A recent manifestation of the new critical trends and the new focus on the politics of architecture can be found in G. Tümer, ed., *İdeoloji, Erk ve Mimarlık* [Ideology, Power and Architecture], the proceedings of a symposium organized by Dokuz Eylül University in April 1996 (Izmir: Dokuz Eylül Üniversitesi, 1996).

20. Salman Rushdie, *The Satanic Verses* (Dover, UK: Consortium, 1992), 49.

21. A cultural history that best captures this profound ambiguity of the modern experience and has been inspirational for my thinking about modernity is Marshall Berman's *All That Is Solid Melts into Air* (New York: Simon and Schuster, 1983).

22. I first encountered the concept of "architectural culture" in the History Theory Program of the Architectural Association in London, and for this I am greatly indebted to Roy Landau's perspective on the historiography of modern architecture. See R. Landau, "The history of modern architecture that still needs to be written," *AA Files*, no. 21 (Spring 1991): 49–54. Since then many programs have adopted a "cultural approach" to architectural history, including the pioneering History, Theory, and Criticism program at MIT, conceived by Stanford Anderson and Henry Millon. Many historians of modern architecture have explicitly adopted the term "architectural culture"—for example, F. Dalco, *Figures of Architecture and Thought: German Architecture Culture 1880–1920* (New York: Rizzoli, 1990).

23. Among others is Beatriz Colomina's *Privacy and Publicity: Modern Architecture as Mass Media* (Cambridge: MIT Press, 1994).

24. See, for example, E. Zürcher, *Turkey: A Modern History* (London: I. B. Tauris, 1993), in which part 2 is titled "Young Turk Era in Turkish History 1908–1950." In F. Ahmad's *The Making of Modern Turkey* (London: Routledge, 1993), three chapters are devoted to the same period. In many other histories, the curbing of the Ottoman sultan's power by a constitution (1908) and the transition to a multiparty democracy (1950) are milestone events.

25. This tendency can be found especially in Üstün Alsaç, *Türkiye'deki Mimarlık Düşüncesinin Cumhuriyet Dönemindeki Evrimi* (Trabzon: KTÜ Yayınları, 1976), and also in İnci Aslanoğlu, *Erken Cumhuriyet Dönemi Mimarlığı* (Ankara: ODTÜ Yayınları, 1980), and in Evin and Holod, *Modern Turkish Architecture*. The only significant exception to this is the recognition of the primarily nationalist character of the entire early republican architecture in

Somer Ural, "Türkiye'nin Sosyal Ekonomisi ve Mimarlık 1923–60," *Mimarlık,* nos. 1–2 (1974): 5–51.

26. Scott, *Seeing Like a State,* 95.

Chapter 1. First Moderns

1. Ahmet Haşim, *Gurabahane-i Laklakan* [1928] (Ankara: Kültür Bakanlığı Yayınları, 1981): 154, 157.

2. Bernard Lewis, *The Emergence of Modern Turkey* (Oxford: Oxford University Press, 1961), 228.

3. The label "First National Style" was to differentiate it from the so-called Second National Style of the 1940s, which looked to traditional Turkish houses rather than monumental Ottoman precedents as the possible source of a Turkish "national style" (see chapter 6). It is important, however, to differentiate between the more cosmopolitan and imperial origins of Ottoman "proto-nationalism" and the more ethnic and linguistic connotations of republican Turkish nationalism. This distinction tends to get obscured by referring to them both as "national styles."

4. A 1903 competition for the ferry stations calling for projects that were "modern" and "uniform" in style is cited in D. Barillari and E. Godoli, *Istanbul 1900: Art Nouvau Architecture and Interiors* (New York: Rizzoli, 1996), 25. There is no mention of this competition in Turkish architectural history sources. But it is very likely that such a competition toward an "image renewal" was a part of the larger administrative and technical reforms launched in 1903 by Şirket-i Hayriye, the Ottoman passenger ferry company, which was responsible for the commissioning, building, and maintenance of the ferry stations and piers. The new Ottoman revivalist style was a perfect response to the need for a repeatable and recognizable "corporate style" for a national Ottoman company at a time of immense debt, when foreign companies dominated Turkey's major transportation enterprises, railroads, and tramlines. See Mümtaz Arıkan, "İskeleler" [Ferry stations], *Dünden Bügüne İstanbul Ansiklopedisi* 4 (Istanbul: Tarih Vakfı Yayınları, 1994): 198–206, and Eser Tütel, *Şirket-i Hayriye* (Istanbul: İletisim Yayınları, 1994).

5. Among the pioneering research on this topic, Yıldırım Yavuz's *Mimar Kemalettin ve Birinci Ulusal Mimarlık Dönemi* [Mimar Kemalettin and the First National Architecture period] (Ankara: ODTÜ Yayınları, 1981) stands out.

6. Günkut Akın's discussion of the earlier Tanzimat period as the introduction of Enlightenment symbols into Ottoman architecture is a compelling one pertaining to the difficulty of dating "modernity" in architectural culture. Yet the isolated nature of the Tanzimat experiments and the absence of a larger program of building or a theoretical discourse justifies the designation of the proponents of the National Architecture Renaissance as the "first moderns." See Akın's discussion of the tomb complex of Mahmut II in Divanyolu (1840) in "Tanzimat ve Bir Aydınlanma Simgesi" [Tanzimat and an Enlightenment symbol], in Z. Rona, ed., *Osman Hamdi Bey ve Dönemi* (Istanbul: Tarih Vakfi Yurt Yayınları, 1993), 123–133.

7. Ahmet Haşim, *Gurabahane-i Laklakan* [1928] (Ankara: Kültür Bakanlığı Yayınları, 1981), 152.

8. The adjective *mürteci* can be translated most closely as "reactionary," with connotations of blocking or resisting progress in history. To this day its noun form, *irtica,* is used to refer to the forces of Islamic religious orthodoxy perceived as the major threat to the secular principles of the republic as established in 1923.

9. Eric Hobsbawm, "Introduction: Inventing Traditions," in E. Hobsbawm and T. Ranger, eds., *The Invention of Tradition* (Cambridge University Press, Canto edition, 1992), 8.

10. The classic example of this is Sir Bannister Fletcher's *A History of Architecture on the Comparative Method* (1896). The book, which appeared in numerous subsequent editions in the twentieth century, was the paradigm of the orientalist tendency to look at non-Western architectures as frozen styles without historical evolution and incapable of modern transformation. For a critical discussion of Fletcher's original book and its subsequent editions, see G. B. Nalbantoğlu, "Toward Postcolonial Openings: Rereading Sir Bannister Fletcher's *History of Architecture,*" *Assemblage* 35 (April 1998): 7–17.

11. Fletcher, *A History of Architecture on the Comparative Method* (New York: Chas. Scribner's Sons, 1958 [1896]), 888ff. In the more recent editions, starting in 1961, the designation "non-historical styles" is removed. For the latest edition, see D. Cruickshank, ed., *Sir Bannister Fletcher's A History of Architecture* (London: Architectural Press, 1996).

12. See, for example, Şerif Mardin's "Religion and Secularism in Turkey," in Albert Hourani et al., eds., *The Modern Middle East* (Cambridge, Mass.: MIT Press, 1995), 348ff, as well as his classic *Religion and Social Change in Modern Turkey* (Albany, NY: SUNY Press, 1989). Hasan Kayalı extends this view to the Young Turks of 1908–1918, rejecting the argument that they were already Turkish nationalists by then. See H. Kayalı, *Arabs and Young Turks: Ottomanism, Arabism, and Islamism in the Ottoman Empire 1908–1918* (Berkeley: University of California Press, 1997), 8–13. Also, for a discussion of "proto-nationalism," see Eric Hobsbawm, *Nations and Nationalism since 1780* (Cambridge: Cambridge University Press, 1990), 73–74.

13. Benedict Anderson, *Imagined Communities: Reflections on the Origins and Spread of Nationalism* (London: Verso, 1983).

14. The Tanzimat (literally, "reforms") period was initiated by the military, financial, and educational reforms of Sultan Mahmut II between 1826 and 1839 and was consolidated and continued during the reign of his son Abdülmecit (1839–1861). Most significantly, the equality before law of all the subjects of the empire, regardless of religion, was recognized, and a modern system of taxation, conscription, and bureaucracy was introduced. This period is regarded as the beginning of the Westernization of Ottoman architecture, especially the proliferation of neoclassic and French Empire styles. In general, many historians and commentators view the institutional reforms and Westernizing agenda of Mahmut II as harbingers of republican modernization a century later.

15. İbrahim Edhem Paşa, ed., *Usul-i Mimari-yi Osmani* (Istanbul, 1873). For the most elaborate and scholarly study of this volume and its historical context, see A. Ersoy, *On the Sources of the Ottoman Renaissance: Architectural Revival and Its Discourse during the Abdülaziz Era, 1861–1876* (Ph.D. diss., Harvard University, 2000).

16. For a selection of Viollet-le Duc's writings and a commentary on the significance of his ideas in the history of modern architecture, see M. F. Hearn, *The Architecture Theory of Viollet-le-Duc* (Cambridge, Mass.: MIT Press, 1992).

17. See C. Perrault, *Ordonnance for the Five Kinds of Columns after the Method of the Ancients* [1683] (Los Angeles: Getty Trust, 1993).

18. See Owen Jones, *The Grammar of Ornament*, 1856 (New York: Portland House, 1986).

19. P. Chatterjee, *Nationalist Thought and the Colonial World* (London: Zed Publications, 1986), 38.

20. Although Edward Said's work is paradigmatic in the linking of orientalist constructs with the politics of imperialism and colonialism, his position is more ambiguous than it is often portrayed. He frequently acknowledges the positive role of Enlightenment thought in nationalist discourses of anticolonial resistance and independence. See E. Said, "Politics of Knowledge," *Raritan* (Summer 1991), 17–31, and also his *Culture and Imperialism* (New York: Alfred A. Knopf, 1992). Also see B. Moore-Gilbert, *Postcolonial Theory: Contexts, Practices, Politics* (London: Verso, 1997), 34–73.

21. He was the son of the minister of public works, İbrahim Edhem Paşa, who commissioned and directed the preparation of *Usul-i Mimari* for the 1873 Vienna Exposition. On Osman Hamdi Bey, see Z. Rona, ed., *Osman Hamdi Bey ve Dönemi* [Osman Hamdi Bey and his period], Proceedings of a Symposium 17–18 December 1992 (Istanbul: Tarih Vakfı Yurt Yayınları, 1993), and M. Cezar, *Sanatta Batıya Açılış ve Osman Hamdi* [Westernization in art and Osman Hamdi Bey] (Istanbul: İş Bankası Yayınları, 1971).

22. For example, J. McKenzie, "Orientalism in Art," in *Orientalism: History, Theory and the Arts* (Manchester: Manchester University Press, 1995).

23. For example, Z. Çelik, "Colonialism, Orientalism and the Canon," *Art Bulletin* 78, no. 2 (June 1996): 202–205.

24. In that sense, Osman Hamdi Bey's "orientalist" paintings are closer to those of artists such as John Frederick Lewis, whose scenes of daily life and domestic settings in Cairo and Istanbul also endowed the "orientals" with personality and contemporariness, than to those of his teacher, Jean Leon Gerome. Orientalist paintings such as those of Osman Hamdi Bey and John Frederick Lewis testify to Albert Hourani's important reminder that "not all orientalists are as orientalist." See Hourani's review of Edward Said's *Orientalism* (1978), *New York Review of Books* 26 (8 March 1979): 27–30.

25. See Z. Çelik, *Displaying the Orient: Architecture of Islam at Nineteenth-Century World's Fairs* (Berkeley: University of California Press, 1992).

26. A large volume of literature exists on the stylistic plurality and eclecticism of late-nineteenth-century Ottoman architecture. See especially Z. Çelik, *The Making of Istanbul: Portrait of an Ottoman City in the Nineteenth Century* (Seattle: University of Washington Press, 1986); C. Can, *İstanbul'da 19. Yüzyıl Batılı ve Levanten Mimarların Yapıları ve Koruma Sorunları* [The buildings of Western and Levantine architects in nineteenth-century Istanbul and their preservation problems] (Ph.D. diss., Istanbul: Yıldız Teknik Üniversitesi, 1993); P. Tuğlacı, *The Role of the Balyan Family in Ottoman Architecture* (Istanbul: Yeni Çığır, 1990); Barillari and Godoli, *Istanbul 1900;* and M. Cezar, *19. Yüzyıl Beyoğlusu* [Nineteenth-century Beyoğlu] (Istanbul: Akbank Yayınları, 1991).

27. For a coherent overview of the history of the architectural profession in Turkey, see G. B. Nalbantoğlu, *The Professionalization of the Ottoman-Turkish Architect* (Ph.D. diss., University of California, Berkeley, 1989).

28. M. Sözen and O. N. Dülgerler, "Konya'da Mimar Muazaffer," *METU: Journal of the Faculty of Architecture* 1, no. 4 (Spring 1978): 117–134.

29. Y. Yavuz, "Mimar Kemalettin Bey," *METU: Journal of the Faculty of Architecture* 1, no. 7 (Spring 1981): 53–76. Also see Yavuz's authoritative monograph *Mimar Kemalettin ve Birinci Ulusal Mimarlık Dönemi* (Ankara: ODTÜ Yayınları, 1981).

30. Yavuz, "Mimar Kemalettin Bey," 69. Yavuz writes that on the eve of the proclamation of the new republic in 1923, Kemalettin Bey moved to Jerusalem to work on the restoration of Islamic monuments, where, "for a brief period of time, his religious sentiments overpowered his nationalism." See Y. Yavuz, "The Restoration Project of the Masjid al-Aqsa by Mimar Kemalettin, 1922–26," *Muqarnas: An Annual on the Visual Culture of the Islamic World* 13 (Leiden: E.J.Brill, 1996): 149–164.

31. Giulio Mongeri had a more stylistically mixed practice than that of Vedat Bey. Before taking up the National Architecture Renaissance and coming to work in Ankara in the late 1920s, he designed a number of neo-Renaissance office buildings and the prominent neo-Gothic church of St. Antoine in Istanbul. On Giulio Mongeri, see Can, *İstanbul'da 19. Yüzyıl Batılı ve Levanten Mimarların Yapıları ve Koruma Sorunları*.

32. Leading members of the 1914 generation were İbrahim Çallı (1882–1960), Nazmi Ziya (1881–1937), Hikmet Onat (1886–1977), Namık Ismail (1890–1935), Feyhaman Duran (1886–1970), and Avni Lifij (1889–1927). Whereas many art historians attribute the rather belated impressionism of these artists to the influence of Paris, others note the formative significance of earlier Ottoman landscape painting traditions. See, for example, G. Renda, "Modern Trends in Turkish Painting," in G. Renda and C. M. Kortepeter, eds., *The Transformation of Turkish Culture: The Atatürk Legacy* (Princeton, N.J.: Kingston Press, 1986), 229–248, and S. Tansuğ, *Çağdaş Türk Sanatı* [Contemporary Turkish art] (Istanbul: Remzi Kitabevi, 1983), 118–135, respectively, for these two explanations.

33. S. Tansuğ, *Çağdaş Türk Sanatı* (Istanbul: Remzi Kitabevi, 1986), 137. Also see C. Baykal, "Yeni Kadın ve İnas Sanayi-i Nefise Mektebi" [The new woman and the sister Academy of Fine Arts], *Boyut* 16 (1983): 6–13.

34. See Nalbantoğlu, *Professionalization of the Ottoman-Turkish Architect,* and E.Ihsanoğlu, *Osmanlı İlmı ve Mesleki Cemiyetleri* [Ottoman scientific and professional societies] (Istanbul: Edebiyat Fakültesi Basımevi, 1987).

35. In 1921 the society renamed itself the Union of Turkish Artists (Türk Sanatçılar Birliği); it opened its first exhibition in Ankara in 1923 when the republic was proclaimed.

36. For example, one could come across architects such as Ali Talat (1869–1922), most notably the designer of the Beşiktaş and Kuzguncuk ferry stations in Istanbul (1913), who studied painting at the academy and then graduated from the engineering school.

37. Nalbantoğlu, *Professionalization of the Ottoman-Turkish Architect,* 117.

38. C. E. Arseven, *Sanat ve Siyaset Hatıralarım* (Istanbul: İletişim Yayınları, 1993), 40–42.

39. "Arif Hikmet Koyunoğlu: Sıradışı Bir Yaşam Öyküsü" [Arif Hikmet Koyunoğlu: an extraordinary life], *Arkitekt* (new series) 4 (1991): 37.

40. "Türk Güzel Sanatlar Birliği Mimari Şubesinde Mukayyet Mimarların İsim ve Adresleri," *Mimar* 1, no. 1 (Kanunisani 1931).

41. *Türk Yüksek Mimarlar Birliği Azaları ve Yüksek Mimarlık Mesleğiyle Âlakadar Mevzuat* (Istanbul: Cumhuriyet Matbaasi, 1940).

42. H. Kayalı, *Arabs and Young Turks*, 4.

43. This point is also emphasized in Barillari and Godoli, *Istanbul 1900*. It should also be noted that the authors of *Usul-ı Mimari-yi Osmani* (1873) were a cosmopolitan group including an Italian, two Armenians, a Frenchman, and a Muslim Turk.

44. For a discussion of Osman Hamdi Bey in similar terms, see S. Deringil, "Son Dönem Osmanlı Aydın Bürokratının Dünya Görüşü Üzerine Bir Deneme" [An essay on the worldview of the educated late Ottoman bureaucrat], in Z. Rona, ed., *Osman Hamdi Bey ve Dönemi*, Proceedings of a Symposium 17–18 December 1992 (Istanbul: Tarih Vakfı Yurt Yayınları, 1993), 9.

45. See, for example, Ernest Gellner, *Nations and Nationalism* (Oxford: Blackwell, 1983), in the first group and Leah Greenfeld, *Nationalism: Five Roads to Modernity* (Cambridge, Mass.: Harvard University Press, 1992), 18, in the second group.

46. Concerning the debates over the cultural meaning of Gothic style during the construction of the Crimean Memorial Church in Istanbul (1864–1868), see M. Crinson, *Empire Building, Orientalism and Victorian Architecture* (London: Routledge, 1996), 124–166.

47. Nasser Rabbat, "The Formation of a Neo-Memluk Style in Modern Egypt," in M. Pollak, ed., *The Education of the Architect* (Cambridge, Mass.: MIT Press, 1997), 363–386. Also see his *The Citadel of Cairo* (Leiden: E. J. Brill, 1995), 18–49. Interestingly, in the manner in which the sources of the National Architecture Renaissance went back to *Usul-i Mimari* (1873), inspired by French architectural theories of the time, the sources of neo-Memluk Egyptian national style were the earlier designs of the French architect Pascal Coste for the Citadel Mosque.

48. Şerif Mardin talks about "a progressive breaking of the social pact" that traditionally existed between Ottoman rulers, bureaucrats, and the people. The "nineteenth-century Ottoman state may have been more efficient, better organized and more modern," he observes, "but it was weaker in substantial terms." See Ş. Mardin, "The Just and The Unjust," *Daedalus* 120, no. 3 (Summer 1991): 113–129.

49. Ziya Gökalp, *Türkleşmek, İslamlaşmak, Muasırlaşmak* (1918). A major portion of this text is published in English in N. Berkes, ed., *Turkish Nationalism and Western Civilization: Selected Essays of Ziya Gökalp* (New York: Columbia University Press, 1959). The quotations are from p. 97.

50. Gökalp, *Türkleşmek, İslamlaşmak, Muasırlaşmak*, quoted from Berkes, *Turkish Nationalism and Western Civilization*, 76, 104.

51. A number of Turkish artists trained in military schools during the Young Turk era (and still known as the "soldier painters") painted scenes of the Gallipoli defense and the nationalist War of Independence, which are among the treasured works of official republican art. Some of the best portraits of Mustafa Kemal and other heroes of the nationalist War of Independence were painted by members of the 1914 generation, further illustrating the continuities between the final years of the empire and the early republic.

52. S. Özkan and Y. Yavuz, "Finding a National Idiom: The First National Style," in A. Evin and R. Holod, eds., *Modern Turkish Architecture* (Philadelphia: University of Pennsylvania Press, 1983), 56.

53. A. H. Koyunoğlu, "Kendi Kaleminden" [In his own words], *Arkitekt* (new series) 4 (1991): 39–50.

54. Ibid., 47.

55. Examples are from *TC Dahiliye Vekaleti, Mahalli İdareler Umum Müdürlüğü Raporu* (Istanbul: Holivut Matbaasi, 1933) and İ. Aslanoğlu, *Erken Cumhuriyet Dönemi Mimarlığı* (Ankara: ODTÜ Yayınları, 1980).

56. See U. Tanyeli, "Çağdaş İzmir'in Mimarlık Serüveni" [The architectural adventures of Izmir], in S. Beygu, ed., *Üç İzmir* (Istanbul: Yapı ve Kredi Bankası Yayınları, 1992), 331–333.

57. In the introductory section of her comprehensive survey of early republican architecture, Inci Aslanoglu writes: "In the 1920s, in spite of the fact that with the new developments in Europe, ornamentation and facadism in architecture had given way to functionalism, rationalism and social concerns, Turkish architects were looking back to revive the old, thus contradicting the new climate of the Kemalist reforms." See I. Aslanoğlu, *Erken Cumhuriyet Dönemi Mimarlığı* (Ankara: ODTÜ Yayınları, 1980), 13.

58. See Mardin, "Religion and Secularism in Turkey," 364.

59. Mardin, "The Just and the Unjust," 127.

60. İsmail Safa, "Yeni Türk Ocağı," *Türk Yurdu* 4/24, no. 27/28 (1930): 82–83.

61. Mehmet Asım in *Vakit*, 22 March 1930, quoted in *Türk Yurdu* 4/24, no. 27/28 (1930), 84–86.

62. Cited in Nalbantoğlu, *Professionalization of the Ottoman-Turkish Architect*, 130.

63. As mentioned in Özkan and Yavuz, "Finding a National Idiom," 65–66.

64. See *Deutscher Werkbund und Deutsch-Turkish Vereinigung: Haus Der Freundschaft in Konstantinopel* (Munich: Verlag von F. Bruckman A.G., 1918).

65. Süha Özkan, "Türk-Alman Dostluk Yurdu Öneri Yarışması 1916" [The Turkish-German House of Friendship Competition], *ODTÜ Mimarlık Fakültesi Dergisi* 1, no. 2 (1975), 177–210.

66. "Adana Erkek Muallim Mektebi Tadil Insaati" [Remodeling of Adana Teachers' School for Boys], *Mimar* 3, no. 3 (1933): 71.

67. Aptullah Ziya, "Sanatta Nasyonalizm" [Nationalism in art], *Mimar* 4, no. 2 (1934): 51–54. "Tulip Era" designates the infiltration of European tastes and aesthetic sensibilities in the eighteenth century, during the reign of Ahmed III (1703–1730).

68. Ibid., 52.

69. Alan Colquhoun, "Three Kinds of Historicism," *Oppositions* 26 (Spring 1984): 29–39. Like Colquhoun, I use "historicism" in the way *Webster's Ninth New Collegiate Dictionary* (1988: 573) defines it: as "a theory that emphasizes the importance of history as a standard of value or as a determinant of events." Another historian-theorist who recognizes the "historicist" nature of modernism is David Watkin, in his *Morality and Architecture* (Oxford: Clarendon Press, 1977).

70. Behçet Ünsal, reminiscences in the special issue "Mimarlığımız 1923–50," *Mimarlık* (Journal of the Turkish Chamber of Architects) 112 (1973): 35.

71. See Sibel Bozdoğan et al., *Sedad Eldem: Architect in Turkey* (Singapore: Concept Media, 1987; reprint, London: Butterworth, 1990).

72. Sedad Çetintaş, *Türk Mimari Anıtları: Osmanlı Devri* [Turkish Architectural Monuments: The Ottoman period] (Istanbul: TC Milli Eğitim Eski Eserler ve Müzeler Röleve Bürosu, 1946).

73. Kandemir, "Mektepli Türk Mimarlarının Piri Mimar Vedat" [The master of schooled Turkish architects: Vedat Bey], *Yedigün* 8, no. 205 (1937): 16.

Chapter 2. İnkilap Mimarisi

1. Quoted from Bernard Lewis, *The Emergence of Modern Turkey* (Oxford: Oxford University Press, 1961), 268.

2. Behçet and Bedrettin, "Türk İnkilap Mimarisi," [Architecture of Turkish revolution], *Mimar* 3, no. 9–10 (1933): 265.

3. Notably Ş. Mardin, *The Genesis of Young Ottoman Thought* (Princeton, N.J.: Princeton University Press, 1962). For a general comprehensive reference on Turkish intellectual history, see H. Z. Ülken, *Türkiye'de Çağdaş Düşünce Tarihi* [The history of contemporary thought in Turkey] (Istanbul: Ülken Yayınları, 1966).

4. M. Matossian, "Ideologies of Delayed Development," in J. Hutchinson and A. D. Smith, eds., *Nationalism* (Oxford: Oxford University Press, 1994), 218–225.

5. Quoted from Lewis, *The Emergence of Modern Turkey*, 269.

6. In the French case, the "model revolutionary" was described as wearing trousers, an open shirt, a short jacket, boots, and a liberty cap, replacing the *culottes*, waistcoats, and powdered wigs of the ancien régime. In the Ottoman case, the fez replaced the turban as mandatory headgear during the modernizing reforms of Sultan Mahmut II in 1829, roughly a century before it was replaced, in turn, by the hat. These examples are cited in R. Kasaba, "Kemalist Certainties and Modern Ambiguities," in S. Bozdoğan and R. Kasaba, eds., *Rethinking Modernity and National Identity in Turkey* (Seattle: University of Washington Press, 1997), 24.

7. Behçet and Bedrettin, "Mimarlıkta İnkilap" [Revolution in architecture], *Mimar* 3, no. 8 (1933): 245–247.

8. Behçet and Bedrettin, "Türk İnkilap Mimarisi," 265–266.

9. Quoted in D. Doordan, *Building Modern Italy: Italian Architecture 1914–1936* (New York: Princeton Architectural Press, 1988), 129. Also see A. Hewitt, *Fascist Modernism: Aesthetics, Politics, and the Avant-Garde* (Stanford, Calif.: Stanford University Press, 1993), and S. Falasca-Zamponi, *Fascist Spectacle: The Aesthetics of Power in Mussolini's Italy* (Berkeley: University of California Press, 1997).

10. Aptullah Ziya, "İnkilap ve Sanat" [Revolution and art], *Mimar* 3, no. 9–10 (1933): 317.

11. For example, Y. Yavuz and S. Özkan, "Finding a National Idiom: The First National Style," in R. Holod and A. Evin, eds., *Modern Turkish Architecture* (Philadelphia: University of Pennsylvania Press, 1983), 65.

12. Ü. Alsaç, *Türkiye'deki Mimarlık Düşüncesinin Cumhuriyet Dönemindeki Evrimi* [The evolution of architectural thought in Turkey in the republican period] (Trabzon: KTÜ Yayınları, 1976), 19.

13. *Yabancı Gözüyle Cumhuriyet Türkiyesi* [Republican Turkey through foreign eyes], (Ankara: Dahiliye Vekaleti Matbuat Umum Müdürlüğü, 1938).

14. Behçet and Bedrettin, "Yeni ve Eski Mimarlık" [New and old architecture], *Mimar* 4, no. 6 (1934): 175.

15. N. Von Bischoff, *Ankara: Eine deutung des neuen Werdens in der Turkei* (Vienna: A. Holzhausens Nfg., 1935), translated into Turkish by B. Belge as *Ankara: Türkiye'deki Yeni Oluşun Bir İzahı* (Ankara, 1936); excerpts in "Yeni Türkiye'nin Kalbi Çankaya" [The heart of new Turkey: Çankaya], *Yedigün* 7, no. 172 (24 Haziran 1936): 20.

16. See B. Georges-Gaulis, *La nouvelle Turquie* (Paris, 1924), E. Pittard, *Le visage nouveau de la Turquie* (Paris, 1931), G. Jaschke, "Ankara, Die Haupstadt der Turkischen Republik," *Die Moderne Turkei* (Stuttgart, 1936), L. Linke, *Allah Dethroned: A Journey through Modern Turkey* (New York: Alfred A. Knopf, 1937), J. Parker and C. Smith, *Modern Turkey* (London, 1940), A. Ritter von Kral, *Kamal Atatürk's Land* (Vienna-Leipzig, 1938), and K. Kruger, *Kemalist Turkey and the Middle East* (London: George Allen and Unwin Ltd., 1932).

17. It can be added that little has changed since then when it comes to the indignation most modern Turks feel when they are considered to be "orientals" inadmissible to the "Western club."

18. "Le Corbusier ile Mülakat" [Interview with Le Corbusier by S. Demiren], *Arkitekt* 19, no. 11–12 (1949): 230–231.

19. Ayşe Öncü discusses this as a broader constituent theme of republican culture by which the contrast was given a strong moral charge: Istanbul, seat of the "traitors," the sultan, the caliph, and the minorities, versus Ankara, locus of superior morality and nationalist consciousness; Istanbul, place of corrupt and decadent lives, versus Ankara, city of decent and respectable people; and so forth. See A. Öncü, "Istanbul'u Nasıl Anlamalı?" *İstanbul*, Türk Tarih Vakfı Yayınları, no. 2 (1992): 72.

20. "Ankara-Istanbul," *La Turquie Kemaliste* 47 (1943): 38–39.

21. See G. Tankut, *Bir Başkentin İmarı: Ankara 1929–39* [The construction of a capital] (Ankara: ODTÜ Yayınları, 1990), 29. Also see F. Yavuz, *Ankara'nın İmarı ve Şehirciliğimiz* [The construction of Ankara and planning in Turkey] (Ankara: Güney Matbaacılık ve Gazetecilik, 1952).

22. Tankut, *Bir Başkentin İmarı*, 30.

23. From *Vilayetlerimiz: Ankara* (Istanbul: Kanaat Kütüphanesi, 1932).

24. "Asya'da Bir Avrupa Şehri: Ankara," *Yedigün* 8, no. 191 (4 Ikinciteşrin 1936).

25. Tankut, *Bir Başkentin Imari*, 28, and also the section on "Designed Capitals" in L. Vale, *Architecture, Power, and National Identity* (New Haven, Conn.: Yale University Press, 1992), 56–162.

26. Z. Kezer, "Irreconcilable Landscapes: Vision and Division in Early Republican Ankara," unpublished paper for the conference "Rethinking the Project of Modernity in Turkey," MIT, March 10–12, 1994. For a critical analysis of the spatial politics in the making of Ankara, see Z. Kezer, "The Making of a National Capital: Ideology, Modernity, and Socio-Spatial Practices in Early Republican Ankara" (Ph.D. diss., University of California, Berkeley, 1998).

27. "Eski Ankara Nasıl Gençleşiyor" [How old Ankara is becoming younger?], *Haftalık Yeni Hayat* 26 (15 Ağustos 1936): 8.

28. See Fehmi Yavuz, "Başkent Ankara ve Jansen," *METU: Journal of the Faculty of Architecture* 7, no. 1 (1981): 25–33, and Tankut, *Bir Başkentin İmarı*.

29. See Bernd Nicolai, *Moderne und Exil: Deutschsprachige Architekten in der Turkei 1925–1955* (Berlin: Verlag fur Bauwesen, 1998).

30. See Fritz Neumark, *Zuflucht am Bosporous: Deutsche Gelehrte, Politiker und Kunstler in der Emigration* (Frankfurt: Knecht, 1980; also published in Turkish in 1982); Ernst E. Hirsch, *Aus des Kaisers Zeiten durch Weimarer Republik in das Land Atatürks: Eine Unzeitgemasse Autobiographie* (Munich, 1982; also published in Turkish in 1985); and Regine Erichsen, "Sığınmacı Alman Bilim Adamlarının Etkisi" [Influence of German refugee professors], in *Ankara 1923–50: Bir Başkentin Oluşumu* (Ankara 1923–50: The making of a capital), symposium proceedings (Ankara: Turkish Chamber of Architects, 1994), 24–36 (in Turkish with German summary).

31. Erichsen, "Sığınmacı Alman Bilim Adamlarının Etkisi," 31.

32. "Neue Bauten Von Ernst Egli, Ankara," *Der Baumeister* 34, no. 2 (1936): 68–71; also in C. E. Arseven, *Yeni Mimari* [New architecture] (Istanbul: Agah Sabri Kütüphanesi, 1931), 9–10.

33. See Sibel Bozdoğan, "Against Style: Bruno Taut's Pedagogical Program in Turkey 1936–38, in M. Pollak, ed., *The Education of the Architect* (Cambridge, Mass.: MIT Press, 1997), 163–192.

34. A. Batur, "To Be Modern: Search for a Republican Architecture," in Holod and Evin, *Modern Turkish Architecture*, 80.

35. The sports stadium was named "19 May" after the date of Mustafa Kemal's arrival in Anatolia in 1919 to start the nationalist War of Independence.

36. P. Vietti-Violi, "Les installations sportives d'Ankara," *La Turquie Kemaliste* 13 (June 1936): 12.

37. "Ankara Gençlik Parkı," *Nafia İşleri Mecmuası* 2, no. 3 (1935): 35–37.

38. Z. Uludağ, "Cumhuriyet Döneminde Rekreasyon ve Gençlik Parkı Örneği" [Recreation in the republican period and the case of the Youth Park], *Bilanço '98: 75 Yılda Değişen Kent ve Mimarlık* (Istanbul: Tarih Vakfı ve Türkiye İş Bankası Yayınları, 1998), 65–74.

39. "La Ferme Orman a Ankara," *La Turquie Kemaliste* 32–40 (August 1939–December 1940): 40.

40. Muallim Afet, "Eski Hükümet Şekli ile Cumhuriyet Arasındaki Fark" [The difference between the old form of government and the republic], *Türk Yurdu* 5/25, no. 35/229 (1930): 4–10.

41. See, for example, Ş. Tekeli, ed., *Kadın Bakış Açısından 1980'ler Türkiye'sinde Kadın* (İstanbul: İletişim, 1990); Y. Arat, *The Patriarchial Paradox: Women Politicians in Turkey* (Princeton, N.J.: Princeton University Press, 1989); N. Göle, *The Forbidden Modern* (Ann Arbor: University of Michigan Press, 1996), and Z. Arat, ed., *Deconstructing Images of "the Turkish Woman"* (New York: St. Martin's Press, 1998).

42. Z. Arat, "Turkish Women and the Republican Reconstruction of Tradition," in F. M. Göçek and S. Balaghi, eds., *Reconstructing Gender in the Middle East* (New York: Columbia University Press, 1994), 57–78.

43. N. Muhittin, *Türk Kadını* [The Turkish woman], (İstanbul: Numune Matbaası, 1931), 76.

44. A. Rıdvan, "Istanbul Kara Çarşaftan ne Zaman Kurtulacak?" [When will Istanbul be free of the veil?], *Yedigün* 5, no. 124 (24 Temmuz 1935): 9.

45. Naci Sadullah, "Son Posta," *Yedigün* 3, no. 66 (13 Haziran 1934): 14.

46. The building was also published in "Son Posta İdarehanesi," *Mimar* 3, no. 3 (1933): 74–75.

47. Hikmet Feridun, "Bayan Saadet: Apartman Yaptıran Kadın Doktor" [Bayan Saadet: The woman doctor who commissioned an apartment building] *Yedigün* 5, no. 127 (14 Agustos, 1935): 7.

48. Zeki Salah, "Rontgen Apartmanı," *Mimar* 3, no. 8 (1933): 231.

49. *Margarete Schütte-Lihotzky: Soziale Architektur Zeitzeugin eines Jahrhunderts* (Vienna: Bohlau Verlag, 1996), 174–178.

50. Y. Navaro, "Using the Mind at Home: Dialogues on Taylorism and Housework in Early Republican Turkey, 1928–40" (unpublished paper, 1996). Navaro writes that the number of women attending these schools rose from 505 in 1923–1924 to 16,500 in 1940–1941.

51. Photographs in *La Turquie Kemaliste* 47 (1943): no page number.

52. See İ. Aslanoğlu, *Erken Cumhuriyet Dönemi Mimarlığı* [Architecture of the early republic] (Ankara: ODTÜ Yayınları, 1980), 101–102.

53. Server Rıfat, "Ismet Paşa Kız Enstitüsünde," *Yedigün* 2, no. 45 (17 İkincikanun, 1934): 10–12.

54. Z. Sayar, "Mektep İnşaatında Plan Tip'in Mahsurları" [The problems with prototype plans in school design], *Mimar* 1, no. 4 (1931): 124, and "Mektep Binalarında Estetik" [Aesthetics in school design], *Mimar* 1, no. 8 (1931): 254.

55. A. Mortaş, "Tire'de Orta Mektep Projesi" [A middle school project in Tire], *Arkitekt* 7, no. 9 (1937): 252–254.

56. B. Ünsal, "Bir İlk Mektep Projesi" [An elementary school project], *Arkitekt* 9, no. 9–10 (1939): 212.

57. Z. Sayar, "Mektep İnşaatında Plan Tip'in Mahsurları," 124–125, and "Devlet İnşaatında Tip Plan Usülünün Mahzurları" [The problems of prototype plans in state buildings], *Arkitekt* 6, no. 9 (1936): 259–260.

58. From a Ministry of Education booklet of plan types and elevations, *Muallim Evleri ve Mekteplerin Planları* [Plans of village schools and teachers' lodgings], 1935 (no publisher or publication information).

59. See "Typentwurfe Dorfschulen fur Anatolien," in *Margarete Schütte-Lihotzky*, 176–178.

60. Editorial in the inaugural issue of *Ülkü* [Ideal], the journal of "People's Houses" (*Halkevleri*), 1, no. 1 (1933): 1–2.

61. A. Çeçen, *Halkevleri* [People's houses] (Ankara: Gündoğan Yayınları, 1990).

62. Among numerous references to Italian, Hungarian, German, and Russian examples in *Ülkü*, see Selim Sırrı, "İtalya'da Halk ve Gençlik Teşkilatı" [Popular and youth organizations in Italy], *Ülkü* 1, no. 3 (1933): 241–243, and Reşit Saffet, "Garp Memleketlerinde Halk Terbiyesi" [Popular education in Western countries], *Ülkü* 1, no. 4 (1933): 295–306.

63. For basiç references, see A. Çeçen, *Halkevleri* (Ankara: Gündoğan Yayınları, 1990), and *Atatürk ve Halkevleri: Atatürkçü Düşünce Üzerine Denemeler* (Ankara: Türk Tarih Kurumu, 1974).

64. See N. G. Yeşilkaya, *Halkevleri: İdeoloji ve Mimarlık* [People's Houses: Ideology and architecture] (Istanbul: İletişim Yayınları, 1999).

65. This is discussed, with many examples, in N. G. Yeşilkaya, *İdeoloji Mimarlık İlişkisi ve Türkiye'de Halkevi Binaları, 1932–1946* [Architecture-ideology relationship and people's houses in Turkey 1932–46] (Master's thesis, Gazi Universitesi, Ankara, 1997).

66. Nusret Kemal, "Halk Terbiyesi" [Popular training], *Ülkü* 2, no. 7 (1933): 16–20.

67. H. Zübeyr, "Halk Terbiyesi Vasıtaları" [Means of popular training], *Ülkü* 1, no. 2 (1933): 152.

68. *CHP Programı*, 1935, quoted in Yeşilkaya, *Halkevleri*, 86.

69. Yeşilkaya, *Halkevleri*, 150–152. To make her point about the tower/chimney element, she cites the example of İzmit Halkevi (1937), with a tall chimneylike element attributed to the architect Seyfi Arkan.

70. "Hilversum Belediye Binası" [Hilversum Town Hall], *Mimar* 1, no. 11–12 (1931): 375–377, and "Sabaudia Şehir Planı" [Sabaudia town plan], *Arkitekt* 6, no. 3 (1936): 76–78.

71. After 1939 an architectural office within the Ministry of Public Works took over the design of people's houses, responding to the "need for a planned and systematic approach" to enable each small town to acquire one such building. With the appointment of Sabri Oran as the chief architect, prototype plans were prepared for people's houses of three different sizes, and these were published in both *Ülkü* and *Arkitekt* in 1940.

72. "Küçük Bir Kasaba İçin Halkevi" [A people's house for a small town], *Yedigün* 11, no. 275 (14 Haziran 1938): 22.

73. Yeşilkaya, *Halkevleri*, 80.

74. "Manisa Halkevi," *Arkitekt* 8, no. 10–11 (1938): 295; "Karamürsel Halkevi," *Arkitekt* 6, no. 5–6 (1936): 142–144; "Gerede Halkevi," *Arkitekt* 6, no. 12 (1936): 330–332.

75. A. Ziya, "Cumhuriyette Köy Yapımı" [Village building in the republic], *Ülkü* 2, no. 10 (1933): 333–336.

76. Regarding the American missionary analogy, see Sabri Gültekin, "Melez Terbiye" [Hybrid training], *Ülkü* 2, no. 7 (1933): 60.

77. Nusret Kemal, "Köy Misyonerliği" [Village missions], *Ülkü* 2, no. 8 (1933): 150.

78. A. Mortaş, "Köy Projesi-Mimar Burhan Arif," *Arkitekt* 5, no. 11–12 (1935): 320.

79. A. Ziya, "Cumhuriyette Köy Yapımı," 333.

80. See Y. Sey, "Cumhuriyet Döneminde Konut" [Housing in the republican period], in Y. Sey, ed., *75 Yılda Değişen Kent ve Mimarlık* [75 years of city and architecture] (Istanbul: Tarih Vakfı ve Türkiye İş Bankası Yayınları, 1998), 277.

81. G. B. Nalbantoğlu, "Silent Interruptions: Urban Encounters with Rural Turkey," in Bozdoğan and Kasaba, *Rethinking Modernity,* 192–210. The source she cites for the ideal village plan is Afet Inan, *Devletçilik İlkesi ve Türkiye Cumhuriyetinin Birinci Sanayi Planı* [Statist principles and the first industrial plan of the Turkish republic] (Ankara: Türk Tarih Kurumu, 1933).

82. Z. Sayar, "İç Kolonizasyon" [Interior colonization], *Arkitekt* 6, no. 2 (1936): 47.

83. Ibid., 46–51.

84. Z. Sayar, "İç Kolonizasyon-Başka Memleketlerde" [Interior colonization in other countries], *Arkitekt* 6, no. 8 (1936): 231–235.

85. On the former, see J. Fiedler, ed., *Social Utopias of the Twenties: Bauhaus, Kibbutz and the Dream of the New Man* (Wuppertal: Muller and Busmann Press, 1995). On the latter, see D. Ghirardo, *Building New Communities: New Deal America and Fascist Italy* (Princeton, N.J.: Princeton University Press, 1989), as well as G. Gresleri et al., *Architettura italiana d'oltremare 1870–1940* (Venice: Marsilio Editori, 1993).

86. A. Ziya, "Köy Mimarisi" [Village architecture], *Ülkü* 1, no. 5 (1933): 370–374.

87. A. Ziya, "Köy Mimarisi," *Ülkü* 1, no. 8 (1933): 37–41.

88. Ibid., 38.

89. A. Ziya, "Gün Geçiminde Kerpiç Köy Yapısı" [Mudbrick village house], *Ülkü* 2, no. 3 (1934): 66–70.

90. A. Ziya, "Köy Mimarisi," *Ülkü* 1, no. 8 (1933): 40.

91. Nalbantoğlu suggests that Nusret Köymen's writings in *Ülkü* on village reform constitute one exception to the journal's dominant ideology in their more sophisticated understanding of the inequality and incommensurability of the voices of reform and the objects of reform. See Nalbantoğlu, "Silent Interruptions," 200–202.

Chapter 3. Aesthetics of Progress

1. Yakup Kadri Karaosmanoğlu, "Kültür ve Medeniyet" [Culture and civilization], *Kadro* 15 (1933): 25.

2. Aptullah Ziya, "Yeni Sanat" [The new art], *Mimar* 2, no. 4 (1932): 97–98.

3. Z. Gökalp, *Türkleşmek, İslamlaşmak, Muasırlaşmak* (1918), quoted from N. Berkes, ed., *Turkish Nationalism and Western Civilization: Selected Essays of Ziya Gökalp* (New York: Columbia University Press, 1959), 73–74.

4. Y. K. Karaosmanoğlu, "Kültür ve Medeniyet," 25–27.

5. *Atatürk'ün Söylev ve Demeçleri* 2 (Ankara: Türk Tarih Kurumu, 1959), 212.

6. Ibid., 207.

7. See M. Matossian, "Ideologies of Delayed Development," in J. Hutchinson and A. D. Smith, eds., *Nationalism* (Oxford: Oxford University Press, 1994), 220.

8. In his discussion of "the dilemmas of cultural identity" that comprise Turkish consciousness, Çağlar Keyder points out that "having withstood overt colonization and preserved

the integrity of the state, Ottoman nationalists perceived their predicament in the paradigm of the European interstate system and in the perspective of intricate alliances and enmities that fueled the world of the Great Powers. For this reason, nationalist ideology, which is ordinarily tinted with a good dose of anti-colonialism, sat uncomfortably in their arsenal." See Ç. Keyder, "Dilemmas of Cultural Identity on the Margins of Europe," *Fernand Braudel Center Review* 16 (Winter 1993): 22.

9. Behçet and Bedrettin, "Mimarlıkta İnkilap" [Revolution in architecture], *Mimar* 3, no. 8 (1933): 245.

10. I. Berlin, *The Hedgehog and the Fox: An Essay on Tolstoy's View of History* (New York: Simon and Schuster, 1953).

11. Mehmet Emin, "İnkilapçilik" [Revolutionism], *Ülkü* 1, no. 1 (1933): 44–48.

12. Müderris İsmail Hakki, "Mimaride Kübizm ve Türk Ananesi" [Cubism in architecture and the Turkish tradition], *Darülfünun İlahiyat Fakültesi Mecmuası* 3, no. 11 (1929): 111.

13. Ibid., 118.

14. Burhan Arif, "Türk Mimarisi ve Beynelmilel Mimarlık Vasıfları" [Turkish architecture and international characteristics of architecture], *Mimar* 1, no. 11–12 (1931): 366.

15. Behçet and Bedrettin, "Mimarlıkta İnkilap," 246.

16. Behçet and Bedrettin, "Yeni ve Eski Mimarlık" [The new and the old architecture], *Mimar* 4, no. 6 (1934): 175.

17. S. Süleyman, "İnkilap ve Kültür Birbirinden Ayrı Şeyler Midir? [Are revolution and culture different things?], *Resimli Ay* (Haziran 1930): 8.

18. K. Atatürk, *Nutuk* [Speech)], 1927 (Istanbul: Milli Eğitim Basımevı, 1962), quoted from T. Parla, *Türkiye'de Siyasal Kültürün Resmi Kaynakları: Atatürk'ün Nutku,* vol. 1 (Istanbul: İletişim Yayınları, 1991), 34–39. Parla observes the way Mustafa Kemal presented himself as the progressive destiny of the Turkish nation, whose consciousness he represented, disclosing this "national secret" only in increments and whenever the appropriate time came. Parla elaborates on this point as a symptom of Mustafa Kemal's authoritarian tendencies.

19. Mehmet Emin, "İnkilapçılık," 45.

20. S. Giedion, *Mechanization Takes Command* [1948] (New York: W. W. Norton, 1969), 3.

21. B. Asaf, "Neden Sanatsızız?" [Why do we not have art?], *Kadro* 13 (1933): 32–34.

22. Ibid., 34.

23. N. Ata, "Sanat ve Makina" [Art and the machine], *Yedigün* 4, no. 89 (1934): 20.

24. Editorial: "Maksad: Türk Rönesansı" [The aim: A Turkish renaissance], *İnsan* 1, no. 1 (1938): 1–2.

25. For example, Le Corbusier, "Makina Medeniyetinden Bekledigimiz Ev" [The house we expect of machine civilization], trans. A. Cemgil, *İnsan* 1, no. 3 (1938): 228–232, and H. Ziya Ülken, "Le Corbusier Gözüyle İstanbul" [Istanbul through Le Corbusier's eyes], *İnsan* 1, no. 10 (1939): 845–846.

26. S. Giedion, *Space, Time, and Architecture* [1941] (Cambridge: Harvard University Press, 1967), 2–28.

27. A. Behne, "Art, Handicraft, Technology" [1922], *Oppositions* 22 (Fall 1980): 96–104, and A. Behne, "Discussion of Ernst Kallai's Article on Painting and Photography," in *Bauhaus Photography* (Cambridge, Mass.: MIT Press, 1985), 134–135.

28. S. Saim, "Lo Korbüziye'nin Muasır Şehri" [The contemporary city of Le Corbusier], *Mimar* 1, no. 2 (1931): 44–48.

29. "Modern Şehir Mimarisi" [Modern urban architecture], *Hakimiyet-i Milliye* (18 Eylül 1930), excerpted and translated from L. Hilbersheimer, *Grosstadt-Architektur* (Stuttgart, 1927).

30. L. Marx, "The Idea of Technology and Postmodern Pessimism," in L. Marx and M. R. Smith, eds., *Does Technology Drive History?* (Cambridge, Mass.: MIT Press, 1995), 237–257.

31. Şemsettin Gündoğdu, "Bu Memleket Böyle Kalmayacak" [This country will not stay as it is], *Sanayi* (Subat 1918), quoted in *Endustri* 25, no. 1 (1939): 1.

32. "Değişmek Bir Zarurettir" [It is necessary to change], *Muhit* 1, no. 4 (1929): 425–428.

33. "New York Belediyesinin Misli Görülmemiş Bir Teşebbüsü" [The unique enterprise of metropolitan New York], *Muhit* 4, no. 43 (1932): 26.

34. "Müstakbel Şehirler" [Cities of the future], *Resimli Ay* 2 (March 1924); Harvey Wiley Corbett, "La ville future," *L'Illustration*, 9 August 1913; Hugh Ferris, *The Metropolis of Tomorrow* (New York: I. Washburn, 1929). For the inspirational status of American skyscrapers and futuristic imagery among the modernist avant-garde in the 1920s and 1930s, see J. L. Cohen, *Scenes of the World to Come: European Architecture and the American Challenge 1893–1960* (Paris: Flammarion and Canadian Center for Architecture, 1995).

35. "Modern Şehirler" [Modern cities], *Muhit* 1, no. 10 (1929): 764.

36. See J. Herf, *Reactionary Modernism: Technology, Culture and Politics in Weimar and the Third Reich* (Cambridge: Cambridge University Press, 1984).

37. B. Anderson, *Imagined Communities: Reflections on the Origins and Spread of Nationalisms* (London: Verso, 1983), 12.

38. From the publicity brochure *Karabük Demir ve Çelik Fabrikaları* (Istanbul: Sümer bank, 1937).

39. S. Süreyya, "Beynelmilel Fikir Hareketleri Arasında Türk Nasyonalizmi" [Turkish nationalism among international ideological currents], *Kadro* 20 (August 1933): 13.

40. See "Ankara Garı Resim Müsabakası" [Ankara railway station mural competition], *Arkitekt* 7, no. 9 (1937): 250–251. Also mentioned in Y. Yavuz, "Ankara Garı ve Mimar Şekip Sabri Akalın," *Ankara,* Ankara Büyükşehir Belediyesi Dergisi, 2, no. 5 (1993): 33–55.

41. See, for example, M. Şevki, "Elektrikli Türkiye" [Electrified Turkey], *Kadro* 13 (Ikinci Kanun 1933): 35–41. "Covering the motherland . . ." is from the lyrics of the "Tenth-Year March," composed on the occasion of the tenth anniversary of the republic in 1933.

42. Başmühendis Kemal, "Memleketimizde Köprücülüğe bir Bakış: Yeni Şose Köprülerimiz" [An overview of bridge building in our country], *Nafia İşleri Mecmuası* 1, no. 1 (1934): 2–11.

43. Ali Süreyya, "Demiryolu Siyasetimiz" [Our railroad policy], *Ülkü* 1, no. 1 (1933): 56–62.

44. In comparison with these early examples of abstract cubic formal compositions of modest scales, Şekip Akalın's Ankara railroad station, inaugurated in 1937, displays the classicizing monumental tendencies of the late 1930s, when an intensified state nationalism took over the architectural culture. Photographs of the opening ceremony of the station testify to the connection between this monumental modernism and state power, something discussed in more detail in chapter 6.

45. "Memleketimizde Silo İnşaatı" [Construction of grain silos in our country], *Arkitekt* 7, no. 4 (1937): 127–128.

46. "Çubuk Barajı, Ankara," *Arkitekt* 6, no. 10–11 (1936): 275–282.

47. See "Le barrage de Çubuk et la station de filtrage," *La Turquie Kemaliste* (1936), and *La Turquie Moderne* 6 (November 1935).

48. Mentioned in T. Gillespie, "Sir Owen Williams" (Master's thesis, Architectural Association, History and Theory Program, London, 1984). Mentioned in J. F. Pinchon, ed., *Rob Mallet-Stevens: Architecture, Furniture, Interior Design* (Cambridge, Mass.: MIT Press, 1990), 130.

49. See F. A. Breuhaus, *Bauten und Raume* (Berlin-Charlottenburg: E. Wasmuth, 1935).

50. For a comprehensive reference on the history of Sümerbank, see Zafer Toprak, *Sümerbank* (Istanbul: Sümerbank Holding AŞ, 1988).

51. "1936/37 Senesinde Türkiye'nin Ekonomik Vaziyeti," *Sümerbank* 3, no. 9–10 (Ankara 1937): 3ff.

52. J. Parker and C. Smith, *Modern Turkey* (London: George Routledge and Sons, 1940), 108–111.

53. Şevket Süreyya, "Le programme quinquennal industriel de la nouvelle Turquie," *La Turquie Kemaliste* 2 (August 1934).

54. See "Notre nouvelle activite industrielle," *La Turquie Kemaliste* 20 (August 1937): 18–21.

55. For example, U. Tanyeli, "Seyfi Arkan: Bir Direnme Öyküsü," *Arredemento Dekorasyon* 3 (March 1992): 88–94.

56. R. Wohl, *A Passion for Wings* (New Haven, Conn.: Yale University Press, 1995).

57. A. Ziya, "Binanin İçinde Mimar" [The architect inside the house], *Mimar* 1, no. 1 (1931): 14–19.

58. Published as "Elektrik Evi, Kadıköy" [The house of electricity, Kadıköy], *Arkitekt* 7, no. 1 (1937): 1–4.

59. "Onuncu Yıl Tak ve Sütunları" [Tenth-year commemorative structures], *Mimar* 3, no. 11 (1933): 351–353.

60. See, for example, the feature articles "1936 İzmir Fuarı," *Arkitekt* 6, no. 10–11 (1936): 283–290, "1938 İzmir Enternasyonal Fuarı," *Arkitekt* 8, no. 9 (1938): 243–252, and "1939 İzmir Beynelmilel Fuarı," *Arkitekt* 9, no. 9–10 (1939): 198–211.

61. J. C. Scott, *Seeing Like a State: How Certain Schemes to Improve the Human Condition Have Failed* (New Haven, Conn.: Yale University Press, 1998), 99.

62. Z. Toprak, *Sümerbank* (Istanbul: Sümerbank Holding AŞ, 1988), preface.

63. See "Sümerbank Proje Müsabakası" [Sümerbank architectural competition], *Arkıtekt* 5, no. 3 (1935): 65–85.

64. *10.Yıl Iktisat Sergisi Kılavuzu* [Guide to the tenth-year economy exhibition] (Ankara: Milli İktisat ve Tasarruf Cemiyeti, 1933), 7.

65. Ibid., 9.

66. "Sergi Binası Müsabakası" [Exhibition Hall competition], *Mimar* 3, no. 5 (1933): 131.

67. "Sergi Evi, Ankara" [Exhibition Hall, Ankara], *Arkitekt* 5, no. 4 (1935): 97.

68. Dr. Wadler, "Die erste Ausstellung im neuen Ausstellungs Gebäude in Ankara," *La Turquie Kemaliste* 4 (December 1934): 23–28.

69. See O. Pferschy, "Die erste Photoausstellung in Ankara," *La Turquie Kemaliste* 12 (April 1936): 18–20.

70. "L'Exposition internationale de la houille a Ankara," *La Turquie Kemaliste* 19 (June 1937): 12–16.

71. Lyrics of a song by the popular composer Sadettin Kaynak, 1939. The Turkish lyrics are *Güzelim İzmir'e bak, altından zincire bak / Akdeniz'in incisi, üründe birincisi / Alıcı verici alsın, cihan hayrette kalsın / Türk işçisi baş alsın, cihan hayrette kalsın / Fuar dolup boşalsın, buluşalım Fuar'da.* See E. R. Üngör, *Türk Musikisi Güfteler Antolojisi* (Istanbul: Eren Yayınları, 1981), 1280.

72. See "La Foire Internationale d'Izmir," *La Turquie Kemaliste* 15 (October 1936): 15–19, and "1936 İzmir Fuarı," *Arkitekt* 6, no. 10–11 (1936): 283–290.

73. Numbers are from "The 1938 International Fair of Izmir," *La Turquie Kemaliste* 23–24 (April 1938): 21, and *Arkitekt* 8, no. 9 (1938): 243.

74. Bernd Nicolai tells us that Taut's Kültür Pavyonu design was based on his 1910 design for the Trager Verkaufskontor in Berlin. See B. Nicolai, *Moderne und Exil: Deutschsprachige Architekten in der Turkei 1925–1955* (Berlin: Verlag fur Bauwesen, 1998), 145.

75. Editorial, "1938 Izmir Enternasyonel Fuarı" [Izmir International Fair], *Arkitekt* 8, no. 9 (1938): 251–252.

76. See "1939 İzmir Beynelmilel Fuarı" [Izmir International Fair], *Arkitekt* 9, no. 9–10 (1939): 205. The Italian pavilion was a variation on the palace of Libya's governor general in Tripoli, transformed for La Mostra della Colonizzazione Libica. See "Funzione autarchica della Fiera di Tripoli," *Africa Italiana* (February 1939): 25–28.

77. See J. L. Cohen, "America: A Soviet Ideal," 3 5 (1984): 33–40, and J. L. Cohen, *Scenes of the World to Come: European Architecture and the American Challenge, 1983–1960* (Paris: Flammarion and Canadian Center for Architecture, 1995).

78. Mentioned in G. Scognamillo, *Türk Sinema Tarihi* [History of Turkish cinema] (Istanbul: Metis Yayınları, 1987), 73–74. The title of Nazım Hikmet's screenplay bears a conspicuous resemblance to that of the Russian futuristic play "Victory over the Sun" (1913), for which the avant-garde constructivist artist Kazimir Malevich was the set designer.

79. The founding members of Group D were Nurullah Berk (1904–1982), Cemal Tollu (1899–1968), Bedri Rahmi Eyüboğlu (1913–1975), Sabri Berkel (1909–?), Zeki Faik İzer (1905–1988), Abidin Dino (1913–1993), and the sculptor Zühtü Müridoğlu (1906–1992). The group published the journal *Ar* and continued as a group until 1946.

80. Z. Sayar, "İnşaatta Standard" [Standardization in building contsruction], *Mimar* 1, no. 1 (1931): 11.

81. See T. P. Hughes, *American Genesis: A History of the American Genius for Invention* (New York: Penguin Books, 1990), 249–284.

82. On the ideological appropriation of technology by German nationalism under the Third Reich, see Herf, *Reactionary Modernism*.

83. I. Berlin, *Two Concepts of Liberty* (Oxford: Clarendon Press, 1958).

84. As outlined by R. Poggioli, *The Theory of the Avant-Garde* (Cambridge, Mass.: Harvard University Press, 1968).

85. P. Safa, "Medeniyet ve Sürat" [Civilization and speed], *Yedigün* 8, no. 2056 (1937): 4.

86. Such glorification can be seen especially in T. Marinetti and A. San't Elia, "Futurist Architecture" [1914], in U. Conrads, ed., *Programs and Manifestoes on Twentieth-Century Architecture* (Cambridge: MIT Press, 1970), 34–38.

87. P. Safa, "Kuvvet ve Teknik" [Power and technique], *Yedigün* 10, no. 251 (1938): 3.

88. P. Safa, "Çarpık Resim Yaşayacak Mı?" [Will distorted art survive?], *Yedigün* 13, no. 326 (1939): 10–11.

89. A. Sami Boyar, "Sanat Varlığımızda Resmin Yeri" [The place of paintings in our artistic existence], *Ülkü* 5 (Ikincikanun 1934): 398.

90. S. Tansuğ, *Türk Resminde Yeni Dönem* [The new era in Turkish painting] (Istanbul: Remzi Kitabevi, 1995), 86.

91. G. B. Nalbantoğlu, *The Professionalization of the Ottoman-Turkish Architect* (Ph.D. diss., University of California, Berkeley, 1989), 250–252.

92. See J. L. Cohen, "America: A Soviet Ideal," *AA Files* 5 (1984): 33–40, and also J. L. Cohen, *Scenes of the World to Come: European Architecture and the American Challenge, 1893–1960* (Paris: Flammarion and Canadian Center for Architecture, 1995).

Chapter 4. *Yeni Mimari*

1. "Yeni Mimari: Mimarlık Aleminde Yeni Bir Esas" [New architecture: A new principle in the world of architecture], *Hakimiyet-i Milliye* (2 Kanunisani 1930).

2. Ibid. Although the author of the article was not identified, the text is identical with that of Celal Esat Arseven's important little book *Yeni Mimari* [New Architecture], published in Istanbul in 1931, suggesting that Arseven probably allowed the newspaper to use his manuscript.

3. This was more than a metaphor in the late 1920s. It was through the competition for the League of Nations headquarters in Geneva in 1927 that the Modern Movement made its first major appearance on the international scene. The rejection of Le Corbusier's entry was the crucial event that outraged modernist architects everywhere and mobilized them to act in solidarity as an international group organized around the CIAM.

4. For example, a Prime Ministry document shows that the official order to send architect Burhan Arif (who worked for the urban planning office of the Ministry of Public Works) to the

Eighth International Congress of Architects in Rome in 1935 was approved by the government on 8 August 1935. The document was signed by President Atatürk, Prime Minister İsmet İnönü, and the entire cabinet. Attachments included the petition of the Ministry of Public Works for an official passport to be issued to Arif and the Ministry of Finance letter approving the expenses of the trip (Order no. 2/3092, Prime Ministry Archives of the Turkish Republic, Ankara).

5. J. C. Scott, *Seeing Like A State: How Certain Schemes to Improve the Human Condition Have Failed* (New Haven, Conn.: Yale University Press, 1998), 96.

6. For the most comprehensive account of the making of an architectural profession in Turkey, see Gülsüm Baydar Nalbantoğlu, *The Professionalization of the Ottoman/Turkish Architect* (Ph.D. diss., University of California, Berkeley, 1989).

7. The Royal Institute of British Architects (RIBA) in England was established in 1834, and the American Institute of Architects (AIA) in the United States in 1851. For basic references on the professionalization of architecture, see M. S. Larson, *Rise of Professionalism: A Sociological Analysis* (Berkeley: University of California Press, 1977); A. Saint, *The Image of the Architect* (New Haven, Conn.: Yale University Press, 1983); D. Cuff, *Architecture: The Story of Practice* (Cambridge: MIT Press, 1991); M. Woods, *From Craft to Profession: The Practice of Architecture in Nineteenth-Century America* (Berkeley: University of California Press, 1999); and S. Bozdoğan, *Towards Professional Legitimacy and Power: The Struggle, Achievements, and Dilemmas of the Architectural Profession in Chicago, 1871–1909* (Ph.D. diss., University of Pennsylvania, 1983).

8. Nalbantoğlu, *Professionalization of the Ottoman/Turkish Architect,* 120.

9. *Neue Sachlichkeit,* or "new objectivity," was an idea embraced by radical modernist architects of the Marxist persuasion in Germany—Hannes Meyer, Mart Stam, and Hans Schmidt in particular—along with the Russian El-Lissitsky. It was an extreme anti-aesthetic position claiming that architecture had nothing to do with art: it was a matter of technical, scientific, and economic organization toward a new society. See M. Hays, *Modernism and the Post-Humanist Subject: The Architecture of Hannes Meyer and Ludwig Hilbersheimer* (Cambridge: MIT Press, 1992).

10. The Association of Independent Painters and Sculptors (Mustakil Ressam ve Heykeltraşlar Birliği) was established in 1929. It was open to a wide range of experiments that sought to apply the influence of cubism and other European trends to landscape, figure, and still-life paintings with Turkish subject matters. Group D was founded in 1932 with a stronger commitment to cubist and constructivist precepts.

11. See C. Esat Arseven, *Yeni Mimari* (Istanbul: Agah Sabri Kutuphanesi, 1931), and Andre Lurcat, *L'Architecture* (Paris: Rene Hilsum, 1929). Arseven's book modified Lurcat's original title, adding the word "new." Referring to the formal canons and rationalist, functionalist principles of interwar modernism, the usage of "yeni mimari" was similar to that of *Neues Bauen* in Germany. At the same time, the influence of Le Corbusier and his journal *L'Espirit Nouveau* also contributed to the emphasis on the word "new."

12. C. E. Arseven, *Yeni Mimari,* 11–13.

13. Ibid., 59.

14. C. E. Arseven, *Sanat ve Siyaset Hatıralarım* [My memoirs of art and politics] (Istanbul: İletişim Yayınları, 1993), 55.

15. "Review of Muallim Celal Esat's *Yeni Mimari*," *Mimar* 1, no. 11–12 (1931): 381.

16. "Güzel Sanatlar Akademisi Mimari Şubesinde Talebe Nasıl Çalışıyor" [How do the Academy of Fine Arts students work in the architectural section?], *Mimar* 1, no. 1 (1931): 25–26.

17. F. Galip, "Güzel Sanatlar Akademisi Talebe Sergisi" [Academy of Fine Arts students' exhibition], *Mimar* 1, no. 7 (1931): 241–243.

18. "Güzel Sanatlar Akademisi Mimari Şubesi Diploma Projesi" [Academy of Fine Arts architectural section diploma project], *Mimar* 4, no. 9–10 (1934): 257–274.

19. B. Taut, *Mimari Bilgisi* [Lectures on architecture] (Istanbul: Güzel Sanatlar Akademisi, 1938). The book was published in Japanese in 1948 and in German as *Architekturlehre* (Hamburg: Verlag fur der Studium der Arbeiterbewegung GmbH, 1977). These lectures were delivered in German and translated into Turkish by Taut's assitants and colleagues. Adnan Kolatan translated the final text of *Mimari Bilgisi*. On Taut's two years in Turkey, see S. Bozdoğan, "Against Style: Bruno Taut's Pedagogical Program in Turkey, 1936–38," in M. Pollak, ed., *The Education of the Architect: Historiography, Urbanism, and the Growth of Architectural Knowledge* (Cambridge, Mass.: MIT Press, 1997), 163–192.

20. For example, Burhan Arif, "Yeni Şehirlerin İnkişafı ve Siedlunglar" [The development of new cities and the *Siedlungen*], *Mimar* 2, no. 6 (1936): 213–216.

21. In Martin Wagner's numerous writings there were discussions of the role of capitalism and economics in urbanism, of urban, demographic, and transportation problems of Istanbul, and of planning guidelines (*Arkitekt* 6, nos. 5–6, 7, 8, 9, 10–11, 12 [1936], and 7, nos. 2, 3, 4, 5–6, 10–11 [1937]). He also wrote about the design of streets and roads (*Arkitekt* 8, nos. 1, 2, 3 [1938]) and standardized housing for earthquake-prone regions (*Arkitekt* 10, nos. 1, 2 [1940]). Wilhelm Schütte began publishing his writings on similar topics after 1940.

22. See *Vier Berliner Siedlungen der Weimarer Republik* (Berlin: Bauhaus Archiv and Argon Verlag, 1987).

23. "Tip ve Sıra Evler" [Typified and row-houses], *Arkitekt* 7, no. 8 (1937): 211–218.

24. Taut, *Mimari Bilgisi*, 313.

25. See Bozdoğan, *Towards Professional Legitimacy and Power*.

26. Müderris İsmail Hakkı, "Mimaride Kübizm ve Türk Ananesi" [Cubism in architecture and the Turkish tradition], *Darülfünun İlahiyat Fakültesi Mecmuası* (Nisan 1929): 118–119, 121.

27. Z. Sayar, "İnşaatta Standard" [Standardization in building construction], *Mimar* 1, no. 1 (1931): 10.

28. İsmail Hakkı, "Mimaride Kübizm ve Türk Ananesi," 115.

29. Ibid., 119–120.

30. Arseven, *Yeni Mimari*, 4. He wrote in Turkish, "*Mimarlık şekil ve bediiyat sahasından ihtiyaç ve mantık sahasına girdi.*"

31. Ibid., 29.

32. Behçet and Bedrettin, "Mimarlıkta Basitlik ve Moda" [Simplicity and fashion in architecture], *Mimar* 4, no. 7 (1934): 213.

33. Z. Sayar, "Mektep Binalarında Estetik" [Aesthetics in school design], *Mimar* 1, no. 8 (1931): 254.

34. Z. Sayar, "Mektep İnşaatında İktisadi Düşünceler" [Economic considerations in school design], *Mimar* 1, no. 6 (1931): 205.

35. Samih Saim, "Yeni Unsurlar" [New elements], *Mimar* 1, no. 4 (1931): 133. It is ironic that this "scientific" argument for the New Architecture was published in the "Ideology" section of the magazine, which was something like a "think-piece" or "theory" section.

36. B. Ünsal, "Kübik Yapı ve Konfor" [Cubic building and comfort], *Arkitekt* 9, no. 3–4 (1939): 60.

37. Mimar Faruk Galip, "Şehirde Mimar" [The architect in the city], *Yeni Türk Mecmuası* 1, no. 5 (1933): 411.

38. A. Ziya, "Binanın İçinde Mimar" [The architect inside the building], *Mimar* 1, no. 1 (1931): 19.

39. See M. McLeod, "Le Corbusier, Taylorism, and Technocracy," *Art Journal* (Summer 1983): 132–147, and J. Louis Cohen, *Le Corbusier and the Mystique of the USSR* (Princeton, N.J.: Princeton University Press, 1992).

40. A. Ziya, "İnkilap ve Sanat" [Revolution and art], *Mimar* 3, no. 10 (1933): 31.

41. Arif Hikmet Koyunoğlu, "Kendi Kaleminden," *Arkitekt* (new series) 1, no. 4 (1991): 48. Arif Hikmet's journalistic pieces on architecture appeared in the official republican newspaper *Hakimiyet-i Milliye* and in the popular weekly magazine *Yedigün*.

42. A. Ziya, "Sanatta Nasyonalizm" [Nationalism in art], *Mimar* 4, no. 2 (1934): 53.

43. Z. Sayar, "Devlet İnşaatında Tip Usülünün Mahzurları" [Problems of prototype design in state buildings], *Arkitekt* 6, no. 9 (1936): 260.

44. Behçet and Bedrettin, "Türk İnkilap Mimarisi" [The architecture of the Turkish revolution], *Mimar* 3, no. 9–10 (1933): 266.

45. Naci Meltem, "Mimaride Güzellik" [Beauty in architecture], *Arkitekt* 8, no. 5–6 (1938): 164.

46. Le Corbusier, *The Decorative Arts of Today* [1925] (Cambridge, Mass.: MIT Press, 1987), 81.

47. Macaroğlu Sami, "Mimaride His ve Mantık" [Feelings and logic in architecture], *Mimar* 3, no. 1 (1933): 25.

48. Taut, *Mimari Bilgisi*, 26–27.

49. Notable among the recent publications on Bruno Taut in Turkish are the catalog of the exhibition *Bruno Taut, 1880–1938* (Istanbul, November 1982–February 1983, Berlin Academy of Fine Arts and German Cultural Association in Turkey) and *Thinking for Atatürk: Two Architects, Bruno Taut and Emin Onat* (Istanbul: Istanbul Technical University, 1998). Also see Bozdoğan, "Against Style," 163–192.

50. Behçet and Bedrettin, "Mimarlıkta İnkilap" [Revolution in architecture], *Mimar* 3, no. 8 (1933): 246.

51. S. Anderson, "Fiction of Function," *Assemblage* 2 (1987): 19–31, and T. Benton, "The Myth of Function," in P. Greenhalg, ed., *Modernism in Design* (London: Reaktion Books, 1990), 41–53.

52. "İzmir Ziraat Mektebi," *Mimar* 2, no. 7–8 (1932): 197–199, and "Gazi İlk Mektebi İzmir," *Mimar* 4, no. 7 (1934): 191–193.

53. On the residential architecture of the 1930s, an informative recent study is Ömer Kanıpak's "Modernism and Dwelling: Residential Architecture in Republican Turkey" (Master's thesis, History Theory Criticism Program, Department of Architecture, MIT, Spring 1998).

54. See W. Lesnikowski, ed., *East European Modernism* (New York: Rizzoli, 1996); M. Toy, ed., *Beyond the Revolution: The Architecture of Eastern Europe* (London: Academy Editions, and New York: St.Martin's Press, 1996); N. Leach, ed., *Architecture and Revolution: Contemporary Perspectives on Central and Eastern Europe* (London: Routledge, 1999); and *Tel Aviv Neues Bauen 1930–39* (Berlin: Wasmuth, 1993).

55. Mimar B. Ö. Celal, "Büyük İnkilap Önünde Milli Mimari Meselesi" (The question of national architecture with respect to the great revolution), *Mimar* 3, no. 6 (1933): 164.

56. See C. Otto and R. Pommer, *Weissenhof 1927 and the Modern Movement in Architecture* (Chicago: University of Chicago Press, 1991).

57. İ. Aslanoğlu, "Evaluation of Architectural Developments in Turkey within the Socio-Economic and Cultural Framework of the 1923–38 Period," *ODTÜ Mimarlık Fakultesi Dergisi* 7, no. 2 (1986): 15–41.

58. Z. Sayar, "İnşaatta Standard," 10–11.

59. See "L'Ecole de construction d'Ankara," *La Turquie Kemaliste* (9 October 1935): 20–21.

60. K. Kaflı, "Ankara'da Yapı Ustası Okulunda Bir Saat" [An hour in the Building Crafts School of Ankara], *Yedigün* 11, no. 279 (1938): 10–12, 24.

61. Prime Ministry document approving the appointment of Hungarian Spevak to work at the Ankara Building Trade School, dated 9 November 1939 (Order no. 2/12316, Prime Ministry Archives of the Turkish Republic, Ankara).

62. "Ankara İnşaat Usta Mektebi" [Ankara Building Crafts School], *Arkitekt* 8, no. 7 (1938): 191–193.

Chapter 5. Living Modern

1. Y. K. Karaosmanoğlu, *Ankara* [1934] (Istanbul: İletişim Yayınları, 1991), 141.

2. For a discussion of this, see Uğur Tanyeli, "Westernization-Modernization in the Ottoman *Wohnkultur:* The Evolution of a New Set of Symbols," in Y. Sey, ed., *Housing and Settlement in Anatolia: A Historical Perspective* (Istanbul: Turkish History Foundation, 1996), 284–297.

3. P. Dumont, "Said Bey: The Everyday Life of an Istanbul Townsman at the Beginning of the Twentieth Century," in A. Hourani, P. Khoury, and M. C. Wilson, eds., *The Modern Middle East* (Berkeley: University of California Press, 1993), 284.

4. C. Behar and A. Duben, *Istanbul Households: Marriage, Family and Fertility, 1880–1940* (Cambridge: Cambridge University Press, 1991).

5. Ibid., 239.

6. Ibid., 242.

7. N. Göle, *The Forbidden Modern: Civilization and Veiling* (Ann Arbor: University of Michigan Press, 1997), 74.

8. "Ev Nedir ve Bir Ev Nasıl Kurulmalı?" [What is a home and how should it be organized?], *Modern Türkiye Mecmuası* 1, no. 1 (1938): 16.

9. A. Ziya, "Binanın İçinde Mimar" [The architect inside the building], *Mimar* 1, no. 1 (1931): 14.

10. Behçet Ünsal, "Kübik Yapı ve Konfor" [Cubic building and comfort], *Arkitekt* 9, no. 3–4 (1939): 60.

11. I. Bilgin, "Modernleşmenin ve Toplumsal Hareketliliğin Yörüngesinde Cumhuriyetin İmarı" [Republican construction in the orbit of modernization and social transformation], in Y. Sey, ed., *75 Yılda Değişen Kent ve Mimarlık* [Seventy-five years of urbanism and architecture] (Istanbul: Tarih Vakfı ve Türkiye İş Bankası, 1998), 255–272.

12. For example, in a photo essay titled "Siz de bu saadete katılmak isterseniz düşünmeyiniz, karar verip hemen evleniniz" [if you want to participate in this happiness, decide now and get married], *Modern Türkiye Mecmuası* 1, no. 11 (1938): 12–13. It used photographs of couples from European sources talking, dining, rowing, and socializing together, with the husband as "breadwinner" and "protector" of the wife, "introducing her to the world of knowledge, arts, and taste and to his business friends and associates." Some of the other essay titles from 1938 in this magazine were "One of Our Social Ills: Divorce" (no. 11), "Learning How to Dance" (no. 14), and "Women's Soul and Husbands" (no. 20).

13. On this topic see especially Victoria Grazia, *How Fascism Ruled Women* (Berkeley: University of California Press, 1992) and E. D. Heineman, *What Difference Does a Husband Make?* (Berkeley: University of California, 1999).

14. The nationalization of modern architecture and the modern house in Italy was first addressed in a paradigmatic essay by G. Ponti, "La Casa Italiana," *Domus* 1, no. 1 (1928): 7.

15. For example, Doktor Demir Ali, "Türkün Sağlığı, Türkiye'nin Sağlamlığıdır" [The health of the Turk is the health of Turkey], *İnkilap* 1, no. 6 (1933): 41.

16. P. Safa, "Modern Türk Kızı I" [Modern Turkish woman I], *Modern Türkiye Mecmuası* 1, no. 1 (1938): 4.

17. P. Safa, "Modern Türk Kızı IV" [Modern Turkish woman IV], *Modern Türkiye Mecmuası* 1, no. 6 (1938): 9.

18. Hüseyin Cahit Yalçın, "Değişen Kadın" [The changing woman], *Yedigün* 7, no. 158 (1936): 5, and "Ev Kadını" [Housewife], *Yedigün* 5, no. 124 (1935): 5.

19. Yalçın, "Değişen Kadın," 5.

20. For example, M. Muzaffer, "Memuriyet Sizin Olsun: Yeni Kavuştuğum Evim Bana Yeter" [I don't want employment: My new home is enough for me], *Muhit* 4, no. 46 (1932): 36–37.

21. "Yazlık Köşk" [A summer villa], *Yenigün* 1, no. 13 (1939): no page number.

22. Y. Navaro cites a book on Taylorism written in 1936 by Süheyla Arel, a girls' institute teacher, which was published in Istanbul in 1936. Y. Navaro, "Using the Mind at Home: Dialogues on Taylorism and Housework in Early Republican Turkey 1928–40" (unpublished paper, 1996).

23. *Die Frankfurter Küche von Margarete Schütte-Lihotzky* (Vienna: Ernst & Sohn, 1993), and *Margarete Schütte-Lihotzky: Soziale Architektur Zeitzeugin eines Jahrhunderts* (Vienna: Bohlau Verlag, 1996).

24. *Margarete Schütte-Lihotzky*, 174–178.

25. B. Taut, *Die Neue Wohnung: Die Frau Als Schöpferin* (Leipzig: Verlag Klinckhardt und Biermann, 1925).

26. İncila Yar, "Modern Ev Idaresi: Evimizde Taylorizm" [Modern household management: Taylorism in our homes], *İzmir Cumhuriyet Kız Enstitütsü Yıllığı* (1935–1936): 40–42, quoted in Navaro, "Using the Mind at Home."

27. Samih Saim, "Güzel Ucuz Sıhhatlı Ev" [Beautiful, healthy, economical house], *Muhit* 1, no. 7 (1929): 498–501.

28. Samih Saim, "Mösyö Jak'ın Asri Villası" [The contemporary villa of Monsieur Jacques], *Muhit* 1, no. 11 (1929): 866–867.

29. Samih Saim, "Kübik Bir Ev" [A cubic house], *Muhit* 1, no. 10 (1929): 786–787.

30. "Üç Katlı Akdeniz Tarzı Güzel bir Villa" [A beautiful three-story Mediterranean-style villa], *Yedigün* 11, no. 276 (1938): 22.

31. Series in *Muhit*: "Güzel Ucuz Sıhhatli Ev" [Beautiful, economical, and healthy house], 1, no. 7 (1929): 498–501; "Amerikan Tertibi Yazlık" [American-style summer house], 1, no. 8 (1929): 128–129, 136; "Asri Hayat Şartlarına Uygun bir Ev" [A house suitable for contemporary life], 2, no. 17 (1930): 1356; "Güzel ve Kullanışlı Evler" [Beautiful and functional houses], 2, no. 18 (1930): 1426–1427; and "Pratik bir Sayfiye Evi" [A practical summer house], 2, no. 21 (1930): 235.

32. "Klasik bir Ev" [A classical house], *Muhit* 3, no. 30 (1931): 66–67.

33. Model designs in *Yedigün*: "Nefis bir Amerikan Villası" [An exquisite American villa], 12, no. 293 (1938): 22; "Bir Amerikan Villası" [An American villa], 12, no. 305 (1939): 22; "Bir Amerikan Villası" [An American villa], 12, no. 308 (1939): 22; and "Iki Katlı ve Çok Kullanışlı bir Amerikan Villası" [A two-story and very functional American villa], 12, no. 309 (1939): 22.

34. "Kutu gibi Sevimli, Üç Odalı bir Ev" [A cute boxlike house with three rooms], *Yedigün* 4, no. 93 (1934): 16; "Hayalinizde Yaşayan Evler" [The houses of your dreams], *Yedigün* 13, no. 202 (1937): 21, and 9, no. 210 (1937): 8; "Beş Odalı fakat Çok Kullanışlı bir Villa" [A five-room, very functional house], *Yedigün* 12, no. 290 (1938): 22.

35. "Modern bir Villa" [A modern villa], *Yedigün* 9, no. 221 (1937): 22.

36. From the signature under the designs, it is likely that the architect was Ferruh (Orel) or Feridun (either Kip or Kunt), all three of whom were graduates of the academy in the early 1930s.

37. No major research or publication exists on the life and career of Emin Necip Uzman, with the exception of a relatively recent feature article, "Profile: Emin Necip Uzman" (essays by U. Tanyeli, O. Barkul, H. Kuruyazıcı, and İ. Aydemir), *Arredemento Dekorasyon* 9 (1995): 70–85.

38. Designs in the "Ev" (House) section of *Yedigün* 11, no. 269 (1938): 19; 11, no. 273 (1938): 22; 12, no. 302 (1938): 22; and 11, no. 270 (1938): 22.

39. Designs by Emin Necip Uzman in *Yedigün* 11, no. 281 (1938): 22; 11, no. 284 (1938): 22; 11, no. 286 (1938): 22; 12, no. 295 (1938): 22; and 12, no. 296 (1938): 22.

40. Such instructions appeared, for example, in "Ecnebilerden Odalarımızın Tezyini ve Tefrişi Hakkında Neler Öğrenebiliriz" [What can we learn from Westerners on the decoration and furnishing of our rooms], *Muhit* 1, no. 4 (1929): 302–303; "Güzel Ev" [Beautiful house], *Muhit* 2, no. 14 (1929): 1112–1113; and "Modernist bir Yatak Odası" [A modernist bedroom], *Muhit* 2, no. 15 (1930): 1186–1187.

41. "Ev Nedir ve Bir Ev Nasıl Kurulmalı?" [What is a home and how should it be organized?], *Modern Türkiye Mecmuası* 1, no. 1 (1938): 16–17.

42. Celal Esat Arseven, *Yeni Mimari* [New Architecture] (Istanbul: Agah Sabri Kütüphanesi, 1931), 32.

43. A. Ziya, "Binanın İçinde Mimar," 19.

44. That Atatürk *ordered* women to dance is cited in N. Göle, *The Forbidden Modern: Civilization and Veiling* (Ann Arbor: University of Michigan Press, 1997): 61.

45. "Güneşin Saltanatı" [The reign of the sun], *Yedigün* 2, no. 39 (1934): 11.

46. Dr. Ali Ridvan, "Bahçesiz Ev Ciğersiz Adam" [House without a garden: Man without lungs], *Yedigün* 3, no. 54 (1934): 23.

47. A. Ziya, "Binanin İçinde Mimar," 14, 19.

48. "Yarının Evi" [Tomorrow's house], *Yedigün* 6, no. 148 (1936): 6–7.

49. Ünsal, "Kübik Yapı ve Konfor," 60.

50. Abidin Mortaş, "Evlerimiz" [Our houses], *Arkitekt*, 6, no. 1 (1936): 24.

51. Ünsal, "Kübik Yapı ve Konfor," 61.

52. Bekir İhsan, "Ev Projeleri" [House projects], *Mimar* 3, no. 1 (1933): 17–18, and "Küçük Ev Projeleri" [Small house projects], *Mimar* 3, no. 2 (1933): 53–54.

53. The organization Bund fur Heimatchutz was established in Germany in 1903 with goals ranging from preservation of the natural environment and traditional culture to the promotion of middle-class and "German" values against the discontents of industrial, modern society. References to vernacular architecture (especially pitched roofs) and traditional domestic culture distinguished Heimatschutz housing projects from those of the Bauhaus and the socialist cooperatives of the Weimar period. For a summary, see C. F. Otto, "Modern Environment and Historical Continuity: The Heimatschutz Discourse in Germany," *Art Journal* 43, no. 2 (Summer 1983): 148–157.

54. B. Arif, "Yeni Şehirlerin İnkişafı ve Siedlung'lar" [The development of new cities and *siedlungen*], *Mimar* 2, no. 6 (1932): 213–216.

55. Arseven, *Yeni Mimari*, 33.

56. See A. Şule Özüekren, "Cooperatives and Housing Production," in Y. Sey, ed., *Housing and Settlement in Anatolia: A Historical Perspective* (Istanbul: Turkish History Foundation, 1996), 355–365.

57. Ibid., 357–358.

58. S. Arkan, "Adana'da Ucuz Evler Mahallesi" [A neighborhood of low-cost housing in Adana], *Arkitekt* 6, no. 1–2 (1936): 33–35.

59. For example, extensive studies of Western town planning and housing practices were published by the engineer-planner Celal Ulusan, a member of the Urban Planning Scientific Committee of the Ministry of Public Works. See C. Ulusan, "Şehir İmar Planları nasıl Tanzim Edilmelidir?" [How should urban master plans be prepared?], *Nafia İşleri Mecmuası* 5, no. 2 (1938):48–63, and "Ucuz Kiralık Evler Nasıl Yapılır ve Bunların Şehir Planlarının Tanzimi" [How can we design low-cost rental homes and their urban planning layout?], *Nafia Vekaleti Dergisi* 5, no. 4 (1938): 28–34.

60. M. Wagner, "Türk Şehirleri ve Mevcut Sahalardan İstifade Ekonomisi" [Turkish cities and the economics of land use], *Arkitekt* 8, no. 3 (1938): 83.

61. From T. Bulutay, Y. S. Tezel, and N. Yıldırım, *Türkiye Milli Geliri 1923–1948* (Ankara: Ankara Üniversitesi Siyasal Bilgiler Fakültesi Yayınları, 1974), cited in İnci Aslanoğlu, *Erken Cumhuriyet Dönemi Mimarlığı* (Ankara: ODTÜ Yayınları, 1980), 217, Table 4.

62. State Institute of Statistics of the Republic of Turkey (Türkiye Cumhuriyeti Devlet İstatistik Enstitüsü) (1995), cited in S. Osmay, "1923'ten Bugüne Kent Merkezlerinin Dönüşümü" [The transformation of urban centers since 1923], in Y. Sey, ed., *75 Yılda Değişen Kent ve Mimarlık*, 140.

63. See M. Balamir, "Kira Evlerinden Kat Evlerine Apartmanlaşma: Bir Zihniyet Dönüşümü Tarihçesinden Kesitler," [From rental apartments to flat ownership: The history of a mental transformation], *Mimarlık* 260 (1994): 29–33.

64. "Güzel Evler: Yurdumuzun her Köşesini Böyle Güzel Yuvalarla Dolu Görmek İstiyoruz" [Beautiful homes: We want to see such homes in every corner of our country], *Yedigün* 7, no. 178 (1936).

65. "Ankara'da Apartman Proje Musabakası" [Architectural competition for an apartment building in Ankara], *Mimar* 4, no. 5 (1934): 139–143.

66. For example, Naci Sadullah, "Tellalın Elinden Yerin Dibine Giren ve Göklere Çıkan Apartmanlar" [Apartments digging into the ground and scraping the skies], *Modern Türkiye Mecmuası* 1, no. 35 (1938): 10–11.

67. Hüseyin Cahit Yalçın, "İstanbul'u Kurtarmak İçin" (To save Istanbul), *Yedigün* 11, no. 266 (1938): 5.

68. See Georg Simmel, "Metropolis and Mental Life" [1898] in K. Wolff, ed., *The Sociology of Georg Simmel* (New York: Free Press, 1964), and Marshall Berman, *All That Is Solid Melts Into Air* (New York: Simon and Schuster, 1982).

69. Halide Edip Adıvar, "Tatarcık: Büyük Milli Roman," *Yedigün* 12, no. 305 (1939): 12–13.

70. As early as May 1933, an editorial by Osmanoğlu Lemi proposed that Turkish youths should follow the "bright and sacred path" of the Nazis. Osmanoğlu Lemi, "Almanya'dan Alınacak Dersler" (Lessons to be learned from Germany), *İnkilap* 1, no. 2 (1933): 1–3. The name of the journal was changed from *İnkilap* (Revolution) to *Milli İnkilap* (Nationalist Revolution) in its second year, 1934.

71. For example, Peyami Safa, "Çarpık Resim Yaşayacak mı?" [Will distorted art survive?], *Yedigün* 13, no. 326 (1939): no page number.

72. I. Aleattin Gövsa, "Güzel Sanatlarda Acayip Meslekler" [Strange occupations in the fine arts], *Yedigün* 10, no. 238 (1937): 10.

73. Peyami Safa, "Bizde ve Avrupa'da Kübik" [Cubic in Turkey and abroad], *Yedigün* 8, no. 1888 (1936): 6–7.

74. Ibid., 7.

75. Hüseyin Cahit Yalçın, "Ev sevgisi" [Love of home], *Yedigün* 5, no. 119 (1935): 5.

76. Hüseyin Cahit Yalçın, "Eski Istanbul" [Old Istanbul], *Yedigün* 9, no. 219 (1937): 5.

77. Hüseyin Cahit Yalçın, "Ev ve Apartman" [House and apartment], *Yedigün* 9, no. 265 (1938): 5.

78. Ünsal, "Kübik Yapi ve Konfor," 60.

79. Behçet Ünsal, "Mimarlıkta Gerçeklik" [Reality in architecture], *Arkitekt* 5, no. 4 (1935): 116.

80. Abidin Mortaş, "Evlerimiz" [Our houses], *Arkitekt* 6, no. 1 (1936): 24.

81. Ibid., 24–25.

82. Bruno Taut, "Türk Evi, Sinan, Ankara" [Turkish house, Sinan and Ankara], *Her Ay* (1 Şubat 1938): 93.

Chapter 6. *Milli Mimari*

1. Sedad Hakkı Eldem, "Milli Mimari Meselesi" [The question of national architecture], *Arkitekt* 9, no. 9–10 (1939): 220, 221.

2. B. Anderson, *Imagined Communities: Reflections on the Origins and Spread of Nationalism* (London: Verso, 1983), 11.

3. E. Hobsbawm, *Nations and Nationalism since 1780* (Cambridge: Cambridge University Press, 1990), and "Introduction: Inventing Traditions," in E. Hobsbawm and T. Ranger, eds., *The Invention of Tradition* (Cambridge: Cambridge University Press, 1983), 1–14.

4. In 1931, the Türk Tarihi Tetkik Cemiyeti (Society for Turkish History Research) and the Türk Dili Tetkik Cemiyeti (Society for Turkish Language Research) were established to carry out scientific studies of the linguistic and historical origins of Turks. Their names were changed, respectively, to Türk Tarih Kurumu (TTK) in 1935 and Türk Dil Kurumu (TDK) in 1936. See F. Çoker, *Türk Tarih Kurumu: Kuruluş Amacı ve Çalışmaları* (Ankara: Türk Tarih Kurumu Basımevi, 1983), and S. Özel et al., eds., *Atatürk'ün Türk Dil Kurumu ve Sonrası* (Ankara: Bilgi Yayınevi, 1986).

5. See C. Kafadar, *Between Two Worlds* (Berkeley: University of California Press, 1995). Much of the modern history of the Ottoman Empire–Turkey from the nineteenth century into the present can also be seen as a confrontation between official Turkish claims to be part of Europe and European efforts to leave them out.

6. Heinrich Gluck, *Die Kunst der Osmanen* (Leipzig: Seemann, 1922); Albert Gabriel, *Monuments Turcs d'Anatolie* (Paris, 1931–1934), and *Voyages archeologiques dans la Turquie orientale* (Paris, 1940).

7. See Celal Esat Arseven, *Sanat ve Siyaset Hatıralarım* (Istanbul: İletişim Yayınları, 1993).

8. Celal Esat Arseven, "Türklerde Mimari: Eti ve Selçuk Mimarileri," *Türk Tarihinin Ana Hatları Eserinin Musveddeleri*, series 2, no. 28 (Istanbul: Akşam Matbaasi, 1932): 3–7.

9. Ibid., 7–28.

10. Celal Esat Arseven, *Türk Sanatı Tarihi: Menşeinden Bugüne Kadar Mimari, Heykel, Resim Süsleme ve Teyzini Sanatlar* (Istanbul: Milli Eğitim Basımevı, 1984), 10.

11. Ibid., 5.

12. Ibid., 7, 10.

13. Ibid., 10.

14. Oktay Aslanapa, *Turkish Art and Architecture* (New York: Praeger, 1971).

15. See B. Ünsal, *Turkish Islamic Architecture in Seljuk and Ottoman Times, 1071–1923* (London: Academy Editions, 1973), 89–90.

16. For the decontextual biases of republican architects and architectural historians in viewing Ottoman architecture, I am indebted to Gülru Necipoğlu for sharing with me the introduction to her manuscript in progress, "Ottoman Architectural Culture in the Age of Sinan: Mosque Complexes as Sites of Collective Identity, Memory and Decorum."

17. Sedad Çetintaş, *Türk Mimari Anıtları: Osmanlı Devri* (Istanbul: TC Milli Eğitim Bakanlığı, Eski Eserler ve Müzeler Röleve Bürosu, 1946).

18. Arseven, *Türk Sanatı Tarihi*, 10.

19. Aptullah Ziya, "Sanatta Nasyonalizm" [Nationalism in art], *Mimar* 4, no. 2 (1934): 51–54.

20. Behçet Sabri and Bedrettin Hamdi, "Mimarlık ve Türklük" [Architecture and Turkishness], *Mimar* 4, no. 1 (1934): 17.

21. Arseven, *Türk Sanatı Tarihi*, 8.

22. E. Egli, *Sinan, der Baumeister Osmanischer Glanzzeit* (Erlenbach-Zürich: Verlag für Architektur, 1954).

23. Bruno Taut, "Türk Evi, Sinan, Ankara," *Her Ay* (1 Subat 1938): 95.

24. See Ş. Mardin, "Consequences of the Collapse of the Ottoman Empire," in K. Barkey and M. Von Hagen, eds., *After Empire: Multi-Ethnic Societies and Nation-Building* (Boulder: Westview Press, 1997), 119.

25. Y. K. Karaosmanoğlu, *Ankara* [1934] (Istanbul: İletişim Yayınları, 1991), 147.

26. From the RPP program of 1935, cited in N. G. Yeşilkaya, *Halkevleri: Ideoloji ve Mimarlik* (Istanbul: İletişim Yayınları, 1999), 88.

27. M. Katoğlu, "Cumhuriyet Türkiyesinde Eğitim, Kültür, Sanat" [Education, culture, and the arts in republican Turkey], in Sina Akşin, ed., *Türkiye Tarihi: Çağdaş Türkiye 1908–1980* [History of Turkey], vol. 4 (Istanbul: Cem Yayinevi, 1990), 426.

28. The quoted passage is the way Bartok himself recorded his mission in 1937. The idea of inviting him was proposed by Professor Laszlo Rasonyi, then the head of the Hungarian Language Department at Ankara University. See B. Suchoff, ed., *Bela Bartok Essays* (Lincoln: University of Nebraska Press, 1997), 137–147. His notes on Turkish music are also published in Turkish as B. Bartok, *Küçük Asya'dan Türk Halk Musikisi* [Turkish folk music from Asia Minor] (Istanbul: Pan Yayıncılık, 1995).

29. B. Bartok, "Hungarian Folk Music" (1929), in Suchoff, *Bela Bartok Essays*, 3.

30. B. Bartok, "What Is Folk Music?" (1931), in Suchoff, *Bela Bartok Essays,* 6–8.

31. B. Bartok, "Why and How Do We Collect Folk Music?" (1936), in Suchoff, *Bela Bartok Essays,* 9–24.

32. B. Bartok, "Folk Song Research and Nationalism" (1937) and "Race Purity in Music" (1942), in Suchoff, *Bela Bartok Essays,* 25–32.

33. B. Bartok, "Folk Song Collecting in Turkey" (1937), in Suchoff, *Bela Bartok Essays,* 147.

34. S. Tansuğ, *Türk Resminde Yeni Dönem* [The new period in Turkish painting] (Istanbul: Remzi Kitabevi, 1995), 86.

35. In music, for example, the synthesis of polyphonic Western classical genres with Turkish folk sources has not taken hold, in spite of state promotion and sponsorship. The most popular genres of pop, arabesque, and religious music are produced and consumed outside of official circles. See M. Özbek, *Popüler Kültür ve Orhan Gencebay Arabeski* (Istanbul: İletişim Yayınları, 1991), and M. Stokes, *The Arabesk Debate: Music and Musicians in Modern Turkey* (New York: Oxford University Press, 1992).

36. See G. B. Nalbantoğlu, "Between Civilization and Culture: Appropriation of Traditional Dwelling Forms in Early Republican Turkey," *Journal of Architectural Education* (November 1993): 66–74, and S. Bozdoğan, "Vernacular Architecture and Identity Politics: The Case of the "Turkish House," *Traditional Dwellings and Settlements Review* 7, no. 2 (Spring 1996): 7–18.

37. The term "rationalism," used interchangeably with modernism in architecture, should not be confused with rationalism in the philosophical sense, as the opposite of empiricism—that is, starting with a priori axioms (or forms in architecture). In modern architecture it simply meant "rational" or "reasonable" and was therefore not contradictory to an "empirical" approach to design.

38. Behçet Sabri and Bedrettin Hamdi, "Mimarlıkta Basitlik ve Moda" [Simplicity and fashion in architecture], *Mimar* 4, no. 7 (1934): 215.

39. Ernst Egli, "Mimari Muhit" [Architectural context], *Türk Yurdu,* no. 30-224 (Haziran 1930): 32–33.

40. Ibid., 36.

41. N. Von Bischoff, *Ankara: Eine deitung des neuen Werdens in der Turkei* (Vienna: A. Holzhausens, 1935), translated into Turkish by B. Belge as *Ankara: Türkiye'deki Yeni Oluşun*

Bir İzahı (Ankara, 1936). Quoted from excerpts in "Yeni Türkiye'nin Kalbi Çankaya," *Yedigün* 2, no. 172 (1936): 19–20.

42. Behçet Sabri and Bedrettin Hamdi, "Mimarlık ve Türklük" (Architecture and Turkishness), *Mimar* 4, no. 1 (1934): 18, 20.

43. Ibid., 20.

44. Aptullah Ziya, "Sanatta Nasyonalizm" [Nationalism in art], *Mimar* 4, no. 2 (1934): 54.

45. Bruno Taut, *Mimari Bilgisi* [Lectures on architecture] (Istanbul: Güzel Sanatlar Akademisi Matbaası, 1938), 66.

46. See S. Bozdoğan, "Against Style: Bruno Taut's Pedagogical Program in Turkey, 1936–38," in M. Pollak, ed., *The Education of the Architect* (Cambridge, Mass.: MIT Press, 1997), 163–192.

47. Taut, *Mimari Bilgisi*, 16–17.

48. Ibid., 56.

49. Ibid., 54.

50. On Sedad Hakkı Eldem, see S. Bozdoğan et al., *Sedad Eldem: Architect in Turkey* (Singapore: Concept Media, 1987; reprint, London: Butterworth, 1991).

51. S. H. Eldem, "Türk Evi" [Turkish house], in *Sedad Hakkı Eldem: 50 Yıllık Meslek Jübilesi* (Istanbul: Mimar Sinan Üniversitesi, 1983): 19.

52. Interviews with Sedad Eldem in 1996; and Bozdoğan et al., *Sedad Eldem: Architect in Turkey*.

53. "The measure of modern architecture is the beauty of the reinforced concrete frame," wrote Eldem, contrasting Perret's profound awareness of this principle with Le Corbusier's tendency to plaster over the frame. S. H. Eldem, "Le Corbusier ve Perret'nin Etkileri" [Influences of Le Corbusier and Perret], in *Sedad Hakkı Eldem: 50 Yıllık Meslek Jübilesi*, 33.

54. S. H. Eldem, "Frank Lloyd Wright'in Etkileri" [Influences of Frank Lloyd Wright], in *Sedad Hakkı Eldem: 50 Yıllık Meslek Jübilesi*, 33.

55. S. H. Eldem, "Türk Evi," in *Sedad Hakkı Eldem: 50 Yıllık Meslek Jübilesi*, 16.

56. Ibid., 19.

57. Halim Baki Kunter, "Ev Kültürü: Eski Türk Evlerinden İki Örnek" [House culture: Two examples of traditional Turkish houses], *Arkitekt* 6, no. 6 (1936): 158–162.

58. S. H. Eldem, *Köşkler ve Kasırlar* [Kiosks and pavilions] (Istanbul: Güzel Sanatlar Akademisi, 1969); *Köçeoğlu Yalısı* (Istanbul: Güzel Sanatlar Akademisi, 1977); *Sa'dabad* (Istanbul: Kültür Bakanlığı Yayınları, 1977); *İstanbul Anıları* [Reminiscences of Istanbul] and *Boğaziçi Anıları* [Reminiscences of the Bosporus], 2 vols. (Istanbul: Alarko Kültür Yayınları, 1979). Also see S. H. Eldem, *Türk Evi* [Turkish house], 3 vols. (Istanbul: Taç Vakfı, 1984).

59. Albert Gabriel, "Türk Evi" [Turkish house], *Arkitekt* 8, no. 5–6 (1938): 149–154.

60. "Güzel Sanatlar Akademisi" (Publicity brochure of the Academy of Fine Arts, Istanbul, 1937).

61. Taut, "Türk Evi, Sinan, Ankara," 93–98.

62. Ibid., 95; also Taut, *Mimari Bilgisi*, 333.

63. Taut, "Türk Evi, Sinan, Ankara," 94.

64. For a more detailed discussion of this, see S. Bozdoğan, "The Legacy of an Istanbul Architect: Type, Context and Urban Identity in Sedad Eldem's Work," in V. M. Lampugnani, ed., *Die Architektur, die Tradition und der Ort*, pp. 528–55 (Ludwigsburg: Wustenrot Stiftung, 2000).

65. Eldem, "Türk Evi," in *Sedad Hakkı Eldem: 50 Yıllık Meslek Jübilesi*, 16.

66. From the catalog of the exhibition, *Yeni Alman Mimarisi* (Ankara, 1943). Bonatz worked as a consultant to the Turkish Ministry of Culture between 1943 and 1946 and taught at Istanbul Technical University between 1946 and 1953. See B. Nicolai, *Moderne und Exil: Deutscsprachige Architekten in der Turkei, 1925–1955* (Berlin: Verlag für Bauwesen, 1998). Also see P. Bonatz, *Leben und Bauen* (Stuttgart: A. Spemann, 1950).

67. S. H. Eldem, "Milli Mimari Meselesi" [The question of national architecture], *Arkitekt* 9, no. 9–10 (1939): 220–223, and "Yerli Mimariye Dogru" [Toward a native architecture], *Arkitekt* 10, no. 3–4 (1940): 69–74.

68. Eldem, "Milli Mimari Meselesi," 221.

69. Taut, *Mimari Bilgisi*, 333–334.

70. See Yıldırım Yavuz, "Ankara Garı ve Mimar Şekip Sabri Akalın," *Ankara Dergisi*, Ankara Büyükşehir Belediyesi 2, no. 5 (1993): 33–56.

71. *Fotoğraflarla Ankara Garı* (Istanbul: Alaadin Kral Basımevi, 30 İlkteşrin 1937).

72. Abidin Mortaş, "Yeni Alman Mimari Sergisi" [The New German Architecture exhibition], *Arkitekt* 13, no. 3–4 (1943): 67–70.

73. Paul Bonatz, "Yeni Alman Mimarisi" [The new German architecture], *Arkitekt* 13, no. 3–4 (1943): 74.

74. These words in praise of engineering structures reflect the larger German intellectual trend toward incorporating modern technology into the mold of a higher and nobler national culture—a trend that Jeffrey Herf characterizes as "reactionary modernism" going back to Oswald Spengler and other romantic philosophers. See J. Herf, *Reactionary Modernism: Technology, Culture and Politics in Weimar and the Third Reich* (Cambridge: Cambridge University Press, 1984).

75. Bonatz, "Yeni Alman Mimarisi," 75.

76. Nicolai, *Moderne und Exil*, 161–196.

77. For example, Üstün Alsaç, "The Second Period of National Architecture," in R. Holod and A. Evin, eds., *Modern Turkish Architecture* (Philadelphia: University of Pennsylvania Press, 1983), 94–104.

78. "Kamutay Müsabakası Program Hülasası" [Summary of the Grand National Assembly competition program], *Arkitekt* 8, no. 4 (1938): 110.

79. Bruno Taut, "Kamutay Müsabaksı Fikir Krokisi," *Arkitekt* 8, no. 4 (1938): 132, and "Türk Evi, Sinan, Ankara," 97.

80. See Hüseyin Gezer, *Cumhuriyet Dönemi Türk Heykeli* [Turkish sculpture in the republican period] (Ankara: Türkiye İs Bankası Kültür Yayınları, 1984). See also Gültekin Elibal, *Atatürk ve Resim Heykel* (Istanbul: Is Bankasi Kultur Yayinlari, 1973).

81. Thorak, one of the most prominent National Socialist sculptors, would go to work in "the world's largest studio" near Munich, designed by Albert Speer, and put his signature on the most famous (and gigantic) sculptures and monuments of the Third Reich. See P. Adam, *Art of the Third Reich* (New York: Harry N. Abrams, 1992).

82. A. Batur, "Üslup Ötesi ve Zaman Dışı Bir Tasarım veya Büyük Ölümün Patetik Yontusu" [A design beyond style and time or the pathetic sculpture of the great death], in *Atatürk İçin Düşünmek* [Thinking for Atatürk] (Istanbul: İstanbul Teknik Üniversitesi Yayını, 1998), 74–80 (also in English and German).

83. Zeki Sayar, "Anıt-Kabir Müsabakası Münasebetiyle" [On the occasion of the Anıt-Kabir competition], *Arkitekt* 13, no. 1–2 (1943): 1–21.

84. Today Anıt-Kabir is contested by a more recent monument, the Kocatepe Mosque, on another hill of Ankara, the two structures symbolizing the confrontation between secular nationalism and the recent rise of Islam. See M. Meeker, "Once There Was, Once There Wasn't: National Monuments and Interpersonal Exchange," in S. Bozdoğan and R. Kasaba, eds., *Rethinking Modernity and National Identity in Turkey* (Seattle: University of Washington Press, 1997), 157–191.

85. See Nurettin Can Gülekli, *Anıt-Kabir Rehberi* (Ankara: Kültür Bakanlığı Yayınları, 1993); also see Murat Ural, "Anıt-Kabir'de Sanat" [Art in Anıt-Kabir], in *Atatürk İçin Düşünmek,* 98–107.

86. Emin Onat and Orhan Arda, "Anıt-Kabir," *Arkitekt* 25, no. 2 (1955): 55–59.

87. "Çanakkale Zafer ve Meçhul Asker Anıtı Müsabakası" [The competition for the Victory and Unknown Soldier Monument of Çanakkale], *Arkitekt* 14, no. 3–4 (1944): 52–65.

Conclusion

1. Bruno Taut, *Mimari Bilgisi* [Lectures on architecture] (Istanbul: Güzel Sanatlar Akademisi, 1938), 333.

2. Mary McLeod, "Le Corbusier and Algiers," *Oppositions* 19–20 (1980): 55. On the inadequacy of functionalist and rationalist doctrines for determining form, see Stanford Anderson, "The Fiction of Function," *Assemblage* 2 (1987): 19–32, and Tim Benton, "The Myth of Function," in P. Greenhalgh, ed., *Modernism in Design* (London: Reaktion Books, 1990), 41–53.

3. Architectural culture at large had to wait until after World War II to realize that the canonic works of the Modern Movement had in reality been aesthetic objects, not historically inevitable expressions of the new materials, construction techniques, and lifestyles of the machine age as claimed. The first important discussion of this was in R. Banham, *Theory and Design in the First Machine Age* (London: Architectural Press, 1960).

4. For the "missing bourgeoisie" and efforts to create it nationally, see C. Keyder, *State and Class in Turkey: A Study in Capitalist Development* (London: Verso, 1987).

5. J. Habermas, "Modernity: An Incomplete Project," in H. Foster, ed., *The Anti-Aesthetic: Essays on Post-Modern Culture* (Port Townsend, Wash.: Bay Press, 1983): 3–15.

6. Susan Buck-Morrs, "Modernity: A Culture Out-of-Bounds," unpublished public lecture delivered for the History Department and the History, Theory, and Criticism section of the Department of Architecture at MIT, 1996.

7. See, for example, Gülsüm Baydar Nalbantoğlu, "Silent Interruptions: Urban Encounters with Rural Turkey," in S. Bozdoğan and R. Kasaba, eds., *Rethinking Modernity and National Identity in Turkey* (Seattle: University of Washington Press, 1997), 192–210. Music presents an interesting case that can highlight new directions in architectural studies. In spite of all the official sponsorship and encouragement of the Kemalist state, neither classical Western music nor Turkish compositions using folk tunes in classical Western modes have taken much hold in society beyond a small circle of republican elites. Meanwhile, classical Turkish music (with its roots in the Ottoman court and in religious orders) has never lost its appeal with large sectors of the population in spite of many years of republican neglect. More pervasively, hybrid and popularized formations, which draw on a range of sources from Turkish classical music and Arab music to Western pop, have proliferated since the 1960s with a popularity unmatched by any other kind of music supported by the state. Cultural historians who have recently looked at this phenomenon conclude that the roots of such hybrid music (the so-called arabesque as well as Turkish pop) go back to the austere cultural politics and impositions of the republic, which deprived the population of traditional music forms dear to them.

8. See Sencer Ayata, "Kentsel Orta Sınıf Ailelerde Statü Yarışması ve Salon Kullanımı" [The status contest among urban middle-classes and the use of living rooms in apartments], *Toplum ve Bilim* 42 (1988): 5–25.

9. For an important first effort to assess this ambiguous moment from a critical and interdisciplinary perspective, see S. Bozdoğan and R. Kasaba, *Rethinking Modernity and National Identity in Turkey*. For an overview of developments in recent history, see N. Pope and H. Pope, *Turkey Unveiled: A History of Modern Turkey* (Woodstock, N.Y.: Overlook Press, 1997).

10. On the topic of historical consciousness, the efforts, symposia, and publications of the Turkish Economic and Social History Foundation have been invaluable. In particular, a series of publications on the occasion of the seventy-fifth anniversary of the republic have covered the architecture, culture, fashion, and social life of the early republican years with ideas similar to those informing this book. See Y. Sey, ed., *75 Yılda Değişen Kent ve Mimarlık* [75 years of architecture and urbanism]; *Üç Kuşak Cumhuriyet* [Three generations of republic]; and *Cumhuriyet Modaları: 75 Yılda Değişen Yaşam, Değişen İnsan* [Republican fashions: Changing lives, changing people in 75 years] (Istanbul: Türk Tarih Vakfı Yayınları, 1998 [all three]).

Bibliography

Periodicals surveyed for 1928–42

AR Resim, Heykel, Dekorasyon, Arkeoloji (Istanbul 1937–)
Arkitekt (Istanbul, 1934–)
Bayındırlık İşleri Dergisi (Nafia İşleri Mecmuası) (Ankara 1935–)
Belediyeler Dergisi (Ankara 1935–)
Demiryolları Mecmuası (Istanbul 1925–)
Hakimiyet-i Milliye (Ankara, 1920–34)
Her Ay (Istanbul, 1938–)
İnkilap (Istanbul, 1933–)
İnsan Sanat ve Kültür Dergisi (Istanbul 1938–)
Kadro (Istanbul, 1932–35)
La Turquie Kemaliste (Ankara 1931–)
La Turquie Moderne (Istanbul 1935–)
Milli İnkilap (Istanbul 1933–)
Mimar (Istanbul, 1931–34)
Modern Türkiye Mecmuası (Istanbul 1938–)
Muhit (Istanbul, 1928–)
Resimli Ay (Istanbul 1924–)
Türk Yurdu (Istanbul 1911–)
Ülkü (Halkevleri Mecmuası) (1933–41)
Yedigün (Istanbul, 1933–)
Yeni Kültür (Ankara 1936–)
Yeni Türk Mecmuası (1932–)
Yenigün (Istanbul, 1939–)

References on Early Republican Turkey

Ankara 1923–50: Bir Başkentin Oluşumu (Ankara: The making of a capital). Ankara: Turkish Chamber of Architects, 1994.

Ankara Posta Kartları ve Belge Fotoğrafları Arşivi (Ankara postcard and photograph archives). Ankara: Belko, 1994.

Atatürk'ün Söylev ve Demeçleri (The speeches of Ataturk). Ankara: Türk Tarih Kurumu, 1959.

Bayındırlık Bakanlığı: Yapı İşlerinde 50 Yıl (Ministry of Public Works: 50 years of building). Ankara: T. C. Bayındırlık Bakanlığı, 1973.

Belediyeler (Municipalities), T. C. Dahiliye Vekaleti Mahalli İdareler Umum Müdürlüğü. Istanbul: Holivut Matbaası, 1933.

Fotoğraflarla Ankara Garı (Photography album of Ankara railway station). Istanbul: Alaaddin Kral Basımevi, 1937.

İstanbul Devlet Güzel Sanatlar Akademisi (Istanbul Academy of Fine Arts). Late 1930s pamphlet, no date.

Mimarlığımız 1923–50, special issue of *Mimarlık,* Journal of the Turkish Chamber of Architects, n.2 (1973).

Muallim Evleri ve Mekteplerinin Planları (Plans of village schools and teachers' lodgings). Ankara: T. C. Maarif Vekaleti, 1935.

Once Upon a Time Ankara. Ankara: The Greater Ankara Municipality, 1993.

Onuncu Yıl İktisat Sergisi Klavuzu (Guide to the 10TH year of the Republic, Economy Exhibition). Ankara: Milli İktisat ve Tasarruf Cemiyeti, 1933.

Sanayi İstatistikleri 1932–35 (Industrial statistics 1932–35). Ankara: Mehmed İhsan Matbaası, 1937.

Sedad Hakkı Eldem: 50 Yıllık Meslek Jübilesi (Sedad Hakkı Eldem: 50 years in the profession). Istanbul: Mimar Sinan Üniversitesi, 1983.

Türk Yüksek Mimarlar Birliği Azaları (Roster of the Turkish Architects' Union). Istanbul: Cumhuriyet Matbaası, 1940.

Yabancı Gözüyle Cumhuriyet Türkiyesi (Republican Turkey through foreign eyes). Ankara: Dahiliye Vekaleti Matbuat Umum Müdürlüğü Neşriyatı, 1938.

Yeni Alman Mimarisi (New German Architecture) exhibition catalog, Ankara (1943).

Ağaoğlu, A. *Devlet ve Ferd* (State and individual). Istanbul: Sanayi-i Nefise, 1933.

Ahmad, F. *The Making of Modern Turkey.* London: Routledge, 1993.

Akman, H. *Türk Ulusallığı* (Turkish nationalism). Izmir: Cumhuriyet Basımevi, 1936.

Akşin, S., ed. *Türkiye Tarihi: Çağdaş Türkiye 1908–1980* (History of Turkey: Contemporary Turkey 1908–1980). Istanbul: Cem Yayınevi, 1990.

Alp, T. *Kemalizm.* Istanbul: Cumhuriyet Matbaası, 1936.

Alsaç, Ü. *Türkiye'deki Mimarlık Düşüncesinin Cumhuriyet Dönemindeki Evrimi* (The evolution of architectural thought in Turkey in the republican period). Trabzon: KTÜ Yayınları, 1976.

Arat, Z., ed. *Deconstructing Images of "the Turkish Woman."* New York: St. Martin's Press, 1998.

Araz, N. *Mustafa Kemal'in Ankarası* (Mustafa Kemal's Ankara). Istanbul: Apa Ofset Basımevi, 1994.

Arseven, C. E. *Yeni Mimari* (New architecture). Istanbul: Agah Sabri Kitaphanesi, 1931.

_____. *Türk Tarihinin Ana Hatları Eserinin Müsveddeleri* (Drafts of an outline of Turkish history). Istanbul: Akşam Matbaası, 1932.

_____. *Türklerde Mimari* (Architecture of the Turks). Ankara: Başvekalet Müdevvenat Müdürlüğü; Istanbul: Akşam Basımevi, 1934.

_____. *Türk Sanatı Tarihi: Menşeinden Bugüne Kadar Mimari, Heykel, Resim, Süsleme ve Teyzini Sanatlar* (History of Turkish art: architecture, sculpture, painting and decorative arts from their origins to the present). Istanbul: Milli Eğitim Basımevi, 1984.

_____. *Sanat ve Siyaset Hatıralarım* (My memoirs of art and politics). Istanbul: İletişim Yayınları, 1993.

Aslanapa, O. *Turkish Art and Architecture.* New York: Praeger Publishers, 1971.

Aslanoğlu, İ. *Erken Cumhuriyet Dönemi Mimarlığı* (Early republican architecture). Ankara: Orta Doğu Teknik Üniversitesi, 1980.

Ataman, D., ed. *Anıtkabir Yarışma Projeleri Sergisi* (Exhibition of Anit-Kabir competition projects). Istanbul: Mimar Sinan Üniversitesi, 1984.

Aygün, T. *Fotoğraflarla Atatürk* (Atatürk in photographs). Ankara: Milli Egitim Basımevi, 1963.

Baltacioğlu, İ. H. "Mimaride Kübizm ve Türk Ananesi" (Cubism in architecture and the Turkish tradition), *Darülfünun İlahiyat Fakültesı Mecmuası* (Nisan 1929): 110–30.

Bartok, B. *Küçük Asya'da Türk Halk Musikisi* (Turkish folk music in Asia Minor). Istanbul: Pan Yayıncılık, 1995.

Baydar, O., and D. Özkan, eds. *75 Yılda Değişen Yaşam, Değişen İnsan: Cumhuriyet Modaları* (75 years of changing lives, changing people: Republican fashions). Istanbul: Tarih Vakfı Yayınları, 1999.

Behar, C., and A. Duben. *Istanbul Households: Marriage, Family and Fertility 1880–1940.* Cambridge: Cambridge University Press, 1991.

Berk, N. *Modern Sanat* (Modern art). Istanbul: Semih Lütfü Basımevi, 1935.

Berkes, N. *Turkish Nationalism and Western Civilization: Selected Essays of Ziya Gökalp.* New York: Columbia University Press, 1959.

Beygu, S., ed. *Üç İzmir* (Three Izmirs). Istanbul: Yapı ve Kredi Bankasi Yayınları, 1992.

Bischoff, N. von. *Ankara: Türkiye'deki Yeni Oluşun bir İzahı* (Ankara: An account of the new formation in Turkey); trans. from German by B.Belge. Ankara, 1936.

Bozdoğan, S., et al. *Sedad Eldem: Architect in Turkey.* Singapore: Concept Media, 1987; reprint, London: Butterworth, 1990.

_____. "Against Style: Bruno Taut's Pedagogical Program in Turkey, 1936–38," in *The Education of the Architect,* ed. M. Pollak. Cambridge, Mass.: MIT Press, 1997.

Bozdoğan, S., and R. Kasaba, eds. *Rethinking Modernity and National Identity in Turkey.* Seattle: University of Washington Press, 1997.

Çeçen, A. *Atatürk'un Kültür Kurumu Halkevleri* (Ataturk's cultural institution: Peoples' Houses). Ankara: Gündoğan Yayınları, 1990.

Cemal, A. *Ankara.* Istanbul: Kanaat Matbaası, 1932.

Çetintaş, S. *Osmanlı Türk Mimarisi* (Ottoman Turkish architecture). Ankara: Başvekalet Basımevi, 1934.

_____. *Türk Mimari Anıtları: Osmanli Devri* (Turkish architectural monuments: Ottoman period). Istanbul: T. C. Milli Eğitim Bakanlığı, Eski Eserler ve Müzeler Rölöve Bürosu, 1946.

Cezar, M. *Sanatta Batıya Açılış ve Osman Hamdi* (Westernization in art and Osman Hamdi Bey). Istanbul: İş Bankası Yayınları, 1971.

Çoker, F. *Türk Tarih Kurumu: Kuruluş Amacı ve Çalışmaları* (Turkish Historical Society: Objectives and activities). Ankara: Türk Tarih Kurumu Basımevi, 1983.

Elibal, G. *Atatürk ve Resim Heykel* (Ataturk, painting and sculpture). Istanbul: Türkiye İş Bankası Kültür Yayınları, 1973.

Ersoy, A. "On the Sources of the Ottoman Renaissance: Architectural Revival and Its Discourse during the Abdulaziz Era, 1861–1876." Ph.D. diss., Harvard University, 2000.

Evin, A., and R. Holod, eds. *Modern Turkish Architecture.* Philadelphia: University of Pennsylvania Press, 1983.

Gabriel, A. *En Turquie.* Paris: Paul Hartmann, 1935.

_____. *Monuments Turc d'Anatolie* (Turkish monuments of Anatolia). Paris: E. de Boccard, 1931–34.

Galip, M. *Ankara.* Ankara: Maarif Vekaleti, 1925.

Georges-Gaulis, B. *La Nouvelle Turquie* (The new Turkey). Paris: A. Colin, 1924.

Gezer, H. *Cumhuriyet Dönemi Türk Heykeli* (Turkish sculpture in the Republican period). Ankara: Turkiye İş Bankası Kültür Yayınları, 1984.

Göle, N. *The Forbidden Modern: Civilization and Veiling.* Ann Arbor: University of Michigan Press, 1997.

Gülekli, N. C. *Anıt-Kabir.* Ankara: T. C. Milli Eğitim Bakanlığı Eski Eserler ve Müzeler Genel Müdürlüğü, 1964.

_____. *Anıt-Kabir Rehberi* (Anit-Kabir Guide). Ankara: Kültür Bakanlığı Yayınları, 1993.

Haşim, A. *Gurabahane-i Laklakan* (1928). Ankara: Kültür Bakanlığı Yayınları, 1981.

Hirsch, E. *Hatıralarım: Kayzer Dönemi, Weimar Cumhuriyeti, Ataturk Ülkesi* (My memoirs: Kaiser period, Weimar republic and Ataturk's land). Ankara: Banka ve Ticaret Hukuku Araştırma Enstitüsü, 1985.

İnan, A. *Türk Tarih Kurumunun Arkeoloji Faaliyetleri* (Archaeological activities of the Turkish Historical Society). Istanbul: Devlet Basımevi, 1937.

_____. *Devletçilik İlkesi ve Türkiye Cumhuriyetinin Birinci Sanayi Planı* (Statist principles and the first industrial plan of the Turkish republic). Ankara: Türk Tarih Kurumu, 1933.

Karabuda, B. *Goodby to Fez: A Portrait of Modern Turkey.* London: D. Dobson, 1959.

Karaosmanoğlu, Y. K. *Ankara* (1934). Istanbul: İletişim Yayınları, 1991.

Kazancigil, A., and E. Özbudun, eds. *Atatürk: Founder of a Modern State.* Hamden, Conn.: Archon Books, 1981.

Keyder, Ç. *State and Class in Turkey*. London: Verso, 1987.

Kezer, Z. "The Making of a National Capital: Ideology, Modernity and Socio-Spatial Practices in Early Republican Ankara," Ph.D. diss., University of California, Berkeley, 1998.

Köker, L. *Modernleşme, Kemalizm ve Demokrasi* (Modernization, Kemalism and democracy). Istanbul: İletişim Yayınları, 1990.

Kruger, K. *Kemalist Turkey and the Middle East*. London: George Allen & Unwin Ltd., 1932.

Landau, J. M. *Atatürk and the Modernization of Turkey*. Leiden: Brill, 1984.

Lewis, B. *The Emergence of Modern Turkey*. Oxford: Oxford University Press, 1961.

Linke, Lilo. *Allah Dethroned: A Journey through Modern Turkey*. New York: Alfred A.Knopf, 1937.

Mardin, Ş. *Religion and Social Change in Modern Turkey*. Albany, NY: SUNY Press, 1989.

_____. *Türk Modernleşmesi* (Turkish modernization). Istanbul: İletişim Yayınları, 1991.

Müderrisoğlu, A. *Kurtuluş Savaşında Ankara* (Ankara during the War of Independence). Ankara: Büyükşehir Belediyesi Yayınları, 1993.

Muhittin, N. *Türk Kadını* (Turkish woman). Istanbul: Numune Matbaası, 1931.

Nalbantoğlu, G. B. "The Professionalization of the Ottoman-Turkish Architect." Ph.D. diss., University of California, Berkeley, 1989.

Navaro, Y. "Using the Mind at Home: Dialogues on Taylorism and Housework in Early Republican Turkey 1928–1940." Manuscript.

Neumark, F. *Boğaziçine Sığınanlar: Türkiye'ye İltica Eden Alman Ilim Siyaset ve Sanat Adamları 1933–53* (Exiles on the Bosphorous: German refugee scientists, political activists and artists, 1933–53). Istanbul: İstanbul Üniversitesi İktisat Fakultesi Yayınları, 1982.

Nicolai, B. *Moderne und Exil: Deutschsprachige Architekten in der Turkei 1925–1955*. Berlin: Verlag fur Bauwesen, 1998.

Özel, S., et al., eds. *Atatürk'ün Türk Dil Kurumu ve Sonrası* (Atatürk's Turkish Language Society). Ankara: Bilgi Yayınevi, 1986.

Parker, J., and C. Smith. *Modern Turkey*. London: George Routledge & Sons Ltd., 1940.

Pittard, E. *Le visage nouveau de la Turquie: A travers l'Asie-Mineure*. Paris: Societe d'Editions Geographiques, Maritimes et Coloniales, 1931.

Renda, G. *Başlangıcından Bugüne Çağdaş Türk Resim Sanatı* (Modern Turkish painting from its beginning to the present). Istanbul: Tiglat Basımevi, 1980.

Renda, G., and C. M. Kortepeter, eds. *The Transformation of Turkish Culture: The Atatürk Legacy*. Princeton: The Kingston Press, 1986.

Ritter von Kral, A. *Kamal Atatürk's Land: The Evolution of Modern Turkey*. Trans. K. Benton. Vienna and Leipzig: Wilhelm Braumuller, 1938.

Rona, Z., ed. *Osman Hamdi Bey ve Dönemi* (Osman Hamdi Bey and his period). Istanbul: Tarih Vakfı Yurt Yayınları, 1993.

Saygun, A. A. *Bela Bartok's Folk Music Research in Turkey*. Budapest: Akademiai Kiado, 1976.

Sey, Y., ed. *Bilanço '98: 75 Yılda Değişen Kent ve Mimarlık* (Report '98: Changes in urbanism and architecture in 75 years). Istanbul: Tarih Vakfı ve Türkiye İş Bankası, 1998.

Sönmez, Z. *Güzel Sanatlar Eğitiminde 100 Yıl* (100 years in fine arts education). Istanbul: Mimar Sinan Üniversitesi, 1983.

Sözen, M. *Cumhuriyet Dönemi Türk Mimarlığı 1923–83* (Republican period Turkish architecture, 1923–83). Ankara: Türkiye İş Bankası Kültür Yayınları, 1984.

Sözen, M., and M. Tapan. *50 Yılın Türk Mimarisi* (50 years of Turkish architecture). Istanbul: İş Bankası Yayınları, 1973.

Suchoff, B., ed. *Bela Bartok Essays*. Lincoln and London: University of Nebraska Press, 1997.

Tankut, G. *Bir Başkentin İmarı: Ankara 1929–39* (The making of a capital: Ankara, 1929–39). Ankara: ODTÜ Mimarlık Fakultesi Yayınları, 1991.

Tansuğ, S. *Cağdaş Türk Sanatı* (Contemporary Turkish art). Istanbul: Remzi Kitabevi, 1991.

Tanyeli, U., ed. *Üç Kuşak Cumhuriyet* (Three generations of the Republic). Istanbul: Tarih Vakfı Yayınları, 1998.

Tomlin, E. W. F. *Life in Modern Turkey*. London and New York: T. Nelson and Sons Ltd., 1946.

Toprak, Z. *Sümerbank*. Istanbul: Sümerbank Holding AŞ, 1988.

Tümer, G., ed. *İdeoloji, Erk ve Mimarlık* (Ideology, power and architecture). Izmir: Dokuz Eylül Üniversitesi, 1996.

Tunçay, M. *Tek Parti Yönetiminin Kurulması 1923–31* (The establishment of the single-party regime, 1923–31). Istanbul: Cem Yayınevi, 1992 (1981).

Üken, H. Z. *Turkiye'de Çağdaş Düşünce Tarihi* (The history of contemporary thought in Turkey). Istanbul: Ülken Yayınları, 1966.

Ünaydin, R. E. *Hatıralar: Türk Dili Tetkik Cemiyeti, kuruluşundan ilk Kurultaya kadar* (Memoirs: Turkish Language Research Society from its inception to the first Congress). Ankara: Recep Ulusoğlu Basımevi, 1943.

Ünsal, B. *Mimari Tarihi* (History of architecture). Istanbul: Kurtuluş Basımevi, 1949.

_____. *Turkish Islamic Architecture in Seljuk and Ottoman Times 1071–1923*. London: Academy Editions, 1973.

Vefik, A. *Milliyetçilik* (Nationalism). Istanbul: Bozkurt Matbaası, 1936.

Weiker, W. *The Modernization of Turkey*. New York: Holmes & Meier Publications, 1981.

Yavuz, F. *Ankara'nin İmarı ve Şehirciliğimiz* (The construction of Ankara and planning in Turkey). Ankara: Güney Matbaacılık ve Gazetecilik, 1952.

Yavuz, Y. *Mimar Kemalettin ve Birinci Ulusal Mimarlık Dönemi* (Mimar Kemalettin and the First National Architecture period). Ankara: ODTÜ Yayınları, 1981.

Yeşilkaya, N. G. *Halkevleri, İdeoloji ve Mimarlık* (Peoples' Houses, ideology and architecture). Istanbul: İletişim Yayınları, 1999.

Zürcher, E. *Turkey: A Modern History*. London: I. B.Tauris, 1993.

Selected References on Nationalism and Modern Architecture

Adam, P. *Art of the Third Reich*. New York: Harry N. Abrams Inc., 1992.

Alsayyad, N., ed. *Forms of Dominance*. Aldershot and Brookfield, Vermont: Avebury, 1992.

Anderson, B. *Imagined Communities: Reflections on the Origins and Spread of Nationalisms*. London: Verso, 1983.

Balibar, E., and I. Wallerstein. *Race, Nation, Class*. London: Verso, 1991.

Barkey, K., and M. Von Hagen, eds. *After Empire: Multi-Ethnic Societies and Nation Building*. Boulder, Col.: Westview Press, 1997.

Berman, M. *All That Is Solid Melts into Air*. New York: Simon and Schuster, 1983.

Bowe, N. G., ed. *Art and the National Dream: Search for a Vernacular Expression*. Dublin: Irish Academic Press, 1993.

Chatterjee, P. *Nationalist Thought and the Colonial World*. London: Zed Publications, 1986.

Cleveland, W. L. *A History of the Modern Middle East*. Boulder, Col.: Westview Press, 1994.

Curtis, W. J. R. *Modern Architecture Since 1900*. Oxford, U.K.: Phaidon Press, 1982.

Doordan, D. *Building Modern Italy: Italian Architecture 1914–1936*. New York: Princeton Architectural Press, 1988.

Etlin, R., ed. *Nationalism in the Visual Arts*. Washington, D.C.: National Gallery of Art, 1991.

Falasca-Zamponi, S. *Fascist Spectacle: The Aesthetics of Power in Mussolini's Italy*. Berkeley: University of California Press, 1997.

Fiedler, J., ed. *Social Utopias of the Twenties: Bauhaus, Kibbutz and the Dream of the New Man*. Wuppertal: Müller and Busmann Press, 1995.

Frampton, K. *Modern Architecture: A Critical History*. New York: Thames and Hudson, 1980.

Gellner, E. *Nations and Nationalism*. Oxford, U.K.: Blackwell, 1983.

Ghirardo, D. *Building New Communities: New Deal America and Fascist Italy*. Princeton, N.J.: Princeton University Press, 1989.

Giedion, S. *Space, Time and Architecture*. Cambridge, Mass.: Harvard University Press, 1941.

Greenfeld, L. *Nationalism: Five Roads to Modernity*. Cambridge, Mass.: Harvard University Press, 1992.

Greenhalg, P., ed. *Modernism in Design*. London: Reaktion Books, 1990.

Herf, J. *Reactionary Modernism: Technology, Culture and Politics in Weimar and the Third Reich*. Cambridge, U.K.: Cambridge University Press, 1984.

Hertzfeld, M. *Anthropology Through the Looking Glass: Critical Ethnography in the Margins of Europe*. Cambridge, U.K.: Cambridge University Press, 1987.

Hewitt, A. *Fascist Modernism: Aesthetics, Politics and the Avant-Garde*. Palo Alto, Calif.: Stanford University Press, 1993.

Hitchcock, H. R., and P. Johnson, eds. *The International Style: Architecture since 1922*. New York: Museum of Modern Art, 1932.

Hobsbawm, E. *Nations and Nationalism since 1780*. Cambridge, U.K.: Cambridge University Press, 1990.

Hobsbawm, E., and T. Ranger, eds. *The Invention of Tradition*. (Cambridge, U.K.: Cambridge University Press, Canto edition, 1992).

Hourani, A., et al., eds. *The Modern Middle East*. Cambridge, Mass.: The MIT Press, 1995.

Hutchinson, J., and A. D. Smith, eds. *Nationalism*. Oxford, U.K.: Oxford University Press, 1994.

Lash, S., and J. Friedman, eds. *Modernity and Identity*. Oxford, U.K.: Basil Blackwell, 1992.

Leach, N., ed. *Architecture and Revolution: Contemporary Perspectives on Central and Eastern Europe*. London: Routledge, 1999.

Levin, M. *White City: International Style Architecture in Israel*. Tel Aviv: Tel Aviv Museum, 1984.

Lesnikowski, W., ed. *Eastern European Modernism*. New York: Rizzoli, 1996.

Lurcat, A. *L'Architecture*. Paris: Rene Hilsum, 1929.

Moravanszky, A. *Competing Visions: Aesthetic Invention and Social Imagination in Central European Architecture 1867–1918*. Cambridge, Mass.: The MIT Press, 1998.

Nerdinger, W., et al., eds. *Tel Aviv Neues Bauen 1930–1939*. Tubingen/ Berlin: Ernst Wasmuth Verlag, 1993.

Sartoris, A. *Gli elementi dell'architettura funzionale*. Milan: Ulrico Hopeli, 1932.

Silberman, N. A. *Between Past and Present: Archaeology, Ideology and Nationalism in the Modern Middle East*. New York: Henry Holt & Co., 1989.

Scott, J. C. *Seeing Like a State: How Certain Schemes to Improve the Human Condition Have Failed*. New Haven, Conn.: Yale University Press, 1998.

Taut, B. *Mimari Bilgisi* (Lectures on architecture). Istanbul: Güzel Sanatlar Akademisi, 1938.

Taut, B. *Modern Architecture*. London: The Studio, 1929.

Toy, M., ed. *Beyond the Revolution: The Architecture of Eastern Europe*. London: Academy Editions; New York: St. Martin's Press, 1996.

Vale, L. *Architecture, Power, and National Identity*. New Haven, Conn.: Yale University Press, 1992.

Yorke, F. R. S. *The Modern House*. London: The Architectural Press, 1934.

Figure Sources

1.15   Archives of the Municipality of Ankara. Reproduced from *Ankara Posta Kartları ve Belge Fotoğrafları Arşivi* (Ankara: Belko, 1994)

1.16   *La Turquie Kemaliste*, n.18 (April 1937)

1.17   Archives of the Municipality of Ankara. Reproduced from *Ankara Posta Kartları ve Belge Fotoğrafları Arşivi* (Ankara: Belko, 1994)

1.18   Photograph and drawing: Courtesy of Yıldırım Yavuz

2.1   Painting reproduced from G.Elibal, *Atatürk ve Resim Heykel* (İstanbul: İş Bankası Kültür Yayınları, 1973)

2.2   *Mimar,* 3, n.8 (1933)

2.3   Reproduced from L.Linke, *Allah Dethroned: A Journey Through Modern Turkey* (New York: Alfred A. Knopf, 1937)

2.4   *Yabancı Gözüyle Cumhuriyet Türkiyesi* (Ankara: Dahiliye Vekaleti Matbuat Umum Müdürlüğü, 1938)

2.5   F.R.S.Yorke, *The Modern House* (London: The Architectural Press, 1934)

2.6   *La Turquie Kemaliste*, n.6, (April 1935)

2.7   *La Turquie Moderne*, 1 November 1935

2.8   Photographs (top and middle): *Der Baumeister,* n.2, (February 1936)
        Photograph (bottom): *La Turquie Kemaliste*, n.47 (1943)

2.9   Photographs by the author

2.10   Author's collection

2.11   Reproduced from *Nafia İşleri Mecmuası* 2, n.3 (1935)

2.12   *La Turquie Kemaliste*, n.47 (1943)

2.13   Postcards courtesy of Supsun Güralp

2.14   Cover of *Yedigün*, 22 February 1938

2.15   *La Turquie Kemaliste*, n.29 (February 1939)

2.16   *Yedigün* 5, n.127 (1935)

2.17   Schütte-Lihotzky Archives. Reproduced from *Margarete Schütte-Lihotzky: Soziale Architektur Zeitzeugin eines Jahrhunderts* (Vienna: Bohlau Verlag, 1996)

2.18   *La Turquie Kemaliste*, n.47 (1943)

2.19   *La Turquie Kemaliste*, n.6 (April 1935)

2.20   Ankara State Art Gallery. Reproduced from *Ankara Resim ve Heykel Müzesi* (Ankara: Kültür Bakanlığı, no date)

2.21   *Arkitekt* 7, n.9 (1937)

2.22   Pamphlet. *Muallim Evleri ve Mekteplerinin Planları* (1935)

2.23   Schütte-Lihotzky Archives. Reproduced from *Margarete Schütte-Lihotzky: Soziale Architektur Zeitzeugin eines Jahrhunderts* (Vienna: Bohlau Verlag, 1996)

3.20   *Arkitekt* 6, n.10-11 (1936)

3.21   Photograph (top): *Arkitekt* 6, n.10-11 (1936)
         Photograph (bottom): *La Turquie Kemaliste,* n.15 (October 1936)

3.22   Postcard (top): Courtesy of Supsun Güralp
         Photograph (bottom): *Arkitekt* 8, n.9 (1938)

3.23   *Arkitekt* 9, n.9-10 (1939)

3.24   Photograph (top): *Arkitekt* 9, n.9-10 (1939)
         Postcard (bottom): Courtesy of Supsun Güralp

3.25   Cover of *Yedigün,* 25 October 1938

4.1   *Mimar* 1, n.1 (1931)

4.2   *Mimar* 4, n.9-10 (1934)

4.3   Publicity brochure, *Güzel Sanatlar Akademisi* (1937)

4.4   *Arkitekt* 7, n.8 (1937)

4.5   Author's collection

4.6   Photograph (top): Archives of the Municipality of Ankara. Reproduced from
         Ankara Posta Kartları ve Belge Fotografları Arşivi (Ankara: Belko, 1994)
         Photograph (middle): *La Turquie Kemaliste,* n.17 (February 1937)
         Photograph (bottom): *Fotograflarla Yeni Ankara Garı* (1937)

4.7   Photograph (top): *Mimar* 2, n.7-8 (1932)
         Photograph (bottom): *Mimar* 4, n.7 (1934)

4.8   Archives of the Municipality of Ankara. Reproduced from *Ankara Posta Kartları
         ve Belge Fotografları Arşivi* (Ankara: Belko, 1994)

4.9   *Arkitekt* 5, n.11-12 (1935)

4.10   Photograph (top): *Arkitekt* 7, n.8 (1937)
         Photograph (middle): *Arkitekt* 9, n.3-4 (1939)
         Photograph (bottom): *Arkitekt* 6, n.9 (1936)

4.11   Photograph (left) by Ömer Kanıpak
         Photograph (right): *Arkitekt* 9, n.5-6 (1939)

4.12   Advertisements from the 1930s issues of *Arkitekt*

4.13   Archives of Sümerbank architectural offices, Ankara

4.14   *Arkitekt* 8, n.7 (1938)

5.1   *Yenigün* 1, n.13 (1939)

5.2   *Yedigün* 1, n.7 (1933)
         Photograph (bottom right): Reproduced from *Assemblage,* n.2, February 1987
         (Source: J.Buekshmitt, *Ernst May,* Stuttgart: A.Koch, 1963, p.47)

6.1   Postcard (top): Author's collection
        Photograph (bottom) by the author

6.2   Author's collection

6.3   Painting (left): reproduced from *Boyut,* n.1–2 (1982)
        Painting (right): reproduced from N.Berk, *Modern Painting and Sculpture in Turkey* (New York: Turkish Information Office, 1955)

6.4   Sedad Hakkı Eldem Archives, Istanbul

6.5   Photograph by Haldun Dostoğlu

6.6   Sedad Hakkı Eldem Archives, Istanbul

6.7   Sedad Hakkı Eldem Archives, Istanbul

6.8   Sedad Hakkı Eldem Archives, Istanbul

6.9   Sedad Hakkı Eldem Archives, Istanbul

6.10   Sedad Hakkı Eldem Archives, Istanbul

6.11   Photograph by the author

6.12   Courtesy of Bernd Nicolai

6.13   Photograph by the author

6.14   Photograph by the author

6.15   *Arkitekt* 14, n.11–12 (1944)

6.16   Sedad Hakkı Eldem Archives, Istanbul

6.17   From the photo album *Fotoğraflarla Yeni Ankara Garı* (1937)

6.18   From the photo album *Fotoğraflarla Yeni Ankara Garı* (1937)

6.19   *Arkitekt* 9, n.7–8 (1939)

6.20   *Arkitekt* 8, n.4 (1938)

6.21   Drawing (top): *Arkitekt* 8, n.4 (1938)
        Photograph (bottom): Archives of the Municipality of Ankara. Reproduced from *Ankara Posta Kartları ve Belge Fotoğrafları Arşivi* (Ankara: Belko, 1994)

6.22   *Arkitekt* 8, n.4 (1938)

6.23   *Arkitekt* 8, n.4 (1938)

6.24   *Arkitekt* 14, n.3-4 (1944)

6.25   Postcard (left): Author's collection
        Postcard (right): Courtesy of Supsun Güralp

6.26   Archives of the Municipality of Ankara. Reproduced from *Ankara Posta Kartları ve Belge Fotoğrafları Arşivi* (Ankara: Belko, 1994)

6.27   *Arkitekt* 13, n.1 (1943)

6.28   *Arkitekt* 13, n.1 and n.2 (1943)

6.29   *Arkitekt* 13, n.1 and n.2 (1943)

6.30   Postcard: Author's collection

Index

Boldface numbers indicate illustrations.

357